D1745121

Listed Buildings and Conservation Areas

Charles Mynors
MA (Arch), MA (TP), Dip Law, MRTPI, ARICS
of the Middle Temple, Barrister

First edition

KINGSTON UPON THAMES
HERITAGE UNIT

Longman

© Longman Group UK Ltd 1989

Published by:
Longman Group UK Ltd,
21–27 Lamb's Conduit Street, London WC1N 3NJ

Associated offices:
Australia, Hong Kong, Malaysia, Singapore, USA

ISBN 085121–408–8

A CIP Catalogue record for this book is available from the British
Library.

All rights reserved. No part of this publication may be reproduced,
stored in a retrieval system, or transmitted in any form or by any means,
electronic, mechanical, photocopying, recording or otherwise, without
either the prior written permission of the publishers, or a licence
permitting restricted copying issued by the Copyright Licensing Agency
Ltd, 33–34 Alfred Place, London WC1E 7DP.

Typeset by Input Typesetting Ltd, London
Printed and Bound in Great Britain by
Bell & Bain Ltd, Glasgow

KINGSTON UPON THAMES
HERITAGE UNIT

K85

ALL   CLASS   711
HS   MYN
CAT   REFS

P   ENB
25-95

Contents

Foreword

As recent vociferous criticism has made clear, few modern buildings in England are universally admired. There is much greater general acceptance of past styles of architecture, since on the whole the majority of the public find that they can relate more easily to the scale and style of buildings which were built by previous generations.

It is therefore fortunate that, despite the destruction which occurred to our cities during the last war and the activities since that time of no doubt well-intentioned but misguided local authorities, developers and planners, we still have a great architectural inheritance of which we can be proud. The situation would be probably very different were it not for the legislation with which this book is concerned. Because of this legislation we should be able to pass on this inheritance to the next generation not only in as good, but in a better condition than that in which it was received.

However, if this is to happen it is essential that the provisions of the legislation should be readily accessible to and easily understood by the increasing number of people whom it affects. Unfortunately the legislation is in fact spread over 12 Acts of Parliament as well as a body of subordinate legislation and ministerial directions. Furthermore, from my own personal experience both at the Bar and on the Bench, I can state with confidence that the meaning of the legislation is not always as clear as it should be.

All those concerned with conservation should therefore rejoice in the publication of this book. It will now no longer be necessary to search through the index of the well-known, admirable, but vast encyclopaedias on planning law and compulsory purchase to ascertain what are the consequences of a building being listed or included in a conservation area. This book gathers together and

then marshals in an orderly manner all the basic provisions of the
law from their different sources. In clear and simple language
the reader is taken step by step to his required destination by the
most straightforward route.

I am sure that all those who are involved from time to time
with listed buildings or conservation areas whether they be lawyers
(including judges), surveyors, architects, administrators or poli-
ticians will find this book indispensable. It is also capable of being
readily understood by the ordinary member of the public who is
concerned with the legislation because, for example, he lives in a
listed building or one of the increasing number of conservation
areas. By reading this book he will readily understand the
responsibilities and rights which he has. If he is adversely affected
by a proposal or a decision he will be able to ascertain what are
the steps which he can take to protect his interests. If he is an
occupier of an historic building he will be able to obtain guidance
as to the financial resources which are available to assist him in
restoring, improving or maintaining the building and the duties
which he has to ensure the safety of those visiting him.

Having resorted to this book, it may still be necessary for the
reader to turn to the encyclopaedias to which I have referred or
to a book dealing specifically with procedure if proceedings in the
High Court are contemplated. However, I will be surprised if it
is necessary to look beyond the covers of this book in order to
resolve the majority of problems in which the professional or the
member of the public is likely to become involved.

Mr Mynors has put his amazing combination of qualifications
in town planning, surveying and the law to very good use. He is
to be congratulated on what he has achieved. I am confident that
this book is destined to become a standard work on the area of
the law with which it deals.

December 1988   The Rt Hon Lord Justice Woolf

Preface

It is indeed sad that in this Town and Country Planning matter, ordinary, reasonable individuals and a reasonable and responsible local authority should not be able to know, without coming to this Court, where they stand about listed building consent in what must be a fairly usual situation. That they did not know where they stand is, in my view, the fault of the Town and Country Planning Act 1971, which, in its relevant parts, uses words and phrases . . . which, in my judgment, can only lead to confusion.

R v *North Hertfordshire District Council, ex p Sullivan* (1981) per Comyn J.

The reason for this confusion (which, unfortunately, was only made worse by the judgment which opened with these words; see 8.1(*d*)) is not hard to find. Those parts of the law which deal with listed buildings and conservation areas are being constantly altered. The relevant provisions in the Town and Country Planning Act 1971 have increased from 24 sections when it was first enacted to 36 in 1988, and the principal Government Circular on the subject has increased in length from 129 paragraphs in 1977 to 154 ten years later. Consequently, the alterations are often hard to find, and are phrased in obscure language.

This book aims therefore to describe as clearly as possible all the relevant law and procedure in the hope that this will assist solicitors, barristers, planners, conservation officers, surveyors, developers, architects, and amenity groups—both those who are trying to preserve Britain's heritage of historic buildings and areas, and those who are trying to overcome the restrictions which these inevitably impose on development. It may also be of interest and use to those who merely live in them.

Some of this book is based on one I wrote for the Royal

Borough of Kensington and Chelsea in 1983, and I am grateful to the Borough Council for allowing me to write that, and now to them and to the Architectural Press for generously enabling me to re-use parts of it. I am also grateful to the editor of the *Journal of Planning and Environmental Law* for allowing me to use material first published there, and to him and to Roger Suddards for their friendship and general support over the last few years. Thanks too to those who have read parts of the manuscript and made helpful comments, and to a number of others who have patiently answered my questions. The responsibility for any errors that remain, and for any views expressed, is however entirely mine. Finally, many thanks to those at Longman who have been involved with this project since its inception, for their encouragement, help—and tolerance!

The extracts from Department of the Environment Circulars and from statutes and other Parliamentary material are Crown copyright, and are reproduced by kind permission of the Controller of Her Majesty's Stationery Office. The examples in Figures 8.2, 8.5 and 8.7 are entirely fictional, and no reference is intended to any persons living or dead.

As always, the major debt is to my wife Janet and to my children, for putting up with me never (well, hardly ever) being around. It is therefore to them, and, in particular, this time to Katherine, that this book is dedicated, with love and thanks.

The law stated in this book is, I hope, accurate as at 1 November 1988; but I have been able to take on board one or two later developments, including the provisions of the new General Development Order, which came into force on 5 December 1988, and the Norfolk and Suffolk Broads Act, the relevant parts of which are expected to come into effect on 1 April 1989.

December 1988   Charles Mynors

Table of Cases

Table of Statutes

Table of Statutory Instruments

Table of Circulars

Abbreviations

These have been used solely in order to shorten as far as possible the references in the text to statutes and statutory instruments.

AMAAA	Ancient Monuments and Archaeological Areas Act
GDO	Town and Country Planning General Development Order
HA	Housing Act
HBAMA	Historic Buildings and Ancient Monuments Act
HPA	Housing and Planning Act
LGA	Local Government Act
LGPAA	Local Government and Planning (Amendment) Act
LGPLA	Local Government, Planning and Land Act
NHA	National Heritage Act
NSBA	Norfolk and Suffolk Broads Act
TCAA	Town and Country Amenities Act
TCP	Town and Country Planning
TCPA	Town and Country Planning Act
TCP (LBCA) Regs	Town and Country Planning (Listed Buildings and Buildings in Conservation Areas) Regulations

Chapter 1

Introduction

1.1 Background

Ever since 1877, when William Morris founded the Society for
the Protection of Ancient Buildings, there has been a growing
awareness of the need for certain older buildings to be given some
measure of special protection. Ancient monuments have therefore
been scheduled and protected since 1882, and listed buildings
since 1932. By October 1988, there were some 13,000 scheduled
monuments, and no less than 422,411 listed buildings in England
alone.

In the last 25 years the conservation lobby has grown even
stronger. There has, in particular, been a movement to protect
areas of special character, as well as individual buildings. Accordingly, local authorities have been designating conservation areas
since 1967. By April 1988, there was only one district in England
which did not contain at least one; and 6,121 areas had been
designated throughout the country—so there must by now be well
over a million buildings which are in a conservation area.

It is not enough merely to schedule monuments, to list buildings, and to designate areas. There must be a control mechanism
to back this up with special protective measures, with the force
of law. To some extent, this can be achieved through the normal
mechanisms of planning control. When planning permission is
sought for a proposal involving the loss or alteration of a historic
building, the local planning authority should be able to use its
development control powers to ensure that unsuitable proposals
are not allowed. However, this has in the past proved inadequate.
This is possibly because there have been insufficient planners with
appropriate skills and knowledge. It is also because the legislation
provides that planning permission is not required for demolition,

1

as opposed to alteration, or for many small works—particularly in the case of dwellinghouses.

So, in addition to *planning permission*, a developer may now require in appropriate cases *listed building consent, scheduled monument consent* or, since April 1987, *conservation area consent*. In each case, the legislation has been gradually strengthened since it was first passed. Both the statutes themselves and the regulations which provide the fine tuning have thus been frequently amended and there has been an increasing amount of case law to assist with the interpretation of the legislation. Departmental Circulars have also been issued and themselves amended and updated, providing much helpful guidance and advice.

The problem is that the law is now of considerable complexity, especially as much of the recent statutory material is in the form of alterations to earlier Acts. This book therefore aims to provide a comprehensive guide to the legislation intended to protect historic buildings and areas and to control their alteration and demolition. It has been written in the hope that it may help to clarify this area of law, and thus in the long run assist in informing those involved in the debate on conserving the country's built heritage.

The book looks first in some detail at those parts of the Town and Country Planning Act 1971 which provide for the creation of a statutory list of buildings of special interest (Chapters 2 and 3) and the designation of conservation areas (Chapter 4).

Often the most pressing problem with older buildings is repair and maintenance. The book therefore describes the various provisions, within the 1971 Act and elsewhere, regarding buildings in need of repair—when does a building owner have to carry out the necessary works; what steps can be taken if he does not; what financial help is available (Chapters 5 and 6)?

As for development involving listed buildings, the general rules of planning control apply, but subject to slight modifications (see Chapter 7). In addition, as explained above, there are further provisions regarding listed building consent (Chapter 8). If works are carried out without consent being obtained, there are a number of possible consequences (described in Chapter 9).

In conservation areas, rules regulate consent for the demolition of unlisted buildings, works to trees and the display of advertisements (Chapters 10, 11 and 12, and Appendix).

Finally, there are different statutory codes which apply in two special cases: churches (see Chapter 13), and scheduled monuments (Chapter 14). The book concludes with a chapter on rescue archaeology (Chapter 15).

1.2 The sources of the law

(a) Primary legislation

The backbone of planning law in England and Wales is the *Town and Country Planning Act 1971* (referred to in the remainder of this book as 'TCPA 1971'). This broadly consolidated all the preceding legislation. The basic rules regarding planning control—the need for planning permission, and how it is obtained—are in Part III. The special rules on listed buildings (which area also partially applied to unlisted buildings in conservation areas) are in Part IV. The enforcement of both codes is in Part V.

The 1971 Act has however been adapted in a number of ways—particularly in the field of historic buildings; and these alterations, taken together, have in some cases made a considerable difference. The principal statutes by which it has been amended are shown in Figure 1.1.

The Department of the Environment has sensibly issued a booklet containing the complete text of the relevant sections of the Act, including all amendments up to 1 April 1987, when the relevant portions of the Housing and Planning Act 1986 came into force (*Town and Country Planning Act 1971: Current Wording of the Provisions Relating to Historic Buildings and Conservation Areas*, pub HMSO, price £5.50). This is a vital tool for anyone working in this area—the 1971 Act as originally published is of almost no use at all.

(b) Statutory instruments

In addition to primary legislation, a new set of regulations has recently been made: the Town and Country Planning (Listed Buildings and Buildings in Conservation Areas) Regulations (referred to in this book as TCP (LBCA) Regs 1987) (SI No 349). These came into force on 1 April 1987, replacing the 1977 Regulations, and provide the detailed implementation of the 1971 Act. They also introduce the term 'conservation area consent' (TCPA 1971, s 55(3A), applied by TCP (LBCA) Regs 1987, Sched 3).

Figure 1.1 Sources of legislation: (1): principal Acts of Parliament

Historic Buildings and Ancient Monuments Act (HBAMA) 1953 — provides for grants by Historic Buildings and Monuments Commission and the Secretary of State for buildings of outstanding interest; amended by NHA 1983

Local Authorities (Historic Buildings) Act 1962 — provides for historic buildings grants by local authorities

Town and Country Planning Act (TCPA) 1971 — the principal statute containing the basic provisions as to planning permission, listed buildings, conservation areas and enforcement; much altered since it was first passed

Local Government Act (LGA) 1972 — altered details of local authorities responsible for administering planning

Town and Country Planning (Amendment) Act 1972 — provided limited control over demolition in conservation areas (superseded by TCAA 1974); also conservation area and town scheme grants

Town and Country Amenities Act (TCAA) 1974 — provided for comprehensive control over unlisted buildings and trees in conservation areas; superseded TCP (Amendment) Act 1972

Ancient Monuments and Archaeological Areas Act (AMAAA) 1979 — provided for complete system of control over works to scheduled monuments; introduced archaeological areas

Local Government, Planning and Land Act (LGPLA) 1980 — made a number of alterations, mostly as to procedural details

Local Government and Planning (Amendment) Act (LGPAA) 1981 — tightened up the enforcement provisions

National Heritage Act (NHA) 1983 — set up the Historic Buildings and Monuments Commission for England (English Heritage) with consequential amendments to procedure

Local Government Act (LGA) 1985 — altered details of local authorities, again; and provided for historic building control in London to be administered by the Commission, alongside the borough councils

Housing and Planning Act (HPA) 1986 — altered a number of details

The recently issued Town and Country Planning General Development Order (GDO) 1988 is also relevant in some contexts. This replaces the GDO 1977, and a host of subsequent amending orders.

(c) Government Circulars

At least as important as the actual legislation itself is the advice issued from time to time by central Government, primarily in the form of Circulars from the Department of the Environment and the Welsh Office. These contain advice to local authorities, and also give useful general guidance as to the interpretation and implementation of the law.

In particular, a major new Circular (No 8/87, *Historic Buildings and Conservation Areas—Policy and Procedures*) was issued by the Department of the Environment on 1 April 1987. This replaces Circulars 23/77, 12/81, 8/84 and 23/84, the letter issued to London authorities in March 1986, and para 4 of the direction issued to the London Docklands Development Corporation in July 1986. Figure 1.2 shows the paragraphs of the Circular dealing with the topics covered by each chapter of this book.

The new Circular also contains, as did its predecessors, a number of important directions by the Secretary of State. These directions (which are noted at appropriate points in the text) have the force of law, even though they are not directly approved by Parliament.

As to the views of the Secretary of State contained in it, the Circular emphasises that 'there are essentially no changes in the Government's policy, and it remains their resolve to preserve the architectural heritage to which listed buildings and conservation areas make such an important contribution' (para 3). It repeats the old message that 'public opinion is now overwhelmingly in favour of conserving and enhancing the familiar and cherished local scene'. But it adds a new note of warning:

It is extremely important that public support for conservation policies should be retained. As more buildings are listed and conservation areas designated, more people are likely to become involved with listed building control. Their experience of this control will doubtless colour their view of conservation (para 5).

Figure 1.2 Sources of legislation: (2): Government Circulars

Topic	England *(DOE Circ 8/87)* paras	Wales *(WO Circ 61/81)* paras
Introduction	1–18	1–7
Listed buildings	33–45, 49–52, and App I	8–17, 22–5, and App I
Building preservation notices	46–8	18–21
Conservation areas	53–71	27–33, 42–5
Buildings in disrepair	107, 124–38, and App V	79, 96–105, and App V
Finance	139–52 and App VI	106–24 and App VI
Planning permission: special provisions	19–32, 38, 52, 61–4, and App II	26, 34–7, 57, 58, and App II
Works to listed buildings	72–93, 99–117, 118, 120, 122, 123, and Apps III, IV	46–66, 73, 74, 79, 80, 82–94, Apps III, IV
Unauthorised works	74–8, 119	90
Demolition of unlisted buildings in conservation areas	72–81, 94–117	67–72, 74
Churches	21, 103–5, 129	63, 75–7, 99
Ancient monuments	49–52	23–6

1.3 Regional variations

(a) England

The law as described in this book generally applies throughout England. There are, however, three cases where the rules are slightly different—although these differences are more as to procedures than as to substance.

First, London has always been slightly different from the rest of England with regard to planning law in general, and historic buildings law in particular. This was emphasised in 1986 when the Greater London Council was abolished. In the course of the emotional debate over abolition, much special pleading was made for the GLC's Historic Buildings Division, which had an international reputation for its high standards. As a result, the Division emerged from the ashes as the London Division of the Commission.

Therefore, the detailed procedures for handling applications are somewhat different in Greater London. The Commission has a larger role than elsewhere, and the Secretary of State a correspondingly reduced one. See Chapter 8 for full details.

Secondly, within the urban development areas set up under the Local Government, Planning and Land Act 1980, the elected local councils are not the planning authority. Instead, the relevant urban development corporation has most of the powers and duties of a local planning authority. This arrangement is not inevitable— it depends on what powers the Secretary of State chooses to give to each new corporation when it is set up (LGPLA 1980, s 149 and Sched 29). In practice however, he gave to each English urban development corporation when it was set up all the powers relevant to the issues considered in this book. The relevant statutory instruments are as follows:

Merseyside Development Corporation (Planning Functions) Order 1981 (SI No 561)

London Docklands Development Corporation (Planning Functions) Order 1981 (SI No 1081)

Trafford Park Development Corporation (Planning Functions) Order 1987 (SI No 739)

Black Country Development Corporation (Planning Functions) Order 1987 (SI No 1340)

Teesside Development Corporation (Planning Functions) Order 1987 (SI No 1341)

Tyne and Wear Development Corporation (Planning Functions) Order 1987 (SI No 1342)

Black Country Development Corporation (Planning Functions) (Wolverhampton) Order 1988 (SI No 1399)

Leeds Development Corporation (Planning Functions) Order 1988 (SI No 1551)

Central Manchester Development Corporation (Planning Functions) Order 1988 (SI No 1552)

Sheffield Development Corporation (Planning Functions) Order 1988 (SI No 1553).

Thirdly, the Norfolk and Suffolk Broads Act 1988 (the relevant parts of which come into force on 1 April 1989) provides for the setting up of the Broads Authority to replace the previous non-statutory joint committee. The new authority is to be the sole district planning authority for the Broads for the purpose of applications for planning permission, listed building consent, conservation area consent and related enforcement procedures (TCPA 1971, s 273A, inserted by the 1988 Act). It is also to have concurrent powers with respect to many other functions under the 1971 Act.

(b) Wales

Readers in Wales should note that the law regarding listed buildings and conservation areas is not always the same there as in England.

In particular, since the remit of the Historic Buildings and Monuments Commission does not extend to Wales, the changes introduced to the 1971 Act by the National Heritage Act 1983 largely apply to England only. Thus in law the Secretary of State for Wales has all the powers and duties ascribed in England either to the Secretary of State for the Environment or to the Commission. In practice, however, the agency of the Welsh Office dealing with historic buildings is very similar to the Commission. It is known as *Cadw*, a Welsh verb meaning 'keep, preserve or save'.

Significantly, Department of the Environment Circular 8/87, in common with its predecessors, does not apply in Wales (see Figure 1.2). The Welsh Office have not yet issued a new Circular replacing 61/81, although one is expected in due course. The directions applying either side of the marches are now therefore significantly different (see in particular 8.4(*h*) and 10.2).

In addition, there are other odd procedural quirks—such as the detailed rules regarding which classes of applications must be notified to the Secretary of State, and which appeals can be decided by inspectors. These largely arise as a result of the much smaller number of listed buildings in Wales.

Finally, the arrangements described above with regard to urban development areas have not been applied, so far, in Wales. The Cardiff Bay Development Corporation does not therefore have any of the powers and duties of a planning authority—these have been retained by Cardiff City Council.

These and other divergences are noted in the text. In general, however, it may be safely assumed that the law is the same in England and Wales—although, except as noted, references to 'the Secretary of State' need to be construed appropriately.

Chapter 2

Listed Buildings

2.1 Lists of buildings of special interest

(a) Introduction

If special protection is to be given to certain buildings of particular merit or interest, it follows that the first requirement is that they should be identified.

In an ideal world, it should be possible for the architectural and historic interest of a building to be taken into account automatically by all those considering the desirability of any proposal affecting it. In reality, however, opinions are bound to differ widely as to the merits of a particular building; and this is particularly so when it is under threat. It is remarkable that a building that has stood totally unnoticed for years can suddenly be extolled by amenity groups as having been a gem of its particular type— the day after it has been demolished. Of more concern, perhaps, is the fate of a building which is widely admired and enjoyed, but condemned by a developer as being a mediocre example of an uninteresting style.

The Town and Country Planning Act 1971, following all the Planning Acts since 1947, therefore recognises that certain buildings have to be identified as being not just of some interest, but of 'special architectural or historic interest'. The Secretary of State is thus under a duty to compile a list of such buildings (TCPA 1971, s 54(1)). Works to these buildings are then subject to the need for *listed building consent* (see Chapter 8); and those responsible for unauthorised works can be penalised (see Chapter 9).

The present system of listed building consent replaces, incidentally, the old system of *building preservation orders* in force prior to 1 January 1969. Any building that was then subject to such an order became in effect a 'listed building' (s 54(10)). As to *building preservation notices*, see Chapter 3.

(b) Principles of selection

Listed buildings are chosen according to a set of definite criteria, drawn up by the Historic Buildings Council (the forerunner of the Historic Buildings and Monuments Commission). Those currently applying to pre-1914 buildings are as follows (Circ 8/87, App I):

Before 1700: all buildings which survive in anything like their original condition are listed;

1700 to 1840: most buildings are listed, though selection is necessary; and

1840 to 1914: only buildings of definite quality and character are listed, and the selection is designed to include the principal works of the principal architects.

In choosing buildings, particular attention is paid to:

(1) special value within certain types, either for architectural or planning reasons or as illustrating social or economic history (for instance, industrial buildings, railway stations, schools, hospitals, theatres, town halls, markets, exchanges, almshouses, prisons, lock-ups, mills);

(2) technological innovation or virtuosity (for instance, cast iron, prefabrication, or the early use of concrete);

(3) association with well known characters or events; and

(4) group value, especially as examples of town planning (for instance, squares, terraces or model villages).

As to the last of these criteria, the Secretary of State has since 1968 been obliged to consider the contribution (presumably architectural or historic) that a building makes to any group of which it forms part. This requirement (now TCPA 1971, s 54(2)) was possibly introduced in the light of the decision by the Court of Appeal in *Earl of Iveagh* v *Minister of Housing and Local Government* [1964] 1 QB 395 that a building might be of special architectural or historic interest by reason of its setting as one of a group.

As to more recent buildings, selected examples of high quality are now being listed from the inter-war period. The criteria here are 'designed to enable full recognition to be given to the varied architectural output of the period. Three main building styles (broadly interpreted) are represented: modern, classical, and others. The building types which may be considered cover nine categories, as follows:

(1) churches, chapels, and other places of public worship;

(2) cinemas, theatres, hotels, and other places of public entertainment;

(3) commercial and industrial premises including shops and offices;

(4) schools, colleges, and other educational buildings;

(5) blocks of flats;

(6) houses and housing estates;

(7) municipal and other public buildings;

(8) railway stations, airport terminals, and other places associated with public transport; and

(9) miscellaneous.

The selection includes the work of the principal architects of the period' (Circ 8/87, App I).

A few outstanding buildings built after 1939 have now been listed. In April 1987, it was announced by the Government that all buildings over thirty years old will be eligible for listing in England. This change brings England into line with Scotland and Wales, although the English policy also allows 'in very exceptional circumstances' for the listing of buildings when they are only ten years old. Although this might at first appear startling, it is perfectly logical—it is surely more important to preserve one of the few excellent buildings of 1970 than one of the many mediocre buildings of 1870. The only difficulty is to agree on which recent buildings are to be selected; out of the many buildings suggested following the announcement, only a handful were chosen— including, for example, Stockwell Bus Garage in London and Coventry Cathedral.

Finally, when considering whether or not to list a particular building (of any period), the Secretary of State is to take into account the merits of not only the building itself, but also those of any object or structure on or near the building or in its curtilage (see 2.5(c), (d)).

(c) Grades

Not all listed buildings are of equal worth, however. They are classified into three grades, as follows (again, summarised in Circ 8/87, App I):

(1) *Grade I*: buildings of exceptional interest (only about 2 per cent of listed buildings so far are in this grade);

(2) *Grade II**: particularly important buildings of more than special interest (some 4 per cent of listed buildings);

(3) *Grade II*: buildings of special interest, which warrant every effort being made to preserve them.

Churches may be included in the list; but Church of England buildings were until recently classified as Grades A, B or C (see 13.1).

Older lists used to contain some buildings classified as Grade III. These were buildings of local interest, but not statutorily 'listed' buildings. They do not therefore obtain the protection afforded to buildings of other grades. However, when these earlier lists are revised, such buildings are frequently upgraded to Grade II—particularly where they are of group value. In addition, many of them will also be in conservation areas, and their demolition will for that reason require consent (see Chapter 10).

The full significance of the grading of listed buildings will become apparent when considering the availability of financial assistance for repairs and the details of procedure for processing listed building consent applications and appeals (see Chapters 6 and 8).

It will be seen that buildings and structures are also deemed to be listed if they have been within the curtilage of a listed building since before June 1948. However, they are not normally mentioned in the list, and are therefore not allocated a grade. This can cause problems where an authority has to decide what procedure to follow with regard to an application for works to a building, not listed in its own right, that is within the curtilage of two buildings of different grades. In practice, where there is any doubt it would seem to be sensible to regard such a building as being of the higher of the two grades, since works to it could be said to affect the setting of the more important of the admittedly listed buildings. Where the curtilage building is obviously of no interest at all so that this would be absurd, and the procedure appropriate to the lower grade is therefore followed, the reason for this should be clearly recorded, to protect against any subsequent legal challenge.

(d) Number of listed buildings

The first listing programme ran from 1947 to 1968. The lists produced were somewhat patchy—especially the earlier ones. A second nationwide resurvey was therefore carried out from 1969. It was accelerated in 1982, and the fieldwork for it was completed by the end of 1987; although some areas have yet to receive their new lists.

The total number of listed buildings in England at the beginning of October 1988 was 422,411. These included 6,059 buildings of Grade I, and an estimated 20,000 of Grade II*. Approximately 30,000 buildings were added to the list during 1985, 27,657 in 1986, and 32,603 in 1987. The number of Grade I buildings rose in the same three years by 129, 104 and 171.

The distribution of listed buildings throughout the country is, as might be expected, far from even. Outside Greater London (which contains 37,768), Kent has the most buildings of all grades (20,808), followed by Devon (19,205), Avon (16,699), and Essex (16,227) If the counties are compared on a population basis, however, it is notable that the highest density of listed buildings per head of population is in the three neighbouring counties of Gloucestershire, Wiltshire, and Hereford and Worcester. As to Grade I buildings, Greater London had 917, followed by Avon (679, including 614 in Bath), East Sussex (274), Oxfordshire (257), and North Yorkshire (220).

The resurvey has so far proceeded much more slowly in Wales. There were at the beginning of October 1988 12,224 listed buildings in the principality, of which 236 were of Grade I, and a further 612 of Grade II*.

2.2 Listing procedure

(a) Production of the list

The Secretary of State is to compile a list of buildings of special architectural or historic interest. He may approve lists produced by others—such as local authorities, consultants, or amenity groups. In particular, he may (in England) approve lists prepared by the Historic Buildings and Monuments Commission (TCPA 1971, s 54(1), amended by NHA 1983).

In practice, the Department of the Environment compiles a list for the area of each local authority (district or borough council). The first lists came into force in the 1940s; and they are constantly being amended. Amendment usually takes the form of:

(1) the inclusion of one or more new buildings in the list;

(2) the alteration of the grade ascribed to a building already on the list;

(3) the removal of a building from the list (because it has been altered, demolished, or burned, or its merit proves to have been misjudged, or it was listed in error); or

(4) the issue of a complete new list for an authority's area.
The last of these will be done only as part of a programmed resurvey of the whole country (see above); and the list produced will normally include all buildings listed previously, although possibly with updated descriptions or grades. This is likely to be less frequent in future, now that the major resurvey is complete. More common is likely to be the ad hoc addition to the list of a particular building, terrace or group (see 2.2(c)).

The Secretary of State, in compiling the list, is required to consult with experts in the field of historic buildings (including specifically the Commission) (s 54(3), amended by NHA 1983). In practice, the survey work is carried out in England by a team of specialist inspectors—in England, employed by the Commission and, in Wales, employed by the Welsh Office (Cadw).

There is no requirement for the Secretary of State to consult the owners of buildings to be listed, or local authorities, or anyone else. Indeed, it used to be a notable feature of the listing process that the Department's inspectors who actually assessed the buildings on site usually carried out only an external survey. They did not normally contact the occupiers or owners concerned—who only became aware of the listing after it had taken effect. 'The evidence with regard to [the listed building procedures] [was] rather startling' (*Amalgamated Investment and Property Co Ltd* v *John Walker and Sons Ltd* [1976] 3 All ER 509 per Buckley LJ at 512).

Inspectors have now been instructed to be more communicative (if only as a matter of politeness); and the Code of Conduct for resurvey teams emphasises the need for publicity before a survey is carried out, and seeking cooperation while it is in progress. Except where an inspector has been warned or has reasonable grounds to suspect that there is a threat of pre-emptive demolition, he will now make himself known to the owner or occupier of the property he is inspecting—or leave a visiting card. The subsequent letter from the Department, notifying the owner of a building that it has been listed, has been made more 'user-friendly'.

There is nevertheless a statutory power for anyone duly authorised by the Secretary of State to enter any land at any reasonable time to survey any building in connection with a proposal to include it in, or exclude it from, the statutory list (TCPA 1971, s 280(2)). There must, therefore, presumably be at least some grounds for thinking that the building is worthy of being listed (or de-listed, as the case may be). A person carrying out such a survey must, if required, give at least 24 hours' notice; and, if he damages the property, compensation is payable (s 281(1),(4); *Six Carpenters' Case* (1610) 8 Co Rep 146a). Moreover, anyone obstructing him is liable to a fine not exceeding level 2 on the standard scale (s 281(2); *R v Chief Constable of Devon and Cornwall, ex parte CEGB* [1981] 3 All ER 826).

Once a building has been surveyed, and considered by the inspector to be suitable for listing, it must then be considered and approved—with or without amendments—in due course by the appropriate (administrative) civil servant in the Department of the Environment or Welsh Office. Eventually, if approved, the amendment to the list (or, as appropriate, new list) is typed, signed and dated by a principal on behalf of the Secretary of State. It is this date that determines conclusively when the building becomes listed.

This process was examined in some detail in the *John Walker* case. The details, in that case, proved to be of crucial importance: on 25 September 1973, the parties signed a contract in which the defendants agreed to sell a Victorian warehouse to the plaintiffs, with a view to its demolition prior to the redevelopment of the site, for £1,710,000. Two days later, on 27 September, the list (containing 1,500 other buildings throughout the London Borough of Tower Hamlets as well as the warehouse) was signed, and the warehouse became effectively 'listed'. The evidence was that, once listed, it was worth only £210,000.

(b) Notification of local authority, owners and occupiers

Once a list or an amendment has been signed, a copy is immediately sent to all the local authorities covering the area concerned (county council, district or borough council, national park planning board and the Broads Authority) (TCPA 1971, s 54(4), amended by LGA 1972; s 54(13), inserted by NSBA 1988). Usually a certified copy is sent to the town clerk or chief executive, with extra copies for general use as required. A copy of any list in Greater London is also sent to the Commission (s 54(5), amended by LGA 1985).

In addition, letters are sent by the Department to 'the owner/occupier' of every building newly listed. However, these will not reach everyone with an interest in the building, particularly where it is leasehold, or in multiple occupation, or currently vacant. The local authority (district or borough council) is therefore under a duty to inform every owner and occupier of the building 'as soon as may be' after being notified by the Secretary of State (s 54(7), amended by LGA 1972). This means that the authority first has to find out who are all the owners (including absent freeholders, tenants of blocks of flats, etc) and occupiers. This can be done by personal inspection, or using the authority's statutory powers to obtain information (TCPA 1971, s 284; Local Government (Miscellaneous Provisions) Act 1976, s 16) — possibly using a standard questionnaire.

This can take place almost immediately in the case of a single building being added to the list; but where a new list is produced for the whole of the authority's area, the paperwork involved can be very time-consuming, and has to be fitted in amongst other routine work. It is not surprising, therefore, that notification can be delayed for several months. The actual notification is to be 'in the prescribed form' (TCPA 1971, s 54(7); TCP (LBCA) Regs 1987, Sched 4).

Since the listing (and hence the need for listed building consent: see 8.1) takes effect from the date the list is signed (see above), and since in certain circumstances the owner may not be informed of it until some while later, there is a real risk that the owner can carry out works to the building which require consent, without being aware of the need for it. He may thus, quite unintentionally, commit an offence punishable by imprisonment—which is particularly unfortunate now that (since *R* v *Wells Street Metropolitan Stipendiary Magistrate, exp Westminster CC* [1986] 1 WLR 1046: see 9.2(*a*)) it has been established that the offence is one of strict liability.

The fact that a building is listed, upgraded, or deleted from the list is to be a local land charge (s 54(6), amended by Local Land Charges Act 1975). This has the effect of ensuring that any future prospective purchaser of the building, as well as the present owners and occupiers, is made aware of its listing, and can therefore find out from the planning authority what effect this may have on any proposed development he wishes to carry out.

Thus, in *Aquis Estates* v *Minton* [1975] 1 WLR 1452, a property company had agreed to purchase the remaining few years of a long leasehold of an old factory in Southwark, subject to there being no adverse entry on the purchaser's local land charge search. The building was subsequently listed, largely for its industrial historical interest. The purchaser then sought to rescind the contract. It was held that the listing did constitute an 'adverse entry', since it would clearly hamper a developer in plans to convert the building for office use. However, although this amounted to a breach of a term of the contract which would have allowed the purchaser to rescind, he had chosen to continue to negotiate, and had invited the vendor to make a non-statutory appeal against the listing (see 2.3). That, not surprisingly, was unsuccessful. But the purchaser, having thus elected to affirm the contract by negotiating, could not repudiate it now.

(c) Spot-listing

Anyone (including a local authority) may request the Secretary of State to include a building on the statutory list. Since it is he and not the authority that has the power to list buildings, there is no point in a private individual or an amenity group asking an authority to do so. Nevertheless it is prudent to obtain its support since it may be able to point out that the building in question was recently proposed for listing, but rejected.

> The request should be made to:
> *England*: Department of the Environment, Listing Branch (HSD2), Lambeth Bridge House, London SE1 7SB (tel 01–211 3000)
> *Wales*: Cadw–Welsh Historic Monuments, Brunel House, 2 Fitzalan Road, Cardiff CF2 1UY (tel 0222–465511).

It should be in writing, and accompanied by a location plan (such as an Ordnance Survey map extract), and up-to-date photographs of the main elevations and any significant features of the building (not photocopies or slides), as well as any other information that may be known about the building—such as the date(s) of its construction; its historical associations, if any; its architect; its group value in the street; and details of any interior features (Circ 8/87, para 39).

Once such a request is received, an investigator will be dispatched to inspect the building, except in a case of urgency where the information supplied is adequate for the building to be assessed without a visit. It will then, if appropriate, be listed in the normal way. This is sometimes known as 'spot-listing.'

It is however inevitable that there will be some delay:

> Public concern for the conservation of old and familiar buildings is increasing and buildings under threat of redevelopment are being brought to the Department's notice in growing numbers. Many of these notifications are made at a very late stage in the formulation of proposals for redevelopment, and intervention by the Secretary of State invariably

means delay and even abandonment of redevelopment schemes, as well as other difficulties and hardship (Circ 8/87, para 38).

It is therefore important that a request to list a building is made as early as possible, preferably before planning permission is granted.

(d) Where to inspect the list

Lists must be kept available for inspection by the public at reasonable hours, free of charge, by all local authorities, by the Commission (lists for Greater London only), and by the Secretary of State (TCPA 1971, s 54(8), amended by LGA 1985).

Lists for the whole of England are available at the Royal Commission on Historical Monuments's National Monuments Record, 23 Savile Row, London W1X 1AB. Queries about the contents of the lists should be sent to the Department of the Environment's Listing Branch (see above). Lists for Wales are available at Cadw–Welsh Historic Monuments (see above).

It is more prudent for enquirers to apply to the appropriate local authority for information, however, for they will then also be able to find out whether or not the building is in a conservation area. If it is, it will be subject to some control (notably over demolition) even if it is not listed.

(e) Removal of a building from the list

A building should obviously be removed from the list if it is demolished. It can also be removed if it is no longer considered to be of special architectural or historic interest, because it has been substantially altered, or because it was entered on the list by mistake, or (rarely) because someone has successfully appealed against the listing (see 2.3). For one or other of these reasons, 451 buildings were in fact removed from the list in 1984, 805 in 1985, 451 in 1986, and 702 in 1987.

Once the Secretary of State has decided or agreed to remove a building from the list, or to alter its grade, the procedure is exactly as for listing (see 2.2(a), (b)).

2.3 Appeals against listing

There is no statutory right to appeal against the inclusion of a building in the list. But anyone can at any time write to the Secretary of State claiming that a building should not be listed (after an initial survey has been carried out), or that it should be removed from the list.

The Department of the Environment has issued a leaflet *How to Appeal Against Listing*, available from the Listing Branch (see 2.2(*c*)). There are no forms to fill in, no set procedures to go through, and no time limits.

You should be aware, however, that buildings are listed for their special architectural or historic interest. . . . We cannot take a building off the list just because an owner feels aggrieved. We have to be convinced that a mistake has been made in adding the building in the first place; or that a building has become so altered or mutilated over the years that it is no longer worthy of listing.

The information required is as for spot-listing (see above)— location plan, photographs and other details as appropriate.

In practice, however, such approaches only rarely lead to a decision being overturned. Certainly in the *Aquis Estates* case (see 2.2(*b*)) none of the parties held out any hope that it would be successful, and the listing was referred to as being 'in practice impossible to rescind'. In fact only three dozen such appeals were received by the Department of the Environment in 1985 (compared to some 23,000 buildings being listed that year); and of those only five were successful.

There was much discussion in the House of Lords during the debate on the Housing and Planning Bill, as to the possibility of a statutory right of appeal against listing. However, after a some-what confused debate in Committee, their lordships voted at report stage not to provide for such a right. But it seems almost inevitable that the issue will reappear at some stage.

There is of course at present a statutory right to appeal against the listing of a building if listed building consent is refused for works to it (TCPA 1971, Sched 11, para 8(2)), or if a listed building enforcement notice is issued (TCPA 1971, s 97(1)(*a*), substituted by LGPAA 1981). This is the first time when the listing of a building directly affects its owner adversely. As to the uncertainty resulting from listing (in other words, from the need to obtain listed building consent), this is no worse than that which arises from the need to obtain planning permission for development.

2.4 Certificates of immunity from listing

Partly as a result of the *John Walker* case (see 2.2(*a*)), it was recognised that the listing of a building at a late stage in redevelopment proposals can cause great inconvenience or hardship. It is therefore possible to apply for a *certificate of immunity from listing*. This is a legal guarantee that a building will not be listed during the five years starting with the date on which the certificate is signed (TCPA 1971, s 54A(2), inserted by LGPLA 1980). It also prevents the local authority from serving a building preservation notice on the building during that period (see Chapter 3).

An application for a certificate can be made by anyone, whether or not they own the building, provided that planning permission has been granted for works involving its alteration or demolition or that a planning application has been submitted for such works (s 54A(1)). This means that it is not possible for a vendor (or prospective purchaser) to apply for a certificate before placing a property on the market, in order to assist in determining its value. In such a case, however, it would presumably be possible to make an application after first submitting a token application for a minor alteration.

The application is made to the Department's Listing Branch or to Cadw–Welsh Historic Monuments (see 2.2(*c*)). There is no form. Nor is there any charge—although there will of course be a fee payable for the planning application which must have preceded the application for a certificate. A copy of the application for a certificate, and of all the accompanying material, must also be sent to the following:

(1) *in a national park*: the county council or joint board;
(2) *in Greater London*: the borough council and the London Division of the Historic Buildings and Monuments Commission;
(3) *in the Broads*: the district council and the Broads Authority;
(4) *elsewhere*: the district or borough council.

The application should include:

(1) the full address of the building;
(2) a copy of the relevant planning application or permission;
(3) a site location plan;
(4) clear, recent photographs; and
(5) confirmation that the application has been copied to the appropriate authority (as above).

On receipt of the application, a thorough inspection of the

building will be arranged and the Department will ask the local authority if it wishes to make any comments.

A certificate takes the form of a letter to the applicant, signed on behalf of the Secretary of State. If one is issued, the Department will notify the district or borough council and the county council (and, in London, the Commission). The existence of a certificate is not a local land charge; but it has been suggested that it should be disclosed in response to enquiries by prospective purchasers (Circ 8/87, para 44).

Note that a certificate does not preclude the local authority from including the property within a conservation area, which would mean that consent could still be required for its demolition. 'It is not considered practicable to extend the certificate procedure to secure immunity from the effects of designation of a conservation area' (para 45). This is no doubt realistic, but it arguably renders the whole procedure slightly pointless.

If a certificate is not issued, the building will of course be listed; but at least this removes the uncertainty.

2.5 The extent of listing

(a) Introduction

A 'listed building' is thus a building included in a list of buildings of special architectural or historic interest compiled by the Secretary of State under s 54 of the 1971 Act. But it is further defined, to include the following (TCPA 1971, s 54(9), amended by HPA 1986):

(1) the building itself;
(2) any object or structure fixed to the building; and
(3) any object or structure within the curtilage of the building, but only if it has been within that curtilage since before 1 July 1948.

It is important to know just what is comprised within the listing, as this will help to determine whether or not listed building consent is needed for any works proposed. Each of the three headings is now considered in turn.

(b) The building itself

The phrase 'the building itself' refers to the principal building which is described in the list. In the old 'provisional' lists, and in the most recent statutory lists (sometimes referred to as 'greenback' lists), there is a description provided for each building. This is there purely to aid identification, and does not mean that any feature not noted is of no importance—it would be possible to write a substantial book on one of the larger listed buildings (a cathedral, for instance), without mentioning every one of its notable features. But the description does (or at least it should) make clear which building is being highlighted. This can be useful, especially where an older building or structure is itself within the grounds of a newer one (such as a medieval wall enclosing the garden of a nondescript Victorian house).

A 'building' is defined to include any structure or erection, and includes any part of any building as so defined (TCPA 1971, s 290, amended by HPA 1986). This means, first, that a 'building' can be as large as a palace or as small as a bollard. In fact a surprising variety of objects have been listed—including, for example, memorials, gravestones, embankments, train sheds, water troughs, lamp posts, mews, arches, and tunnels.

Secondly, every part of a listed building is in law equally 'listed'. The interior is thus just as much listed as the exterior—whether or not it is in itself of any interest. See, for example, the appeal reported at [1983] JPL 751, regarding works to the interior of a late Victorian pub. Here, all the features on the exterior of the building are equally listed. Listed, too, would be any unattractive later additions to an old building including the modern replacement of windows and doors. Statements that, for example, the exterior of a building, or a particularly fine period shop-front, are listed mean nothing—the exterior, or the shopfront, may be the reason why the building has been included in the list; but either the whole building is listed, including the interior, or none of it.

(c) Objects and structures attached to a listed building

Secondly, a listed building is defined to include 'any object or structure fixed to the building' (TCPA 1971, s 54(9), as amended by HPA 1986). This is a fairly general phrase, and would seem to include almost anything—a sundial, a conservatory, an immediately adjoining building (which would clearly be a 'structure')—or even a climbing plant (unless that is outside the definition of 'object').

There is thus no doubt that any man-made object that is fixed to the building, inside or outside, will be listed. This is intended to bring within control the alteration or removal of objects which are part of the historic fabric or are of architectural interest, such as panelling, chimney-pieces and wrought-iron balustrades. In cases of doubt, the critical test to determine whether or not an object is included would be whether it is a 'fixture' (such as carved wood panelling: *Corthorn Land and Timber Co* v *Minister of Housing and Local Government* (1966) 17 P & CR 210, and *Re Chesterfield* [1911] 1 Ch 237) or a 'fitting' (such as furniture or paintings). The usual rules for distinguishing real and personal property will therefore apply. These may sometimes lead to uncertainty, however—tapestries, fixed to the wall, were held not to be fixtures in *Leigh* v *Taylor* [1902] AC 157; but they were considered fixtures in *Re Whaley* [1908] 1 Ch 615. In the second of these two cases, it was considered that 'the ornaments were inserted primarily for the purpose of creating a beautiful room as a whole, and not intended for the mere display and enjoyment of the chattels themselves'. In a notable borderline case carved figures on the stairs, sculptured marble vases in the hall, a pair of marble lions at the head of a flight of garden steps and sixteen stone garden seats, all of which merely rested on their own weight, were all held to be fixtures; the test was whether the items were 'part of the architectural design . . . and put in there as such, as distinguished from mere ornaments to be afterwards added' (*D'Eyncourt* v *Gregory* (1866) LR 3 Eq 382 per Lord Romilly MR at 396).

Note that whether the fixture is part of the 'listed building' is independent of any merit that the fixture may or may not possess. Whether or not its alteration or removal will need listed building consent depends on whether the works will affect the character of the building as a building of special architectural or historic interest (1971 Act, s 55(1)). Clearly the removal of fine fifteenth century carvings, as in the *Corthorn* case, will affect the building's special character, and will therefore require consent; the removal of a bath tap (just as much a fixture) will not.

More difficult, however, is the case where the 'structure' attached to the listed building is itself a building—such as a garage, attached to a (listed) house; or even one house (not listed in its own right) attached to another (listed). Is the 'attached' structure in each case to be considered as much subject to listed building control as the admittedly listed building to which it is attached? This was the subject of attention by the Court of Appeal in *A–G, ex rel Sutcliffe, Rouse & Hughes* v *Calderdale BC* [1983] JPL 310 and by the Court of Appeal and the House of Lords in *Debenhams PLC* v *Westminster City Council* [1986] JPL 671, overturned by [1987] JPL 344.

In *Calderdale*, the building which was listed in its own right was a disused mill at Hebden Bridge. Attached to this was a stone bridge, and attached to the other end of the bridge was a terrace of 15 millworkers' cottages, also disused. The dispute centred on the contention that, since a structure (B) fixed to a listed building (A) is deemed to be part of the building, structure (C) fixed to structure (B) is also part of building (A).

In the opinion of Stephenson LJ, the purpose of s 54(9) was to bring within control works to objects and structures which might not be intrinsically of interest, but which were so closely related to a listed building that their removal might adversely affect it (see, for example, TCPA 1971, s 56(3), and Circ 8/87, para 25). On this basis, he favoured a broad approach to the construction of the subsection, and thus concluded that 'although at first sight it seemed unlikely that [the far end] of this terrace could be regarded as fixed to the mill, he thought the judge [at first instance] was right in concluding that this terrace was a structure fixed to the mill in the ordinary sense of those words'.

The *Debenhams* case concerned a group of several buildings which were within the same hereditament for rating purposes, but only some of which (including the former Hamley's toy shop in Regent Street) were listed in their own right. 27–28 Kingly Street was not, but had been linked to the others by a footbridge at second floor level and a subway. The two buildings are in fact entirely different in character, and were only ever linked for a short period by an accident of history. It was held in the Court of Appeal (following *Calderdale*) that No 27–28 was a structure fixed to the admittedly listed building, and was therefore part of it.

However, this was overturned by the majority on appeal to the House of Lords. Lord Keith there considered that the word 'structure' is intended to convey a limitation to such structures as are ancillary to the listed building itself, for example a stable block of a mansion house, either fixed to the main building or within its curtilage. In his opinion, the concept envisaged is that of principal and accessory.

Finally, under this heading, note that a post-1948 addition to a listed building is still 'listed;' it is only post-1948 structures in the curtilage of the building, not fixed to it, that were in 1987 excluded from the listing (HPA 1986, Sched 9, para 1).

(d) Objects and structures in the curtilage of a listed building

It is not surprising that a listed building is defined to include objects and structures fixed to the building. They are, after all, very obviously part of the building. It is perhaps less immediately apparent that the listing extends to 'any object or structure within the curtilage of the building which, although not fixed to the building, forms part of the land and has done so since before 1 July 1948' (TCPA 1971, s 54(9), amended by HPA 1986).

This means that any object or structure is subject to listed building control if:

(1) it is in the 'curtilage' of a clearly listed building (that is, one that is identified and described in the statutory list itself); and

(2) it has been there since June 1948.

The listing thus extends to any object (such as a statue or birdbath) or structure (such as a garden pavilion or wall) in the curtilage of the building. This protection obviously makes sense in the case of, for example, a large country house whose grounds contain numerous temples, statues, grottoes and so on; they may indeed in some cases be one of the reasons, or indeed the principal reason, why the building was listed (s 54(2)(*b*); see 2.1(*b*)). On the other hand, they are still affected by the restrictions involved in the listing process even if they are of no interest whatsoever (such as a decaying garden shed).

As with objects and structures fixed to the building (see above), the first critical test is not any merit that the object or structure may or may not possess, but whether it 'forms part of the land'. The normal rules for distinguishing between fixtures and fittings will therefore apply. Thus greenhouses, not secured to the ground but standing by their own weight on concrete dollies, were held not to be part of the land (*HE Dibble* v *Moore* [1970] 2 QB 181, CA); whereas a dry stone wall was clearly a fixture (*Holland* v *Hodgson* (1872) LR 7 CP 328). Also see *D'Eyncourt* v *Gregory* (1866) LR 3 Eq 382 (2.5(*c*) above) and see 11.4 on gardens generally.

The effect of this has been somewhat mitigated by the amendment, which took effect on 1 April 1987, whereby such structures were not subject to listed building control if they had not been part of the curtilage since before 1948. This would remove from the need for consent many trivial operations in the grounds of listed buildings. It incidentally also removed the ridiculous anomaly whereby one could in some circumstances require listed building consent for the demolition of a garden shed erected (quite possibly under permitted development rights) in the 1950s. Where consent has already (before the coming into force of the 1986 Act) been refused for works to structures which are, as a result of this change, no longer deemed to be listed, work may now proceed with impunity—subject, obviously, to any need for planning permission (HPA 1986, Sched 9, para 1(2)).

(e) Definition of curtilage

This still leaves, however, the vexed question of what is the extent of the *curtilage* of a building. The definition often cited is 'the ground which is used for the comfortable enjoyment of the house or other building . . . although it has not been marked off or enclosed in any way. It is enough that it serves the purpose of the house or building in some necessary or reasonably useful way' (*Sinclair-Lockhart's Trustees* v *Central Land Board* (1951) 1 P & CR 195 at 204). This is not very precise; and it might also include, for example, a neighbour's garden which could serve a house in a very useful way by providing an attractive view. Thus in *Re St George's, Oakdale* [1975] 2 All ER 870, it was held that the territorial extent of the curtilage 'will depend on the facts of the individual case and the circumstances of the particular site'. And in *Methuen-Campbell* v *Walters* [1979] QB 525, Buckley LJ held that it was not enough that the land and its curtilage were conveyed or demised together. Nor is the test whether the enjoyment of one is advantageous or convenient or necessary for the full enjoyment of the other.

. . . for one corporeal hereditament to fall within the curtilage of another, the former must be so intimately associated with the latter as to lead to the conclusion that the former in truth forms part and parcel of the latter. There can be very few houses indeed that do not have associated with them at least some few square yards of land, constituting a yard or a basement area or passageway or something of the kind . . . which on a reasonable view could only be regarded as part of the messuage and such small pieces of land would be held to fall within the curtilage of the messuage. This may extend to ancillary buildings, structures or areas such as outhouses, a garage, a driveway, a garden and so forth. How far it is appropriate to regard this identity as parts of one messuage or parcel of land as extending must depend on the character and circumstances under consideration. To the extent that it is reasonable to regard them as constituting one messuage or parcel of land, they will be properly regarded as all falling within one curtilage; they constitute an integral whole (at pp 543–4).

Reference was made in *A–G ex rel Sutcliffe, Rouse & Hughes* v *Calderdale BC* [1983] JPL 310 (see 2.5(*c*) for the facts) to *Methuen-Campbell* and to a number of other cases (notably *Pilbrow* v *Vestry of the Parish of St Leonard's, Shoreditch* [1895] 1 QB 433 and *Vestry of St Martin's-in-the-Fields* v *Bird* [1895] 1 QB 428), showing the difficulty of finding a clear definition. The only test which emerged was to consider in each instance:

(1) the physical layout of the listed building and the structure;
(2) their ownership, past and present; and
(3) their use or function, past and present.

Stephenson LJ, as noted above, favoured a broad interpretation of the Act, so that even 'a block of flats replacing the stables of a mansion house might have to be treated as part of the mansion house because within the curtilage of the mansion'. He therefore came to the conclusion ('not without doubt') that the terrace had definitely been within the curtilage of the mill when they were both built in 1870, and that it not been taken out of its curtilage by the changes which had subsequently taken place. Similarly, in *Debenhams PLC* v *Westminster CC* [1986] JPL 671 at 674 (see 2.5(*c*)), the footbridge between the buildings was removed towards the end of the period in question. But the Kingly Street building was reckoned by the Court of Appeal to be still within the curtilage of the listed building since it was nearby, in the same ownership, and (when occupied) in the same use.

This view, however, was overturned by the majority opinion in the House of Lords in *Debenhams*. The curtilage issue was only raised in passing, but by implication Lord Keith disagreed with the decision of the Court of Appeal (and hence also with their decision in *Calderdale*), since in his opinion 27–28 Kingly Street was an independent building and not part of the listed building under the 1971 Act ([1987] JPL 344 at 347). The possibility of extending the scope of the listing of a building is thus definitely limited.

The most recent case on this point (*Dyer* v *Dorset CC* [1988] 3 WLR 213) concerned a similarly worded provision in the Housing Act 1980 (Sched 1, amended by HA 1985). The Court of Appeal here had to decide the meaning of the phrase 'the dwellinghouse either forms part of, or is within the curtilage of, the building'. It was held that the issue of whether a particular dwellinghouse was within the curtilage of another building, being a question of fact and degree, was primarily for the trial judge. This particular case concerned a college of agriculture, which comprised an estate of about 100 acres containing the main house, which was its headquarters, extensive gardens, a park and a mass of outbuildings—a situation similar to a number of larger listed buildings in extensive grounds used for institutional purposes. The lecturers' houses, including the one whose status was in dispute, were on the edge of the estate, facing a road which provided the only vehicular access. They were fenced off at the back, although there was pedestrian access to the rest of the college grounds.

Lord Donaldson MR examined various authorities and concluded that the word 'curtilage' seemed always to have to be read in context. Accordingly, if in this case the relevant words were the 'curtilage of the college', he would have had little doubt that, despite the fact that the house was on the edge of the campus and divided from it by a fence, it would have rightly been held to have been within that curtilage. But those were not the relevant words, and he was quite unable to find that the house lay within the curtilage of any other college building or collection of buildings.

The practical effect of the inclusion in the listing of buildings within the curtilage is anyway limited by the requirement that, as already noted, listed building consent is only needed for works to the 'listed building' (as thus defined) where they affect its character (TCPA 1971, s 55(1)). So, to take Stephenson LJ's example in *Calderdale* of the block of flats (see above), many if not almost all works to the new block would not need listed building consent as they would not affect the character of the mansion house. Of course, if the flats were erected since 1948, they would now—since the amendment discussed above—only be included within the listing if they were actually (directly or indirectly) 'attached' to the mansion.

There was an attempt in the House of Lords debate on the Housing and Planning Bill to insert into the 1971 Act a statutory definition of 'curtilage'. This would have limited it to land not exceeding one hectare, but otherwise followed the *Calderdale* test almost verbatim. This was unsuccessful but it did provoke from Lord Montagu (the chairman of the Historic Buildings and Monuments Commission) the comment that:

the practice of the Department now and of my officers who advise the

Department is to consider individually all the structures and buildings on a site which can be construed as separate buildings and to list those, and only those, which qualify. The new lists therefore will leave little room for doubt whether a building is listed or not (*Hansard* (HL) Deb, 13 October 1985, col 625).

Only time will tell whether this optimism is justified.

(f) Cases of doubt

In view of the preceding comments, it will be clear that it will not always be easy to determine whether or not a particular building, object or structure is within the scope of the listing.

If in doubt, therefore, the only safe course is to ask the local planning authority. It is, after all, the authority that decides whether or not to take enforcement action or to institute a prosecution if works are carried out for which listed building consent should (in its view) have been obtained. It is always possible, when served with a copy of a listed building enforcement notice, to appeal against it on the ground that consent was not required for the works (TCPA 1971, s 97(1)(*b*), substituted by LGPAA 1981 and see 9.4(*f*)). However, it is more sensible to ask for the authority's view in the first place.

There is, incidentally, no procedure, akin to a s 53 determination, to enable an owner to ascertain formally whether or not listed building consent would be required for a particular operation he has in mind. Any opinion offered by a local authority officer must, therefore, be just that—it will not and cannot legally bind the authority (*Western Fish Products* v *Penwith DC* [1981] 2 All ER 204).

2.6 The consequences of listing

The effect of a building being listed is that it is declared openly to be 'of special architectural and historic interest' (TCPA 1971, s 54(1)). This does not imply that there is any presumption in favour of the building being preserved—compare the definition of a conservation area, which states that it is an area 'the character or appearance of which it is desirable to preserve or enhance'. But it is stated in the Act that the inclusion of a building in the list is 'with a view to the guidance of local planning authorities in the performance of their functions under this Act in relation to historic buildings'.

The most important of these functions is probably the determining of applications for planning permission and listed building consent. Accordingly, the Act provides that:

In considering whether to grant planning permission for development which affects a listed building or its setting, and in considering whether to grant listed building consent for any works, the local planning authority or the Secretary of State, as the case may be, shall have special regard to the desirability of preserving the building or its setting or any features of special architectural or historic interest which it possesses (TCPA 1971, s 56(3), amended by LGPLA 1980).

Again, note that there is here no presumption in law in favour of the building being preserved—but the planning authority is at least to consider the desirability of that being achieved (see also 7.6 and 8.7). 'Listing' a building therefore in theory means precisely that—merely including it in a list, as an aide memoire to all concerned to ensure that it is not demolished or damaged by unsuitable alterations without at least some thought being given to its preservation.

In practice, however, there is as a matter of policy a presumption in favour of buildings of special interest being preserved (Circ 8/87, para 91; quoted at 8.7(*b*)). To assist in achieving this, the legislation has over the years been developed so that there are now a number of special provisions regarding listed buildings. These are summarised in Figure 2.1, and explored in more detail in the remainder of this book.

As to the financial consequences of a building being listed, it has already been noted that in some cases these can be disastrous for an owner or prospective purchaser (*Amalgamated Investment and Property Co Ltd* v *John Walker and Sons Ltd* [1976] 3 All ER 509; see 2.2(*a*)). In other cases listing may be advantageous, as is shown by the number of estate agents' particulars which make a feature of it. Either way it has been accepted, both explicitly in the *John Walker* case and implicitly in *Aquis Estates* v *Minton* [1975] 1 WLR 1452 (see 2.2(*b*)), that the possibility of a building being listed is something that vendors and purchasers alike have to accept as an inherent hazard of property ownership and transfer.

Figure 2.1 The consequences of listing

Buildings in disrepair
The local authority is able to take some steps to ensure that a listed building is maintained in good repair (see Chapter 5)

Financial assistance
Limited financial assistance may be available for the repair and restoration of a listed building (see 6.2 to 6.4); VAT is not payable on alterations for which listed building consent is needed and has been obtained (see 6.8(*a*)); and rates are not payable if the building is unoccupied (see 6.8(*b*))

The need for planning permission
The 'permitted development' limits are significantly more restricted (see 7.3(*b*)); and the procedure for making Article 4 directions is slightly different (see 7.4(*b*))

Planning applications
Extra publicity is given to applications affecting the setting of a listed building (see 7.5(*b*), (*c*));
the authority is to consider the desirability of preserving the building and its setting when considering any planning application affecting it (see 7.6); and if the building is owned by a local authority, it may not give itself planning permission to carry out its own works (see 7.5(*e*))

Listed building consent
Listed building consent is required for the demolition of a listed building, or for any other works which affect its special character (see Chapter 8)

Unauthorised works
The local authority may take enforcement action or institute a criminal prosecution if unauthorised works are carried out (see Chapter 9)

Chapter 3

Building Preservation Notices

(a) The need for building preservation notices

The listing process is inevitably slow; and it is also incomplete. A building of merit may therefore be at risk until it is listed at the next routine resurvey of the area. Or it may have been over-looked in the last one—particularly if its distinctive features are not readily apparent from an external survey.

In such a case the local authority, an amenity group or any individual can always write to the Department of the Environ ment, requesting that the building be 'spot-listed' (see Chapter 2). In the majority of cases, however, even this process takes considerable time. It is therefore not suitable where a building of special interest is under immediate threat of demolition or drastic alteration.

To help solve this problem, a provision was introduced in the Town and Country Planning Act 1968 (see now s 58 of the 1971 Act), whereby a local planning authority may serve a *building preservation notice* on the owner and occupier of a historic building that is at risk. 'Some authorities have already made good use of these powers, but there is still further scope for their employment. Too frequently, the Department is asked to assess or list a building immediately, when the service of a building preservation notice by the local authority would be quicker and more expedient as a short-term measure' (Circ 8/87, para 46).

(b) Procedure

The need to serve a building preservation notice will often be urgent, not allowing for decisions to be taken by committees. The power to take the initial decision to serve one may usefully be delegated to appropriate officers of the authority, so as to save

33

C

time (LGA 1972, s 101; Circ 8/87, para 46). Once the decision has been taken to serve a notice, it should be prepared as soon as possible, and a copy served on all those involved. The most important person is usually the occupier of the building; it will be prudent wherever possible to ensure that he is given a copy personally. Where there are several occupiers (as, for example, with a residential building in multiple occupation, or an urban building with different retail tenants on the ground floor), postal service by recorded delivery may be more practical. A copy must also be served on the owner (if different, such as in the case of leasehold property).

Given that, in most cases, a building preservation notice is only used where there is a development proposal pending, it is obviously sensible for the authority to serve a copy on all those involved in the development (who will usually be known)—these might include architects, project managers, contractors and (not the least important, if matters have progressed to an advanced stage) demolition contractors. In each case, again, delivery is best by hand or by recorded mail.

Where any of the above cannot be found, a notice can be fixed to the building or to a prominent object on the site (such as the main gate or doorway). This may often be a sensible course of action anyway in addition to serving copies, especially in cases of urgency. This power was introduced in 1972 (TCPA 1971, s 58(6), overturning *Maltglade Ltd* v *St Albans RDC* [1972] 1 WLR 1230).

The notice must:

(1) state that the building appears to the authority to be of special architectural or historic interest;
(2) state that the Secretary of State has been asked to list it; and
(3) explain the effect of the notice (see below).

Where a notice is handed or sent to any of those noted above, it will usually be helpful to attach an accompanying letter in clear English saying what it means; the 'explanation' demanded by the Act is often itself not as clear as it might be.

At the same time as serving the notice, the authority must also immediately request the Secretary of State formally to list the building. Such a request should include a copy of the notice, a location plan, and photographs of the building (Circ 8/87, para 47).

There is no statutory right of appeal by the owner or occupier against serving of a building preservation notice. But, as with listing, it is always possible to make an informal appeal to the Secretary of State (see 2.3). If listed building consent is subsequently applied for, and refused or granted subject to adverse conditions, it is possible to appeal on the ground (amongst any others) that the building should not be listed (TCPA 1971, Sched 11, para 8(2)(*b*)).

A building preservation notice may be served by:

(1) *in urban development areas* (except Cardiff Bay): the urban development corporation (see 1.3(*a*));

(2) *elsewhere in Greater London*: the borough council (TCPA 1971, s 58(1)) or the Historic Buildings and Monuments Commission (s 58(7), inserted by LGA 1985);

(3) *in a national park (outside a metropolitan area)*: the county council (LGA 1972, s 182(4)) or Planning Board (LGA 1972, Sched 17);

(4) *in the Broads*: the Broads Authority (TCPA 1971, s 273A, inserted by NSBA 1988); and

(5) *elsewhere*: a district council (TCPA 1971, s 58(1)).

A building preservation notice may not be served on an ecclesiastical building or a scheduled monument (s 58(2); see Chapters 13 and 14 respectively). Nor may it be served on a building which has been the subject of a certificate of immunity from listing within the previous five years (TCPA 1971, s 54A(2), inserted by LGPLA 1980; see 2.4).

(c) The consequences of a building preservation notice

The effect of a building preservation notice is that, from the date of its issue, and for as long as it remains effective, the building is effectively a listed building (see Chapter 2). In particular, works for its alteration or demolition require listed building consent (see Chapter 8). If such works are carried out without consent being obtained, the local authority can take enforcement action or can institute criminal proceedings (see Chapter 9).

The only provision that applies to a building that is actually listed but not, for some reason, to one that is merely subject to a building preservation notice, is the specific offence of criminal damage to a listed building (TCPA 1971, s 57; see 9.3).

However, such protection lasts only for six months. If within that period the Secretary of State decides that he will list the building, then he will notify the owner and occupier and the local authority in the usual way (see 2.2(*b*)), and the building will thereafter have precisely the same status as that of any other listed building. If, in the interim, the authority has refused listed building consent for certain works, it may be liable to pay compensation under s 171 of the 1971 Act once the listing is confirmed (s 173(2); and see 8.10). A claim for compensation in such circumstances should be submitted to the authority immediately after the adverse decision is received.

Alternatively, the Secretary of State may decide not to list the building. In that case, he will notify the planning authority, which will in turn notify the owner and occupier (TCPA 1971, s 58(5)(a)). The effect of the notice will lapse (s 58(3)); and any application for listed building consent that is outstanding will lapse, as will any outstanding enforcement proceedings (TCPA 1971, Sched 11, paras 15, 16). However if unauthorised work was carried out while the notice was in force, anyone responsible is still liable to criminal prosecution (Sched 11, para 14), and any expenses incurred by the authority in taking enforcement action will still be recoverable (para 16).

If the service of the notice caused any financial damage, including any damages resulting from a breach of contract for building or demolition works, the authority is then liable to pay compensation; although only to anyone who had an interest in the building at the time when the notice was served (TCPA 1971, s 173(3), (4)). This means that anyone else who may be out of pocket (contractors, etc) can only recover damages if they are able successfully to sue the building owner, who could then recover from the authority.

A claim for compensation under this provision must be submitted within six months (TCP (LBCA) Regs 1987, reg 9).

Finally, if the Secretary of State decides not to list the building, the local authority may not serve another building preservation notice on it within twelve months of his decision (TCPA 1971, s 58(5)(b)), which contains the interesting implication, borne out by experience, that the perceived architectural or historic interest of a building may change significantly in only a year!

If, however, the Secretary of State takes no action within the six-month period, the notice will also lapse. The consequences will be the same as if he had decided formally not to list the building (see above); except that, in this case, there is nothing to stop the authority immediately serving another notice, and thus in effect prolonging the original notice for a further six months.

Chapter 4

Conservation Areas

4.1 Background

Some twenty years after the production of the first lists of buildings of special interest, it was recognised that whole areas could also need special protection. They might not contain any buildings of particular architectural merit or historical importance; but they could be very much part of the 'familiar and cherished local scene' (see below).

The Civic Amenities Act 1967, a private members' bill introduced by Duncan Sandys (who had ten years earlier founded the Civic Trust, and was until his death in April 1988 its president), therefore introduced the concept of *conservation areas*. Four were designated that year, and twenty-one years later it was estimated that there were over 6,121 conservation areas in England alone. The number of buildings in each area varies from a handful to several thousand; there must by now be around a million buildings within a conservation area—twice as many as are listed in their own right. Of all the districts in England, only one now has not a single conservation area—Castle Point in Essex (better known as Canvey Island). There were at the start of April 1988 a further 335 conservation areas in Wales.

The provisions of the 1967 Act were re-enacted by the Town and Country Planning Act 1971, but the sole protection afforded to such areas was the requirement for extra publicity to be given to planning applications affecting them (see now TCPA 1971, ss 28, 29 as amended by no less than five subsequent Acts; see 7.5(*b*), (*c*)). Otherwise, the original s 277 (located, significantly, right at the end of the 1971 Act in 'Part XV—Miscellaneous and Supplementary Provisions') merely placed upon local authorities the duty to pay special attention to the desirability of preserving the character or appearance of conservation areas. This duty has in itself been considered by the courts to be important (*Richmond-upon-Thames BC* v *Secretary of State* (1978) 37 P & CR 151, *R* v *Lambeth LBC, ex parte Sharp* [1986] JPL 201 and *Steinberg* v *Secretary of State* (1988) *The Independent*, 2 December. see 4.3(*b*)). But no more specific provisions were included, and in particular there was no control over demolition.

This was partially altered by the Town and Country (Amendment) Act 1972 and, more substantially, by the Town and Country Amenities Act 1974. The 1974 Act gave a planning authority control over the demolition of all unlisted buildings in any conservation area (TCPA 1971, ss 277 and 277A, inserted by TCAA 1974), subject to certain, important exceptions; see Chapter 10. The 1974 Act also introduced the duty to prepare enhancement proposals (see 4.4(*b*)), and control over works to trees (see Chapter 11).

4.2 Designation of conservation areas

(a) Eligibility for designation

The statutory definition of a conservation area is 'an area of special architectural or historic interest, the character or appearance of which it is desirable to preserve or enhance' (TCPA 1971, s 277(1), substituted by TCAA 1974).

The criteria adopted by different planning authorities, and by a single authority as time goes on, are bound to vary widely. But, on the whole, as 'public opinion is now overwhelmingly in favour of enhancing the familiar and cherished local scene' (Circ 8/87, para 5), the meaning of the critical word 'special' in the definition is being, inevitably, widened—every local scene is 'familiar' to many, and most are 'cherished' by some. The Act does not specify to whom the preservation or enhancement of the area must be desirable; and opinion is scarcely likely to be unanimous.

The Circular offers the following guidance:

Clearly there can be no standard specification for conservation areas. . . . [They] will naturally be of many different kinds. They may be large or small, from whole town centres to squares, terraces and smaller groups of buildings. They will often be centred on listed buildings, but not always. Pleasant groups of other buildings, open spaces, trees, an historic street pattern, a village green or features of historic or archaeological interest may also contribute to the special character of an area. Areas appropriate for designation as conservation areas will be found in almost every town and many villages. It is the character of areas, rather than individual buildings, that section 277 of the 1971 Act seeks to preserve or enhance (Circ 8/87, para 54).

The 6,000 or so areas designated so far have in fact varied widely in character. The first ones were mainly town centres (such as Stamford) and architectural set pieces (such as Bath). Others have included villages, model housing layouts (as at Saltaire), open spaces (Princes Park, Liverpool, with its formal approach) and areas of attractive if unremarkable suburbia. Some include groups of quite recent buildings (such as Silver End Estate in Essex). There are also conservation areas that are almost entirely rural and are very large indeed. Some areas have unfortunately been declared for reasons that were perhaps only tenuously connected with their architectural or historical character (such as parts of Kensington High Street, and Hammersmith Broadway).

Most suitable areas have by now been identified—there are only about 150 new ones designated each year.

There is no 'immunity certificate' procedure available to guarantee against a property being included within a conservation area (see 2.4).

(b) Designation procedure

A conservation area can be designated by the following:
(1) *in most urban development areas* (except Cardiff Bay)· the urban development corporation (see 1.3(*a*));
(2) *elsewhere in Greater London*: the borough council or the Historic Buildings and Monuments Commission (TCPA 1971, s 277(10)(*a*), substituted by TCAA 1974 and amended by LGA 1985);
(3) *in a national park outside a metropolitan area*: the county council (s 277(10)(*b*), substituted by TCAA 1974 and amended by LGA 1985);
(4) *in a metropolitan county*: the borough council (s 277(10)(*aa*), inserted by LGA 1985);
(5) *in the Broads*: the Broads Authority (TCPA 1971, ss 273A, inserted by NSBA 1988); and
(6) *elsewhere*: either the district council or the county council (s 277(10), substituted by TCAA 1974).

The Commission may not designate a conservation area, however, without first consulting the appropriate borough council and obtaining the consent of the Secretary of State. A county council may not designate an area without consulting the relevant district council (TCPA 1971, s 277(5), substituted by LGA 1985). A district council is not under a duty to consult the county before making a designation; but 'it is clearly desirable that there should be continuing consultation between county and district with a view to formulating joint policies and arrangements for making the best use of staff' (Circ 8/87, para 56).

The Secretary of State is also empowered to designate conservation areas, and to cancel designations (s 277(4), substituted by TCAA 1974); but he has almost never used this power. If he does so, he must inform the local planning authority and, if in England, the Commission (s 277(6), substituted by TCAA 1974; s 277 (6A), inserted by LGA 1985).

Once an area has been identified as being suitable for designation, or an existing area for extension, a report will be submitted to the appropriate committee of the authority, and a resolution will be passed to designate the area. The area involved should be specified accurately, since the designation will significantly affect the rights of property owners living within it. In most cases, this is best done by preparing a schedule of all the properties to be included, which should be appended to the resolution.

It will be helpful at an early stage to prepare a map of the proposed area—both for the purposes of public consultation and to inform the members of the authority. In the event of any conflict between the schedule and the map, it is the former which will prevail; and in a densely built-up area a map of sufficient scale to indicate beyond all doubt the boundaries of a large conservation area will have to be of considerable size. A schedule removes any uncertainty as to whether or not a particular property is included—as will be necessary when registering the designation as a local land charge (see below)—and can be transmitted by telephone and more easily photocopied. But both the map and the schedule need to be prepared with care.

It is the date of the appropriate formal resolution by the local authority that is the date of the designation, not the date of any subsequent advertisement.

Finally, every local planning authority is under a continuing duty to consider whether it should designate new conservation areas, or extend existing ones (s 277(2), inserted by TCAA 1974 and amended by LGPLA 1980). It is possible, although very rare, for a past designation to be cancelled (s 277(2), (6), inserted by TCAA 1974).

(c) Publicity

Usually the designation of a conservation area will be preceded by some kind of survey, and possibly by a public consultation exercise. Although there is no statutory requirement for this authorities can, and occasionally do, designate or extend areas without any prior notice. However they have been reminded that it is important that proposals to designate new areas or to extend existing ones should be made known in the locality, so that developers and those living in the area may be aware of the existence of the designation, and thus aware of the need to apply for consent for the demolition of unlisted buildings, and to notify the authority of works to trees (Circ 8/87, para 55). They have also been urged to consider designating areas at the time they prepare local plans and unitary development plans, as this helps to give publicity to any proposals that may emerge (see also 4.4(*a*)).

Once an area has been designated or extended, however, the authority must place an advertisement in at least one local newspaper and in the *London Gazette*. This must contain sufficient details to enable the area to be identified (presumably a schedule of properties included; see above), and a note as to the effects of the designation (TCPA 1971, s 277(7), substituted by TCAA 1974). The authority must also notify the Secretary of State and (in England) the Historic Buildings and Monuments Commission of the designation (s 277(6), substituted by TCAA 1974; s 277(6A), inserted by LGA 1985).

In contrast to the compulsory notification of owners and occupiers of a building that is listed, no notice has to be given to those living or working in the area. Parliament must have either assumed that they will spot the announcement in the local press, which is somewhat naive since it is usually in small print in the 'statutory notices' section, or else considered that to notify them individually would be desirable but impossibly expensive. This means that there is an even greater likelihood of an owner or developer carrying out works without being aware that he needs consent (see 2.2(*b*)). However, the designation is to be registered as a local land charge, which means that future purchasers of property in the area will be warned of its existence (s 277(9), inserted by TCAA 1974 and amended by Local Land Charges Act 1975).

As with listed buildings, there is no statutory right of appeal against a building being included in a conservation area. There is nothing to stop an individual owner writing to the local authority and asking it to cancel the designation; but the chances of success are likely to be remote.

(d) Where to find information

Information as to whether a particular property is within a conservation area, or is likely to be included within one, can be found out from the planning department of the appropriate district council, urban development corporation or (in a national park) special board or county council. There will increasingly often be a 'conservation officer' who will be able to advise on the specific implications of any particular existing or proposed designation.

It should be borne in mind that the precise boundaries of areas are altered from time to time, and new areas designated, so that it is important to ensure that any information is right up-to-date.

4.3 The consequences of conservation area designation

(a) General consequences

In the twenty-one years since the first conservation areas were designated, there has been a slow but steady increase in the number of specific statutory provisions aimed at assisting in their preservation and enhancement. The principal effects of the designation of a conservation area are now as summarised in Figure 4.1. They are explored in more detail in the remainder of the book.

In addition, it may be noted that a simplified planning zone may not include any land within a conservation area (TCPA 1971, s 24E(1)(b), inserted by HPA 1986). It remains to be seen whether this provision will be of any significance, since at the time of writing very few zones had been declared.

(b) Duties of local authorities and others

Once a conservation area has been designated, 'special attention shall be paid to the desirability of preserving or enhancing its character or appearance in the exercise, with respect to any buildings or other land in that area, of any powers under [the Town and Country Planning Act 1971], Part I of the Historic Buildings and Ancient Monuments Act 1953, or the Local Authorities (Historic Buildings) Act 1962' (TCPA 1971, s 277(8), substituted by TCAA 1974). Note that this duty falls not just upon planning authorities, but upon anyone exercising any powers under the

Figure 4.1 Consequences of conservation area designation

Duties of the local planning authority	The local planning authority is under a general duty to ensure the preservation and enhancement of conservation areas (see 4.3(*b*)), and a particular duty to prepare proposals to that end (see 4.4)
Buildings in disrepair	The local authority may be able to take steps to ensure that a building in a conservation area is kept in good repair (see Chapter 5)
Financial assistance	Limited financial assistance may be available for the upkeep of a building in the area (see Chapter 6)
The need for planning permission	The details as to the limits of what works may be carried out without planning permission are somewhat different (see 7.3(*c*))
Planning applications	Extra publicity is given to planning applications affecting conservation areas (see 7.5(*b*), (*c*)); and the planning authority is to take into account the desirability of preserving and enhancing the character of the area when determining such applications (see 7.6)
Conservation area consent	Conservation area consent is required for the demolition of any unlisted building in the area (see 10.1); and the local authority may take enforcement action or institute a criminal prosecution if consent is not obtained (see 10.6)
Works to trees	Notice must be given to the local authority before works are carried out to any tree in the area (see 11.1)
Advertisements	The display of advertisements may be somewhat more restricted (see Chapter 12)

relevant Acts. In particular, this includes the Secretary of State and his inspectors.

The most relevant of the many and various powers under the Town and Country Planning Act 1971 include the following:

(1) the preparation of development plans under Part II of the Act;
(2) the control of development under Parts III and V;
(3) the controls under Parts IV and V relating to listed buildings, trees, advertisements and property in need of maintenance;
(4) the repair of unoccupied buildings under s 101;
(5) the exercise of highways powers under Part X;
(6) the control of demolition under s 277A; and
(7) the preparation of proposals under s 277B.

The 1953 and 1962 Acts concern the giving of grants and loans (see Chapter 6).

These various powers are considered in detail elsewhere in this book, but the nature of the general duty is clear: 'local authorities stand in the vanguard of those protecting historic buildings and areas, and the Secretary of State hopes they will make diligent use of all the powers available to them' (Circ 8/87, para 5).

The precise scope of that duty came under scrutiny in the High Court, in *R* v *Lambeth LBC, ex parte Sharp* [1986] JPL 201. The local authority wished to construct a stadium in part of Brockwell Park in SE London, which was in a conservation area. It used the procedure under the Town and Country Planning General Regulations 1976 (reg 6) whereby it could grant itself deemed permission, and as part of that procedure erected one site notice (see 7.5(*e*)). It also held a well attended public meeting, at which the effect on the conservation area of the proposed development was fully discussed, but it transpired that when the initial decision had been made by the relevant council officer to seek deemed permission, he had not taken into account the fact that Brockwell Park had by then been designated as a conservation area. He had therefore failed to take into account the effect of the proposal on the conservation area, as the council was required to do by the 1971 Act.

The way the council took the decision, including the meeting and the representations received subsequently, indicated, when viewed as a whole, that they were fully aware of the conservation issues. But it was held that the initial failure to consider the council's duty under s 277(8) meant that the notice to seek deemed permission was bad, and that everything that followed was bad, and the deemed planning permission was therefore quashed. This decision was upheld in the Court of Appeal (reported at [1987] JPL 440), although the issue of the council's general duty was not raised there.

Those officers and members of a local authority who are directly and regularly involved in the planning process should be aware of the significance of conservation area designation, and should not cause the authority to be caught out in this way. But the importance of this decision in the present context perhaps lies in its implications for those elsewhere within the authority, in departments such as engineers, housing, recreation, and so on. In this case, 'It was said that the inference to be drawn from the sequence of events was that all [the officer] did was to carry out the policy that the amenity services committee was set on. . . . It was not, however, possible to separate the functions of the borough council' in this way ([1986] JPL 201 at 204 per Croom-Johnson LJ).

The existence of conservation areas, and the implication of designation, therefore needs to be brought to the attention of any officers and members of a local authority who are responsible for carrying out activities that require deemed planning permission.

It has also been recently emphasised that the enhancement of the appearance of a conservation area means more than merely its preservation. A planning authority is thus under no obligation to accept existing eyesores, but may quite properly seek to bring about improvements—for example by the use of discontinuance notices (*Westminster CC* v *Secretary of State* [1988] 3 PLR 104; and see 12.3(*c*)). Similarly, preservation and enhancement is an essentially positive concept and means more than merely avoiding harm to the character of an area (*Steinberg* v *Secretary of State*, (1988) *The Independent*, 2 December; see 7.6(*a*)).

(c) Conservation area advisory committees

Planning authorities have also been asked to consider setting up conservation area advisory committees, consisting primarily of people who are not members of the authority. The composition of such committees will vary, depending on the locality; advice is given in Circ 8/87 (para 68). It may be appropriate to set up a committee for each conservation area, possibly meeting locally; or else one covering the whole of an authority's area.

The role of such a committee is to advise on applications for planning permission, listed building consent and conservation area consent which affect the conservation area(s) in question, to comment on other issues that may affect the area (such as traffic management schemes), and to help formulate positive proposals for its enhancement.

It has in practice sometimes proved difficult to retain the enthusiasm which existed when these committees were first set up. This in part reflects the general acceptance in some areas (for example, Wandsworth in London) of the desirability of conservation, leading to lack of interest or complacency. The committed membership of amenity groups, who often provide the membership for advisory committees, has similarly declined in such areas in recent years. But in other areas (such as neighbouring Lambeth), conservation area designation is perceived by local authorities to be politically undesirable, since it is held to be partially responsible for house prices rising faster. Such councils also feel that conservation deflects resources from other tasks regarded as more important, such as providing homes and jobs. Here advisory committees, where they exist, exercise only marginal influence; and any representations by amenity groups are often counter-productive.

4.4 Policies and proposals

(a) Development plans

It has already been noted that planning authorities should consider the possibility of designating (or extending) conservation areas at the time when they prepare local plans or (in metropolitan areas) unitary development plans.

In addition, it is important for an authority to include appropriate policies within such plans, to clarify its general approach with regard to conservation areas. Issues covered could include:

(1) the promotion of suitable development (such as pedestrian schemes or the creation of open space) to be carried out by the authority itself or by other agencies;

(2) the use of planning gain to bring about improvements;

(3) the control of potentially unsuitable development (either in a particular area, or in all areas); and

(4) the enhancement of the appearance of the area through measures to divert parking and through traffic elsewhere.

Such topics can also in the short term usefully be included in non-statutory plans (see, for example, Circ 22/84, Annex, para 1.14). These can be prepared more rapidly than formal development plans and can thus be a more appropriate format for detailed policies and standards. When a development plan is in due course prepared for the area, it must include these informal policies (*Great Portland Estates* v *Westminster CC* [1985] JPL 108 at 114).

Considerable weight is given at appeals to up-to-date development plans. If therefore an authority wishes to resist new development in a conservation area, and to counter the oft-repeated argument that there is a presumption in favour of permission being granted (see for example Circ 14/85, para 3), it is vital to have available a well-written set of conservation policies in an adopted local plan, not just an attractive but informal series of guidelines.

On the other hand, not all development is unsuitable in every conservation area; and not every existing building must be kept forever. The duty of an authority is after all to enhance, as well as to preserve, the character of its conservation areas (TCPA 1971, s 277(8), substituted by TCAA 1974). 'Often the emphasis will be on control, rather than preservation' (Circ 8/87, para 61; and see 4.3(*b*) and 7.6).

(b) Conservation area proposals

More specifically, authorities are under a duty to 'formulate and publish from time to time proposals for the preservation and enhancement of any parts of their area which are conservation areas' (TCPA 1971, s 277B(1), inserted by TCAA 1974 and amended by LGPLA 1980). No more specific timing is laid down; nor is there in the Act any detailed requirement as to the form or content of such proposals. The Circular, surprisingly, does not elaborate on these points either.

Such proposals might cover, in more detail, the same topics as were mentioned in connection with development plans, as well as other more specific items. Thus 'proposals for preservation' would presumably include policies for the avoidance of unsuitable change, which may need to be supplemented by proposals for Article 4 directions (see 7.4) where the powers available would otherwise be inadequate. They might also include proposals for restoration work assisted by grants or loans, to avoid demolition taking place that would otherwise become necessary.

County councils, where they still exist, may be able to assist district councils in the preparation of such proposals; they may have a larger budget, and relevant facilities such as graphics support; and their officers will often have wider experience of the technical and policy issues involved.

'Proposals for enhancement' of the conservation area would include proposals for:

(1) the removal of all that presently harms its character (such as unsightly street furniture to be removed or upgraded, and vacant sites to be landscaped or sensitively developed); and

(2) the promotion of positive improvements (such as design policies for specific sites or new buildings generally, paving schemes, and grant-aiding the replacement of missing architectural details).

In particular, the 'floorscape' (that is, the treatment of the footways, carriageways and open spaces) often makes a vital contribution to the character of a conservation area: 'Every effort should be made to retain or re-introduce the traditional surfaces, for example natural stone paving or setts wherever possible' (Circ 8/87, para 65). Even statutory undertakers are urged to carry out their reinstatement works in a sensitive manner. It remains to be seen whether these exhortations (introduced for the first time in 1987) will have any effect, particularly in view of the tight restrictions on spending by public authorities. In any event, liaison with the county surveyor, or whoever is responsible for highway maintenance, will be vital.

Local authorities have interpreted the requirement to prepare conservation area proposals in widely differing ways. Some have proposed, and carried out, very imaginative schemes for specific physical enhancements (such as pedestrianising and paving a market square). Others have produced short leaflets setting out detailed policies and proposals for a particular terrace. A few have produced what are virtually (non-statutory) local plans. Most authorities have done little or nothing. The problem is that it is much easier (and cheaper) to 'formulate and publish' proposals than to implement them.

Proposals must be submitted to a public meeting locally, theoretically within the actual conservation area itself (s 277B(2), inserted by TCAA 1974). Usually of more value will be the involvement of local residents, professionals and amenity groups. It may be useful for the authority to jointly form a working party with such groups—to meet both before the proposals are formally prepared, to discuss ideas, and afterwards, to ensure that they are implemented.

Chapter 5

Repairs and Restoration

5.1 Importance of repairs

The second half of this book describes various measures designed to ensure that historic buildings and areas are protected from unnecessary demolition and unsuitable alterations. In practice, however, before any such works are even contemplated, the more immediate problem facing the owner of many a historic building is that of ensuring that it is kept in good repair, and trying to pay for the maintenance and repair that this involves. Where a building has not been properly looked after, so that more or less drastic restoration is now necessary, the problems, and the bills, will be greater still.

Local authorities, too, will be concerned to ensure that the historic buildings in their area are in good repair. It is of little comfort to prevent one fine listed building from demolition if at the same time whole streets of old buildings are falling into disrepair through neglect of repair and maintenance.

Local authorities and private owners alike should remember that quite modest expenditure on repairs needed to keep a building weather-tight, early treatment of dry rot etc and routine maintenance (especially the regular clearance of gutters and downpipes) can prevent much more extensive and expensive repairs becoming necessary at a later date (Circ 8/87, para 124).

Perhaps surprisingly, there is no specific obligation on the owner of a building that is listed or in a conservation area to keep it in good repair. This chapter therefore starts by outlining briefly the general obligation imposed by common law and by statute on any building owner. This may sometimes be particularly relevant in the case of an older building.

In addition, however, there are some powers available to a local authority (acting either as planning authority or housing authority) which it may use in certain circumstances to persuade or, in some cases, to force an owner to carry out repair works. Some of these apply to all buildings, and some specifically to historic buildings. The power to bring about area improvement under the Housing Act 1985 may also be relevant.

Finally, it should be noted that it may be necessary to obtain planning permission or listed building consent before repair works are carried out (see 7.2(*b*) and 8.1(*f*) respectively).

5.2 Obligation to repair

The basic rule is that 'a man has a right to enjoy his own property in his own way' (*Stocker* v *Planet Building Society* (1879) 27 WR 877). This freedom has of course been substantially eroded in the last hundred years (not least by planning and other statutory controls); but it still remains true that there is no general obligation to keep a building in good repair. To this there are, however, certain limited exceptions.

(a) General liability at common law

First, the occupier of any building is under a duty (the 'common duty of care') to anyone other than a trespasser entering it, to take reasonable care to see that he will be reasonably safe for the purpose for which he is there (Occupiers' Liability Act 1957, s 2). For more details, an appropriate detailed text should be consulted.

The duty under the 1957 Act to keep a building safe for visitors normally falls on whoever has control over it. Thus, in the case of leasehold property, the duty is normally placed on the tenant. However where a building is occupied under a licence, the absentee freeholder may be liable (*Wheat* v *Lacon* [1966] AC 552). He will also be liable if he has undertaken to carry out repairs, or if has reserved a power to do so (Defective Premises Act 1972, s 4). If the building is vacant, the last 'occupier' may be liable (*Harris* v *Birkenhead Corpn* [1976] 1 WLR 279).

In the case of a historic building which is wholly or partly in a serious state of disrepair, it may be appropriate to erect signs to warn visitors and passers-by of any danger; but this will not always be sufficient for the occupier of the building to evade liability (1957 Act, s 2(4)(*a*)). It will probably be sufficient where, for example, a farmer allows visitors to view a ruinous castle on his land free of charge, but not in the case of buildings to which the public are admitted for even a small charge, such as historic houses, castles, etc (Unfair Contract Terms Act 1977, s 1(3) [as amended by Occupiers' Liability Act 1984, s 2] and s 2).

Secondly, where a building adjoins a highway, if it becomes dangerous and in a state where it could collapse and injure a passer-by or a neighbour, the occupier will be liable under the law of nuisance (see, for example *Wringe* v *Cohen* [1940] 1 KB 229) particularly if he is under a contractual liability to keep the building in repair, such as a covenant in a lease (see below). Furthermore, he will be liable whether or not he knew or ought to have known of the problem, and even if he had employed a contractor to sort it out (*Tarry* v *Ashton* (1876) 1 QBD 314). In some cases, such as where a small dwellinghouse is let on a short lease, the freehold owner may be responsible as well as the occupier—even if there was no covenant in the lease for the landlord to carry out repairs (*Mint* v *Good* [1951] 1 KB 517, CA).

This could be particularly relevant in the case of older buildings of a more ornate style in urban areas—stucco, for example, is liable to become loose after a bad winter, and portions of details such as ornamental cornices may fall onto the footway.

(b) Repair of leasehold property

The tenant of a leasehold building is under an implied obligation to use the premises in a tenant-like manner—that is, he 'must take proper care of the place' and 'must do the little jobs about the place which a reasonable tenant would do' (*Warren* v *Keen* [1954] 1 QB 15 at 20, CA). He is also bound by any repairing covenants in his lease—typically, 'to repair and keep the demised premises in good tenantable repair and condition'—which will be of greater consequence in most cases. The standard of repair is construed with reference to the age, character and locality of the premises at the time the lease commenced (*Lurcott* v *Wakely and Wheeler* [1911] 1 KB 905, CA):

> The age of the house must be taken into account, because nobody could reasonably expect that a house 200 years old should be in the same condition as a house lately built; the character of the house must be taken into account, because the same class of repair as would be necessary to a palace would be wholly unnecessary to a cottage; and the locality of the house must be taken into account, because the state of repair necessary for a house in Grosvenor Square would be wholly different from the state of repair necessary for a house in Spitalfields (per Lord Esher MR in *Proudfoot* v *Hart* (1890) 25 QBD 42 at 52).

The language of the judgment reflects the times in which it was given; but it remains to be seen what effect, if any, the listing of a building would have on the scope of a tenant's obligation under such a repairing covenant. Certainly there is no liability to repair inherent defects—which may be particularly relevant in the case of historic buildings (see, for example, *Lister* v *Lane and Nesham* [1893] 2 QB 212, CA and *Collins* v *Flynn* [1963] 2 All ER 1068).

A landlord, on the other hand, has in general no obligation to repair leased premises, unless he covenants to do so. But in the case of a dwellinghouse (which in this context includes a flat) let after 24 October 1961 on a lease for a term of seven years or less, he is under an implied obligation to keep in good repair the exterior and structure of the building (HA 1985, ss 11–14). Any purported attempt to include in the lease a clause excluding this liability will be void. And the liability may be extensive in the case of historic buildings—see *Elmcroft Developments* v *Tankersley-Sawyer* [1984] 270 EG 140, CA, where the landlord was held liable to insert a new damp-proof course in order to eradicate dampness in a late Victorian mansion block.

5.3 Intervention by the local authority

(a) Powers available to an authority

Where a building falls into disrepair, the liability under common law and statute outlined so far will rarely be sufficient to ensure that it is restored. The local authority may therefore intervene in certain cases. These are summarised in Figure 5.1, and outlined in more detail in the following sections of this chapter. They fall broadly into two categories.

First, there are limited powers available specifically aimed at the restoration of historic buildings. These are as follows:

(1) where a building is listed or (in certain cases) in a conservation area, an authority may carry out urgent repairs (TCPA 1971, ss 101 and 101A; see 5.4);

(2) where a listed building is not being properly maintained, the authority may seek to compulsorily purchase it (TCPA 1971, ss 114–17; see 5.5); and

(3) where a building is of historic interest (not necessarily either listed or in a conservation area), the authority may seek to acquire it by agreement (TCPA 1971, s 119; see 5.6).

Secondly, there are general powers available whether or not the building in question is listed or in a conservation area:
    (1) where the condition of any building (or other land)

Figure 5.1 Buildings in disrepair: powers available to local authority

Statutory provision	Type of works envisaged	Procedure	Reference for further information
TCPA 1971, ss 101, 101A	Works urgently necessary for preservation of listed building, or part, if it is not in use (also for unlisted buildings in conservation area with approval of Secretary of State)	Notice to owner specifying works; authority can enter, do the works, and reclaim the cost	5.4
TCPA 1971, ss 114–17	Works reasonably necessary for preservation of listed building	Repairs notice to owner; authority can compulsorily purchase	5.5
TCPA 1971, s 119	[Disrepair not necessary]	Acquisition by agreement of any building of interest	5.6
TCPA 1971, s 65	Works necessary to remedy condition of (any) property affecting amenity of the surrounding area	Notice to owner specifying works required; authority can prosecute for non-compliance, or carry out works and reclaim the cost	5.7
Building Act 1984, s 77	Works to make safe (any) dangerous building, including demolition if necessary	Notice to owner specifying works; authority can enter, do the works, and reclaim the cost	5.8
Building Act 1984, s 79	Works for repair or restoration of (any) ruinous or dilapidated building	Notice to owner specifying works; authority can enter, do the works, and reclaim the cost	5.8
HA 1985, s 189	Works to improve house unfit for human occupation	Notice to owner specifying works; authority can enter and do the works at its own expense	5.9

'adversely affects the amenity of the area' (TCPA 1971,
s 65; see 5.7);
(2) where a building is 'dangerous' or 'ruinous' (under the
Building Act 1984 and corresponding legislation in Inner
London; see 5.8); and
(3) where a house is 'unfit for human habitation' or in a clearance area (under the Housing Act 1985; see 5.9).
These powers are not primarily intended to achieve the preservation of historic buildings; but they can in appropriate cases be
used by an imaginative local authority to that end. The expenditure involved will usually be met from environmental health and
housing budgets, which will usually be much larger than the small
allocation specifically earmarked for 'conservation'. On the other
hand, the insensitive or unthinking use of these procedures can
be a real impediment to conservation, especially since (in the case
of powers under the Building and Housing Acts) they are often
administered by officers whose principal aims, quite rightly, lie
elsewhere. Those Acts are therefore now subject to modification
in the case of listed buildings and conservation areas.

(b) Choice of procedure

The law directly relating to listed buildings in poor repair has
always placed greater emphasis on the powers of the local planning
authority than on the duties of either the authority or building
owners. Financial restrictions perhaps make this inevitable.

But even the existence of a power imposes by implication a
duty to consider whether it should be exercised. This emerged
clearly in *R v Stroud DC, ex parte Goodenough* [1982] JPL 246,
where the local authority had served a notice requiring the owners
of two buildings to make them safe or demolish them within eight
weeks. Three members of a local action group thereupon applied
for an order of mandamus to force the authority to take steps to
secure the preservation of the buildings.

It was held in the Divisional Court (per Woolf J):

. . . a planning authority . . . should exercise great circumspection to see
whether or not there was some other alternative open to them to prevent
the demolition taking place when this was not desirable. If a planning
authority did not take into account all its relevant powers when doing
this then it was failing to perform its function properly under the legislation (p 247).

This is no more than a standard principle of administrative law:
'it has been so often decided as to have become an axiom, that,

in public statutes, words only directory, permissory or enabling may have a compulsory force where the thing to be done is for the public benefit or in advancement of public justice' (*R* v *Tithe Commissioners* (1849) 14 QB 459 per Coleridge J at 474). It has now been given statutory force in this context by a new section (56C) inserted into the 1971 Act (by the HPA 1986, Sched 9, para 6(1)). This now provides that, before taking any steps with a view to making a dangerous structure order in respect of a building that is listed or in a conservation area, an authority must consider:

(1) if repair works are urgently necessary, carrying them out under s 101 of the 1971 Act; or

(2) (in the case of a listed building), serving a repairs notice under s 115 of that Act, with a view to then compulsorily acquiring it.

There is a similar provision, enacted on the recommendation of the Law Commission when the housing legislation was consolidated into the Housing Act 1985, whereby a local housing authority, when taking any action under that Act, must have regard to:

(1) the beauty of the landscape or the countryside;

(2) the other amenities of the locality; and

(3) the desirability of preserving existing works of architectural, historic or artistic interest (HA 1985, s 607).

For the meaning of 'amenities', see 5.7(*e*).

The difficulty for interested third parties such as amenity groups or neighbours will still be to prove that an authority has not merely decided not to use these powers, for whatever reasons, but has failed even to consider doing so: 'The very concept of administrative discretion involves a right to choose between more than one possible course of action upon which there is room for reasonable people to hold differing opinions as to which is to be preferred' (*Secretary of State for Education and Science* v *Tameside MBC* [1977] AC 1014 per Lord Diplock at 1064).

A good example of the use of the various procedures, together with grant-aid, featured Pell Wall Hall, a large country house by Soane, near Market Drayton in Shropshire. The owner had allowed it to deteriorate since acquiring it twenty years before, and in 1984 the local authority served a repairs notice under s 115. It then started compulsory purchase proceedings, including in the draft compulsory purchase order a direction for minimum compensation (see 5.5(*g*)). It intended to sell the building to the British Historic Buildings Trust, at a loss of £100,000. The owner appealed without success to the magistrates' court against the order, and thence (equally unsuccessfully) to the Crown Court, the High Court and the Court of Appeal—the latter in July 1987 (reported as *Rolf* v *North Shropshire DC* [1988] JPL 103). In 1986 fire had reduced the building to a shell, and during 1987 emergency works were carried out by the authority, under s 101, with grant-aid from the Commission. The compulsory purchase order was finally confirmed in January 1988, and the building should now pass to the Trust, for refurbishment and conversion into residential units, with the aid of a further grant from the Commission of £200,000—approximately 40 per cent of the total repair cost.

(c) Other options

There are several other ways in which a local authority can effectively intervene to bring about the restoration of historic buildings and areas.

First, a local authority may sometimes be able to intervene to bring about the improvement of a neglected site (under the Building Act 1984, the London Government Act 1963, and the 1971 Act; see 5.8(*c*) and 5.7).

Secondly, an authority has considerable powers (now contained in the Housing Act 1985; see 5.10) to assist in the improvement of whole areas, by means of the designation of housing action areas and general improvement areas. These are not specifically aimed at the repair of historic buildings and areas, but may incidentally achieve this, not least because of the greater availability of grants.

Thirdly, it can offer financial assistance in the form of grants or loans. This is considered in Chapter 6.

Finally, the simplest, cheapest and often the most effective course of action is to offer specialist guidance. This may take the form of advice to building owners from suitably trained officers. Or where the same problems recur frequently, it may be sensible to produce appropriate technical leaflets, possibly in collaboration with other authorities whose areas contain similar buildings.

Owners of listed buildings may require advice on the best way to carry out repairs or alterations. Many will wish to obtain professional advice on their problems or proposals. The Secretary of State hopes that local authorities will give such informal advice to owners as is possible within their staff resources or guide owners to other sources where they can obtain such advice for themselves. The national amenity societies are willing to offer advice wherever possible. The Royal Commission on the Historical Monuments of England may have a record of the building and its reports may be available for guidance. . . . The Historic Buildings and Monuments Commission aims to provide a nationwide advisory service within the limits of its resources (Circ 8/87, para 109).

5.4 Urgent repairs to listed buildings and in conservation areas (ss 101 and 101A)

(a) Buildings eligible

The first of the powers in the 1971 Act specifically designed to deal with the repair of buildings which are listed or in conservation areas concerns urgent repairs. The relevant powers are contained in ss 101 and 101A of the 1971 Act. These were inserted by the HPA 1986 (Sched 9, para 6) in place of the previous s 101, which itself was inserted by the TCAA 1974 in place of the original section. Note that all subsequent references to ss 101 and 101A of the 1971 Act are to those sections in their current form, that is, as inserted by the 1986 Act.

The basic principle of this provision is that an authority may itself carry out urgent works for the preservation of a building if:

(1) it is listed (TCPA 1971, s 101(1)(a)); or
(2) it is in a conservation area, and the Secretary of State has given a direction that the procedure can be used on the grounds that its preservation is important for the maintenance of the character of the area (s 101(1)(b), (2)).

A local authority wishing to use its powers under this section in connection with a particular unlisted building in a conservation area, and amenity groups or individual members of the public attempting to persuade an authority to do so, should ask the Secretary of State to make a direction under s 101(1)(b). In practice, they should write to the appropriate regional office of the Department of the Environment or to the Welsh Office enclosing photographs or other suitable evidence. Before making such a direction, the Secretary of State is to consult with the Historic Buildings and Monuments Commission (s 101(5)(b)).

The power was originally designed for use in connection with unoccupied buildings. However, since 1987, it may also be used in respect of a building that is occupied, but only to secure the preservation of a part of it that is 'not in use' (s 101(3)).

In addition, it should also be borne in mind that (as explained in more detail in 2.5) a 'listed building' includes:

(1) any object or structure fixed to the building (TCPA 1971, s 54(9)(*a*), as substituted by HPA 1986);
(2) any object or structure which has been within the curtilage of the building since before 1948 (s 54(9)(*b*)); and
(3) any part of the building (inside or outside), as so defined (TCPA 1971, s 290(1)).

There is therefore no reason why an authority could not carry out works under s 101 to save a particular feature of a listed building or its curtilage (such as a fine plaster ceiling, or a garden temple). The only requirement is that the part of the building concerned is 'not in use', which is likely to be the case if it requires urgent work for its preservation. Note that s 101 in its present form contains the phrase 'not in use', rather than (as previously) the word 'unoccupied'. This means that, for example, a ceiling void may be eligible under this heading.

This power may not be used in respect of an ecclesiastical building or a scheduled monument (1971 Act, s 101(3); see Chapters 13 and 14 respectively).

(b) Types of works envisaged

The works specified in the notice must be 'urgently necessary for the preservation of the building' (TCPA 1971, s 101(1)). As to what is envisaged, the view of the Secretary of State is as follows:

Any work done on a building under section 101 should be the minimum required for its preservation and carried out at a reasonable cost; expensive permanent repairs should not be carried out under these powers. It is considered that only emergency repairs, for example to keep a building wind and weatherproof or to prevent damage by vandals, which should not involve an owner in great expense, would be appropriate. Inexpensive repairs done in time often arrest the deterioration of a building (Circ 8/87, para 129(i)).

This is self-explanatory. However, it still leaves open the question of what repairs would be appropriate in the case of an unoccupied building that is deteriorating, but only gradually. If repair works are not carried out, the building may stand for some time to come, and it might therefore be difficult to classify them as 'urgent'. Sooner or later the building will collapse and, on the day before that, the works will indeed be 'urgent', and the service of a notice will be too late. This may be a particular problem where only part of a building (such as a room, or a ceiling) is under threat from, for example, dry rot or beetle infestation. In any such case, therefore, it will be a matter for individual judgment by the local authority as to when a s 101 notice can be justified.

In addition, it is now specifically provided that the works may consist of or include temporary support for the building—such as scaffolding, props or shelter (s 101(1)). This overturns the ruling by the Court of Appeal (per Donaldson LJ) in *R v Secretary of State, ex parte Hampshire CC* [1981] JPL 47 at 49).

(c) Procedure

Any person duly authorised in writing by the appropriate local authority may enter any land (including, for example, a building next door to the one in need of preservation):

(1) to determine whether or not the authority should exercise its powers under s 101; and

(2) to carry out in due course any works that it decides are necessary (TCPA 1971, s 280(4)).

The general comments on entry to private property that were made in connection with the survey of buildings for listing (see 2.2(*a*)) would apply here too.

The powers under s 101 are exercisable by the following:

(1) *in most urban development areas* (except Cardiff Bay): the urban development corporation (see 1.3(*a*));

(2) *elsewhere in London*: either the appropriate borough council or the Historic Buildings and Monuments Commission (TCPA 1971, s 101(1), (5)(*a*));

(3) *elsewhere in England*:
   — any local authority (county, district or borough council: ss 101(1), 290(1)) or, within its area, the Broads Authority (s 101(6), inserted by NSBA 1988); or
   — the Commission—but only with the specific authority of the Secretary of State, which is intended to be given in exceptional circumstances only (TCPA 1971, s 101(5)(*c*); Circ 8/87, para 126);

(4) *in Wales*:
   — any local authority (county, district or borough council) (ss 101(1), 290(1)); or
   — the Secretary of State for Wales—but he intends to act only in exceptional circumstances (s 101(1); WO Circ 61/81, para 98).

Before carrying out the work, the authority must give at least seven days' written notice to the owner (s 101(4)). The purpose of this requirement is to enable the owner to discuss the matter with the authority, and perhaps to volunteer to carry out the works himself.

The notice must therefore set out in detail precisely what is intended, with estimates—the latter prepared wherever possible by a quantity surveyor. It is no good requiring the owner 'to support the building in a manner to the satisfaction of the Council to prevent its collapse' (*R* v *Secretary of State for the Environment, ex parte Hampshire CC* [1981] JPL 47), or to carry out 'all such steps as may be necessary to preserve the structure of the building' (*R* v *Camden LBC, ex parte Comyn Ching & Co (London) Ltd and another* [1984] JPL 661 at 661 and 666). The requirement to describe the works in detail is also important in that it enables the owner to decide whether to appeal against the notice (see below), in accordance with the rules of natural justice (see, for example, *Cooper* v *The Board of Works for Wandsworth* (1863) 14 CB (NS) 180).

Once the notice has been served on the owner, he may of course make a satisfactory response. He may volunteer to do the works himself or he may submit an application for listed building consent (and, where appropriate, planning permission—see Chapter 7) to carry out more substantial works of restoration or conversion. He may also seek, or the authority may offer, a grant or loan (see Chapter 6).

If, however, no satisfactory response is forthcoming, the authority (or the Commission, where appropriate) can then proceed to carry out the necessary works itself (s 101(1), (5)(*c*)). If the owner explains that the works will be carried out 'in due course', that would not be satisfactory. In the absence of any firm proposals and given that the works are by definition urgent, the authority would probably be justified in proceeding.

If the authority wishes to reclaim the cost of the works, the owner has a right to appeal (see below). Thus the notice may come under careful scrutiny both from him and from the Secretary of State. It is therefore important for the works carried out by the authority to be carefully considered—both as to their extent and as to their cost. Any decisions need to be fully supported by factual evidence and accurately recorded for use in case of any appeal.

A frugal authority may insist on obtaining several tenders and accepting only the lowest. As a result, the works may be significantly delayed, and eventually carried out to a poor standard, leading to yet further deterioration of the building. On the other hand, an authority carrying out the works immediately, and accepting the first estimate available, may find that the Secretary of State disallows some of the costs on appeal. In practice, speed is often essential to prevent further disrepair.

Where the owner of an unoccupied building is unknown or cannot be traced, the authority may proceed at least seven days after putting up a notice addressed 'to the owner/occupier' and setting out the details of what works are proposed. If no response is received to such a notice within the seven-day period (and a response is for obvious reasons unlikely), the authority may proceed with the works, although it will in practice have to meet the cost from its own resources.

(d) Recovery of the cost of the works

Once the works have been carried out by a local authority, it can then, if it wishes, recover their cost (TCPA 1971, s 101A(1)). To achieve this, it must first serve on the owner of the building a notice setting out the cost, and asking him to pay (s 101A(2)). Such a notice must also mention the right of appeal under s 101A(5) (*Bolton MBC* v *Jolley* (1988) *The Independent*, 19 December). The authority is not obliged to do this, and there is no reason in law why it should not seek to recover only part of the cost, or none. This might be appropriate where, for example, the owner was an individual with limited means, or a charity— particularly in the case of a large building, where even limited repairs are likely to be expensive. In other cases, there might in practice be no way of recovering any of the cost, such as where the owner is overseas, bankrupt or unknown (see above).

The 'owner' in this context will be the freeholder or the lease-holder if he is renting the building at significantly less then the market rent (1971 Act, s 290(1); *London Corpn* v *Cusack-Smith* [1955] AC 337, upheld in *Pollway Nominees* v *Croydon LBC* [1986] 2 All ER 849). The 'owner' from whom the money can be recovered (s 101A(2)) is presumably, in the absence of any more specific provision, the same 'owner' as the one on whom notice was first served of the authority's intention to carry out the works (s 101(4)). There is no provision for the authority to claim it from the new owner; nor can the cost of the works be registered as a local land charge. Therefore, in order to prevent possible problems arising in the event of the property changing hands, the authority should seek to recover the cost as soon as possible after the works have been carried out. If necessary, the cost of the works, together with a reasonable sum in respect of establishment charges, can be recovered as a simple contract debt (s 111; LGA 1974, s 36).

If the Commission has carried out the works, as the agent of the Secretary of State (that is, outside London), it is he who is entitled to recover the cost (TCPA 1971, ss 101(5)(c), 101A(1)).

Within twenty-eight days of receiving a demand for payment, an owner may make representations to the Secretary of State on any of the following grounds:

(1) that some or all of the works were unnecessary for the preservation of the building;

(2) that the amount specified in the notice is unreasonable; or

(3) that the recovery of it would cause hardship (s 101A(4)(a), (c)).

Where the works involved include temporary support or shelter for the building (see above), the continuing expenses involved are recoverable from the owner, and may be billed on an interim basis (s 101A(3)). However, the owner may claim as one of his grounds of appeal against the recovery of expenses that the temporary works have continued for an unreasonable length of time (s 101A(4)(b)).

The Secretary of State will consider the representations in the light of the following (see Circ 8/87, para 129):

(1) the necessity for the works to be done (see above, 5.4(b)); and

(2) the financial circumstances of the owner.

He will then decide whether any of the cost of the works is recoverable, and if so how much. He will notify his decision, and the reasons for it, to the owner, and to the local authority (or the Commission if it carried out the works) (s 101A(5)). In some cases such appeals have been decided only after a long delay, and even then the alterations made to the sums claimed were relatively trivial.

5.5 Compulsory purchase of listed buildings in need of repair (ss 114 to 117)

(a) Need for compulsory purchase

Where a listed building is in poor condition, it is often because its owner is unwilling or unable to carry out the necessary works.

This may be because he is deliberately letting the building fall into disrepair thereby forcing the planning authority to grant listed building consent for its demolition. Or it may be because he would be very willing to repair it, but simply cannot afford to.

If the works are urgent, the s 101 procedure (described above) may be used. But this is only effective in very limited circumstances and cannot, in particular, bring about works other than those immediately necessary. Alternatively, the local authority or the Historic Buildings and Monuments Commission may be willing to offer grants or loans (see Chapter 6). But these will usually only cover part of the cost of the works, and the owner will still need to find the balance, which, again, he may be unwilling or unable to do. Even if a way can be found to assist or persuade the owner to carry out the works needed to bring the building into repair, he still has to keep it in repair in the future, which may (especially in the case of a large building) be a very onerous responsibility.

In these circumstances, the basic problem arises from the ownership of the building. The existing owner cannot or will not maintain it; those who could and would do not own it. The 1971 Act accordingly provides a special procedure whereby a listed building may be compulsorily purchased by a public authority.

Once the building is in public ownership, the acquiring authority then has a number of options. In principle, it can make such arrangements for its management, use or disposal as it considers appropriate to ensure its preservation (TCPA 1971, s 126; and see *Rolf* v *North Shropshire DC* [1988] JPL 103 at 107). It could, for example, carry out the necessary repairs itself, and then either retain it for its own purposes, or sell or lease it to another owner. Alternatively, it could transfer it to another owner straight away, but subject to a requirement that the owner carry out the repairs. If the subsequent owner could be identified prior to the completion of the compulsory purchase, the authority could enter into a conditional contract of sale with him, to be completed at the moment the authority itself acquires the building. In this way, it would receive the proceeds of the subsequent sale at the same time as it had to pay for the initial purchase. The authority would thus not be out of pocket for more than a very short time—and in determining the spending limits of an authority, allowance is made for back-to-back deals of this sort (see Circ 5/87, paras 28–32). Authorities liable to rate-capping would thus need to be particularly careful to ensure that the building was passed on promptly to its new owners, so as to avoid unnecessarily increasing their spending, and thereby attracting financial penalties.

The procedure could thus be used in several different ways. The simplest option is where the owner of a listed building (for example, a town house owned by an absentee landlord and let as flats) has allowed it to fall into very poor condition, but is not interested in doing any repairs (since the capital outlay would not be reflected in extra rental income). Here the local authority can purchase the building, repair it, and sell it to a new owner, who can either continue to use it for the same purpose or apply to change its use. Alternatively the authority could sell the building subject to a requirement that it must be repaired, possibly offering a grant as an inducement to carry out detailed work to the correct specifications.

Secondly, where, for example, a listed building in poor condition is occupied by a charity or other organisation that has very limited capital to carry out repairs, a local authority can purchase the building, carry out the works at its own expense (or with assistance from the Commission), and lease it back to the original occupiers on a lease containing a landlord's repairing covenant.

Thirdly, the procedure could be used where a substantial listed building (such as a country house or a church) is no longer required or suitable for its original function. In such a case, the authority could serve one or more repairs notices setting out precisely what repairs it considers are needed to the building (see below). It can then seek offers from suitable developers for a total rehabilitation scheme, which will include all the specified repairs, together with (probably) a change of use and (possibly) considerable alterations. A contract should then be entered into for the sale of the building by the authority to the developer, conditional on the successful completion of its compulsory purchase from the existing owner. Where planning permission is needed for the proposed works, the contract could be linked to an agreement, to ensure that the necessary repairs are carried out. Such an agreement can be made under s 52 of the 1971 Act or (better) under s 33 of the Local Government (Miscellaneous Provisions) Act 1984. It needs to be very carefully drafted, if it is to bind all parties as intended—many s 52 agreements contain errors, or turn out to be unenforceable.

Fourthly, the authority could sell the building to a building preservation trust (see 6.4), for the trust to carry out the repairs and any appropriate refurbishment works. The financial details of such a transaction would need to be worked out carefully so as to minimise the burden on the trust; it might well be appropriate for the resale to include an element of grant-aid, with the Commission also possibly contributing financially to the authority or to the trust.

These are only a few examples of how the s 114 procedure could be used creatively. What is certain is that, once an authority has acquired experience of the procedure in practice, it is much easier to do it again, and to find ways of maximising the benefit to all concerned. It should be remembered by local authorities that finance may be available from the Commission to assist with the purchase of buildings in appropriate cases (HBAMA 1953, s 5B, inserted by NHA 1983). In Wales, similar assistance may be available from the Secretary of State (HBAMA 1953, s 6, amended by TCPA 1971 and NHA 1983).

A recent instance of the use of this procedure was the action taken by North Shropshire District Council to bring about the repair of Pell Wall Hall (*Rolf* v *North Shropshire DC* [1988] JPL 103; and see 5.3(*b*)).

Note that the s 115 procedure may be used (unlike s 101; see above) to secure the repair of listed buildings which are occupied. But it may not be used in the case of:
(1) an unlisted building in a conservation area (TCPA 1971, s 114(3)); or
(2) an ecclesiastical building in ecclesiastical use, or a scheduled monument (ss 114(3) and 58(2); see Chapters 13 and 14).
An authority may acquire a historic building (including one in the above categories) by agreement, rather than using compulsory purchase powers (1971 Act, s 119; see below).

(b) Acquiring authorities

The Secretary of State may himself compulsorily purchase a listed building (TCPA 1971, s 114(2)). In the case of a building in England, he should only do so after consultation with the Historic Buildings and Monuments Commission (s 114(3A), inserted by NHA 1983). But he has stated that he will only use this power himself in 'very exceptional circumstances' (Circ 8/87, para 130).

Otherwise, compulsory purchase of a listed building under s 114 can be carried out by any of the following:

(1) *in an urban development area in England*: the urban development corporation (see 1.3(*a*));
(2) *elsewhere in Greater London*: the London borough council or the Commission (s 114(1), as amended by LGA 1985);
(3) *in a national park*: the county council or district council or joint planning board (s 114(1), LGA 1972, Sched 16, para 31);
(4) *in a metropolitan area*: the district council (s 114(1));
(5) *in the Broads*: the county council or district council or the Broads Authority (s 114(1); s 114(1A), inserted by NSBA 1988); and
(6) *elsewhere*: the county council or the district council (s 114(1)).

There is no reason why a county council and a district council should not operate together. The former will sometimes have greater specialist expertise in historic buildings matters, and may have experience of using this procedure elsewhere in the county. The latter will be responsible for the grant of planning permission and listed building consent for any subsequent rehabilitation of the building. The Commission may also be involved—both as a source of technical expertise and to provide financial assistance where appropriate.

(c) Repairs notices

The first stage in the procedure is that a 'repairs notice' must be served on the owner and occupier (TCPA 1971, s 115(1)). The notice must 'specify the works which [the authority considers] reasonably necessary for the proper preservation of the building'. This is probably best achieved by means of a detailed report by an appropriately qualified surveyor or architect, with detailed experience of the repair and maintenance of the type of building in question. It is not clear whether the word 'specify', used in the Act, means that the notice must include a 'specification' in sufficient detail to enable it to be used by a builder without more ado, or whether it merely implies a report adequate to form the basis of such a specification. It presumably means a description of the works sufficient to identify exactly what is needed, without specifying the number of bricks to be used.

In practice, it would usually be appropriate to discuss the works specified with whoever is actually going to carry them out. This in turn means that the authority should have clearly thought through what it intends to do once it has purchased the building—

see the comments above for some suggestions. It would also be sensible in many cases for a district council to seek specialist advice from the county council. Note that the authority does not have to take into account the owner's means when specifying the works (*Rolf* v *North Shropshire DC* [1988] JPL 103 at 105)—this contrasts with the s 101 procedure, where the owner can appeal against a claim for recovery of the cost of urgent works carried out on the grounds that it would cause hardship.

The notice should not specify works over and above those that the authority considers to be 'reasonably necessary for the proper preservation of the building' (s 115(1)(*a*)). Thus in *Robbins* v *Secretary of State and Ashford BC* [1988] JPL 349 a notice served under s 115 required works to be done to Willesborough Windmill in Kent which went beyond mere repairs, and included measures aimed at 'restoring it to its former glory'. This did not invalidate the subsequent approval by the Secretary of State of the authority's compulsory purchase order; 'There was an obvious public interest, where listed buildings were concerned, in expecting owners to make reasonable efforts to comply with those parts of repairs notices which they know to require work which could lawfully be required' (p 356), and in this case the owner had carried out no works at all. Authorities should not use this as an excuse to avoid considering carefully what works are currently necessary, as opposed to desirable. More extensive works, however worthwhile, should not be included in the notice, but obviously can be carried out later at the authority's discretion, once it owns the building. The decision of the High Court has been upheld in the Court of Appeal ([1988] JPL 824).

The fact that the notice is to specify the works (presumably all the works) necessary for the preservation of the building which is to be purchased would seem to mean that it is not possible to serve several notices in respect of the same part of a building— although, since 'building' can mean 'part of a building' (TCPA 1971, s 290), there would be nothing to stop several notices being served for one building. In the case of a large complex of buildings (such as a country house with stables, outbuildings, gatehouses, etc, or a terrace of houses all in bad repair), therefore, the correct procedure would be as follows. The authority should first serve a separate notice in respect of each part of the complex, or each house in the terrace. It could then start compulsory purchase procedures in respect of the whole group once two months had elapsed after the service of the last repairs notice of the series.

Alternatively, it could serve a series of compulsory purchase orders, each at least two months after the corresponding repairs notice had been served. In either case, the Secretary of State should be invited to confirm all the orders together (see below). Which is the most appropriate course of action, and in what sequence the various parts of the group are dealt with, will depend on the amount of work involved in preparing the necessary notices and orders.

The repairs notice must also explain the effect of ss 114 to 117 of the Act—that is, it must set out what is the compulsory purchase procedure (including the provisions as to compensation (see below); TCPA 1971, s 115(1)(*b*)). It is to be served on the owner of the building—that is, the freeholder or, where appropriate, the leaseholder or subleaseholder entitled to receive the market rent (ss 115(1), 290). But it would also be sensible to serve a copy of the notice on the occupier(s) of the building, and any other interested parties (such as any prospective purchasers and their professional advisers, the Commission, and the district or county council).

Where a notice has been served under s 115, the owner is barred from serving either a purchase notice or a listed building purchase notice on the authority at any time within the succeeding three months—or, if compulsory purchase proceedings are started within that three-month period, at any time until they are concluded (ss 180(5), (6), 190(4)).

Finally, where the owner of the building is not known or cannot be traced, a notice should be affixed to the building (see the comments at 5.4(*c*) as to the corresponding procedure for s 101 notices). The compulsory purchase proceedings can then be started two months after the notice was put up, under the special procedure in Sched 2 to the Compulsory Purchase Act 1965.

(d) Compulsory purchase procedure

The detailed procedure is broadly as for any compulsory purchase, and is governed by the Acquisition of Land Act 1981 and the Compulsory Purchase of Land Regulations 1982 (TCPA 1971, s 114(5)) although note the special right of appeal to the magistrates' court (s 114(6); see below).

The acquiring authority first makes a draft compulsory purchase order, in the prescribed form set out in the 1982 Regulations. The order may include not only the listed building itself, but also any adjoining land whose purchase is appropriate (s 114(1), (2)). This would apply to land required for preserving the building or its amenities (such as the garden of a town house), or for affording access to it, or for its proper control or management (such as the outbuildings of a country house, or the lodge of an institutional building). The land to be acquired is defined in the order by reference to a map (1982 Regulations, Sched). Authorities have been warned to take care when preparing orders—a high proportion of orders submitted to the Secretary of State for confirmation contain errors or omissions (Circ 6/85, para 3).

The authority then advertises the order for at least two weeks in the local press, and serves separate notices on each owner, lessee and occupier of the land (Acquisition of Land Act 1981, ss 11, 12).

The compulsory purchase of the building cannot start until at least two months after the repairs notice has been served (TCPA 1971, s 115(1)). For this purpose, the 'start' of the compulsory purchase means the service of the notices on the owners etc of the land (TCPA 1971, s 115(4); 1981 Act, s 12). For the timetable in a case involving more than one repairs notice, see above.

The press advertisement and the notice to the owners etc must both state the date by which any objections may be made. This must be at least twenty-one days from the making of the draft order. Any such objections are likely to be in two categories:

(1) those against the principle of compulsory purchase; and
(2) those referring only to the amount of compensation to be paid.

If there are no objections, or if the authority considers that all the objections are in the second category, the Secretary of State is then entitled to confirm the order without further ado. If however there are any objections which are or might be in the first category, he must first hold a public inquiry (1981 Act, s 13). Curiously, objectors other than owners, lessees and occupiers, such as neighbours or amenity societies, have a right to be heard, but the Secretary of State is entitled to disregard their objections (*Middlesex CC* v *Minister of Local Government and Planning* [1953] 1 QB 12, CA). Otherwise, the procedure is as for other similar inquiries (Compulsory Purchase by Public Authorities (Inquiries Procedure) Rules 1976; *Local Government Board* v *Arlidge* [1915] AC 120).

Before confirming the order, in the case of a building in England, he must consult the Historic Buildings and Monuments Commission—except, obviously, in the case of an order made by the Commission itself in London (TCPA 1971, s 114(3A), as inserted by NHA 1983 and amended by LGA 1985).

Of more significance, he must not make or confirm a compulsory purchase order unless he is satisfied as to two matters:

(1) that reasonable steps are not being taken to preserve the building properly (s 114(1), (2)); and

(2) that it is expedient that provision should be made for the preservation of the building (s 114(4)); and consequently

(3) that it is expedient that it should be compulsorily purchased (s 114(4)).

Thus if the works specified in the repairs notice had been carried out in their entirety, the Secretary of State would normally refuse to confirm a compulsory purchase order, on the first ground above—although in theory he could authorise the acquisition in order to ensure that other works, which he considered to be necessary for the preservation of the building but which had not been specified in the notice, were carried out. Note that the requirement is in the present tense—it is no good an owner claiming that he intends to carry out repairs. It would seem that what is required to defeat an order is at the very least a binding contract for the carrying out of the repairs. It may be insufficient to show that he has carried out only some of the works; where a notice contains more than is strictly required for the building's preservation, it would only be necessary for the owner to show that those works that were actually necessary had been carried out (*Robbins*; see p68). Note too that the works must be such as to preserve the building 'properly'—a mere temporary operation would not suffice.

If, however, the order is confirmed, possibly in a modified form, notices must once again be publicised in the press and sent to the owners and occupiers of the land (1981 Act, s 15).

(e) Appeal to magistrates' court

In addition to the normal method of objecting to any compulsory purchase order, described above, there is a further right to appeal to the local magistrates' court. Under this procedure, anyone served with notice of the order may within the following twenty-eight days apply to the court for an order staying further proceedings on the compulsory purchase order (TCPA 1971, s 114(6)).

The procedure to be adopted in the event of such an application is anomalous. On receipt of the complaint by the building owner, the court will issue a summons on complaint (in Form 99; see *Stone's Justices' Manual*, 1988 ed, para 6–952; Magistrates' Courts Act 1980, ss 51, 52; Magistrates' Courts Rules 1981, rr 34, 98). The local authority concerned will then attend to answer the complaint. But there appears to be no provision for the authority to set out a statement of its case; nor for the production of proofs by expert witnesses. For further details, see the article at [1983] JPL 655.

In any event, an order staying the proceedings must be granted if, but only if, the court is satisfied that 'reasonable steps have been taken for properly preserving the building'. But the steps must have already been taken by the date of the hearing; again, a mere promise will not be enough.

Anyone aggrieved by the decision of the magistrates' court can appeal to the Crown Court (s 114(7)). It was as a result of such an appeal that the Pell Wall Hall case eventually reached the Court of Appeal ([1988] JPL 103 at 104; and see 5.3(*b*)).

(f) Compensation

As to the compensation payable if the compulsory purchase order is confirmed, the basic rule is that it is the value of the land 'if sold on the open market by a willing seller' (Land Compensation Act 1961, s 5, rule 2). In determining what this open market value is, the normal rules will apply.

Special problems may arise however in the case of buildings falling to be valued under rule 5—that is, 'where land is, and but for the compulsory acquisition would continue to be, devoted to a purpose of such a nature that there is no general demand or market for land for that purpose'. This would apply to, for example, churches and chapels, and ornamental structures serving no useful purpose. Clearly, in such circumstances, to pay open market value (which might be nil) would be unjust, and the compensation payable is therefore the reasonable cost of equivalent reinstatement elsewhere, if that is bona fide intended by the landowner. However, what cost is 'reasonable' may be difficult to determine. The replacement of monumental Victorian architecture by a modern functional building often makes it difficult to decide what is genuinely 'equivalent' or comparable.

A further problem arises where such a structure is redundant. In this case, rule 5 no longer applies, since the land would no longer be used for its last purpose, even if it were not being compulsorily purchased, and there is no intention to reinstate.

The appropriate value would therefore again be that obtainable on the open market; which would presumably be the value in some alternative use, if there is any, or otherwise might be zero or even negative.

In addition, the planning position needs to be investigated carefully to ascertain what, if any, planning permission might be forthcoming which would increase the value of the property (see Land Compensation Act 1961, ss 14–16). It is to be assumed that listed building consent would be granted for any works involving the alteration or extension of the building (TCPA 1971, s 116). Moreover, it can be assumed that planning permission will be granted for Sched 8 development (principally 10 per cent extensions; TCPA 1971, s 169 and Sched 8), and that listed building consent will be granted for any demolition involved in carrying out such development (TCAA 1974, s 6).

The likelihood of obtaining planning permission for works involving alterations of any significance will, in many cases, be small. The net effect of these provisions would therefore be that the only (small) additional value likely would be that arising from the carrying out of works which require listed building consent, but which:

(1) are not development at all; or
(2) are permitted development; or
(3) are within Sched 8 development.

The planning position may need to be considered more carefully, however, in the case of a compulsory purchase under s 115 of the 1971 Act where the acquiring authority is willing to grant planning permission for refurbishment proposals involving a change of use or some new building works.

But there is no assumption that listed building consent would be granted for any other works amounting to total or partial demolition of the building (TCPA 1971, s 116, as amended by TCAA 1974, s 290). It should be borne in mind here that some works of 'alteration or extension' will include an element of (at least partial) demolition (see 8.1(d)), and that it therefore cannot be assumed that consent will automatically be granted for them. In the case of a building being purchased under s 115, which is likely to be considered to be of particular interest by the acquiring authority, such consent would indeed probably not be forthcoming. This would also put a severe restraint on any additional value to be reflected in the purchase price.

Finally, it may be noted that the comments in this section apply to *any* compulsory purchase of a listed building (s 116; Circ 8/87, paras 137, 138). So, for example, the valuation for the purposes of assessing compensation of a listed building that happens to be included within a town centre redevelopment scheme would be in accordance with the comments above. In such a case the possibility of listed building consent being obtained for demolition would need to be evaluated.

For an example of the assessment of compensation for the purchase of a listed house in bad repair, see *Taylor* v *Cheltenham BC* (1978) 246 EG 923, LT. The Lands Tribunal (to which any dispute over compensation is referred) accepted that logically the property had a minus value, but that nevertheless a purchaser might be prepared to accept it at a 'knock-down price.'

(g) Compensation for building deliberately left derelict

One further feature of compulsory purchase under s 114 of the 1971 Act is that there is a special method of assessing the compensation payable where the listed building to be acquired is deliberately left derelict (TCPA 1971, s 117, as amended by LGA 1974, LGA 1985 and Acquisition of Land Act 1981).

This only applies, however, where the acquiring authority is satisfied that the building has been deliberately allowed to fall into disrepair for the purpose of justifying:

(1) its demolition, and
(2) the development or re-development of the site or any adjoining site (s 117(1), (2), as amended by LGA 1974 and LGA 1985).

In other words, to justify the use of this procedure, it must be proved that the neglect of the building was not merely deliberate or reckless, but also that the underlying motive was to facilitate demolition and redevelopment. Such a claim by the authority would be difficult to justify in the face of a counterclaim by the owner that he had no such motive, but was simply unable to afford to maintain the building properly.

Where such a claim can be substantiated, the authority may include in the draft compulsory purchase order a 'direction for minimum compensation'. If it does so, it must state this in the notice served on the owners and occupiers informing them of the order (s 117(1)–(3), as amended by the 1974, 1981 and 1985 Acts). A model for such a direction is provided in App J to DOE Circ 6/85.

The effect of such a direction is that the compensation payable by the authority for the purchase of the building is not to be assessed on the basis of the usual assumptions as to planning permission contained in the Land Compensation Act 1961 (see above). Instead, it is to be assumed that planning permission and listed building consent would only be granted for those works which are necessary for restoring the building and maintaining it in a proper state of repair (s 117(4)). This would stifle any hope that the owner might have entertained of obtaining an inflated 'development' value for the site. 'It is hoped that authorities will not often have to resort to this power, but its existence should act as a deterrent against the sort of deliberate neglect which has caused the loss of listed buildings in the past' (Circ 8/87, para 136).

Anyone who is served with notice of a compulsory purchase order containing a direction for minimum compensation can apply within twenty-eight days to the local magistrates' court for an order that the direction is deleted from the purchase order. If the court is satisfied that the reason for the state of the building is not to facilitate its demolition and redevelopment, then it must delete the direction from the purchase order (s 117(5), as amended by the 1974, 1981 and 1985 Acts). The procedure for such an application is as for an application under s 114(6) of the 1971 Act (see 5.5(e)). There is also a right of appeal to the Crown Court against the decision of the magistrates' court (s 117(6)).

See *Rolf* v *North Shropshire DC* [1988] JPL 103 at 104 for an example of the use of a minimum compensation direction.

5.6 Acquisition of historic buildings by agreement

(a) Acquisition by local authorities (s 119)

As an alternative to compulsory purchase, a local authority may acquire by agreement any building which appears to be of special architectural or historic interest, together with any adjacent land necessary for its upkeep (TCPA 1971, s 119(1)(b), (c)).

There is no need for the building to be listed, or even in a conservation area. Section 54(1) states specifically that the statutory list is prepared for the guidance of local authorities in performing their functions under the 1971 Act; and there will therefore be a presumption in favour of this power being used in connection with listed buildings only. Nor is there any need for the building to be in disrepair, although that is one obvious reason for the power being exercised. If negotiations break down, however, the authority may wish to use its compulsory powers instead; and this will only be possible if the building is both listed and in need of repair (see above).

Acquisition of property by agreement is more straightforward than compulsory purchase, and will be suitable where the owner and the local authority—possibly after consultation with the Historic Buildings and Monuments Commission—are agreed that purchase by the authority is the best means of securing the future of the building. Since the terms and conditions of the purchase will be by mutual agreement, there is no reason why an authority should not in appropriate cases pay a reduced price for a dilapidated building in need of major restoration.

The Commission (or, in Wales, the Secretary of State) may be willing to make a financial contribution towards the acquisition of buildings by an authority under s 119 (HBAMA 1953, ss 5B(1), 6, inserted and amended by NHA 1983).

The s 119 procedure may also be used in any of the ways described in connection with compulsory purchase—such as resale to a new owner, refurbishment by a developer, or leaseback to the original owner (TCPA 1971, s 126(1); see 5.5(*a*)).

The acquisition of a building under s 119 may be carried out by a county council, district council or London borough council (s 119(1)) or, in a national park, the joint planning board (LGA 1972, Sched 16, para 31).

(b) Acquisition by the Secretary of State and by the Commission

The Secretary of State has power to acquire by agreement, or to accept as a gift, any building which appears to him to be 'of outstanding historic or architectural interest' and any land contiguous or adjacent to such a building (HBAMA 1953, s 5(1)); there is no requirement that the building should be in need of repair. As to the meaning of 'outstanding interest', see 6.2(*a*). The Secretary of State may also accept a capital endowment to provide income for the upkeep of a historic building (s 8). This avoids problems that might otherwise occur, as such an endowment (unless it were charitable) would fail as a non-charitable purpose trust.

The Commission may acquire (by purchase, lease or gift) any property in England that is:

(1) a building of outstanding historic or architectural interest; or

(2) a building that is in a conservation area, and of special historic or architectural interest; or

(3) land associated with a building in either of those categories; or

(4) any other garden or land that is of outstanding historic or architectural interest

(HBAMA 1953, s 5A, inserted by NHA 1983). The Commission too may accept an endowment for the upkeep of such a building or garden (ss 8A, 8B).

The Secretary of State (in England or Wales) or the Commission (in England) may also purchase by agreement, or accept as a gift, any objects (such as paintings or furniture) associated with such a building, provided that the building is in his or its ownership or control or that of the National Trust (ss 5(2), 5A(2)).

The Secretary of State or the Commission may then make whatever arrangements seem to be appropriate for the disposal, custody and management of the property (s 5(3), (3A)).

Any acquisition or disposal of property by the Secretary of State must in any event be the subject of consultation with the Commission (or the Historic Buildings Council for Wales) except in cases of urgency (s 5(4), amended by NHA 1983). Any such action by the Commission must have the consent of the Secretary of State (s 5A(4), inserted by NHA 1983).

5.7 Buildings and other land in need of maintenance (s 65)

(a) Background

A planning authority can only serve a notice under s 101 to bring about urgent repairs to a building. There is little point in serving a repairs notice under s 115 if the authority is not prepared to follow it up with compulsory purchase. A further possibility, which has only been available in the context of a building since 1987, is for it to serve a notice under s 65 of the TCPA 1971 (note that all references to the section are to it in its present form, that is, as substituted by HPA 1986, s 46).

This power was in the past available only in the context of open land. It has therefore been little used in practice. However a s 65 notice can now be served in connection with any 'land' (rather than, as was the case previously, only 'gardens and vacant sites'). Here, 'land' is defined to include 'a building' (TCPA 1971, s 290(1)). It would therefore be perfectly in order for a local authority to serve a notice on the owner and occupier of any building whose condition was 'adversely affecting the amenity of the surrounding area' (s 65(1)). The notice would require the owner and occupier of the building to remedy its poor condition, subject only to a right of appeal to the magistrates' court (s 105). The authority can then carry out the necessary works itself and reclaim the cost from the owner (s 107).

There is no need for the building or land to be listed or in a conservation area, although the s 65 procedure would be particularly appropriate to a neglected historic building. It would be equally applicable to occupied, partly occupied or vacant buildings. It could also be used for churches and scheduled monuments (unlike notices under either s 101 or s 115 of the TCPA 1971; see 5.4(a) and 5.5(a)). The local authority simply has to be satisfied, before serving the notice, that the condition of the property is 'adversely affecting' the 'amenity' of any part of its area or the area of any neighbouring authority (TCPA 1971, s 65(1)).

(b) Initial procedure

A s 65 notice can be served by the following authorities:

(1) *in national parks*: the county council (outside metropolitan counties) or planning board (LGA 1972, s 182(4), Sched 17, paras 1, 3 and 20), or the district council (LGA 1972, s 182(5));

(2) *in urban development areas (except Cardiff Bay)*: the urban development corporation (see 1.3(a));

(3) *in the Broads*: the Broads Authority (TCPA 1971, s 273A, inserted by NSBA 1988); and

(4) *elsewhere*: the district or London borough council (TCPA 1971, s 65(4)).

The authority must 'serve the notice on the owner and occupier' of the land (TCPA 1971, s 65(1)). It will often be prudent for the authority to find out first who are the owners and occupiers (see below).

The notice must specify:

(1) what steps the authority requires to be taken to remedy the condition of the building, and the period within which those steps are to be taken (s 65(2)); and

(2) the period at the end of which it is to come into effect (s 65(3)).

As to the steps to be taken, the notice must specify these with sufficient accuracy for the recipient to know exactly what he has to do, and by when he has to do it. This requirement has been considered at length by the courts in the context of the steps required to be taken by an enforcement notice. See, in particular, the comments of Upjohn LJ in *Miller-Mead* v *Minister of Housing and Local Government* [1963] 2 QB 196 at 232, often followed subsequently. If the notice does not specify the works at all, or is hopelessly vague, it will be a nullity, and the recipient will not be under any duty to comply with it.

The specification of the works required would usually best be done by way of a schedule of repairs attached to the notice (as is standard practice with repairs notices under the Housing Acts; see 5.9(*a*)).

As to what works are suitable to be the subject of a s 65 notice, this will clearly depend on the facts of each case. But a planning authority, when drafting a s 65 notice, and a property owner, when considering whether to appeal against one, should bear in mind that amongst the four possible grounds of appeal (see 5.7(*e*), (*f*)) are:

(1) that the remedial works required to be carried out are excessive; and
(2) that the time within which those works are to be carried out is unreasonably short (TCPA 1971, s 105(1)(*d*), (*e*), as amended by HPA 1986).

(c) Service and coming into effect of notice

A s 65 notice comes into effect at the end of the period stated within it. This must be at least twenty-eight days from the date of service (TCPA 1971, s 65(3)). Note that the wording of this requirement is different from that of the corresponding provision in s 87(13) (TCPA 1971, as amended by LGPAA 1981). Since it is the notice itself, and not a copy, which is served on each owner and occupier, the date on which it comes into force must be the same for each recipient. If, therefore, notices are served on different dates, the periods specified in each must be calculated so as to expire simultaneously. This requires very careful drafting to avoid errors. It is also prudent to choose a date for the notice to come into effect which allows for the possibility of notices not being delivered and having to be re-addressed. If the different recipients of the same notice are in effect told that it is to come into effect on different dates, the notice will probably be a nullity, and all recipients will then be able to ignore it (*Bambury* v

Hounslow LBC [1966] 2 QB 204; *Stevens* v *Bromley LBC* [1972] Ch 39; 400, CA).

Because of potential procedural challenges, therefore, it is best to ensure that, as far as possible, the notice is served on *all* the relevant owners and occupiers on the same date. To achieve this, it will usually be necessary to serve a preliminary notice on any known owner or occupier seeking the full name and address of any others. A planning authority can require these details to be supplied within a period of fourteen days, on penalty of a fine of up to level 5 on the standard scale (Local Government (Miscellaneous Provisions) Act 1976, s 16, as amended by the Criminal Justice Act 1982 and Criminal Penalties (Increase) Order 1984). There is also a power to obtain much more information from owners, to be supplied within a period of up to twenty-one days on pain of a fine of up to level 3 (currently £400) (TCPA 1971, s 284, as amended by Town and Country Planning (Amendment) Act 1977 and the 1982 Act).

Some of these problems arise because the procedural requirements as to the service of s 65 notices have been badly drafted. The section in its revised form still uses the language of the pre-1981 provisions concerning the service of enforcement notices; see, eg, TCPA 1971, s 87(7) as originally drafted. Those were significantly amended by the LGPAA 1981, because a number of practical procedural difficulties arose where there were many owners and occupiers involved. It may therefore be relevant to consult pre-1981 editions of standard texts for details of the possible pitfalls (for both the local authority and the building owner).

(d) Appeal against a s 65 notice

Anyone receiving a s 65 notice may appeal against it—not to the Secretary of State, but to the magistrates' court for the area containing the land (TCPA 1971, s 105(1), (2), as amended by HPA 1986). Such an appeal must be made before the notice comes into effect, which will be at least twenty-eight days after its service to owners and occupiers (see above). There is then a further right of appeal, by either the appellant or the planning authority who served the notice, to the Crown Court (s 106).

Where an appeal is made to the magistrates' court, the notice is suspended until the matter is finally determined (s 105(3)). This means until the time for appealing to the Crown Court has expired—or, if such an appeal has been made, until the appropriate time limits for appeals to higher courts have expired (*Garland* v *Westminster CC* (1970) 21 P & CR 555).

There are now only four possible grounds of appeal against a s 65 notice. These are considered in detail below. Ground (*c*) was repealed in 1987 (by HPA 1986, Sched 11, para 20).

Note that, if a recipient of a notice wants to appeal against it on grounds (*a*) and (*b*) below, an appeal to the magistrates' court is the only way to proceed (TCPA 1971, s 243(3)) unless the notice was incorrectly served, or if other grounds are relied on, when an application for judicial review may be made (under RSC, Ord 53; see 8.9(*b*)).

When determining an appeal against a s 65 notice, the magistrates' court may quash it, or may uphold it with or without alteration. Such alteration may only be made if it does not cause any injustice to the appellant (TCPA 1971, s 105(5)). The court may also correct any informality, defect or error in the notice if it is satisfied that the mistake is not 'material' (s 105(4)). The wording of these provisions again follows that of the pre-1981 enforcement provisions; and the scope of the court's power is thus now considerably narrower than that of the Secretary of State's power to vary enforcement notices (see TCPA 1971, s 88A(1), (2), as substituted by LGPAA 1981).

(e) Grounds of appeal: the condition of the land

The first two grounds of appeal against a s 65 notice are as follows:

(*a*) that the condition of the land to which the notice relates does not adversely affect the amenity of any part of the area of the local planning authority which served the notice;

(*b*) that the condition of the land to which the notice relates is attributable to, and such as results in the ordinary course of events from, the carrying on of operations or a use of land which is not in contravention of Part III of the [TCPA 1971]

(TCPA 1971, s 105(1)(*a*), (*b*), as amended by HPA 1986).

The first of these should be straightforward. Any dispute is likely to be a simple matter of fact or opinion.

The phrase 'adversely affecting' was only introduced by the HPA 1986. Its meaning has not therefore yet been explored by the courts. The requirement in the Act as originally drafted was that the condition of the land should 'seriously injure' its surroundings; the new phrase implies that something less than serious injury would suffice to justify a notice. A building that is 'derelict' would thus almost certainly fall within the scope of the s 65 power; one that was merely 'in disrepair' might or might not. The side-note to the section as amended is 'power to require proper maintenance of land.' This would appear to justify an authority serving a notice on a building that was merely in need of maintenance, rather than only on buildings that were in danger of collapse.

As to the meaning of the 'amenity' of land, it has been defined to be its 'visual appearance and the pleasure of its enjoyment' (*Cartwright* v *Post Office* [1968] 2 All ER 646 at 648). And 'the word may be taken to express that element in the appearance and layout of town and country which makes for a comfortable and pleasant life rather than a mere existence' (*Re Parramatta CC, ex parte Tooth & Co Ltd* (1955) 55 SR (NSW) 282 at 306, 308). More recently, it has been held that 'the word "amenity" still connotes in a statute what Scrutton LJ thought it did [in *Re Ellis and Ruislip-Northwood UDC* [1920] 1 KB 343 at 370] on its first appearance in the Housing, Town Planning etc Act 1909; "pleasant circumstances or features, advantages" ' (*FFF Estates Ltd* v *Hackney LBC* [1981] QB 503, CA).

The second ground of appeal is less straightforward. It means basically that the s 65 procedure can be used either:
(1) where the poor condition of the property arises from a building or other operation or a use of the property that *is* in contravention of planning control (see TCPA 1971, s 87(3), as substituted by LGPAA 1981); or
(2) where the poor condition of the property happens to arise in this case, but need not inevitably arise, from an operation or use of the property that is perfectly in order.

In the second of these situations, therefore, it is necessary to consider whether the poor condition of the property is 'such as results in the ordinary course of events from' that operation or use. So, for example, if planning permission has been granted to use a site for car-breaking, it would not be possible to use a s 65 notice to control the unsightly appearance which would no doubt ensue. Yet if a building is used quite lawfully for residential purposes—or indeed is vacant after such use has stopped—there is no reason why, *in the ordinary course of events*, that use should lead to the building being in poor condition. If therefore such a building is in poor condition, so as to lead to the amenity of the surrounding area being affected, it would be perfectly in order to use the s 65 procedure to bring about its improvement.

(f) Grounds of appeal: the remedial works required

The third and fourth grounds of appeal against a s 65 notice are as follows:

(*d*) that the requirements of the notice exceed what is necessary for preventing the condition of the land from adversely affecting the amenity of any part of the area of the local planning authority who served the notice, or of any adjoining area;

(*e*) that the period specified in the notice as the period within which any steps required by the notice are to be taken falls short of what should reasonably be allowed

(TCPA 1971, s 105(1)(*d*), (*e*), as amended by HPA 1986).

As to ground (*d*), this will normally mean that only external works could be required, such as:

(1) the repair or restoration of crumbling cornices, porticoes, pinnacles and other details;

(2) the repainting of particular details or of a whole facade;

(3) the repair, restoration or repainting of other features such as walls, railings, gates and fences; and

(4) the tidying up of gardens and other open land (particularly where adjacent to a road).

In most cases internal works to a building could not be included since, however necessary they might be for its long-term health, they make little difference to its effect on the amenity of the area. It might be argued that, where a building is in such poor condition as to be on the verge of partial or total collapse, it would be appropriate to prevent this by serving a s 65 notice requiring more substantial structural work. However, this would probably not withstand challenge. A notice can only be served where the amenity of the area is (currently) affected by the condition of the land or building (TCPA 1971, s 65(1)), not where it is merely likely to be affected in the future. Accordingly, the works required in the notice can only be those needed to alleviate a present problem, not those desirable (or even necessary) to prevent a future one.

In addition, the works required should only be the minimum needed to improve the external appearance of the property, since any other specification would be open to being challenged on appeal. In considering what is this minimum level of works, it would be relevant to take into account whether the building is listed or in a conservation area. Thus, for example, suppose that a uniform Grade I terrace of stucco town houses which is other-wise in perfect condition contains one house that has been neglected, with peeling stucco and missing features. Only its complete external restoration to the same state as the others would be adequate to alleviate the effect it currently has on the area. But if the building in poor condition is one of a group of mixed styles within a not particularly distinguished conservation area, then the scope of works which could reasonably be required by a s 65 notice would obviously be more limited.

See also the comments above on 'adversely affect' and 'amenity'.

As to ground of appeal (e), when considering the corresponding ground of appeal against an enforcement notice (now TCPA 1971, s 88(h), as substituted by LGPAA 1981), the courts have held that it is correct to take a realistic approach, looking at the whole history of the site and taking previous delays and prevarications into account (*Mercer* v *Uckfield RDC* (1962) 60 LGR 226).

In general, it will be a matter for the discretion of the magistrates as to whether or not the requirements of the notice are excessive on either or both of these grounds.

(g) Non-compliance with a s 65 notice

Unless it is quashed on appeal, a s 65 notice will sooner or later come into effect—either at the end of the period stated within it, or when any appeals have been finally disposed of. The recipient must then carry out the remedial works specified in it, within the time specified or within such longer period as may be allowed by the authority. If he does not, the local authority can institute a prosecution in the magistrates' court, and he will then be liable on conviction to a fine of level 3 (TCPA 1971, s 104(2), as substituted by LGPAA 1981 and amended by Criminal Justice Act 1982 and Criminal Penalties (Increase) Order 1984).

If, after being convicted, the owner or occupier of the property still does not do everything in his power to ensure that the original notice is complied with, he is guilty of a further offence, and can on conviction be fined up to £40 per day (s 104(7), as substituted by LGPAA 1981 and amended by HPA 1986). To be convicted of the further offence, no further specific act is required; all that is necessary is to take no action to improve the condition of the property.

But if, on the other hand, the recipient of the notice is no longer the owner or occupier of the property, he may substitute as defendant in any prosecution the present owner or occupier (s 104(3)–(5), as substituted by LGPAA 1981). Similarly, if the failure to comply with the notice is through no fault of his, the person who is responsible may be convicted instead (s 104(6), as substituted by LGPAA 1981).

(h) Carrying out of the required works by the local authority

In spite of the possibility of the owner and occupier being convicted under s 104(2) or s 104(7), the required remedial works may still not be carried out. The local authority will then have to step in and carry them out itself. If it does so, it may recover the cost of the works from the current owner of the property (TCPA 1971, s 107(1), as amended by LGPAA 1981).

If the current owner was not responsible for the state of affairs which gave rise to the notice in the first place, he may in turn claim the cost of the works from whoever was responsible (s 107(2), as amended by LGPAA 1981). When a property that is subject to an outstanding s 65 notice is purchased, any prospective purchaser should be aware of the notice as it is a local land charge (Local Land Charges Rules 1977, r 2(2)). He should therefore be in a position to adjust the purchase price accordingly. The liability to pay the expenses recovered by the authority is not however at present registrable as a local land charge, although this may change in the future (s 107(3)). Alternatively, the authority may recover the cost of the works, together with a reasonable sum in respect of its establishment charges, as a simple contract debt (s 111; LGA 1974, s 36).

Finally, if the occupier prevents the authority from carrying out the works, the owner may complain to the magistrates' court. The court may order the occupier to desist (Public Health Act 1936, s 289, as applied with modifications by TCP General Regulations 1976, reg 16).

5.8 Dangerous structures and ruinous buildings

(a) General provisions

Where a building seems to an authority to be not merely in disrepair but dangerous, it may apply to the magistrates' court, and the court may make an order requiring the owner:
(1) to make it safe; or
(2) to demolish all or part of it and remove any rubbish

resulting from the demolition work (Building Act 1984, s 77).

If the owner fails to comply with the notice, the authority can carry out the necessary works itself. It may also recover any expenses incurred; and the owner is liable to a fine of up to level 1 on the standard scale. In appropriate cases, the authority can proceed to carry out the works immediately, without first applying to the court, and claim expenses afterwards. If it takes this course of action, however, the court in awarding expenses may take into account whether the situation were sufficiently urgent to justify the shorter procedure (1984 Act, s 78).

Where a building seems to the authority to be 'ruinous or dilapidated' (but not necessarily dangerous), it may serve on the owner a notice requiring him to carry out works of repair or restoration (1984 Act, s 79). The owner is, however, normally able to demolish all or part of the building as an alternative to carrying out the required works.

The 'works' envisaged in this context are 'something in the nature of semi-permanent work to the building itself which would make it reasonably safe in respect of a person who might happen to go into it' (*Holme* v *Crosby Corpn* (1949) unreported). They might, in particular, include fencing off the building to protect passers-by from possible danger, or merely arranging for it to be watched (1984 Act, s 78(4)).

The Building Act 1984 (like those portions of the Public Health Act 1936 which it replaced) does not apply to Inner London (1984 Act, Sched 3, Part II). Broadly similar provisions are however contained in the London Building Acts (Amendment) Act 1939, although the procedure is somewhat different. The district surveyor is to notify the borough council of any dangerous structure in its area (1939 Act, s 61; *London CC* v *Herring* [1894] 2 QB 522). Either he or the council will then carry out any works necessary, and recover their expenses from the owner, or else the council may prop up the building and require the owner to carry them out (ss 62–6). A notice can also be served on the owner of a neglected structure (s 69).

(b) Modification in the case of listed buildings and conservation areas

A notice under any of these provisions is usually served by the environmental health department of the local authority, who will not be directly concerned with historic buildings matters. The building owner, on its receipt, may not be aware (or may chose to forget) that, if the building is listed or in a conservation area, he will still need consent before demolition can proceed. This supposed reliance upon dangerous structure orders has in the past been a significant loophole in the law, and has led to the demolition of a number of listed buildings—either in good faith and ignorance, or otherwise.

This has been made slightly more difficult by the insertion into the 1984 and 1939 Acts of an explicit requirement that the power to issue such orders is subject to the provisions of the Planning Act regarding listed buildings and conservation areas (1984 Act, ss 77, 79; 1939 Act, ss 62, 65, 69; new final subsections inserted by HPA 1986). The purpose of the new provision, inserted in the House of Lords, is:

> to make it clear that the orders or notices do not override listed building control. That should once and for all dispel any notion that listed building consent is not required if a building is the subject of a dangerous structure order or notice. Either listed building consent must be obtained or notice must be given in accordance with the new provision in Section 55(6) (see 9.2(c)), if the defence offered by that subsection is to be relied on (*Hansard* (HL), 13 October 1986, vol 480, cols 587–8).

Thus any works to a listed building specified in a dangerous structures order require listed building consent—unless they are so minor that they do not affect the special character of the building (see 8.1(c)). Similarly, any demolition required by an order requires conservation area consent if the building concerned is in a conservation area. The amended form of s 55(6) of the 1971 Act provides a defence if consent is not obtained, but it lays a substantial burden of proof on the owner if such a defence is to be successful (see 9.2(c)); it is not enough merely to state that the building was subject to a dangerous structure order. The Secretary of State sensibly suggests that an authority serving a dangerous structure order should remind the building owner of the need to obtain the appropriate consent or give notice under s 55(6)(d) (Circ 8/87, para 107).

(c) Land in poor condition following demolition works

Problems can also arise as a result of the poor condition of a property following the collapse or demolition of a building. Where this leads to such a quantity or type of rubbish or other material lying on the site of the building or on any adjoining land, and where as a result the land is in such a condition as to be 'seriously detrimental to the amenities of the neighbourhood', the local authority may require the owner of the land to take such steps as may be necessary to clear up the site (Building Act 1984, s 79(2)). This in effect gives an authority the power to deal with such a site on a once-only basis.

The corresponding power available to a borough council in Inner London to deal with derelict, neglected or unsightly land is contained in London Government Act 1963, s 40(3), Sched 11, Part II, para 9. Anyone receiving a notice served under this Act may appeal against it to a magistrates' court.

5.9 Unfit houses and clearance areas

(a) General provisions

Where a local housing authority (district council or borough council: Housing Act 1985, s 1) is satisfied that a house is unfit for human occupation, it must serve a repair notice unless it is also satisfied that the necessary works to make it fit would be unreasonably expensive (HA 1985, s 189). It may also serve a repair notice (although it does not have to) if it considers that the house is in such a state of disrepair that substantial works are needed to it (s 190). Anyone receiving such a notice may appeal against it within the following twenty-one days to the county court (s 191); and if the works required are not carried out, the authority may carry them out at its own expense (s 192).

If, on the other hand, the disrepair has advanced to the stage where the cost of remedial works would be unreasonable, the authority must instead serve a 'time-and-place notice' (HA 1985, s 264). This in effect sets a meeting at which the future of the house may be discussed. At the meeting, the owner may undertake either not to use the house, or to carry out works to make it fit. If no undertaking is given, the authority is then obliged to make a demolition order or a closing order. As with a repair notice, there is a right to appeal against either type of order within twenty-one days to the county court (s 269).

If, as a result of an appeal against a repair notice, it transpires that the works required cannot be carried out by the owner at reasonable expense, the authority may purchase it, either using compulsory purchase powers or by agreement (HA 1985, s 192).

Finally, where a whole area contains houses and other buildings which are all unfit for living in, or dangerous or injurious to health, the housing authority is to declare a clearance area (HA 1985, s 289). It must then compulsorily purchase and clear the land by demolishing the offending buildings—together with any other buildings which may have to be demolished to make a sensible geographical area (ss 290, 291).

(b) Modification in the case of listed buildings

These procedures under the Housing Act 1985 are modified in the case of a building that is listed, although not where it is in a conservation area but not listed.

First, a demolition order may not be served on a building if:

(1) it is listed (HA 1985, s 304(2)); or

(2) the Secretary of State has served a notice stating that 'its architectural or historic interest is sufficient to render it inexpedient that it should be demolished pending determination of the question whether it should be a listed building' (s 304(3); note that there is no reference anywhere in the TCPA 1971 to such a notice of 'impending listing'); or

(3) demolition is inexpedient having regard to its effect on another building (HA 1985, s 265(2)).

In such cases, the authority must instead serve a closing order (ss 265(2) and 304(2)). Demolition, either by the owner of the building or by the authority, would still of course require listed building consent; as would alteration or other works affecting its character. When the house has been repaired to the point where it is once again fit to be lived in, however, the closing order is determined—that is, it no longer has any effect (s 278).

Secondly, where a listed building is included in a clearance area, the housing authority must within three months apply to the Secretary of State for listed building consent before it can be demolished (HA 1985, s 305(1)). In practice such an application might well be aired at the inquiry into the compulsory purchase order under s 290. A notice to treat (following the confirmation of the order) may not be served until consent has been granted (s 305(2)). If the building is unfit, and listed building consent is not obtained (that is, consent is not applied for within the three-month period, or is refused), the authority may not demolish it (s 305(5)). It must instead serve a repair notice under s 189, or a closing order under s 265 (see above) either of which would have the effect of the building being restored. Where on the other hand a listed building has been included in a clearance area but is not unfit, the authority must apply to the Secretary of State for listed building consent before it can be demolished; but in this case, if consent is not obtained, the building ceases to be in the clearance area, and the compulsory purchase order ceases to have effect (s 305(4)).

Similarly, if a building is listed after being included in a clearance area and compulsorily purchased, listed building consent must be applied for within three months of the listing (s 306). If consent is not obtained, the authority may not demolish it under s 291, but is instead deemed to have purchased it under Part II of the HA 1985 (that is, to provide housing accommodation) or, if it is not a house, under Part VI of the TCPA 1971 (that is, land purchased for general planning purposes); again, this will mean that the authority will then have to restore the building itself.

If an unlisted building in a conservation area is subject to a demolition order under s 265 or to a compulsory purchase order under s 290 which is confirmed by the Secretary of State following the declaration of a clearance area, the housing authority does not need conservation area consent before it can demolish it (DOE Circ 8/87, para 97(1)(h), (j); WO Circ 61/81, para 70(i); see 10.2(c)). However this is subject to the general duty of the authority, noted above, to have regard to 'the amenities of the locality and the desirability of preserving works of architectural or historic interest' when taking any action under the Act (HA 1985, s 607). As to the meaning of 'amenity', see 5.7(e).

5.10 Area improvement

In addition to its powers with respect to individual buildings, a local authority may also take steps to bring about the improvement of a whole area, under Part VIII of the HA 1985. It may be appropriate in some cases to coordinate this action with other initiatives aimed more specifically at historic buildings.

On the one hand, the declaration of a special area brings with it greater involvement and activity by the authority. If the area contains a number of listed or other historic buildings, any improvement works will need to be carefully monitored to ensure that they take account of the special features of each building.

On the other hand, and more positively, this increased building activity—and financial commitment—can be an excellent opportunity to bring about the restoration of historic buildings and areas on a scale which would otherwise be impossible. This is not least because the improvement programme is financed from the local authority's housing budget, which is usually larger than its planning budget which finances the enhancement of historic buildings. It can also be a good opportunity to carry out general environmental works to an area—landscaping, paving schemes, road closures and so on. These can make a significant improvement to the setting of a listed building or to the appearance of a conservation area. In addition, the declaration of a special area leads to much greater availability of grants (see 6.5).

There are two principal types of area initiative: housing action areas and general improvement areas. Housing action areas were introduced in the HA 1974 (Part V). General improvement areas were introduced earlier (in the HA 1969), as a sign of the change in emphasis away from the then prevailing ideology of slum clearance and redevelopment. They are linked to a local authority's powers and duties under the Housing Acts rather than those under the Planning Acts; accordingly, for more details, a specialist text on housing law should be consulted.

A housing authority (usually the district or borough council) may declare a housing action area (HAA) where 'the living conditions are unsatisfactory and can be dealt with within a period of five years so as to secure an improvement in the housing accommodation in the area, the well being of persons living in the area and the proper and effective management and use of that accommodation' (HA 1985, s 239).

In other words, the overriding aim of a declaration is the improvement of housing in the area. Once an area has been declared (and the declaration approved by the Secretary of State), the authority may then also acquire land (HA 1985, s 243), and carry out environmental works (s 244). To help finance the works, the authority may claim a subsidy from central Government funds of 50 per cent of the attributable debt charges over twenty years, up to a limit of £400 for each dwelling in the area (s 245).

A general improvement area (GIA) is 'a predominantly residential area in which . . . living conditions could be improved by the improvement of the amenities of the area or the dwellings therein or both' (HA 1985, s 253). Here there is an emphasis on the improvement of the area as a whole, rather than merely on that of the housing stock within it.

Again, once an area has been declared, the housing authority may carry out works on its own land, and may assist in the carrying out of works on other land, by grants, loans or otherwise. This will be primarily, but by no means exclusively, the improvement of residential property. It may also acquire, let and dispose of land, as well as carry out pedestrianisation schemes (TCPA 1971, s 212; HA 1985, s 256). Again, financial subsidy is available from central Government.

In either case, environmental works may be carried out. But if the central Government financial subsidy is to be obtained, the authority must first obtain approval from the Secretary of State. He has however stated (in App F to Circ 21/80) that he will automatically approve certain types of works, including the clearance of derelict land, street enhancement schemes, and (in some cases) the re-use of old buildings for community facilities.

Chapter 6

Finance

6.1 Introduction

(a) Justification for grants and loans

The special control mechanisms applying to historic buildings, and indeed the few powers that are available to encourage repairs, inevitably involve an element of restriction on the freedom of the owners of such buildings to do what they like with them. The justification for such restriction is presumably that Parliament has decided that it is desirable that such buildings and areas should wherever possible be conserved in the national interest.

Furthermore, the inclusion of a building in the statutory list or within a conservation area will in many cases sooner or later involve its owner in extra expense. Decaying stone slates that might have been replaced with concrete tiles must be restored with slates to match the original. Crumbling cornices cannot be simply removed; they must be carefully restored to the same pattern. And so on. Almost all works to an old building are expensive; and this should be taken into account by a prudent purchaser when acquiring or renting one. But this is especially so where the building is 'preserved' by law.

Seen from this perspective, listing is a form of compulsory acquisition of owners' rights, but with the critical feature that there is no financial compensation. It might therefore be reasonable to expect that this should be offset by a system of generous grants, loans and other financial incentives to assist repairs and restoration. It might even appear from the legislation that this is so. In fact, however, almost all that is to be found are permissive powers, even though there are a surprisingly large number of them.

This book is primarily concerned to explain the law, and this

93

chapter therefore outlines the relevant statutory provisions enabling local authorities, central Government, the Historic Buildings and Monuments Commission and others to give and lend money. But it must be remembered that all grants and loans, from whatever source, are only discretionary (with the very limited exception of some housing grants; see 6.5), and that the actual availability of assistance in any particular case is critically dependant upon the availability of finance.

(b) General points to be considered by applicants for grant aid

Anyone considering applying for financial assistance would be wise to bear in mind the following points. They are quoted from a leaflet on grants produced by the Commission, but they apply equally to grant aid from any public body:

We expect repair work which we aid to be sympathetic to the character and importance of the buildings in question, and to be done to a standard which will ensure durability and value for money. We can provide full technical advice on these matters.

Do not start work before we have offered a grant unless you have obtained our written approval to do so. We do not pay grants for work which has already been carried out.

The principal types of grant available are summarised in Figure 6.1.

(c) General points to be considered by funding authorities

Grants and loans may be given towards the cost of restoring individual historic buildings of outstanding interest by the Historic Buildings and Monuments Commission (English Heritage) and the Secretary of State for Wales (Cadw—Welsh Historic Monuments) (see 6.2). Finance can be made available for other individual historic buildings (whether or not they are 'outstanding') by local authorities, of either tier, under the 1962 Act (6.3(*a*)–(*c*)), and in London by the Commission, under the LGA 1985 (6.3(*d*)).

These individual grants may be useful in specific cases, particularly where the building to be restored is individually of exceptional interest; but the buildings thus benefiting will tend to be widely scattered geographically, and the overall effect thus very limited. An alternative approach, which in some cases can be much more effective, is for a local authority to concentrate on restoring a specific group of properties, such as a terrace or a row of uniform villas.

Such a restoration scheme can have a number of facets. Grants

Figure 6.1 Repair and restoration of historic buildings: principal sources of grant aid

Statutory provision for grant	Type of work eligible	Further information
A Historic Buildings and Monuments Commission (English Heritage)		
HBAMA 1953, s 3A	Repair and maintenance of buildings and land of outstanding interest	6.2(*a*)
HBAMA 1953, ss 3A, 5B	Works and acquisitions by the National Trust	6.2(*c*)
LGA 1985, Sched 2, para 3	Maintenance or management of any building or place in Greater London	6.3(*d*)
TCP (Amendment) Act 1972, s 10	Works for preservation or enhancement of any conservation area	6.3(*e*)
TCP (Amendment) Act 1972, s 10B	Repair of buildings in town scheme (usually administered by local authority)	6.3(*f*)
B Secretary of State for Wales (Cadw—Welsh Historic Monuments)		
HBAMA 1953, s 4	Repair and maintenance of buildings and land of outstanding interest	6.2(*b*)
HBAMA 1953, ss 4, 6	Works and acquisitions by the National Trust	6.2(*c*)
TCP (Amendment) Act 1972, ss 10, 10B	Conservation areas and town schemes [as for England; see above]	6.3(*e*), (*f*)
C Local authorities		
Local Authorities (Historic Buildings) Act 1962	Repair and maintenance of any building of architectural or historic interest,	6.3(*a*), (*b*)
	including repair of building in town scheme [jointly administered with English Heritage/Cadw]	6.3(*f*)
HA 1985, Part XV	Improvement, conversion and repair of older dwellings, and installation of missing amenities	6.5
Inner Urban Areas Act 1978, ss 5, 6	Area enhancements; restoration or conversion of industrial/commercial buildings	6.6
D National Heritage Memorial Fund		
NHA 1980, s 3	Restoration and acquisition of outstanding buildings etc by public bodies and charities	6.2(*d*)
E Building preservation trusts		
AMAAA 1979, s 49	Purchase, restoration and resale of old buildings	6.4
F Other sources		
	[Various]	6.7

Note: Almost all these schemes may offer loans as well as or instead of grants and loans can be offered for specified improvements (such as painting, or the restoration of particular missing features—cornices, window surrounds, porches, roof slates, and so on). Article 4 directions (see 7.4) can be made in appropriate cases, to ensure that, for example, painting is carried out according to a coordinated colour-scheme. Technical advice can be made available. Publicity can be given to the whole programme, through the distribution of suitable leaflets and visits to individual property owners. In these and other ways, the financial and manpower resources of the authority can be concentrated on a single area, to achieve the maximum effect.

The financial element in such a package can be grants and loans under the 1962 or 1985 Acts (see above). Alternatively or (better) in addition, the Commission may offer Section 10 conservation area grants (6.3(*e*)). Or it may be possible to set up a town scheme, enabling finance to be obtained from both the local authority and the Commission (6.3(*f*)).

In residential areas, it may be appropriate to offer grants under the Housing Act (see 6.5), or to consider declaring a housing action area (HAA) or general improvement area (GIA) (see 5.10), leading to the greater availability of grant aid from the local authority, with subsidies from central Government. It may also be sensible for an authority to carry out some works itself, either to buildings or to the surrounding area.

Procedures for allocating grants and loans need to be considered carefully. The powers of local authorities in this area are entirely discretionary, but such discretion must actually be exercised by the local authority (that is, the full council or the relevant committee or sub-committee as authorised by its standing orders). In practice, it would in many cases be impracticable for a committee or sub-committee to consider every application for grant aid, and an officer will have to do so. This is allowed for by LGA 1972, s 101(1)(*a*), but such delegation must be formally agreed if it is to be valid; and such agreement should state clearly the terms and limits of the delegation. The officer exercising the delegated power may not in turn delegate it to a junior officer.

Similarly, it is probably sensible for an authority to adopt a policy as to the circumstances in which grant aid will normally be given or withheld, so as to maximise consistency and fairness, and minimise the time spent on considering each application. However such a policy should not be followed blindly. Every case must be considered on its own merits and decided as the public interest requires at the time (see, for example, *Att-Gen, ex rel Tilley* v *Wandsworth LBC* [1981] 1 WLR 854; *R* v *Port of London Authority, ex parte Kynoch Ltd* [1919] 1 KB 176 at 185; and *R* v *London County Council, ex parte Corrie* [1918] 1 KB 68). Where an applicant insists on being heard, the relevant committee should at least consider any written representations made, especially in view of the absence of any statutory right of appeal against the refusal of a grant (see *Corrie* at 75).

In particular, it has recently been held that it is unlawful to adhere unthinkingly to a policy of not giving grants for works which are already under way at the time of the application (*R* v *Secretary of State for Transport, ex parte Sheriff* (1986) *The Times*, 18 December). Such a policy may well be prudent—and is indeed widely followed; but individual applications must still be given proper attention.

6.2 Finance for buildings of outstanding interest

(a) Grants and loans from the Historic Buildings and Monuments Commission (English Heritage)

Grants have been available for many years for the repair and maintenance of buildings of outstanding interest. The current provisions are to be found in HBAMA 1953, s 3A (inserted by NHA 1983). Prior to April 1984, grants under this heading were made by the Secretary of State on the advice of the Historic Buildings Council for England under s 4. Since that date, grants have been given (in England) by the Historic Buildings and Monuments Commission (English Heritage), under s 3A(1), and loans under s 3A(2). Under these provisions, the Commission may make grants [or loans] for the purpose of defraying in whole or in part any expenditure incurred or to be incurred:

(1) in the repair or maintenance of a building which appears to be of outstanding historic or architectural interest, or

(2) in the upkeep of any land which comprises, or is contiguous or adjacent to, any such building, or

(3) in the repair or maintenance of any objects ordinarily kept in any such building, or

(4) in the upkeep of a garden or other land which appears to be of outstanding historic interest but which is not contiguous or adjacent to such a building.

The Commission's own interpretation of this is as follows:

E

We give grants for repairs to historic buildings which we judge to be of outstanding national interest. This usually means buildings listed grade I or sometimes grade II*. But occasionally closer investigation reveals something unexpected and outstanding about grade II or even unlisted buildings, so if you seriously believe your building is of national interest it may be worth applying for a grant whatever its present grade.

The standard rate of grant is 40% but a higher or lower rate may be offered where necessary. Grants are available only to help with major repairs which are beyond an owner's means, and we do not normally consider repair programmes costed at less than £10,000. Some grants are made for conserving important contents of outstanding buildings, such as tapestries, wall paintings and sculpture. (*Grants for Monuments, Historic Buildings and Conservation Areas*, HBMC Leaflet, 1988.)

Grants or loans under s 3A may be subject to conditions, and in particular to a condition requiring that the public should be given access to the building (s 3A(4)). In fact almost all of the buildings given grant aid in 1986–87 did offer some form of public access, either through opening to the public generally or by appointment, or by the nature of their use (such as hotels or theatres).

Grants made under s 3A can be recovered under s 4A (inserted by AMAAA 1979 and amended by NHA 1983) in the following circumstances:

(1) if any condition attached to the offer of the grant is not complied with (s 4A(2)); or

(2) if at any time within ten years of the payment of the grant:
the recipient disposes of the building (s 4A(4)); or
the recipient gives the building (other than on death) to another, and he or she disposes of it (s 4A(6), (7)).

A 'disposal' for this purpose means a sale, exchange or lease for twenty-one years or more (s 4A(5)). But it does not include the creation of a mortgage, and a sale by a mortgagee does not therefore result in the grant having to be repaid (*Canterbury CC v Quine* (1987) 55 P & CR 1). This power to demand the repayment of a grant is entirely discretionary.

Loans under s 3A may be subject to terms as to repayment and interest as seem fit to the Commission (s 3A(5)).

Applications have to be on the standard form issued by the Commission, available (with further information) from: English Heritage, Historic Buildings Division, Fortress House, 23 Savile Row, London W1X 2HE (tel 01–734 6010 ext 882).

During the financial year 1986–87, the Commission offered 245 grants under s 3A, amounting to a total of £9.1 million (compared to £6.8 million in 1985–86). In addition a further £5.3 million was

given for places of worship in use (other than cathedrals) which
have been eligible for s 3A grants since 1977.

(b) Grants and loans from the Secretary of State for Wales (Cadw—Welsh Historic Monuments)

A scheme for the repair and maintenance of buildings and other
land of outstanding interest in Wales is operated by Cadw—Welsh
Historic Monuments, under HBAMA 1953, s 4 (amended by
NHA 1983). The terms under which grants are made are identical
to those applying to s 3A grants in England (see 6.2(*a*)), except
that the Secretary of State, before making any grant under this
provision, must consult the Historic Buildings Council for Wales
(other than in cases of urgency) (s 4(4)). A grant made under s 4
can be recovered under s 4A in identical circumstances to a s 3A
grant.

Loans may also be given by the Secretary of State for buildings
of outstanding interest in Wales (HBAMA 1953, s 4(1), extended
by Civic Amenities Act 1967, s 4(1)). Such loans may be on
whatever terms he thinks fit, subject to the approval of the
Treasury.

Applications should be made on the appropriate form, which
is available (together with an explanatory note) from: Cadw—
Welsh Historic Monuments, Brunel House, 2 Fitzalan Road,
Cardiff CF2 1UY (tel 0222 465511).

(c) Grants and loans to the National Trust

Grants and loans may be given by the Commission (in England)
or by the Secretary of State (in Wales) to the National Trust for
the repair and maintenance of buildings of outstanding interest
(HBAMA 1953, ss 3A, 4, as amended by NHA 1983). The normal
rules apply (see 6.2(*a*), (*b*)), except that a grant may take the
form of a capital endowment, the income from which can then be
used to defray the relevant maintenance or repair costs over a
longer period ('so long as it is reasonably practicable to give effect
to the purposes of the endowment') (ss 3A(3), 4(3)). Such an
arrangement may be secured by a contract, trust or other arrangement as appropriate.

It is also possible for the Trust to be given a grant by the
Commission or the Secretary of State to defray all or part of the
cost of acquiring any building of outstanding historic or architectural interest (ss 5B(2)(*a*), 6(2)–(4), amended by NHA 1983). In
England (only) the Trust may be given a grant to enable it to

acquire land adjacent to such a building, or any other garden or land of outstanding historic interest (s 5B(2)(*b*), (*c*), inserted by NHA 1983).

(d) Grants and loans from the National Heritage Memorial Fund

Grants and loans may be made by the National Heritage Memorial Fund under NHA 1980, s 3, to the Secretary of State or to any suitable non-profit making body within the United Kingdom to assist him or it

to acquire, maintain or preserve:
(*a*) any land, building or structure which in the opinion of the Trustees is of outstanding scenic, historic, aesthetic, architectural or scientific interest;
(*b*) any object . . . of outstanding historic, artistic or scientific interest;
(*c*) any collection or group of objects . . . which taken as a whole is . . . of outstanding historic, artistic or scientific interest

(NHA 1980, s 3(1)). Grants can be made by the Fund to bodies such as the National Trust and building preservation trusts. The intention is that it should only be approached when all other options have been tried. In 1986–87, grants of £1.1 million were made for buildings. Further details can be obtained from the Trustees of the Fund at 10 St James's Street, London SW1A 1FF (tel 01–930 0963).

6.3 Other grants and loans for historic buildings

(a) Grants from local authorities for individual buildings

A local authority (in England or Wales) may offer a grant to contribute towards the cost of the repair or maintenance of:
(1) any listed building in or in the vicinity of its area (Local Authorities (Historic Buildings) Act 1962, s 1(1)(*a*), amended by TCPA 1971); or
(2) any other (unlisted) building of architectural or historic interest in its area (s 1(1)(*b*), amended by TCPA 1968).
Advice has been given to local authorities in Appendix VI of Circ 8/87 (App VI of WO Circ 61/81) on the use of their powers under the 1962 Act.

Grants can be given by
(1) county councils, district councils and joint planning boards (1962 Act, s 1(4)), amended by TCPA 1971); and
(2) the Broads Authority (s 1(5), inserted by NSBA 1988).

They may not however be given by urban development corporations. In the case of an expensive programme of works, it may be appropriate for a county council and a district council both to give a grant towards a building in the area of the latter, to achieve the maximum benefit. Similarly, in the case of a listed building on or near the boundary between two districts, it may be desirable for the two district (or county) authorities to share the cost, although in this case the building must be listed (s 1(1)(*a*)). In either of these situations it will often be advantageous for the grant to be administered and the repair works to be checked by only one of the funding authorities, acting as agent for the other (as is provided for by LGA 1972, s 101(1)(*b*)).

Grants may only be by way of a contribution towards the cost of the works, although there is no limit as to the proportion of the cost that can be met by way of grant, provided it is less than 100 per cent. This would seem to mean that, if the works are carried out by the authority itself, the owner of the building must make a contribution (even if only a nominal one) towards the cost.

A building must be of some architectural or historic interest to be eligible for grant aid; but it only has to be actually listed if it is not within the funding authority's area. It is uncertain what would be sufficient 'interest' to justify the giving of a grant; but arguably any building which an authority is prepared to pay money to see repaired and maintained must be of at least some interest.

There is no entirely accurate estimate of how much is spent by local authorities on grants to historic buildings, but in 1986–87 the figure for authorities in England was around £9 million. The availability, and size, of grants varies enormously as between different authorities—a few projects attracting grants of over £100,000, and some trivial amounts. Some authorities allocate funds on a 'first come first served' basis, others according to carefully thought out criteria, for example according to types of building or geographical areas; but see 6.1(*c*) on the application of such criteria.

As a condition of receiving a grant under the 1962 Act, the recipient may be required to enter into an agreement with the authority whereby the public can have access to the building:

A requirement as to access will not be appropriate in all cases. Some buildings may not be sufficiently large or significant to justify this. Sometimes the value of a building attracting a grant may lie in its external appearance seen from a street or other public place. On the other hand where the building is not reasonably visible from a public place or where its value lies partly or wholly in its interior, opportunities for public access at specified times or by appointment to the building or to the appropriate parts of it should be considered.

The extent and duration of public access must clearly be decided with regard to the circumstances of each case. A requirement that would be so onerous upon the owner or occupier of the building as to discourage the acceptance of a grant would, of course, tend to defeat the object of the Act (Circ 8/87, App VI, paras 7, 8).

At the same time as assisting towards the cost of the repair and maintenance of a building under the 1962 Act, an authority may also make a grant towards the cost of the upkeep of any garden that is occupied with it (s 1). 'It will often be unsatisfactory for public funds to be spent on preserving a building if the surrounding garden, which might be part of the architectural concept or at least a pleasant setting for the building, could not be kept in reasonable order' (App VI, para 4). Grants cannot however be given towards gardens other than in connection with grants or loans for buildings associated with them (unlike grants under the 1953 Act; see 6.2).

Details of local authority grants should be sought from the conservation officers of both the district or borough council and the county council (where there is one).

(b) Repayment of local authority grants

A grant made under the 1962 Act can be recovered by the local authority that paid it if, at any time within the following three years, the recipient either:

(1) disposes of the building (s 2(1)); or
(2) gives it (other than on death) to another, and he or she disposes of it (s 2(2)).

A 'disposal' for this purposes means a sale, exchange or lease for twenty-one years or more (s 2(1)). But it does not include the creation of a mortgage, and a sale by a mortgagee does not lead to the grant having to be repaid (*Canterbury CC* v *Quine* (1987) 55 P & CR 1). It would also presumably be possible for an authority to seek to recover the grant if any condition attached to its offer (for example, as to letting the public have access to the building) is not complied with; but there is no statutory provision for this.

This power to demand the repayment of a grant is entirely discretionary:

The object . . . is to deter speculators and to prevent profit-making attributable to the grant from public funds. It will not always be right to recover the grant . . . For example the works towards the cost of which grant was paid might have been done at the request of the local authority in order to retain the architectural advantage of the building, perhaps by having a new stone tile roof instead of concrete tiles or by replacing a decaying ornamental feature, and might have no functional advantage. Again, a preservation society may sometimes propose to buy a building for restoration and apply for a grant, making it clear at the outset that their intention would be to re-sell the building. In such circumstances it would appear right to recover grant only to such extent as is possible after the preservation society have re-couped their expenditure (Circ 8/ 87, App VI, para 11).

(c) Loans from local authorities

As an alternative to making a grant, a local authority may offer a loan for the same purposes (see 6.3(a)) (1962 Act, s 1(1)). This may be upon such terms and conditions as it wishes (s 1(2)). In particular, an authority may make low-interest or interest-free loans; and it may renounce its right to repayment at any time, or subsequently vary the interest rate or other conditions with the agreement of the owner. The generality of the power to impose terms and conditions would seem to admit the possibility of requiring public access, as for grants, although Circ 8/87, App VI, para 6 suggests otherwise.

The setting up of a programme of loans may be a cost-effective way for an authority to bring about the repair, maintenance and restoration of historic buildings, since the funds can be recycled as the loans are repaid. Experience would tend to suggest, however, that such a programme will only be attractive if the loans are interest-free (which implies a hidden element of grant aid), and if the bureaucracy is kept to the absolute minimum.

(d) London grants from the Historic Buildings and Monuments Commission (English Heritage)

The Greater London Council used to have a substantial programme of historic buildings grants, although under the London Government Act 1963, rather than under the 1962 Act. Since the abolition of the Council, the London Division of the Historic Buildings and Monuments Commission (English Heritage) has taken over the programme, and offers 'London grants' for any worthwhile project affecting historic places or buildings.

The statutory basis for this scheme is now contained in the

LGA 1985, which provides that the Commission may 'undertake, or contribute towards, the cost of preserving, maintaining and managing any building or place of historical or architectural interest in Greater London' (Sched 2, para 3(1)(*b*)). This is somewhat wider than the corresponding provision in the 1962 Act (see 6.3(*a*)), since the Commission can carry out the work and pay for the entire cost itself if it wishes. It can also 'preserve' and 'manage' a building, not just 'repair' and 'maintain it'. It may assist any 'place' of interest, rather than just any 'building', which would seem to extend to financing enhancements to the street scene, and other such works.

There is no specific provision however for the recovery of any grant, although in practice grants are often subject to a condition that they must be repaid if the property changes hands within ten years (as for Section 10 grants; see 6.3(*e*)). Nor may the Commission under these powers offer a grant for a building or place outside Greater London.

There are no powers for the Commission to offer a loan under this heading.

Further details, and application forms, can be obtained from English Heritage, London Division, Chesham House, 30 Warwick Street, London W1R 6AB (tel 01–734 8144 ext 83 or 137).

(e) Conservation area grants from English Heritage and Cadw (Section 10 grants)

Section 10 grants are made to assist in 'the preservation or enhancement of the character or appearance of any conservation area or any part of a conservation area'. Prior to 1980, they were only available in conservation areas that were considered to be of 'outstanding interest'; the Civic Trust administered a non-statutory scheme in respect of other areas. The criterion now is that the expenditure to be grant aided should 'make a significant contribution towards preserving or enhancing the character or appearance of that area or part' (TCP (Amendment) Act 1972, s 10(1), substituted by LGPLA 1980 (Wales); s 10(1AA), inserted by NHA 1983 (England)).

Grants are given in England by the Historic Buildings and Monuments Commission (English Heritage) and in Wales by the Secretary of State (Cadw—Welsh Historic Monuments) on the advice of the Historic Buildings Council for Wales. The former comments that:

We cannot provide grants in [every conservation area], and so we have established schemes in about 500 priority areas where grants are available towards the cost of repairing historic buildings, whether listed or not, and for associated environmental works. We are always ready to consider the case for adding to the list of grant-eligible conservation areas.

Work is eligible for grant if it affects the structure and appearance of the building. This can include such items as re-roofing, repointing or repairs to stonework or brickwork, treatment of dry rot, and repair of windows and doors. In some areas the grants concentrate on encouraging the use of particular traditional materials. Routine maintenance, alterations and conversions are not eligible for grant. (*Grants for Monuments, Historic Buildings and Conservation Areas*, HBMC leaflet, 1988.)

The expenditure on Section 10 grants in England was £4.4 million in 1986–87, and 544 grants were offered. Around half of the budget is earmarked for spending in the twenty-three specially selected Programme Towns, so as to maximise their effectiveness. If however the annual allocation has not been committed by mid-year, it is reallocated to non-Programme towns. The criteria for the selection of Programme Towns, and for the distribution of grants generally, were reviewed in 1987. As a result, emphasis is likely to be placed on work in areas of greater need, including industrial towns, historic towns in the north of England, declining seaside towns and rural areas.

Environmental works (such as paving, landscaping and so on), which can make a great difference to the appearance of some conservation areas, are also eligible for Section 10 grants.

Grants under s 10 will usually be for 25 per cent of the cost of eligible works, and will not be given for works costing less than £4,000 except possibly in the case of small properties. Where the cost of the works rises, and an increased grant is sought, the minimum level will be £500, or 25 per cent of the initial offer if lower. Applications for grants of more than £10,000 made by commercial concerns are subject to scrutiny as to both the means of the applicant and the economics of the project generally.

Grants may be subject to any conditions thought suitable (s 10(2)). In particular, they may be recovered in appropriate cases if the property changes within ten years, exactly as for grants under HBAMA 1953 (see 6.2(*a*) for details) (s 10A, inserted by AMAAA 1979).

Loans may also be made under Section 10 powers, and may be subject to any terms as to interest and repayment that seem to be appropriate (s 10(2)–(3A)). Few if any loans have been offered hitherto, but it was stated in 1987 that the Commission hoped to launch a scheme for loans of £50,000 minimum; progress will be monitored.

Further information on Section 10 grants and loans can be obtained from English Heritage, Historic Areas Division, 25 Savile Row, London W1X 1BT (tel 01–734 6010 ext 861), or from Cadw—Welsh Historic Monuments (see 6.2(*b*)).

(f) Town schemes

A town scheme is an arrangement whereby central and local resources are pooled so as to share the cost and maximise the effectiveness of the money spent.

The Commission (or, in Wales, the Secretary of State) and the relevant local authority (or authorities) enter into a 'repair grant agreement', under which they each agree to allocate an annual sum to be given in grants over a specified number of years for the repair of a specified group of properties (TCP (Amendment) Act 1972, s 10B(4), inserted by LGPLA 1980 and amended by NHA 1983). The properties involved (which must be in a conservation area) are included in a 'town scheme list' or on a 'town scheme map' (s 10B(2), (3)).

The repair of any of the buildings in the town scheme can then be assisted by a grant, which comprises two elements:

(1) half from the local authority or authorities concerned (under their powers in the Local Authorities (Historic Buildings) Act 1962; as to which, see 6.3(*a*)); and

(2) half from:
   in England, the Commission (under TCP (Amendment) Act 1972, s 10B(1A), inserted by NHA 1983), or
   in Wales, the Secretary of State, subject to the approval of the Historic Buildings Council for Wales (s 10B(1), (6), (7)).

The grants will be given to the applicant by the Commission or the Secretary of State where they are supervising a scheme. In many cases, however, the local authority (or one of the authorities if two are involved) will handle the administration of the scheme, and will give the applicant the grant (including the element funded by central funds; s 10B(8), (9)). There are currently around 208 town schemes in England, of which some 160 are delegated to local authorities in this way. The total expenditure by the Commission for town schemes in England was £1.8 million in 1986–87.

A town scheme grant is generally given at a rate of 40 per cent of eligible costs. This figure used to be 50 per cent, but has been reduced so as to enable the available funds to be spread more widely. Where both the county council and the district council are involved, they may split the local authority half of the grant between them as they see fit. The Broads Authority is able to enter into a town scheme agreement, but urban development corporations and joint planning boards are not able to enter into town schemes (s 10B(11), amended by NSBA 1988). The minimum level of grant for non-delegated townschemes is £800 grant (that is, 40 per cent of £2,000 of eligible works). The level of grant under delegated schemes will vary according to the policy of the local authority concerned.

Where a property changes hands within three years of a grant being paid, it may be reclaimed by the body that gave it, exactly as for any other local authority grant under the 1962 Act (see 6.3(*b*)) (s 10B(10)).

6.4 Building preservation trusts

A building preservation trust is an organisation set up to bring about the restoration of historic buildings by purchasing them, carrying out the required works, and then reselling them on the open market. The theory is that the addition to the value of each building dealt with in this way will gradually increase the capital assets of the trust, and enable it to buy and restore an ever increasing number of buildings.

A trust can raise money from wherever it wishes, and may apply for grants and loans under any or all of the schemes described so far in this chapter. It can also borrow money on a short-term low-interest loan from the Architectural Heritage Fund, which had working capital of £3.5 million at the start of 1988. The Fund in turn is able to be grant aided by the Secretary of State (in both England and Wales) and by the Commission (under their powers in AMAAA 1979, s 49, amended by NHA 1983). The Fund and the trusts themselves are registered charities.

At the end of 1987, there were 87 trusts in England and one in Wales. Further details are available from the Fund at 17 Carlton House Terrace, London SW1Y 5AW (tel 01–925 0199).

6.5 Housing Act grants

Where historic buildings are in residential use, grants by local authorities under Part XV of the HA 1985 can in some cases be much more effective to bring about their restoration than grants aimed specifically at historic buildings. From the point of view of the building owner, where such grants are available at all they are likely to be easier to obtain, since the authority's funds available for housing are likely to be very much greater than those available for conservation. In a few cases, grants are available as of right. The advantage for the authority is that they will attract financial support from central Government.

In appropriate cases, it may be sensible for an applicant to seek, or an authority to offer, a grant under the 1985 Act in addition to any that may be offered under the 1953, 1962 or 1972 Acts (see 6.2, 6.3), since the former can be used for improvement and conversion works, whereas the latter will be limited to repair and maintenance. This can enable modern amenities to be provided, which in turn can make the restoration of an old house a viable proposition.

Improvement grants are made under ss 467–73 of the 1985 Act. They are available at the discretion of the local authority for the conversion and improvement of older substandard properties, providing certain qualifying conditions are met. The dwelling must normally have been built before 1961 (s 462), and must be owner occupied. It must in addition have a rateable value of not more than £225 if the grant is for improvement works, or £350 if it is for conversion (the corresponding figures for dwellings in Greater London are £400 and £600). An improvement grant can include an element for repair works (which should not, incidentally, be duplicated by a historic buildings grant). The authority has discretion to relax the standards required in appropriate cases, when older buildings by their nature are unable to meet modern standards without drastic alterations (s 468(3)).

Intermediate grants are available as of right for the installation of missing standard amenities such as toilets and baths, again providing certain qualifying conditions are met. The relevant provisions are in ss 473–82 of the Act. Special grants are also available (under ss 483–90) to houses in multiple occupation, to provide standard amenities and means of escape in case of fire.

Repairs grants are available for substantial structural repairs (that is, not routine repairs or rewiring) to dwellings built before 1919. Dwellings built before 3 October 1961 are also eligible if the works consist of the replacement of lead piping. The relevant provisions are in ss 491–8 of the Act and in the Grants by Local Authorities (Repairs) Order 1983; and advice can be found in

Circ 20/81, App B. These grants are generally at the discretion of the local authority (s 495), except where a repairs notice has been served under ss 189 or 190 (see 5.9(a)). They are however only available for dwellings with a rateable value of not more than £225 (or £400 in Greater London).

Figure 6.2 Housing Act grants: limits of eligible expenses

	Unlisted building £	Listed Grade II £	Listed Grade II* £	Listed Grade I £
A Greater London				
Repairs	6,600	6,860	7,130	7,480
Improvements:				
category A	13,800	14,320	14,840	15,540
category B	9,000	9,520	10,040	10,740
Conversions:				
category A	16,000	16,490	17,000	17,700
category B	10,400	10,970	11,480	12,180
B Elsewhere				
Repairs	4,800	5,060	5,330	5,680
Improvements:				
category A	10,200	10,720	11,240	11,940
category B	6,600	7,120	7,640	8,340
Conversions:				
category A	11,800	12,290	12,800	13,500
category B	7,700	8,210	8,720	9,420

Source: Grants by Local Authorities (Eligible Expense Limits) Order 1983, retained in force by the Housing (Consequential Provisions) Act 1985, s 2

Higher limits of eligible expenses have been specified for both improvement and repair grants for works to dwellings which are listed (but not for those which are merely in conservation areas). This reflects the cost of specific works, materials or architectural detail that may be necessary to maintain their character and appearance. Figure 6.2 shows the current limits. Category A refers to priority cases, where the dwelling concerned is in a housing action area (see 5.10), or is occupied by a disabled person or is in need of major works of repair (see the 1983 Order for details). Category B is the remainder. However, local authorities have been asked to bear in mind that, where a historic buildings grant is given in recognition of the importance of conserving a building and its features, it will not normally be appropriate to give a HA grant at the higher eligible expense limit, as this would be to take account twice over of the additional costs which may be incurred to preserve the character and appearance of the building (Circ 8/87, para 146).

6.6 Inner Urban Areas Act grants

Where historic buildings and areas are of a predominantly industrial or commercial character, it may be possible to fund conservation programmes through the use of grants by local authorities under the Inner Urban Areas Act 1978.

Any district may be 'designated' by the Secretary of State if it contains an inner urban area of special social need, where conditions could be improved by the use of the powers contained in the Act (s 1). Any 'designated district authority' may then declare any predominantly industrial or commercial part of the district to be an 'improvement area', if it considers that it could be improved by the offer of grants under s 5 or s 6 (Sched 1). It is then possible for the authority to give grants as follows:

(1) under s 5 for enhancement works benefiting the area:
   —the construction of fencing or walls;
   —landscaping and the planting of trees, shrubs and plants;
   —the clearing or levelling of land;
   —the cleansing of watercourses, whether natural or artificial, or the reclamation of land covered with water;
   —the cleaning, painting, repair or demolition of structures or buildings; and
   —the construction of parking spaces, access roads, turning heads or loading bays; and

(2) under s 6 for:
   —the conversion, extension, improvement or modification of industrial or commercial buildings; and
   —the conversion of other buildings into industrial or commercial buildings.

Section 5 grants are of obvious relevance to programmes aimed at restoring and enhancing the appearance of industrial or commercial conservation areas. Section 6 grants may be useful to assist the restoration or conversion of individual historic buildings (whether or not they are listed). Such grants may of course be even more effective if they are used together with funding from other sources, such as grants or loans from the Commission or the Secretary of State for Wales.

So far, 13 London boroughs have been designated under the Act, 12 districts in or near Merseyside or Greater Manchester, nine in South Wales, seven each in Yorkshire and the North East, four in the West Midlands, as well as Kingston-upon-Hull, Leicester and Nottingham.

6.7 Finance from other sources

In addition to those already described, there are a number of other possible sources of finance for the repair, maintenance and restoration of historic buildings.

First there are a number of charitable trusts concerned with conservation, such as (in alphabetical order) the Ernest Cook Trust, the Historic Churches Preservation Trust, the Landmark Trust, the Leche Trust, the Manifold Trust, the Monuments Trust, the Pilgrim Trust, and many others. Assistance may also be available from bodies such as the city livery companies. Details of the grants made by some of the larger trusts are given in *A Guide to Major Grant-making Trusts* (Directory of Social Change, 1986). It may also be worth inspecting the Register of Local Charities, available both at the offices of the local authority and at the Charity Commission in London. In many areas there are old charities with suitable objects, whose trustees could be approached.

Secondly, it should not be forgotten that the repair, maintenance and presentation of historic buildings and gardens are closely related to the tourist industry. It is for this reason that the English Tourist Board publishes each year the *English Heritage Monitor*, an invaluable guide to the heritage business, and the source of much of the statistical material in this book. It is for the same reason that the national Tourist Boards give grants (under the Development of Tourism Act 1969). The English Board's annual budget for investment in heritage projects is around £9 million. And the Ministry of Agriculture, amongst others, operates a system of grants for tourism projects in rural areas. Local authorities, too, may be more willing to give grants, under any of their various powers, if they can be convinced that a restoration project will boost local tourism.

Thirdly, there are various public sector bodies who make grants which are aimed primarily at other objectives, but which may be used to assist restoration works. British Coal, for example, assists suitable preventive or restoration works to buildings in areas of mining subsidence (under the Coal Mining (Subsidence) Act 1957, s 9). The Council for Small Industries in Rural Areas (COSIRA) and the Countryside Commission both give grants for the conversion of redundant buildings in rural areas. The Welsh Development Agency may assist the creation of jobs through the reuse of redundant buildings. The Sports Council, the Crafts Council and other similar bodies may in appropriate cases be able to help. Details of some of these, and other possibilities, are contained in the *Directory of Public Sources of Grants for the Repair and Conversion of Historic Buildings* (looseleaf, 1988; available at £4 (including postage) from English Heritage Publications Department, Room 236, 23 Savile Row, London W1X 2HE).

6.8 Taxation

(a) VAT on works to historic buildings

Since 1 June 1984, certain works to historic buildings have been accorded privileged status with regard to liability for value added tax. As with many 'concessions', the benefit is more apparent than real. Prior to 1984, all buildings were in the same position, but the relief was then withdrawn except for historic buildings.

The current position (as at September 1988) is, in outline, as follows:

(1) new building works are zero-rated;
(2) 'approved alterations' to 'protected buildings' are zero-rated;
(3) other alterations to protected buildings are liable to tax at 15 per cent; and
(4) repairs to existing buildings ('protected' or otherwise) are liable to tax at 15 per cent.

As to the first, this means that works to replace, for example, railings removed during the war, or other (new) work to enhance a conservation area or the setting of a historic building does not attract tax. This relief is likely to be withdrawn in the 1989 Budget in respect of new works to create non-residential buildings, as a result of European Commission infraction proceedings concluded in 1988.

'Protected buildings' are defined (in VAT Act 1983, Sched 5, Group 8A, Note 1) as follows:

(1) listed buildings under TCPA 1971; and

(2) scheduled monuments under the AMAAA 1979.

This would seem to include buildings and structures attached to a listed building or within its curtilage (TCPA 1971, s 54(9); see 2.5 for a full discussion). But the case for any such building or structure being 'listed' would need to be fully explained to the Customs and Excise if a claim to zero-rating is to be successful. A building which is subject to a building preservation notice, but which has not yet been listed, is not a 'protected building'; nor is an unlisted building in a conservation area.

'Approved alterations' are defined (in Group 8A, note 3) as follows:

(1) alterations to a listed building for which listed building consent is required (see 8.1) and has been obtained;

(2) alterations to a listed building owned by the Crown (see 8.2(c)) for which listed building would be required if it was in any other ownership;

(3) any alterations to a listed building that is in ecclesiastical use (see 13.2(a));

(4) any alterations to a scheduled monument for which scheduled monument consent is required (or would be if it were not owned by the Crown (see 14.3(a)).

Zero-rating applies generally to:

(1) services supplied in the course of approved alterations to protected buildings (for example, by builders, plumbers and so on), other than services of architects, surveyors and others acting as consultants or supervisors (Group 8A, Item 2); and

(2) goods and materials supplied by a person supplying zero-rated services in connection with the supply of those services (Group 8, Item 3), but not domestic electrical or gas appliances or fitted furniture other than fitted kitchen furniture (Group 8, Note 2A).

'Repairs' as such can never be 'alterations', approved or otherwise, even if they are included within the terms of the relevant consent. This distinction has been the subject of much litigation over the years, and has not been (indeed probably cannot ever be) fully resolved.

It seems that the general approach of HM Customs and Excise is to accept that, if listed building consent has been obtained for particular works, it must have been needed, and that those works are therefore approved alterations. It is therefore prudent to include as much as possible in a listed building consent application. The description of the works needs to be given some thought. They should wherever possible be described in terms of 'alteration', 'improvement' or 'extension', rather than 'repair' or 'replacement'. It may be wise to include some phrase such as 'alterations to [elevations, rooms, etc] and all new works shown on Drawings [1, 2, 3]'.

In cases of uncertainty, an approach should be made for a ruling to the local VAT office dealing with the contractor. This should be done by supplying full details of the proposed works, as for the listed building consent application (and using the same numbered drawings) (see 8.3(*c*)). HM Customs and Excise suggest that, to justify zero-rating any works, a contractor will need in addition to the usual records:

(1) for listed buildings, including churches, evidence that it was a listed building when the works were done (either a copy of the entry in the relevant statutory list or in the local land charges register, or a copy of the statutory notice sent out by the local authority at the time the building was listed); see 2.2(*b*); and

(2) for listed buildings other than churches, evidence that the alteration works received listed building consent (a copy of the consent together with any associated schedules, correspondence and drawings showing what works obtained listed building consent).

If a ruling is obtained stating that the works are zero-rated, this should be adequate to convince the contractor not to charge tax. It will in any event normally be honoured by the Customs and Excise should there be any subsequent dispute (*Hansard*, (HL) 21 July 1978, Vol 954 col 426–427).

Further details can be obtained in a useful (free) leaflet produced by HM Customs and Excise, *Protected Buildings (Listed Buildings and Scheduled Monuments)* (No 708/1/85), obtainable from local VAT offices.

(b) Rating of unoccupied historic buildings

If a local authority resolves to charge rates on all or some classes of unoccupied buildings in its area, under General Rate Act 1967, s 17, the charge will not apply in respect of a rating hereditament which:

(1) is the subject of a building preservation notice (1967 Act, Sched 1, para 2(*c*), amended by TCPA 1971); or

(2) is included in the list [of listed buildings] (para 2(c)); or
(3) is included in the schedule of monuments (para 2(d), amended by AMAAA 1979).
The exemption does not apply to an unlisted building in a conservation area.

Problems have arisen with the scope of this exemption, since the extent of a 'hereditament' for rating purposes may be quite different—larger or smaller—than that of a 'listed building' (with, or even without, its curtilage) as defined by TCPA 1971, s 54(9). The first is a concept arising from the characteristics of how a building is occupied; the second arises from its physical (architectural and geographical) features. Therefore in some cases it may not be very meaningful to discuss, as the 1967 Act does, whether or not a hereditament 'is included' in the list.

In *Providence Properties Ltd* v *Liverpool CC* [1980] RA 189, the rating hereditament comprised three warehouses, of which one was listed and two were not. The Divisional Court held that the exemption from rating would not apply in such a case. This was upheld by the House of Lords in *Debenhams PLC* v *Westminster CC* [1987] JPL 344. After finding on the facts (as to which, see 2.5(c)) that one of the two buildings comprising the hereditament was listed and one was not, Lord Keith agreed that the whole hereditament was liable to the payment of rates. He also (at 347–8) specifically considered the position where a building preservation notice is served on one building within a hereditament, so that it could be said without any undue straining of language that the hereditament as such is the subject of the notice, but considered that even here the whole hereditament would be liable to the payment of rates.

The position would presumably be identical if only one building or object within a larger rating hereditament was scheduled as a monument under the AMAAA 1979. Payment would be liable in respect of the whole.

As to whether or not a hereditament is 'unoccupied', so as to give rise to the possibility of the exemption coming into play, this is a matter of general rating law beyond the scope of this book, but see in particular *R* v *St Pancras Assessment Committee* (1877) 2 QBD 581 and *London County Council* v *Wilkins* (1956) 49 R & IT 495.

The general rate is of course due to be abolished in 1990 in England and Wales, to be replaced by the community charge (poll tax) for domestic property and the new uniform non-domestic rate for other property (Local Government Finance Act 1988). Most of the details as to the latter are as yet uncertain; but it seems probable that the existing concession as to unoccupied historic buildings will continue to apply in some form.

(c) Capital taxation

There are some provisions which operate so as to give a measure of relief to the owners of all buildings, which may be particularly relevant to historic buildings. There are other reliefs available only in the case of those which are of 'outstanding' interest.

A historic building will in many cases be the only or principal residence of an individual private taxpayer. Where this is so, capital gains tax (CGT) is not payable on its disposal (CGT Act 1979, ss 101–4). Where the taxpayer owns and occupies two or more houses, he or she may elect as to which is to be treated as the 'principal' one.

Secondly, gifts of property may attract relief from capital gains tax or inheritance tax (IHT). There is a general roll-over relief applicable to a capital gain accruing on the gift of any asset, provided that both the donor and the recipient apply to the Inland Revenue. The net effect of this is to transfer the payment of any capital gains tax due, until (at least) the next disposal of the asset (Finance Act 1980, s 79). Gifts of property to charities and to certain heritage bodies (see below) are subject to a similar roll-over relief (CGT Act 1979, s 146), and are also exempt from inheritance tax if the gift is on the death of the donor (IHT Act 1984, ss 23, 25, 26, 32). A gift of property will not attract inheritance tax anyway if it is made at least seven years before the death of the donor—and if the donor dies within the seven-year period, tax is payable but at a tapering rate (Finance Act 1986).

The heritage bodies referred to in the previous paragraph are those generally concerned with the preservation of 'the heritage', and include the National Trust, the Historic Churches Preservation Trust, the Nature Conservancy Council, any local authority, any Government department, and any university (IHT Act 1984, Sched 3).

A gift of an historic building on the death of the donor will not attract inheritance tax, if the following conditions are met to the satisfaction of the Inland Revenue:

(1) the building is of outstanding historic or architectural interest;

(2) the new owner undertakes that reasonable access will be

provided for the public and that the building will be properly maintained.

Inheritance tax is not payable where such a building is accepted by the Revenue in satisfaction of inheritance tax liability generally (in which case there will be no liability to capital gains tax, stamp duty or value added tax either) (IHT Act 1984, s 231).

Where a fund is set up for the maintenance of a building of outstanding interest, further reliefs are available. Neither capital gains tax nor inheritance tax will be payable on property transferred to the fund when it is set up (IHT Act 1984, s 27(1)), and inheritance tax will not be payable when capital is spent from the fund for a purpose connected with the property (s 76(1)). The person setting up the fund (that is, the owner of the building) can elect that any income from it is to be assessable to income tax on the trustees at a favourable rate, rather than on him or herself, so long as it is spent on such purposes (Finance Act 1977, s 38(2)). The capital of the fund, however, must be used for the preservation or repair of the property, or for providing public access to it, or to meet the expenses of the trustees.

The test of whether a building is 'outstanding' for these purposes is inevitably imprecise. The offer of a grant under HBAMA 1953 (see 6.2) is usually accepted by the Revenue as evidence of sufficient quality; but broadly any building that is listed Grade I or II* might be accepted, and even one of Grade II. Where a building is accepted as being of sufficient interest, any reliefs apply to land and objects associated with the building as they do to the building itself.

The above comments are inevitably only in very broad outline. For further details, see a comprehensive booklet published by the Inland Revenue in December 1986, *Capital Taxation and the National Heritage* (no IR 67). This can be obtained (price £5.25 including postage) from Inland Revenue Reference Room, Room 8, New Wing, Somerset House, London WC2R 1LB.

Chapter 7

Planning Permission

7.1 Planning permission and other forms of consent

The fundamental principle of the planning system is the need for anyone wishing to develop land to obtain *planning permission* from the local planning authority or the Secretary of State. This applies to listed buildings and scheduled monuments just as it does to any other buildings; and applies whether the land in question is within or outside a conservation area or archaeological area.

The need for planning permission, and the process by which it is obtained, is covered in detail in all the standard works on planning law and procedure. The purpose of this chapter is not to duplicate those, but to highlight issues particular to planning applications affecting listed buildings and conservation areas.

7.2 The need for planning permission

(a) The general rule

Planning permission is needed for the carrying out of any *development* (TCPA 1971, s 23(1)), which is defined as:

the carrying out of building, engineering, mining or other operations in, on, over or under land; or the making of any material change in the use of any buildings or other land (s 22(1)).

This definition is subject to some minor exceptions and qualifications, the relevant ones of which are noted below.

To obtain planning permission, it is necessary to submit a planning application to the local planning authority, unless what is proposed is 'permitted development', which is (in most cases) permitted automatically by a development order. The need for a planning application is summarised in Figures 8.1 and 10.1 which deal respectively with listed buildings and with unlisted buildings in conservation areas.

(b) Alterations to existing buildings

The primary means by which a local planning authority controls building works affecting a listed building is that listed building consent is needed for its 'demolition, alteration or extension' (TCPA 1971, s 55(1); see Chapter 8). Planning permission will also be needed, however, for any significant building operations which affect it (see 7.2(*a*)). 'Building operations' are defined to include rebuilding operations, structural alterations of and additions to buildings, and other operations normally undertaken by a person carrying on business as a builder (TCPA 1971, s 290).

In the case of an unlisted building in a conservation area, on the other hand, conservation area consent is needed only for its demolition, but not for its alteration or extension (see Chapter 10). Again, planning permission is needed for building operations of any consequence, including most alterations and extensions to existing buildings. Indeed, the need for planning applications to be made in such cases is often the only means available to a planning authority to control unsuitable alterations to existing buildings, which may cumulatively have a serious effect on the appearance of the conservation area.

Planning permission is not needed for the carrying out of 'works for the maintenance, improvement or other alteration of any building, being works which affect only the interior of the building, or which do not materially affect its exterior' unless they are works for making good war damage, or for the alteration of a building by providing additional space below ground (TCPA 1971, s 22(2)(*a*)).

The precise definition of maintenance etc will depend on the facts in each case. But the restoration to the same design of a building of which only the original foundations, damp course and two walls remained has been held—not surprisingly, perhaps—to be reconstruction, constituting development, and not maintenance or repair (*Street* v *Essex CC* (1965) 193 EG 537). More recently, a proposal to rebuild substantially a derelict, listed, house was held on appeal to require planning permission as well as listed building consent, both of which were refused (see [1985] JPL 807). The replacement of a hedge by a fence has also been held not to be maintenance. The fact that a building is listed or within a conservation area means that certain relatively minor works to it, which would not do so otherwise, could be considered to affect its external appearance 'materially'.

Planning permission will thus usually not be needed for repairs and restoration works. But if a building has been allowed to decay seriously, or even become semi-derelict, then works of repair (however desirable) may well affect its appearance, and therefore be 'development'. They would still not normally require a planning application in the case of a dwellinghouse or an agricultural building, however, as they would be permitted development (GDO 1988, Sched 2, Pt 1, Class A; Pt 6, Class A).

In a borderline case, the planning authority should be consulted as to whether planning permission is needed. If there is any doubt, it will often be prudent to submit an application for planning permission. If the building is listed, an application for listed building consent will almost always be required anyway, and the two applications can therefore be submitted and processed at the same time—the same drawings can after all be used for both. If the building is unlisted, but in a conservation area, both the planning authority and any local amenity groups may be particularly vigilant to spot apparently unauthorised alterations; and the submission of an application may therefore avoid much trouble later on.

A planning application will not be necessary for building operations (as defined above) if they are 'permitted development', that is, permitted by a general or special development order (see 7.3(a)) unless the permitted development 'rights' have been withdrawn by an Article 4 direction.

Finally, note that planning permission is required for the creation of new space below ground, even though there is no effect on the external appearance of the building above ground (TCPA 1971, s 22(2)(a)). In the case of a listed building, this is possibly the only case of building works which might require planning permission but not listed building consent.

(c) Other building and engineering operations

The definition of 'development', for which planning permission is normally required, includes 'building operations' (defined above) and 'engineering operations' (TCPA 1971, s 22(1)). The former is straightforward, and includes the erection of any building or structure, even if as small as a model village (as at

Bekonscot in Buckinghamshire: *Buckinghamshire CC* v *Callingham* [1952] 2 QB 515).

Thus, building works in the grounds of a listed building, not actually affecting the building itself, which will not require listed building consent (see 8.1(*c*)) will require planning permission unless they are permitted development. Such works may significantly affect the setting of the listed building, which is why applications to carry them out require special publicity (see 7.5(*b*)). Conservation area consent is only needed for the demolition of existing buildings. It is never needed for the construction of new ones. The need for planning permission in most such cases thus enables the authority to have some influence over changes in the character of the area (see, for example, *Steinberg* v *Secretary of State* (1988) *The Independent*, 2 December). Again, special publicity is needed.

'Engineering operations' include the formation of any means of access, whether public or private, for vehicles or pedestrians (TCPA 1971, s 290). The laying of hardcore on a garden after the removal of the front and side walls has on appeal been held to be the formation of an access, and hence to constitute development requiring planning permission ([1972] JPL 109). This could be significant in that such development can often have a very unfortunate effect on the character of a conservation area. But note that this will be permitted development, not normally requiring specific permission, if it is within the curtilage of a dwellinghouse or in connection with other permitted development (GDO 1988, Sched 2, Pt 1, Class F; Pt 2, Class B).

Floodlighting is in general not development (*Kensington and Chelsea RLBC* v *CG Hotels* [1981] JPL 190). This would not be the case however if the equipment used to provide the illumination is so substantial or permanently fixed to the building or the ground that its installation amounts to an engineering operation.

(d) Demolition

The conventional view is that planning permission is not needed for the demolition of a building.

This seems to stem from statements to that effect in Circ 67/49 and Development Control Policy Note No 7 (1969, para 3). Both of these are now cancelled, and anyway represented the opinion of the Government of the day, rather than authoritative statements of the law. However, in the leading case of *Coleshill and District Investment Co* v *Minister of Housing and Local Govern-*

ment [1969] 1 WLR 746, the House of Lords were clearly of the opinion that demolition could be development in certain circumstances. In that case, the partial demolition of an ammunition depot was held to be on a sufficient scale as to amount to an engineering operation. In *City of Glasgow DC* v *Secretary of State for Scotland* [1982] JPL 374 it seems to have been assumed (at 375–6) that the demolition of the top two storeys of a building might have required planning permission. It would be bizarre if permission were required from the local planning authority for the partial demolition of a building but not for its total demolition. Thus in *Beecham* v *Metropolitan District Auditor* (1976) LGR 79, DC, it was accepted that the demolition of two hundred houses might be development requiring planning permission.

Certainly it would seem on the face of it that demolition will in most cases constitute either a building operation (see 7.2(*a*)), or an engineering operation, or at the very least an 'other' operation; and it will clearly affect the external appearance of the building concerned. It would thus appear to be development, needing planning permission (TCPA 1971, s 22(1)). The fact that planning authorities do not in practice seek an application probably arises from likely difficulties over enforcing such a requirement, rather than from any clear interpretation of the Act itself.

There is, however, no doubt that listed building consent is needed for the demolition of a listed building, in whole or in part (TCPA 1971, s 55(1)), and that conservation area consent is needed in most cases for the demolition of an unlisted building in a conservation area (TCPA 1971, s 277A(2), as inserted by TCAA 1974). Planning permission should therefore only be sought as well if the proposed works involve alteration in addition to demolition. As to the distinction between alteration and demolition, see 8.1(*d*).

(e) Changes of use

Listed building consent or conservation area consent will only be required for a change in the use of a building if its physical consequences involve some demolition works, or if they affect the character of a listed building. However, planning permission is almost always required for a material change in the use of a building, unless the existing and proposed uses are within the same use class (TCPA 1971, s 22 (1),(2)(*f*)). The use classes are currently prescribed in the TCP (Use) Classes Order 1987.

It will therefore sometimes happen that applications for two types of consent will be needed, eg where a listed house is being converted into offices. In such a case, the two applications will be determined on the basis of different criteria, and it could well happen that one is refused and the other is granted.

7.3 Permitted development

(a) Need for permission

There are a number of categories of minor works for which a planning application is not normally needed, as they are automatically permitted by a general or special development order. They include, for example, the construction of small extensions to dwellinghouses, the painting of buildings, and works by various public bodies. They are known as *permitted development*.

The classes most relevant to listed buildings and conservation areas are currently as shown in Figure 7.1. They are subject in almost all cases to numerous restrictions as to volume, dimensions, location and other details.

The general development order currently in force (TCP General Development Order 1988, referred to in this book as 'GDO 1988') includes seventy-seven 'Classes' of permitted development, grouped into the twenty-eight 'Parts' of Sched 2. This came into force on 5 December 1988, and repealed the GDO 1977. That had been significantly amended by a number of subsequent orders, and modified in its application to conservation areas by a further sequence of Special Development Orders. One welcome new feature of the GDO 1988 is that it sets out the relevant Classes of permitted development both as they apply within conservation areas and as they apply elsewhere.

Note, however, that specific planning permission is needed to carry out works which would otherwise be permitted development in two instances:

(1) where the right to do so has been withdrawn by a previous grant of planning permission or an Article 4 direction (GDO 1988, arts 3(4),4; see 7.4); or

(2) where the works would involve making or widening an access to a trunk or classified road, or would create a danger to the users of any road (art 3(5)).

(b) Permitted development affecting listed buildings

The rules as to what is permitted development were until 1988 almost exactly the same for listed as for unlisted buildings.

However, as a result of changes introduced in the GDO 1988, they are now significantly different, as well as being somewhat more complex than they appear at first sight.

First, almost any development in the curtilage of a listed dwellinghouse now needs specific planning permission, since it is no

Figure 7.1 Permitted development: categories most relevant to listed buildings and conservation areas

GDO 1988, Sched 2, Part 1 Development within the curtilage of a dwellinghouse (*formerly GDO 1977, Sched 1, Class I*)
  A Alterations and small extensions
  B Alterations to the roof affecting its shape
  C Other alterations to the roof
  D Porches
  E Garden structures (sheds, swimming pools etc)
  F Hardstandings for domestic vehicles
  G Storage tanks for heating oil
  H Small satellite antennas

Part 2 Sundry minor operations (*formerly Class II*)
  A Gates, fences and walls
  B Means of access (see 7.2(c))
  C Painting

Part 4, Class A Temporary buildings (*formerly Class IV.1*)

Parts 6 and 7 Agricultural and forestry development (*formerly Classes VI and VII*)

Part 8 Minor industrial and warehouse development (*formerly Classes VIII and XXVIII*)

Parts 9 and 10 Repairs to highways and services (*formerly Classes IX and X*)

Part 11 Development authorised by local or private Acts of Parliament (*formerly Class XII*)

Parts 12 to 18 Minor development by various public bodies (*formerly Classes XIII to XVIII*)

Parts 24 and 25 Telecommunications development (*formerly Classes XXIV and XXV*) (see 7.3(d))

Part 26 Restoration works by or on behalf of the Historic Buildings and Monuments Commission (*formerly Class XXX*) (see 7.3(e))

longer permitted development. Part 1, Class E provides that 'the provision within the curtilage of a dwellinghouse of any building or enclosure, swimming or other pool required for a purpose incidental to the enjoyment of the dwellinghouse, or the mainten- ance, improvement or other alteration of such a building or enclosure' is normally permitted development. But this only applies to operations within the curtilage of a dwellinghouse that is listed if the volume of the building to be built, altered or improved is less than 10 cubic metres (para E.1(*f*)). To make doubly certain, since such an operation if it is in a conservation area is to be treated as though it were the enlargement of the dwellinghouse itself (para A3(*a*)(i); see 7.3(*c*)), it is provided that this still does not mean that the erection of a building in the curtilage of a listed building is permitted development (para A.1(*g*)).

Secondly, the 'erection, construction, maintenance, improve- ment or alteration of a gate, fence, wall or other means of enclosure' is not permitted development if it is within or enclosing the curtilage of a listed building (Part 2, para A.1(*d*)).

These two changes were introduced because such works do not need listed building consent (see 8.1(*c*)), and were until 1988 almost entirely outside the control of the planning authority, even if they had a highly undesirable effect on the setting of a listed building. As to the meaning of 'curtilage', see 2.5.

Thirdly, it seems that almost any extension to a listed building itself, of whatever volume, requires planning permission. This is because Sched 2, Pt 1, para A.1(*g*) provides that 'the erection of a building within the curtilage of a listed building' is not permitted development. The intention of the draftsman was probably to refer only to freestanding buildings. But any statutory instrument must be interpreted in the context of its parent Act. And in this case the TCPA 1971 specifically provides that 'building' includes 'part of a building' (s 290). That is of course 'except in so far as the context otherwise requires', but here the context is that of the enlargement or alteration of a dwellinghouse. The 'building' within the curtilage of the listed dwellinghouse, whose erection is stated not to be permitted development, would thus include an extension to the listed house itself, which, after all, must be within its own curtilage.

For a possible alternative view, see the Scottish case of *Whyte* v *Bruce* (1900) 37 SLT 614 (see 10.2(*b*)). This does not however apply if the extension takes the form of a porch or a dormer on a rear roof slope outside a conservation area, as these are still permitted developments under Part 1, Classes B and D respectively.

(c) Permitted development in conservation areas

Since conservation area consent is not needed for the erection of new buildings or for the alteration of existing ones, the need for planning permission to be obtained is the only way in which a planning authority can control works which may significantly affect the character or appearance of a conservation area. However, if the works are permitted development, then no planning application is normally needed, and the authority has no control at all, except by making an Article 4 direction covering the property and the type of development concerned.

For example, the character of a conservation area that mainly comprises terraces of small Victorian cottages opening off the back of the pavement can be totally transformed by the replacement of the original sliding sash windows by modern glazing. Such work is permitted development (GDO 1988, Sched 2, Pt 1, Class A), and no planning application is therefore required. Therefore unless the cottages are listed or subject to an Article 4 direction, the planning authority is powerless to intervene. Similarly, the painting of brickwork on unlisted buildings is also permitted development (Pt 2, Class C).

The limits of what is permitted development within a conservation area can therefore be of considerable significance in certain cases. They were in the past the same as those applying elsewhere, but were (first) modified somewhat by the TCP (National Parks [etc]) Special Development Order 1981. This was replaced by a further Order in 1985. The modifications are now (since 1988) contained within the body of the GDO itself. They apply in national parks, areas of outstanding natural beauty (AONBs) and areas designated under s 41(3) of the Wildlife and Countryside Act 1981 (notably the Norfolk Broads) as well as in conservation areas—these are together referred to in the Order as 'Art 1(5) land'. And note that (again, only since 1988) the modified limits apply regardless of when the area in question was designated. The principal differences are now as follows.

First, extensions to dwellinghouses in conservation areas are only permitted development if they do not add more than 10 per cent or 50 cubic metres (whichever is greater) to the volume of the original building (Sched 2, Pt 1, para A.1(*a*)(i)). The limits

elsewhere are 15 per cent or 70 cubic metres except in the case
of terrace houses (para A.1(*a*)(i), (ii)). Nor (since 1988) are the
following permitted development within a conservation area:

(1) the cladding of any part of the exterior of a dwellinghouse
    with stone, artificial stone, timber, plastic or tiles (para
    A.2); or

(2) any alterations to the roof of a dwellinghouse resulting in
    a material alteration to its shape, notably dormer windows
    (para B.1(*e*)).

Secondly, it has been noted above (see 7.3(*b*)) that Pt 1, Class E
provides that the erection within the curtilage of a dwellinghouse
of various buildings and enclosures is normally permitted development. This applies generally within a conservation area just as
elsewhere, but if the volume of the building to be built, altered
or improved (the 'curtilage building') is greater than 10 cubic
metres, and the dwellinghouse is in a conservation area, the operation is to be treated as though it were the enlargement of the
dwellinghouse itself (paras E.1(*f*), A.3(*a*)(i)). The relevant limits
in Pt 1, Class A therefore apply, as to height, size, location and
so on. Outside conservation areas, this applies only if the curtilage
building will be within 5 metres of the dwellinghouse (para
A.3(*a*)(ii)). Note that this no longer applies only to garages and
coachhouses, as was the case prior to 1988.

The combined effect of these two provisions is that the overall
amount of building works that can be carried out to a dwellinghouse or in its grounds without a planning application is substantially smaller within a conservation area than elsewhere.

Thirdly, extensions to industrial and warehouse buildings in
conservation areas are only permitted development if they do not
add more than 10 per cent to the volume of the original building,
or 500 square metres to its aggregate floor space; elsewhere the
limits are 25 per cent and 1,000 square metres respectively (Part
8, para A.1(*d*), (*e*)). Exactly the same applies to extensions to
electricity undertakers' buildings (Part 17, para G.1(*b*)).

Fourthly, the provisions regarding telecommunications development are slightly different in conservation areas (see below).

(d) Telecommunications equipment

As a result of advances in the relevant technology, a number
of public companies have been licensed under the provisions of
the Telecommunications Act 1984 as public telecommunications
operators. These include British Telecom and Mercury, cellular

radio companies, and operators of local broadband cable systems. Their licences, issued under the Telecommunications Code in the 1984 Act allow them to install in the street and on private property apparatus such as wires, poles, masts, street cabinets, microwave dishes and other antennas.

Under Pt 24 of Sched 2 to the GDO 1988, such installations, on the Code operator's own land or elsewhere, are permitted development provided that they conform to the terms of the relevant licence. These in most cases require special notifications to or consultation with the local planning authority in the case of installations affecting listed buildings or in conservation areas, and in many cases require new lines and cables to be placed underground. In addition, the installation of antennas (including dish aerials) by Code operators is not permitted development in conservation areas (Pt 24, para A.1(g)). A Code operator must give at least eight weeks' notice to the planning authority of any works which it proposes to carry out within a conservation area on its own land, relying on the permission in Pt 24 (para A.2(3)).

Other telecommunications development, that is, not carried out by Code operators, is never permitted development within conservation areas (Pt 25, para A.2(g)). For further details, see Circular 16/85.

Finally, the installation of satellite antennas on and in the curtilage of dwellinghouses is normally permitted development (Pt 1, Class H). This used not to be so in the case of an antenna in a conservation area if part of it came in front of the front of the dwellinghouse (TCP (National Parks [etc]) Special Development Order 1985, art 3(aa)); but this distinction no longer applies.

Where any installations are attached to a listed building, listed building consent will still be needed in the usual way.

(e) Works by the Historic Buildings and Monuments Commission

In general, development carried out by the Commission on its own land on behalf of the Secretary of State does not require planning permission as such, but will be notified to planning authorities in the same way as development by Government departments (NHA 1983, s 34(2), Sched 3, para 2(3); Circ 18/84, Pt IV, para 2). See 8.2(c), (d) for details of the corresponding procedure for departments to consult local authorities on their proposals for works affecting listed buildings.

Other works by the Commission generally require planning permission to the same extent as works by any other developer.

Certain works for the preservation or repair of buildings or monuments in the Commission's ownership or control are however permitted development (GDO 1988, Sched 2, Pt 26). These include:

(1) the maintenance, repair or restoration of a building or monument (but not its extension);

(2) the erection of protective screens or fencing, for a period of six months (or longer if agreed by the local planning authority); and

(3) works to stabilise any cliff, watercourse or coastline.

This list does not include development associated with the promotion of buildings and monuments as visitor attractions. The construction of car parks, ticket booths, refreshment shops, heritage interpretation centres and the like will thus still need to be notified to the planning authority, or to form the subject of a planning application, depending on whether or not the works are to be carried out in pursuance of a direction of the Secretary of State.

7.4 Article 4 directions

(a) Effect of a direction

A local planning authority may sometimes wish to restrict the right of landowners to carry out certain categories of development which would otherwise be automatically permitted by the General Development Order. This will occur where that type of permitted development would have a particularly unfortunate effect on the appearance of the area (see 7.3).

This can be achieved by making an *Article 4 direction*—it is art 3 of the GDO which 'permits' those classes of development specified in Sched 2, and art 4 that enables a planning authority to restrict that permission. A direction can be made covering one or more properties, and can restrict one or more classes of permitted development, or part of one class (for example, 'alterations to any part of any elevation of the dwellinghouse fronting a highway', currently within Pt 1, Class A of Sched 2). The procedure will often be appropriate to enable a planning authority to control development in a conservation area.

The effect of an Article 4 direction being made on a property in respect of a particular category of permitted development is that development within that category is no longer automatically permitted, that is, it is no longer permitted by the Order, but must instead be the subject of a specific planning application (see below). This does not necessarily mean that the planning authority will refuse permission, but it does enable it to retain some control.

Directions will usually be made covering a group of properties, or a wider area, such as all or part of a conservation area. It has however been held that an Article 4 direction can be made in respect of a single site (*Thanet DC* v *Ninedrive* [1978] 1 All ER 703). The existence of a direction should be entered by the local authority as a local land charge in Part 3 of the register (Local Land Charges Rules 1977, r 2(2)).

(b) Article 4 directions affecting listed buildings

It will not often be necessary to make Article 4 directions concerning alterations and extensions to listed buildings themselves, as these will virtually always require listed building consent, and thus be within the control of the planning authority. It may however be appropriate in a few cases for an authority to make a direction restricting permitted development within the curtilage of a listed building, since this will not require listed building consent and would otherwise be outside control. Since 1988, there are in fact very few types of development affecting a listed building which do not require a specific planning permission (see 7.3(*b*))—one example where a direction might still be appropriate would be to restrict the provision of hard surfaces or satellite antennas in the curtilage of listed dwellinghouses (still permitted development within Pt 1, Classes F and H respectively).

A direction does not normally require the approval or confirmation of the Secretary of State if it relates only to:

(*a*) a listed building;
(*b*) a building which is notified to the authority by the Secretary of State as a building of architectural or historic interest; or
(*c*) development within the curtilage of a listed building

(GDO 1988, art 5(3)). It is not clear to what the second category refers.

In such a case, the direction is therefore made by the planning authority, and notified to the owners and occupiers of the land concerned. It comes into force on the date of the notification (art 5(10)). Note however that it must still be approved by the Secretary of State if it is made to restrict the carrying out of routine works by statutory undertakers (art 5(3)).

(c) Article 4 directions in conservation areas

Bearing in mind the unfortunate effect of certain types of permitted development, particularly in connection with dwelling-houses (see 7.3(*c*), on the character and appearance of conservation areas, it may often be appropriate for planning authorities to make Article 4 directions in order to retain control.

Directions relating to unlisted buildings must however be either approved or confirmed by the Secretary of State. His current policy (originally given as App D to Circ 12/73) is set out as App II to Circ 8/87. In summary,

unless there are obvious and immediate reasons for it, a direction should not be made until it is clear that there will not be adequate public co-operation in the improvement of the area. Although the Secretary of State will generally be in favour of approving directions relating to [conservation] areas, a special need for them must be clearly shown, (such as a known or potential threat to the character of the area) because the fact that they are conservation areas is not in itself a justification for a direction. However, where there is no threat, known or potential, the question of need may be satisfied if the authority can show how a direction would assist a positive policy which they had adopted for enhancing the character or appearance of the conservation area. For example, it would be justifiable to make a direction to bring under control permitted development which would be unsympathetic to a programme or scheme of conservation work (Circ 8/87, para 64).

Directions may thus be particularly useful where an authority wishes:

(1) to prevent completely a particular type of development (such as the painting of previously unpainted brickwork, or alterations to the front elevations of dwellinghouses);

(2) to control the location of development (for example, to allow extensions to dwellinghouses, but only at the rear rather than the side); or

(3) to control the precise details of minor works (such as the design of window surrounds on new side extensions, or the materials used in new front garden walls).

Particular care is needed where a direction is to be made covering painting (Pt 2, Class C) with the aim of bringing about or maintaining a uniform colour scheme for a formal group of buildings. It is in such a case essential to prepare beforehand a colour code, possibly in conjunction with any local amenity group. Such a code should be drafted with reference to the numbered British Standard colours (derived from BS 4800), not to general descriptions (for example, 'cream') or manufacturers' own brand names ('almond blossom'). It is more likely to be effective if a single colour scheme is stipulated, and well publicised. But in practice it may prove very difficult to enforce any scheme without extensive cooperation from property owners.

It is perhaps more realistic only to attempt to control painting in the case of buildings where *any* paint would be highly unfortunate, such as those faced with stone, or with elaborate decorations in terracotta. In such cases it may be best to frame the direction so as to restrict only 'painting of hitherto unpainted parts of the elevation, being development within Pt 2, Class C'; this has the effect of leaving outside control the repainting of woodwork and pipework.

(d) Procedure for making a direction

The planning authority must first draft the direction showing which properties are to be covered and which categories of permitted development are to be restricted (GDO 1988, art 4(1)). These should both be kept to the minimum possible. If the direction covers too much, it is more difficult to draft accurately, more time-consuming to prepare and serve on owners and occupiers, less likely to be approved by the Secretary of State, more likely to be ignored by owners, and less likely to be effectively enforced.

The choice of categories of development to be controlled therefore needs to be considered carefully, particularly where they are within Pt 1, Class A, as this covers a wide variety of different types of work. The direction should thus only aim to restrict precisely those alterations which are likely to be damaging, for example, 'alterations to the elevations of the dwellinghouse fronting the highway' or 'extensions at the rear of the dwellinghouse'. This is partly in order not to restrict the freedom of property owners more than is justifiable. It is also, more pragmatically, so as not to generate more planning applications than are needed, for works which will, inevitably, usually be of little significance. This approach has also been assisted by the division of Class I.1 in the GDO 1977 into Classes A, B and C in Pt 1 in the GDO 1988.

The properties involved must be specified with precision, particularly in the case of a large area, both on a map and by a list. If the direction involves different categories of development for different properties in the same area, it may be best to draw up a matrix table.

When the direction has been drawn up, it must then be sent by the planning authority to the Secretary of State for his approval (GDO 1988, art 5(1)). When it has been approved, with or without modifications, the authority must then wherever possible notify every owner or occupier of any land affected. The direction takes effect in respect of land on the date when it is notified to the owners and occupiers of that land (art 5(10)).

If the authority considers that such notification is impracticable because of the number of owners involved or the difficulty of identifying them, it must pass a resolution to that effect, and then publish an advertisement in a local newspaper explaining the effect of the direction. The direction in this case takes effect on the date when the advertisement is published (art 5(12)–(15)). The advertisement procedure should not be used except where it is unavoidable, as the owners and occupiers concerned are unlikely to become aware of the direction. It is probably best in the case of a direction covering a large area to deliver a notice to each property concerned addressed to 'the owner/occupier', and then to place an advertisement in the press to meet with the formal requirements.

The notice served on owners and occupiers will usually be a formal legal document. It should therefore wherever possible be accompanied by a leaflet explaining in simple language what an Article 4 direction is, and why one has been served in this particular case. The text of such a leaflet might also be a convenient way of explaining to the relevant committee of the authority why the direction should be made in the first place.

Within a conservation area, an Article 4 direction can be made by either the district or the county planning authority; elsewhere normally only by the district (art 4(4)). In any event, a district authority making a direction must give notice of it to the county, and vice versa (art 5(2)). It is also possible for the Secretary of State to make a direction (art 4(1)).

Note incidentally that art 4 of the GDO 1977 has been replaced by arts 4 and 5 of the GDO 1988, the first dealing with the making of a direction, and the second its approval.

(e) Procedure in cases of urgency

Where an authority wishes to make a direction to counter an immediate threat of unsuitable permitted development occurring, the above procedure will take too long. There is accordingly an alternative procedure available in some cases, which can be used where the authority considers that proposed development would be 'prejudicial to the proper planning of their area or would constitute a threat to the amenities of their area' (GDO 1988, art 5(4)). It is however only possible to use this procedure to restrict permitted development in Pts 1 to 4 (see Figure 7.1 for details). This means, in particular, that it cannot be used to stop permitted development carried out by statutory undertakers and Telecommunications Code operators.

Where a direction is made under art 5(4), it does not require the approval of the Secretary of State. As soon as it has been made, notice should be given to the owners and occupiers concerned, or an advertisement be placed in the press, in the same way as when a direction has been approved in a non-urgent case (see 7.4(d)); the direction comes into force on the date of the notice or advertisement (art 5(10), (12)–(15)). It only remains in force for six months, however, unless it is confirmed by the Secretary of State, with or without modifications, within that period. A copy of the direction should therefore be sent to him as soon as it is made (art 5(5), (7), (8)).

When the direction has in due course been either confirmed or disallowed by the Secretary of State, further notice must be given in the same manner (art 5(8), (11)–(15)).

It is probably best for an authority faced with an immediate threat of unsuitable permitted development in one of Pts 1 to 4 to make at once a direction under art 5(4), covering only the property directly affected, and send it for confirmation to the Secretary of State. It should then consider whether similar development is likely to take place elsewhere in the immediate area; if so, it should make a second, more comprehensive direction under the normal procedure covering the wider area (including the first property). It can then cancel the earlier urgent direction once the subsequent one has been approved.

(f) Response to an Article 4 direction

There is no formal right of appeal against the making of an Article 4 direction. But where an owner or occupier becomes aware, by whatever means, that the local planning authority is proposing to make a direction affecting his or her property, it is of course open to him or her to object (as with appealing against a building being listed; see 2.3). Similarly, it is possible to object after receiving notice that a direction has been made under the speedier procedure (see 7.4(e)). Such an objection should be in the form of a letter to the authority, stating why it is considered that the carrying out of the relevant category of permitted development would not be harmful. In the case of a direction requiring the confirmation of the Secretary of State, a second copy of the letter should be enclosed, together with a request that it should be sent to the officer at the Department of the Environment who is dealing with the case.

An informal approach of this kind is not likely to succeed in persuading the authority to cancel the direction; but it may occasionally persuade the Secretary of State not to approve it.

Once a direction has been made and, where necessary, been confirmed by the Secretary of State, it is then necessary for anyone wishing to carry out the relevant type of development to apply for a specific grant of planning permission. If permission is refused, or granted subject to onerous conditions, it will then of course be possible to appeal against the decision to the Secretary of State. At such an appeal, the argument that the development which the authority wishes to restrict is normally permitted automatically will certainly be a very material consideration.

In addition, it may be possible to claim compensation from the authority. In the first of the three cases identified in 7.4(c), if the development that the authority wishes to restrict consists of an alteration to a building that would increase its value (such as an extension), it may have to pay compensation (TCPA 1971, s 165). In the second case, the law is uncertain as to whether compensation would be payable. In the third case, it is almost certainly not payable.

Where compensation is payable, it will be quantified as the difference between the value of the land if the development were to have been carried out and its value in its existing state, but in arriving at the latter figure it is to be assumed that some Sched 8 development (notably rebuilding or the construction of an extension of up to 10 per cent in volume) would be allowable (s 164(4), applied by s 165(2)). A further sum will also be payable by the authority in respect of any work that is rendered abortive by the making of the direction (s 164(1),(2), applied by s 165(2)). The calculation of the total sum is a complex matter, requiring specialist legal and valuation advice.

7.5 Planning applications: procedure

(a) Details required with application

In general, works to a listed building which require planning permission almost always require listed building consent as well. Accordingly, two applications will be required. There used to be a provision whereby a grant of planning permission for works to a listed building operated automatically as a grant of listed building consent as well (TCPA 1971, s 56(2)), but this was repealed in 1980 (LGPLA 1980, Sched 15).

The forms required for each application can be obtained from the local planning authority, who will also be able to advise on what drawings should be submitted, and in what quantity. Since in general the drawings required for the listed building consent application will need to be in considerable detail (see 8.3(*c*)), they will almost certainly be adequate for the planning application as well.

Ownership certificates will be required for the planning application as well as for the listed building consent application; the requirements under the two codes are identical (TCPA 1971, s 27; see 8.3(*d*)). In appropriate cases, therefore, notice can be given to other owners of the land (where certificates B or C are used), and advertisements placed in the press (where certificates C or D are used), at the same time for both applications.

As to planning applications in conservation areas, whether or not they are accompanied by applications for other types of consent, the usual rules apply as to the submission of forms and supporting material (formerly in the GDO 1977; see now TCP (Applications) Regulations 1988, reg 3). But in practice the requirements of planning authorities as to the amount of information that should be submitted about the materials and details of proposed development will often be more demanding within conservation areas than elsewhere.

Some authorities go further, and will only accept detailed planning applications in some or all of their conservation areas. An authority is entitled to do this wherever it is of the opinion that in a particular case an outline application for planning permission would be unsuitable, because the general principle involved 'ought not to be considered separately from all or any of the reserved matters' (GDO 1988, art 7(2)). The Secretary of State has advised that this power should be used only sparingly, even in conservation areas (Circ 22/80, para 9; Circ 8/87, para 61). It used to be possible for an applicant wishing to submit an outline application to appeal to the Secretary of State against an authority's insistence on a detailed application in any particular case (GDO 1977, art 5(2)). Unfortunately since 1988 this is no longer possible.

Where works to an unlisted building in a conservation area include some demolition, both planning permission and conservation area consent will be required. Here too, the two applications should normally be submitted at the same time with the same drawings.

A fee is required with a planning application (unlike applications for listed building consent and conservation area consent), except where the proposed development requires only specific permission because of a condition on an earlier permission or an Art 4 direction (TCP (Fees [etc]) Regulations 1983 and 1985, regs 5, 5A).

(b) Publicity for planning applications

It has already been noted that there are a number of categories of development affecting historic buildings and areas which require neither listed building consent nor conservation area consent, in particular, new buildings in conservation areas or in the curtilage of listed buildings. The need for planning permission to be obtained is therefore the only means open to a local planning authority to exercise any control in these cases. It is therefore not surprising that the authority is under a duty to publicise such applications, in order to obtain a wider cross-section of public opinion.

This duty applies where the application is for development which, in the opinion of the planning authority, would affect the character or appearance of a conservation area or the setting of a listed building (TCPA 1971, s 28(1), amended by LGA 1974 and TCAA 1974). As to how far this extends, the advice from the Secretary of State is:

The 'setting' of a building may be limited to the immediate surroundings of a building, but often may include land some distance from it. For example, where a listed building forms an important visual element in a street, it would probably be right to regard any development in the street as being within the setting of the building. A proposed high or bulky building might also affect the setting of a listed building some distance away. The character and appearance of a conservation area could be affected by proposed development outside the designated area but visible from it. This provision should therefore not be interpreted too narrowly and, if there is doubt, it is better to advertise (Circ 8/87, para 27).

The publicity is to take the form of:
(1) a notice in a local newspaper (normally in small print in the 'Statutory Notices' section); and
(2) a notice on or near the land concerned, which must be displayed for at least seven days.

Each notice must indicate the nature of the development in question, and must name a place where further details (that is, the drawings and supporting material) can be inspected. Those details must then be obtainable there for at least twenty-one days from the date of the press notice (TCPA 1971, s 28(2), amended by LGA 1972 and LGA 1985). Note that it is the planning authority that is under a duty to give such publicity, not the applicant.

Whether such publicity is of value must remain open to question. Most authorities in any event choose to publicise many applications (including those outside conservation areas) much more widely than they are required to by law. They will thus often inform neighbours and local amenity groups.

The planning authority must not determine the application until twenty-one days after the appearance of the press notice or the putting up of the site notice, whichever was the later (s 28(3)). And they must take into account any representations received during that period as a result of the publicity (s 29(4)).

(c) Notification of planning applications

As well as publicising all planning applications affecting listed buildings and conservation areas, planning authorities must notify the more significant ones (in England) to the Historic Buildings and Monuments Commission (TCPA 1971, s 28(2A)–(2C), inserted by NHA 1983). Authorities should send a copy of the press notice (see above), and 'appropriate supporting information, eg plans' (Circ 8/87, para 30).

The duty to notify the Commission arises in the following cases (which apply in all conservation areas in England):
(1) development affecting the setting of a listed building of Grade II* or Grade I; and
(2) development affecting the character or appearance of a conservation area, involving:
—the erection of a new building of more than 3000 cubic metres volume or 1000 square metres floorspace;
—the alteration or extension of an existing building, where the alteration or extension is above that size; or
—the change of use of a building of above that size

(TCPA 1971, s 28(2B), inserted by NHA 1983; Circ 8/87, para 29). The former requirement that all applications in about five hundred named conservation areas should be notified to the Commission no longer applies (Circ 8/87, para 28).

In addition, since 1988 the Commission must be notified of any planning application for development 'likely to affect the site of a scheduled ancient monument' (GDO 1988, art 18(1)(*n*); and see 14.3(*f*)).

Finally, within Greater London the planning authority must notify the London Division of the Commission in the following cases:

(1) development affecting the setting of a listed building of Grade II (TCPA 1971, s 28(2B), inserted by NHA 1983; Circ 8/87, para 29); and

(2) development involving the total or partial demolition or 'material alteration' of a listed building of any grade (TCPA 1971, s 58A, inserted by LGA 1985; GDO 1988, art 18(1)(*m*)).

The aim of this procedure is to enable the Commission to comment helpfully on applications at the earliest possible stage and before authorities have reached their own conclusions. All that is strictly necessary is to send the briefest details. In practice, however, some 12,000 applications are notified each year, and it is almost impossible for the Commission to discriminate between them or to make any very useful response. Authorities are therefore encouraged to send some more details, at least in the more significant cases. If, however, an authority does not hear from the Commission within twenty-eight days, it can be assumed that it has no comment (Circ 8/87, para 30). It does not in any event have a right to require the authority to determine an application in a particular way—it can merely make representations, which the authority must 'take into account' (TCPA 1971, s 29(4); GDO 1977, art 15(5)).

There is no corresponding requirement that planning applications affecting listed buildings and conservation areas in Wales should be notified to the Welsh Office (Cadw).

In some areas, district planning authorities also notify county authorities of planning applications affecting listed buildings and conservation areas. This enables the specialist conservation officers in the county authority to provide helpful advice, both to the district authority and to the applicant. The proportion of applications notified in this way varies from nil in some districts to almost all in others.

Applications will, as noted above, often be notified to neighbouring landowners and local amenity groups. Authorities have also been urged to send notification of the most significant ones for comment to the Royal Fine Arts Commission (Circ 8/87, para 26).

(d) Development by Government departments

Development by the Crown does not require planning permission, but Government departments consult planning authorities before proceeding with any development proposal for which permission would otherwise be required (Circ 18/84, para 4). Where such a proposal affects the character of a conservation area or the setting of a listed building, authorities have been asked to advertise it and notify the Historic Buildings and Monuments Commission wherever they would do so if the development were to be carried out by any other developer (Circ 18/84, para 18; Circ 8/87, para 28).

(e) Development by local authorities

In most cases local authorities wishing to carry out their own development may in effect grant themselves planning permission, by the relevant committees merely passing the appropriate resolutions. However, where the development consists of or includes the alteration or extension of a listed building (of any grade), the authority must apply to the Secretary of State for permission (TCP General Regulations 1976, reg 7(1)(a)). An application in such a case is deemed to have been made to the authority and referred to the Secretary of State for his decision.

This reflects the fact that an application by a local authority for listed building consent for its own works, which would also be required in such a case, must be made to the Secretary of State (see 8.2(e)). The two applications can thus be dealt with together. It also incidentally prevents any abuse by an unscrupulous authority of its power to grant itself planning permission in the case of works to a listed building (which can sometimes be politically sensitive).

Provided that a proposal does not include any alteration or extension to a listed building, a local authority is entitled to grant itself planning permission even if the proposal affects the setting of a listed building or the character of a conservation area. But the authority, like any other prospective developer, must advertise the proposal on site and in the press (TCP General Regulations 1976, reg 4(2)(c)). Because of the possibility of abuse, the courts have interpreted these requirements very strictly. Thus in *R* v *Lambeth LBC ex p Sharp* [1987] JPL 440, concerning a proposal by a London Borough Council to build an athletics track in a conservation area, the Court of Appeal held that the mere failure to specify in the press notice the time within which representations were to be made to the authority was sufficient to render the subsequent grant of deemed planning permission a nullity (see 4.3(*b*)).

A local authority should also notify the Commission of its own development proposals in cases where any other developer would have to do so (see 7.5(*c*); Circ 8/87, para 28).

7.6 Planning applications: decision-making

(a) General principles

In considering whether to grant planning permission for any development which affects a listed building or its setting, planning authorities and inspectors are required to 'have special regard to the desirability of preserving the building or its setting or any features of special . . . interest which it possesses' (TCPA 1971, s 56(3), amended by LGPLA 1980). The extent of the 'setting' of a listed building has been considered above (see 7.5(*b*)).

Similarly, authorities and inspectors are under a duty to consider the desirability of preserving or enhancing the character of a conservation area when determining any planning applications affecting it (TCPA 1971, s 277(8), substituted by TCAA 1974).

Often the emphasis will be on control rather than preservation, to allow the area to remain alive and prosperous but at the same time to ensure that any new development accords with its special architectural and visual qualities. It will be important to see that every new building is designed not as a separate entity, but as part of a larger whole, which has a well established character of its own (Circ 8/87, para 61).

As an example of the second of these principles, the inspector deciding an appeal regarding a proposal to build a nursing home in a conservation area in Sheffield considered that the primary consideration in such cases was whether the proposal would preserve or enhance the area's character ((1986) 1 PAD 263). More recently, an inspector's decision granting planning permission for a new house in a North London conservation area was overturned because he had stated that his duty was to consider whether the proposed development would harm the character of the area:

In his Lordship's judgment there was a world of difference between the issue which the inspector defined and the need to pay special attention to the desirability of preserving or enhancing the character or appearance of the conservation area. . . . The concept of avoiding harm was essentially negative. The underlying purpose of section 277(8) seemed to be essentially positive' (*Steinberg* v *Secretary of State* (1988) *The Independent*, 2 December).

And in *Penwith DC* v *Secretary of State* (1985) 277 EG 194 it was held that it had been reasonable for an inspector to decide that, in general, an amusement arcade was not appropriate in a conservation area, unless particular circumstances suggested otherwise.

(b) New uses for historic buildings

Much of the literature on conservation stresses that the key to preserving old buildings often lies in finding new uses for them. Planning authorities have therefore been urged to relax controls over land use allocation, density, plot ratio and daylighting, and to apply Building Regulations and fire safety legislation sensitively and sensibly, where this would enable historic buildings to be given a new lease of life (Circ 8/87, para 19).

This theme is central to the reasoning behind many decisions (by local planning authorities and by inspectors at appeals) on applications for changes of use of listed buildings. It also applies, although to a lesser extent, to unlisted buildings in conservation areas. It is usefully developed in the Circular:

The best use for an historic building is obviously the use for which it was designed and wherever possible, this original use, particularly if it is a residential use, should continue. If the use of the building has been changed from its original purpose, it should be considered whether it can revert to it. But in many cases it must be accepted that the continuation of the original use is not now a practical proposition and it will often be essential to find appropriate alternative uses. In considering whether a use is appropriate, authorities should pay particular attention to the architectural and historic features of the building and endeavour to find a use which will preserve them. If, for example, a large house with fine staircases and plaster ceilings can only be converted into flats with excessive subdivision that will destroy the internal features of interest, then a use needing large rooms such as offices, which will enable the staircases and ceilings to be left intact, might be preferable. Even if internal alterations are not proposed, it is important to find a use which will not damage the fabric of the building or result in damage from increased floor loadings. Unsympathetic development in close proximity to a listed building can mar its appearance or make its future use unattractive or untenable or, on some occasions, physically damage its structure, for example if it brings heavy traffic close to the building.

The greatest problems arise when large buildings, built for needs which have ceased to exist, become vacant, eg mills, maltings, breweries or former military establishments. Because of their bulk and position in the townscape or landscape, their demolition would cause a radical change in the appearance and ambience of the locality. This is particularly important when the buildings are along a waterfront of historic interest. Several successful conversion schemes have been carried out. Old warehouses and granaries, etc are now being used for housing, workshops, squash courts, restaurants, hotels, community and arts centres. Alternative uses are also sometimes needed for historic buildings found in gardens or parks . . .

Changing patterns of farming and rural life also means [sic] that new uses must be found for buildings such as stables, coach houses, barns, and oast houses that play such an important part in the history and appearance of the countryside. All possible solutions should be explored. If these buildings are used as workshops, craft studios or as holiday accommodation, they can often make a contribution to the rural economy by providing employment.

Local authorities should therefore be flexible in dealing with planning applications for changes of use of buildings of architectural or historic interest or other applications for consent for works associated with a change of use. It is suggested that they should, wherever possible, make a survey of such buildings in their area and make a provisional assessment of the types of new uses which they would be prepared to accept. This is particularly important when the buildings are empty, either in their entirety or on the upper floors. With this information available, authorities should be able to respond more quickly when applications for a change of use are submitted.

Authorities are reminded that when owners are having difficulties in disposing of historic buildings, help is available from the Buildings at Risk Unit of the Commission. (The Society for the Protection of Ancient Buildings offers an analogous service to their members also extending to buildings not on the statutory list.) Authorities are asked to keep in mind the possibility of using listed buildings themselves and to draw attention to the availability of premises in their areas if they receive enquiries from potential employers. (Circ 8/87, paras 20–4).

A typical example of how these principles work out in practice is given by an appeal against the refusal of planning permission for the conversion into offices of a residential building in Winchester (then listed Grade II, and about to be upgraded to II*). The

Inspector in his report dismissing the appeal ([1988] JPL 285) said at 286–8:

> In my opinion the main issues in this appeal are whether the change of use of the Mill House to offices is necessary in order to preserve this listed building; and whether such a use would maintain the integrity of the structure and the attractiveness of its setting.
>
> I agree with the parties that the Mill House is a fine listed building and all steps should be taken to ensure its preservation. In my opinion national and local policies would justify granting planning permission for the change of use to offices provided it could be established that because there was no demand for a residential use the house would not again be used for that purpose and would fall into decay if permission were not granted. . . .
>
> From the evidence submitted I am not satisfied that the Mill House is incapable of continued residential use. . . . Bearing in mind the quality of the house and its setting, the likely cost of such works is not so great as to mean that the house would not command a reasonable price for residential use in today's market.
>
> The other main issue which I identified only falls to be considered in detail if it is established that the Mill House is incapable of residential use. While an office use could on your evidence provide a sufficient return to enable the property to be restored and maintained in good order, such a use would in my view make it difficult to retain the integrity of structure, as works beyond those necessary for domestic use would be needed if the house were to be used for offices.

A more unusual example of this principle being applied was in *Tower Hamlets LBC* v *Secretary of State for the Environment and Lane* [1983] JPL 315, where permission was granted for the conversion of a listed residential building into offices, which would otherwise have been against policy, in order to secure its restoration. In that case, the restoration works were carried out, but the new use was not implemented. When permission was sought to renew the permission, it was held that it was legitimate for the inspector to take into account the benefit of the restoration works which had already taken place.

Accordingly, where permission is sought for a package of works including alterations to a building in connection with a change in its use, it may be desirable for the applicant to produce detailed financial calculations to show that the continuation of the present use is not sufficiently profitable to enable the building to be restored.

(c) Design

Where an existing building that is listed or in a conservation area is altered or extended, the general design, detailing and choice of materials of the new work should obviously respect those of the original building. In some cases, such as alterations to a Grade I or II* listed building, this may mean that the new work must match the old exactly. Elsewhere, it may be possible to incorporate new designs, but thought should still be given to such details as matching up storey heights, and echoing the rhythm of solid and void in the original elevation. The choice of materials will also need particularly careful consideration.

It should also be borne in mind when considering the desirability of proposed alterations to an existing building that they will have an effect not just on the appearance of the building itself but also on that of the area in which it is set. Thus, for example, where planning permission was sought for the addition of an extra floor in the form of a mansard roof on a listed house within the Kingsdown Conservation Area in Bristol, the recommendation of the inspector (that it should be allowed) was influenced both by the effect of the extra storey on the appearance of the house and by its impact on the skyline of the conservation area as a whole ([1984] JPL 525; and see 8.7(*d*)).

Where an entirely or largely new building is erected that affects the character or appearance of a conservation area or the setting of a listed building, it will be important to ensure that it is sensitively designed. There will be more scope for new designs here than would be the case with alterations to an existing building (pastiche neo-Georgian is not always, or even often, the right answer) but local authorities (and amenity groups) will understandably be more concerned with architectural and aesthetic aspects of new proposals in such locations than they would be elsewhere.

In general, planning authorities have been criticised, both by architects and developers and by the Government, for becoming too involved in the design of proposed new development; but it has been recognised that historic buildings and areas are a special case. The current advice is therefore as follows:

Planning authorities should recognise that aesthetics is an extremely subjective matter. They should not therefore impose their tastes on developers simply because they believe them to be superior. Developers should not be compelled to conform to the fashion of the moment at the expense of individuality, originality or traditional styles. Nor should they be asked to adopt designs which are unpopular with their customers or clients.

Nevertheless control of external appearance can be important especially for instance in environmentally sensitive areas such as national parks, areas of outstanding natural beauty, conservation areas and areas where the quality of environment is of a particularly high standard. Local planning authorities should reject designs which are out of scale or character with their surroundings. They should confine concern to those aspects of design which are significant for the aesthetic quality of the area. Only exceptionally should they control design details if the sensitive character of the area or the particular building justifies it. Even where such detailed control is exercised it should not be over fastidious in such matters as, for example, the precise shade of colour of bricks. They should be closely guided in such matters by their professionally qualified advisers. This is especially important where a building has been designed by an architect for a particular site. Design guides may have a useful role to play provided they are used as guidance and not as detailed rules.

Control of external appearance should only be exercised where there is a fully justified reason for doing so. If local planning authorities take proper account of this policy there should be fewer instances of protracted negotiations over the design of projects and a reduction in the number of appeals to the Secretaries of State on matters of design. When such appeals are made the Secretaries of State will be very much guided by the policy advice set out in this circular in determining them. (Circ 22/80, paras 19–21; repeated as Circ 31/85).

See also the comment in Circ 8/87 (para 61) on the design of new buildings in conservation areas, and the decision of the High Court in *Steinberg* v *Secretary of State*, at 7.6(*a*)

(d) Restoration of historic buildings as planning gain

It has already been noted that the preservation of a historic building may be a factor justifying the grant of planning permission for an otherwise unacceptable change in its use. This principle has in some cases been carried further, where the preservation of one building is only possible if funds are made available through the realisation of profits from another, otherwise unacceptable, development.

Thus in one case (*Brighton BC* v *Secretary of State for the Environment* (1978) 39 P & CR 46), a school sought permission to develop an unused area of one of their playing fields as a housing estate. On appeal, the decision to grant permission (against the policies of the development plan) was influenced by the desire of the school to realise sufficient profit from the sale of the site to allow them to refurbish the main school buildings, which were listed Grade II and in a conservation area.

The *Brighton* case was cited with approval in a more recent case, concerning the partial redevelopment of Covent Garden Opera House in London. Here the planning authority was satisfied that the restoration of the principal parts of the (Grade I) Opera House (only half of the cost of which could be raised by donations) justified the raising of finance by demolishing other listed buildings of less importance in order to carry out an otherwise unacceptable office development. The local residents objected, and challenged by way of judicial review the resolution of the authority to grant planning permission (*R* v *Westminster CC, ex p Monahan* [1988] JPL 557). Webster J in the High Court held that the fact that the finances made available from the commercial development would enable the improvements to be carried out was capable of being a material consideration, and could thus be taken into account by the authority. This decision was subsequently upheld by the Court of Appeal ((1988) *The Independent*, 20 October).

It may also be appropriate for a planning authority to seek by means of an agreement with the developer the restoration of an historic building as a screen for a proposed new building nearby (see Circ 23/83, para 12).

Chapter 8

Listed Building Consent

8.1 The need for listed building consent

(a) Introduction

An explanation has been given of how buildings are listed, and what is the extent of the listing. It has been shown that a building preservation notice confers upon a building for six months the same status as being listed. Merely to record buildings of merit is not however enough (except very occasionally) to save them; what, then is the extra protection given to listed buildings?

The previous chapter has already described the requirement for extra publicity to be given to planning applications for development affecting listed buildings, and for the extra care that is to be taken by planning authorities in processing such applications. Over and above this, however, is the need for almost all works to a listed building to be given separate *listed building consent* by the appropriate local planning authority. The 1971 Act provides that:

if a person executes or causes to be executed any works for the demolition of a listed building or for its alteration or extension in any manner which would affect its character as a building of special architectural or historic interest, and the works are not authorised . . . he shall be guilty of an offence (TCPA 1971, s 55(1)).

It should be noted that the carrying out of unauthorised works (that is, works for which listed building consent is needed but has not been obtained) is a criminal offence. This is in contrast to the carrying out of development for which planning permission is required but has not been obtained, which is only a breach of planning control—the criminal offence in that case only occurs if the planning authority chooses to serve an enforcement notice,

148

and the developer fails to comply with it. See Chapter 9 for a further discussion of unauthorised works.

It should also be borne in mind when considering which works need listed building consent that, as explained in detail in Chapter 2, a 'listed building' includes:

(1) the building itself;
(2) any object or structure fixed to it; and
(3) any freestanding object or structure that has been in its curtilage since 1948 (TCPA 1971, s 54(9), as amended by HPA 1986).

And of course a 'building' also includes any part of a building as so defined (TCPA 1971, s 290).

The need for consent for different categories of works to a listed building is summarised in Figure 8.1.

(b) Demolition

First, then, listed building consent is needed for the demolition of a listed building (TCPA 1971, s 55(1)). Given that a building includes part of a building, it logically follows that almost any works affecting it in any way—or any object or structure fixed to it or within its curtilage—must, at least in theory, include demo-lition, and therefore require consent. Note that there is no equi-valent in listed buildings legislation to the 'permitted development' mechanism whereby some minor works are granted planning permission automatically (see 7.3). Certainly listed building consent would normally be needed under this heading for works such as the demolition of an internal wall or front garden railings, or the removal of a fireplace, an external or internal plaster cornice or a wrought-iron balcony. It was held on appeal that consent should have been obtained for the removal of pilaster mouldings, even though accidental ([1981] JPL 443).

In addition, where proposed works include any demolition, notice must be given before starting to the Royal Commission on Historical Monuments (TCPA 1971, s 55(2)(*b*); and see 8.4(*d*)). In many cases, the local authority and others (such as neighbours and various statutory authorities) may have to be notified under requirements of the Building Act 1984, ss 80–83 although note that this does not apply in Inner London. Planning permission, on the other hand, is not normally required for demolition as such (see 7.2(*d*)), although it will of course be needed if there are any alterations or other building or rebuilding works associated with the demolition.

Figure 8.1 Works to a listed building: consents needed

Type of work	Listed building consent	Planning permission
1 Total demolition of building	Always needed	Never needed in practice (see 7.2(*d*))
2 Partial demolition	Always needed	Only needed if associated with other development
3 External alteration or extension of building (not 'permitted development'; see 7.3)	Always needed	Always needed
4 External alteration or extension of building (permitted development)	Needed where the works affect the character of the building as one of special interest	Needed only where required by an Article 4 direction (see 7.4) or by a condition on a previous permission
5 Minor external alteration to building (not 'development'; see 7.2(*a*))	Needed only where the works affect the special character of the building	Never needed
6 Alteration to interior of building	Needed only where the works affect the special character of the building	Never needed
7 Demolition of building in 'curtilage' of listed building (see 2.5(*e*))	Always needed	As for 1 and 2 above
8 Alteration or extension of building in curtilage of listed building	Needed where the works affect the special character of the 'building' (that is, the listed building itself plus the curtilage building)	As for 3 to 6 above
9 Erection of new building in curtilage of listed building (not touching it)	Not needed	Almost always needed
10 Works to a listed religious building	Not often needed; see 13.2	As for 1 to 6 above
11 Works to a listed scheduled monument	Never needed; but note that scheduled monument consent will almost always be needed (see 14.3)	As for 1 to 6 above

There are however two practical limitations to this. The first is the general principle that the law is not concerned with trifles (*de minimis non curat lex*); and works that are genuinely trivial can therefore be reasonably carried out without consent. But caution is needed here—what may seem trivial to a property owner or developer may be of monumental importance to an enthusiastic conservationist or local authority. Whether or not any particular works proposed are substantial enough to come within control can only be finally determined by the courts; but to embark on litigation in such a case would almost always be absurd. If in doubt, therefore, an owner should seek the advice of the authority, or to be on the safe side apply for consent anyway—there is no fee for listed building consent applications.

The second limitation is that proposed works may more sensibly be categorised as the 'alteration or extension' of a listed building, rather than 'demolition' as such. If they are, they will only require listed building consent if they alter or extend the building in such a way as to affect its character. As to the difference between these categories, see 8.1(*d*).

The other point to be considered here, related to this second limitation, arises from an ambiguity in the drafting of s 55(1) of the Act. The description of the types of work for which listed building consent is required is as follows:

the demolition of a listed building or . . . its alteration or extension in any manner which would affect its character . . .

It is unfortunately not clear whether the limitation ('in any manner' etc) refers just to the 'alteration or extension' or also to the 'demolition'—and there is no punctuation to help either. Commonsense would tend to suggest that the limitation does not apply to 'demolition'; if the intention had been otherwise, the phrase should have read 'the demolition, alteration or extension of a listed building in any manner . . .' In practice, too, there will not be many works of demolition which will not alter the character of a building—although, since the 'building' includes some structures in its curtilage, it is possible to envisage works which would clearly be 'demolition' (the removal of a pre-war potting shed within the curtilage of a country house but at some distance from it, for example) but which might equally clearly not affect the character of the 'building' (that is, the listed building itself plus all the buildings and structures in its curtilage; s 54(9)).

On balance, therefore, it would seem that listed building

consent will be required for any works which can be described as 'demolition' (whether of the whole building or merely part of it) as opposed to 'alteration', unless they are so trivial as to be capable of being ignored.

(c) Alterations and extensions

Listed building consent is required for any alterations or extensions to a listed building 'if they would affect its character as a building of special architectural or historic interest' (TCPA 1971, s 55(1)). This covers a larger spectrum of works than those for which planning permission is required. It includes in particular almost all the types of works which are defined in the GDO as being 'permitted development' (and which do not therefore normally need to be the subject of a planning application; see 7.3). It also includes many works which are not 'development' at all either because they affect only the interior of the building or because they do not 'materially' affect its external appearance (see 7.2(*b*)). The grade of the listed building is irrelevant in this context.

What types of works are sufficient to 'affect the character' of a listed building as a building of special architectural or historic interest? The phrase is a fairly general one, and is open to wide interpretation. By way of example, it has been held by the Secretary of State in recent appeals that listed building consent was required for the erection of shutters ([1981] JPL 607), the installation of new double glazed windows ([1988] JPL 194), the replacement of Victorian stained glass with clear glazing ([1984] JPL 899), the removal of a partition and other internal alterations to a smoke room in a public house ([1983] JPL 751), and the painting of stonework ([1979] JPL 782; and see 8.1(*e*)).

It is perhaps important to repeat here that the description (if any) of the building in the statutory list does not necessarily include all of its features of merit. Thus to alter a feature not noted in the description of a building, and in particular the interior, might still be to affect its character, and therefore require listed building consent. Note that, contrary to a popular misconception, this applies regardless of the grade of the building (it does not just apply to buildings of Grade I or II*).

On the other hand, in considering the character of 'the building' as one of special interest, what is at issue is the character of the whole building—that is, the whole of the building listed in its own right plus all the pre-1948 structures and objects in its curtilage (s 54(9), as amended by HPA 1986), and not just that of either the main building by itself or the particular structure or building to be altered. However, in the case of a listed building set in large grounds, presumably to alter a minor structure (such as an outhouse) at some distance from either the main building or any subsidiary buildings that are intrinsically of any interest would not affect the character of the whole, and would not therefore require consent.

As with demolition works (see above), the courts are the ultimate arbiter of whether proposed works would affect the character of a listed building sufficiently to require listed building consent. In practice, however, commonsense will usually supply the answer—consent will only very exceptionally be needed, for example, for very minor works such as rewiring or redecorating. But, again, remember that sincerely held views on such matters can differ strongly; and remember, too, that failure to obtain listed building consent when it is required can end up in a fine, or worse. If in any doubt, anyone contemplating virtually any works to a listed building (of any grade) should seek advice from the planning authority, or just submit an application to be safe.

It should also be borne in mind that, if listed building consent is sought and obtained for proposed works, their cost will not be subject to value added tax (see 6.8(*a*)). This may be a powerful incentive to outweigh any delay involved in applying for consent.

Listed building consent will not incidentally be required for the erection of a new building within the curtilage or affecting the setting of a listed building, unless it is physically attached to the existing building, since the definition of a listed building does not include the ground (*Cotswold DC* v *Secretary of State and Pearson* [1985] JPL 407; and see the appeal at [1984] JPL 55). The new building will of course usually require planning permission, and the special procedures as to publicity for such proposals (see 7.5(*b*)) will apply. For similar reasons, it was held on appeal that the placing of two strips of York stone paving in the front garden of a listed house did not need consent ([1975] JPL 690).

(d) The distinction between demolition and alteration

Listed building consent is needed for works to a listed building if they involve either:

(1) its demolition; or

(2) its alteration or extension in any manner which affects its

character as a building of special interest (TCPA 1971, s 55(1)).

(This adopts the interpretation of the Act explained in 8.1(*b*)). Accordingly, as noted above, it may sometimes be important to decide whether works are 'demolition' or whether they are 'alteration or extension', in order to determine whether listed building consent is required.

In addition, the distinction between 'demolition' and 'alteration or extension' may be important in other contexts:

(1) to determine the correct procedure for handling applications and appeals, in particular, the degree of publicity required (see 8.4);

(2) to determine whether or not the Royal Commission on Historical Monuments has to be allowed to record the building (see 8.4(*d*));

(3) to determine the availability of compensation for the refusal of listed building consent (see 8.10(*a*)); and

(4) to determine whether or not conservation area consent is needed for proposed works to an unlisted building in a conservation area (see 10.1).

The problem is considered in Circ 8/87 (at para 81):

It is often asked whether works which do not involve total demolition of a building should nevertheless be regarded as 'works for the demolition of a building'. The Secretary of State cannot give an authoritative interpretation of the law, but draws attention to section 290(1) in which 'building' is defined as including any part of a building. The demolition of a part of a building should thus be regarded as the demolition of a building for the purposes of section 55 (and also section 277A).

This wording is identical with that of Circ 23/77, para 66, which was considered totally unhelpful in *R* v *North Hertfordshire DC, ex parte Sullivan* [1981] JPL 752 at 753. The difficulty is that almost every alteration or extension includes some demolition, but (in the scarcely more helpful words of Comyn J at 754) 'not every piece of work by way of alteration or extension necessarily amounted to demolition'. That case involved the extension of a Grade II listed farm house by the erection of a new addition. 'He [Comyn J] thought any court would be prepared to overlook and be prepared to treat as an extension rather than demolition something small, by way of interference with a listed building, but certainly not anything as elaborate as the case here shown in the plans and shown in the affidavit.'

A few months after *North Hertfordshire*, however, Webster J in the same court took the opposite line, in *Long and Long* v *Secretary of State and North Norfolk DC* [1981] JPL 886. In this case, works were to be carried out to a barn which was within the curtilage of a Grade II listed house, and thus listed itself. Planning permission and listed building consent had (in effect) been given for alteration of the barn, but not for its demolition. However, it transpired that, because of its poor construction, it had first to be demolished almost to the ground and rebuilt to the altered design. 'He [Webster J] considered that it was possible that the word "demolition" in [section 55] did not necessarily include demolition followed by immediate rebuilding, but he did not arrive at any conclusion about it. . . . even if an offence had been committed, which he doubted, it must have been an offence of the most technical kind' (at p 889). It is questionable whether Ms Sullivan (the owner of the neighbouring property who instigated the proceedings in *North Hertfordshire*) would have agreed that such an offence was merely 'technical'.

It seems in the light of the above that any owner faced with this problem should obtain the advice of the local planning authority. Any authority in doubt should err on the side of caution, to avoid being faced with the kind of challenge which succeeded in overturning the decision of *North Hertfordshire*.

(e) Painting

One particular category of work that has recently come before the courts is external painting.

There can be little doubt that painting a hitherto unpainted listed building (or a hitherto unpainted part of one) affects its character, and thus requires listed building consent. Thus, as noted above, it has been held on appeal ([1979] JPL 782) that consent should have been obtained for the painting of stonework. In one case in Lincolnshire, the owner of a listed stone building who had painted it red was successfully prosecuted in the magistrates' court, and had to remove the paint ([1984] JPL 578).

Repainting existing paintwork in a different colour can be more difficult. In a 1972 appeal (noted at [1972] JPL 650), the Secretary of State considered that listed building consent should have been obtained for the repainting of a front door of a listed building (22 Royal Crescent in Bath, listed Grade I). On the planning merits, however, he went on to find that, since the repainting, the colour of the door had faded to such an innocuous shade of pale primrose yellow that it no longer affected the building's character. Since the effect of time and weathering had been such as to eliminate that particular breach of listed building control, the listed building enforcement notice was suitably varied.

In *Windsor and Maidenhead RBC v Secretary of State* [1988] JPL 410, on the other hand, the offending paintwork was rather more noticeable. A listed building enforcement notice had been served on the owners of 2 and 2A Clarance Crescent in Windsor alleging a breach of listed building control by 'painting the exterior of the building in colours of deep pink with black detailing on, *inter alia*, pilasters, string course, window cills, window frames, the base area of the main wall on the front elevation and the front porch'. The inspector reported that 'It is my view that the character of the appeal premises has been altered to a point which constitutes a contravention of section 55 of the Act'. However, the Secretary of State in his decision disagreed:

There are occasions when the painting of the facade of a listed building is undoubtedly an alteration which affects its character because it obliterates features of interest, eg brickwork, timbering or lettering or other details which are architecturally or historically important. In such cases, consent is, in the opinion of the Secretary of State, needed. In the present case he notes that the facade of the building was already painted and the action of repainting cannot therefore be said to have constituted works of alteration (p 411).

This echoed his advice as it then was in Circ 8/87 (para 93). But Mann J considered (at p 414) that the critical question is whether the repainting affects the character of the building as a building of special interest as it did here. He did not think that there was any sensible distinction to be drawn between painting and repainting, and accordingly remitted the matter to the Secretary of State with a direction to dismiss the appeal and uphold the enforcement notice. Paragraph 93 of Circ 8/87 has subsequently been amended (by Circ 18/88) to reflect this judgment.

It is submitted that this decision is obviously correct. It makes it clear that the need for consent turns on the extent to which the painting or repainting affects the character of the building. Thus in a terrace of white stucco town houses, to paint one house cream would probably not need listed building consent; but to paint one scarlet would need consent—and would probably not get it!

Painting and repainting are both permitted development (GDO 1988, Sched 2, Part 2, Class C); and if the proposed repainting could be shown to increase the value of the building, compensation would be payable (under TCPA 1971, s 171) if listed building consent were refused. In cases such as the Windsor one, it would seem to be difficult to prove that such an increase in value was likely.

Painting the interior of a building can never be development, and can therefore never require planning permission (s 22(2)(*a*)). But to paint the interior of a listed building, or even some feature of the interior, may require listed building consent, if it affects the character of the building. Thus the painting of wooden panelling at Sutton Place, Surrey (listed Grade I) was held by the Secretary of State, disagreeing with his inspector, to be an alteration requiring consent, although he agreed with the inspector that consent should be granted, as the painting unified the appearance of the panelling, which was of mixed dates and styles, and some of which was of poor quality (see [1984] JPL 899 at 902, 904).

(f) Repairs

Repairs and restoration works to a listed building may well require listed building consent if they comprise alterations which would affect its special character. The fact that the works may be required by a dangerous structures order or repair notice is irrelevant (Building Act 1984, ss 77, 79; London Building Acts (Amendment) Act 1939, ss 62, 65, 69; final subsections inserted by HPA 1986; see 5.8(*b*)). It is also irrelevant that the proposed works may have been the subject of an offer of a grant, from whatever source.

Careful thought needs to be given to the precise way in which the repairs are carried out, and the materials used. If the details of the works are appropriate, then not only is listed building consent more likely to be granted, but it may not be needed at all—since a repair using materials virtually identical to those used in the original building and carried out to the same design can scarcely be said to affect its character.

On the other hand, the carrying out of repairs using new materials may constitute works affecting the character of the building, and may therefore require consent. In *Bath CC* v *Secretary of State and Grosvenor Hotel* [1983] JPL 737, for example, it was agreed by all the parties involved, including the owner of the (Grade I) building, that the replacement of a leaking roof comprising some Welsh slates and some asbestos 'slates' with a new roof of just asbestos slates was an alteration requiring consent. It was also held in this case that the supposed urgency of the works in no way obviated the need for consent at least to be applied for before works were started. If it had been, the owners would have immediately become aware both that listed building consent would only be granted for reroofing entirely in Welsh slates, and that financial assistance might be available to assist with the cost of the works. See 9.4(*g*) for further details of this case.

As to cleaning and restoration, the view of the Secretary of State is that 'simple cleaning of a listed building using water would not normally require listed building consent but other methods or more extensive restoration work might well need consent' (Circ 8/87, para 93). This is probably correct, and means that methods of cleaning such as sand blasting should only be carried out after consultation with the local planning authority or, in more significant cases, the Historic Buildings and Monuments Commission or the Welsh Office.

(g) Urgent works

Works may sometimes have to be carried out to a listed building as a matter of urgency, either by way of emergency repairs, or to forestall imminent collapse. This might involve the demolition of a whole building which is suddenly found to be unsafe; or it might mean something less drastic (for example, hacking off the remainder of a stucco cornice after part had fallen onto the street below). Such works will require listed building consent just as in any other case—that is, if they amount to demolition or if they affect the special character of the building. The fact that the works may be required by a dangerous structures order or similar notice is irrelevant (see above).

Wherever possible, listed building consent should be obtained, or at least applied for, in advance. If there should be any subsequent dispute, the application will be a useful indication, if not proof, that the applicant is not attempting to flout the law. The conservation officer of the local authority may be able to give some guidance on how the works could best be carried out.

In some cases, however, the urgency may be such that it is not practical to obtain consent in advance. It will then be necessary to obtain listed building consent to retain the works which have already been carried out (TCPA 1971, s 55(2A), inserted by LGPLA 1980). In all cases, written notice (even if not a formal application for consent) must be given to the local planning authority 'as soon as reasonably practicable', either before or after the works, to avoid any possible liability to criminal prosecution. Such

notice must justify in detail why the works are being or were carried out, and in particular:
(1) that they were urgently necessary in the interests of safety or health or for the preservation of the building;
(2) that the same result could not be achieved by repair works or temporary support or shelter; and
(3) that the works were limited to the minimum measures immediately necessary

(TCPA 1971, s 55(6), as substituted by HPA 1986; and see 9.2(c)).

8.2 Special cases

(a) Churches

Churches have always been to a large extent outside the need for listed building consent. However, the rules were marginally changed in 1987 (TCPA 1971, s 58AA, inserted by HPA 1986). The current position is described in detail in Chapter 13, but is broadly as follows:
(1) listed building consent is almost never required for works to a listed Church of England church, whether it is in use or redundant;
(2) consent is only required for works to a listed church of any other Christian denomination if the religious use of the building has ceased;
(3) it is likely that the law will in due course be changed so that consent will be required for works to a listed church of any other Christian denomination if they involve the loss of any of its significant architectural features; and
(4) it is uncertain whether consent is required for works to listed religious buildings of other faiths.

(b) Scheduled monuments

It is possible for a listed building also to be a scheduled monument under the AMAAA 1979. Thus some agricultural buildings, such as medieval barns or dovecotes, are both scheduled and listed, as are some bridges, urban buildings (for example, market halls and guildhalls) and, increasingly, industrial monuments.

Almost any works to a scheduled monument require scheduled monument consent (see 14.3). However, if the monument is listed, listed building consent would not be needed as well (TCPA 1971, s 56(1)(b), as amended by AMAAA 1979).

This avoids duplication of controls. It is in some cases unfortunate that, since applications for scheduled monument consent are determined solely by the Secretary of State, the local planning authority conservation officers, who may have considerable local knowledge, are not necessarily involved.

(c) Works by Government departments

Buildings owned and occupied by the Crown, including departments of central Government, health authorities, and the Metropolitan Police, may be, and frequently are, listed (TCPA 1971, s 266(1)(c)).

Listed building consent is not however required for works carried out by the Crown to its own listed buildings. Instead, the developing department (that is, the Government department or whatever) submits a notice to the local planning authority that it is intending to carry out the works, under the arrangement described in Part IV of Circ 18/84 (para 9). The authority then deals with the notification as if it were a normal application for listed building consent, and advertises it in the press, notifies the national amenity societies and so on, in the usual way (see the remainder of this chapter for details). Any objections received are passed to the developing department, who will then consider whether to proceed. Any unresolved dispute between that department and the planning authority is referred to the Department of the Environment, who will either deal with the matter on the basis of written representations, or hold a non-statutory public inquiry (see Circ 18/84, Part IV, paras 31–3 and 25).

Listed building consent is however required before a listed building can be lawfully demolished, altered or extended by the owner of any other interest in Crown land (such as a lessee or licensee) (s 266(1)(b)). In such a case, the relevant Crown department would need to be consulted by the owner under the normal arrangements for notifying other owners (TCP (LBCA) Regs 1988, reg 6; and see 8.3(d).

Where a Government department wishes to dispose of its interest in land containing a listed building, and considers that the land would be more valuable if the building were altered or demolished, it may seek listed building consent from the local planning authority (TCPA 1984, s 1). Such an application is dealt with in the same way as if it were made by any other owner.

(d) Works by the Historic Buildings and Monuments Commission

When the Commission was first set up, it was provided that it was to have the same status as a Government department in respect of works carried out on behalf of the Secretary of State—that is, works to any monuments, buildings or land owned by the Department of the Environment which it is managing on behalf of the department (NHA 1983, s 34(2), Sched 3, para 2(3); Circ 18/84, Part IV, para 2). Accordingly, where it would otherwise need listed building consent for such works, it will notify the planning authority under the procedure in Circ 18/84 (see above).

Where it needs consent for any other works—where, for example, it is seeking approval for works to be carried out to buildings which it is proposing to purchase—an application for listed building consent will be needed. Planning authorities have been directed to refer direct to the Secretary of State for his decision 'all applications for listed building consent made by [the Commission] in respect of the carrying out of works to any building which is in its ownership, guardianship or otherwise under its control or of which it is the prospective purchaser' (direction in Circ 8/87, para 102). Authorities should advertise such applications in the usual way and forward any comments received, together with their own comments, to the Department of the Environment regional office.

In Wales, on the other hand, Cadw—Welsh Historic Monuments is an integral part of the Welsh Office. Works carried out by Cadw to its listed buildings are therefore in the same position as works carried out by any other Government department (see WO Circ 61/81, para 73).

(e) Works by local authorities

A local authority, unlike a central Government department, must apply for listed building consent before it can demolish, alter or extend any listed building (TCPA 1971, s 271, substituted by TCAA 1974; TCPA 1971, Sched 21, Part VI). All the principles outlined above regarding the need for listed building consent apply to works by local authorities as to those by any other property owner. The difference is that applications are made to the Secretary of State (TCP (LBCA) Regs 1987, reg 13(2)), that is, the authority may not grant itself 'deemed listed building consent'.

This incidentally means that where an authority wishes to dispose of a listed building on the open market, it may grant itself planning permission for a change of use; but if the change involves any alterations to the building, listed building consent (and planning permission where required) must still be obtained from the Secretary of State.

The application for listed building consent is made in the form of an application to the authority, and is deemed to have been referred to the Secretary of State under the call-in provisions (see 8.5(*d*)). The authority must therefore advertise the application on site and in the press, and elsewhere as it deems fit, and notify the national amenity societies where appropriate (see 8.4(*c*), (*d*)). It must then send to the Secretary of State with the application any representations received (reg 13(3)–(6)). An application by a district council is made direct to the Secretary of State, and one by a county council is made to the district council, who pass it on to him (reg 13(7)).

The Secretary of State will then reach a decision, after holding a public inquiry if the authority wishes (reg 13(3); TCPA 1971, Sched 11, para 4). 'The Secretary of State is particularly concerned about the number of applications to demolish which are being submitted by local authorities in respect of their own buildings and asks them to set an example to other owners by making a diligent search for a new use and, if necessary, a new owner (such as a building preservation trust), before seeking consent to demolish' (Circ 8/87, para 101).

Local authorities are also under a special duty to preserve any listed buildings (and indeed any 'features of interest' even if not listed) when they are in the process of appropriating, developing and disposing of land for general planning purposes (TCPA 1971, s 125). This might apply where, for example, an authority is assembling land for a town centre redevelopment scheme.

8.3 Applications for listed building consent

(a) Sources of procedural rules

The rules of procedure regarding applications for listed building consent are to be found in several places. First, Sched 11 to the Act provides the basic rules (TCPA 1971, s 56(6)).

Secondly, that Schedule gives the Secretary of State powers to make regulations setting out detailed procedures (TCPA 1971, Sched 11, para 1(1A), substituted by HPA 1986). The regulations currently in force are the TCP (Listed Buildings and Buildings in Conservation Areas) Regulations 1987 (SI 1987 No 349; referred to throughout this book as TCP (LBCA) Regs 1987). These came into force on 1 April 1987, and replace Regulations of the same name made in 1977. The differences are not substantial, except in respect to conservation areas (see Chapter 10).

Thirdly, the Secretary of State is also empowered to give directions exempting certain types of application from compliance with some of those procedures (Sched 11, para 7, as amended by LGA 1985 and HPA 1986). The directions currently in force in England are included in Circ 8/87. These replace, and in some cases significantly differ from, previous directions given in Circs 23/77 and 23/84 and in the letter to London authorities in March 1986, and the direction issued to the London Docklands Development Corporation in July 1986. The directions in force in Wales are in WO Circ 61/81.

(b) Local planning authorities

Applications for listed building consent, outside national parks and the Broads, are determined by the following authorities:

(1) *in urban development areas except Cardiff Bay*: the urban development corporation (see 1.3(*a*));

(2) *elsewhere in metropolitan counties*: the district or borough council (TCPA 1971, s 1(1)(*b*), substituted by LGA 1985);

(3) *elsewhere in Greater London*: the borough council (s 1(1)(*c*), substituted by LGA 1985); and

(4) *elsewhere*: the district or borough council (s 1(1)(*a*), substituted by LGA 1985; LGA 1972, Sched 16, para 25).

This will also be the authority to whom an application should initially be made.

Although applications are thus in most cases to be determined formally by district or borough planning authorities, in some areas the county planning authority may provide a team of staff with appropriate specialist skills—since the range of advice needed is often beyond the resources of a single authority (particularly in the case of a small council whose area contains few listed buildings). In practice, therefore, some district authorities refer to the county council almost all applications; others refer none. In addition, authorities (of either tier) are of course able to call upon the advice of the Historic Buildings and Monuments Commission or the Welsh Office in significant or difficult cases, even where they are not obliged to consult them formally. Some authorities obtain specialist assistance from private consultants.

The Secretary of State does have power (under LGA 1972,

Sched 16, paras 58. 59) to require district planning authorities to submit for his approval details of the arrangements they have made for carrying out their functions with respect to listed buildings and conservation areas, and to make appropriate directions if he is not satisfied. He has stated (in Circ 8/87, para 7) that he does not intend to issue any such formal directions, but that he hopes that 'within the resources available to them, authorities will continue to ensure that they obtain the best possible advice'.

In national parks, an application for listed building consent (and indeed any accompanying application for planning permission) should be made initially to the district or borough council, unless it relates to a building in a metropolitan county (TCP (LBCA) Regs 1987, reg 7(1)). That council will then pass it straight on to the authority that will determine it. This will be the Peak District Joint Planning Board, the Lake District Special Planning Board, or the county council in any other national park (LGA 1972, s 182(4), amended by LGA 1985, and Sched 17, paras 1, 3, 20). If the application relates to a building in a part of the Peak District within a metropolitan county, it should be made direct to the Joint Planning Board (TCP (LBCA) Regs 1987, reg 7(2)).

In the Broads, applications for listed building consent will actually be determined by the new Broads Authority (TCPA 1971, s 273A, inserted by NSBA 1988). It is however likely that they will be processed by the relevant district councils, and that they should initially be submitted to them (LGA 1972, s 101; s 265A(1)(c), inserted by NSBA 1988). At the time of going to press, however, the detailed delegation arrangements had yet to be finalised.

Normal listed building control applies in enterprise zones and simplified planning zones.

(c) Submission of applications

Before submitting a formal application for listed building consent, a prospective applicant should always consider whether it might be fruitful to have a preliminary meeting with the planning authority. Wherever possible, such a meeting should be with the conservation officer of the authority which will deal with the application, and it may usefully involve officers of the county authority or the Commission as well (see above). It could be either on site or in the authority's offices. In the latter case, detailed photographs of the buildings should be available. The timing of a pre-application meeting needs thought. It should be after sufficient details of the proposed works have been considered for the scheme to be clear, but before it has become unchangeable.

The quality of the advice received will vary widely. In Essex, Hampshire and Derbyshire, for example, there are a large number of officers with specialised training and experience; and the London Division of the Commission (and its predecessor, the Historic Buildings Division of the Greater London Council) has always had a very high reputation. In Northumberland, on the other hand, there are apparently no specialist conservation officers either in the county council or in any of the district councils. A new professional organisation, the Association of Conservation Officers, was formed in 1983 to promote good practice.

The actual application must be submitted to the appropriate local planning authority—generally the district or borough council or urban development corporation (see above)—on the relevant form issued by it (see Figure 8.2). Three copies of the form should be submitted (TCP (LBCA) Regs 1987, reg 3(1)).

The application form must be accompanied by three copies of:

(a) sufficient particulars to identify the building to which it relates, including a plan; and

(b) such other plans and drawings as are necessary to describe the works which are the subject of the application (TCPA 1971, Sched 11, para 1(1), substituted by HPA 1986).

This will include detailed drawings of any alterations proposed (including specifications of materials to be used in any new works or repairs). In addition, 'it is helpful if applications . . . are accompanied by photographs of all elevations if consent is sought for demolition, or for the part affected by alterations and extensions (including the interior). The photographs need not be taken professionally, but should clearly show the architectural details of the building' (Circ 8/87, para 76).

In certain cases it may also be sensible for an applicant to submit a financial appraisal of the proposed works (see 8.7(c)).

There is no fee payable for an application for listed building consent. But if an application for planning permission is submitted at the same time, the correct fee (if any) should be submitted with it, otherwise both applications may be delayed.

(d) Ownership certificates

The application should also be accompanied by one copy of a certificate indicating the ownership of the building (TCP (LBCA) Regs 1987, reg 6). This will be one of the following:

Figure 8.2 Application for listed building consent

Please read the accompanying notes before completing any part of this form

Form LB1

Application for listed building consent

Town and Country Planning Act 1971

Application no.	For official use only
Date received	

Three completed copies of this form and plans should be sent to the City, Borough or District Council.

1. Applicant (in block capitals)

Name ..... UNIVERSAL COMPUTER PRODUCTS PLC

Address ..... UCP HOUSE, THE BROADWAY,

..... LONDON W15 7EX

Tel. No. 01-334 5778

Agent (if any) to whom correspondence should be sent (in block capitals)

Name ..... OXBRIDGE DESIGN GROUP

Address ..... ABBEY CHAMBERS, HIGH STREET,

..... OXBRIDGE OB1 3QZ

Tel. No. ..... OXBRIDGE 242167

2. Full address or location of the building to which this application relates.

142 LONDON ROAD, OXBRIDGE

3. Particulars of the applicant's interest in the building (e.g. owner, lessee, prospective purchaser, etc.).

Owner of 99-year lease expiring 25th December 2086

4. Describe briefly the proposed works, (e.g. demolition, alteration, extension) and give the reasons why the works are considered necessary.

Internal alterations and refurbishment of main building; demolition of 1930s extension; construction of new extension at rear

5. List of drawings and plans submitted with the application.

Plans   LR 1 - 4   Details   LR 11 - 14
Elevations LR 5 - 8   Photographs LR 15
Sections LR 9, 10

Note: The plans should be sufficient to identify the building and all alterations and extensions should be shown in detail; the works should also be shown in relation to any adjacent buildings.

I/We hereby apply for listed building consent to execute the works described in this application and the accompanying plans and drawings and in accordance therewith.

Date   6th June 1988

Signed   A. Harcourt

On behalf of   Universal Computer Products Plc
(insert applicant's name if signed by an agent)

The Town and Country Planning (Listed Buildings and Buildings in Conservation Areas) Regulations 1977 provide that an application for listed building consent shall not be entertained unless it is accompanied by one of 4 certificates. If you are the sole owner of all the land, certificate A, which is printed below, is appropriate: only one copy need be completed. If you cannot complete certificate A you will have to give notice to the other owners and complete certificate B. Certificates C and D are appropriate only if you have made efforts to trace the other owners and have failed. The forms of these notices and certificates are as prescribed in the Regulations.

Town and Country Planning Act 1971

Certificate A

I hereby certify that no person other than * ~~XXXXX~~ the applicant   was an owner (a) of the building to which the application relates at the beginning of the period of 20 days before the date of the accompanying application.

Signed   A. Harcourt

*On behalf of   Oxbridge Design Group

Date   6th June 1988

Note: (a) "Owner" means a person having a freehold interest or a leasehold interest the unexpired term of which was not less than 7 years.

*Delete where inappropriate

A The applicant is the only owner of the building.

B The applicant has informed all the other owners of the building of the application.

C The applicant has informed all the other known owners of the building of the application, and has taken reasonable steps (in practice, usually by inserting a notice in the local press) to notify the unknown owners of it.

D The applicant does not know of any of the owners of the building, but has taken reasonable steps to notify them of the application.

The 'owner' in this context means anyone who, twenty days before the date of the application, had a freehold interest in the building, or a leasehold interest with at least seven years unexpired. The certificates and notices to be used are set out as Sched 2 to the 1987 Regulations.

To submit a false certificate deliberately or recklessly is a criminal offence, punishable by a fine of up to level 3 (TCPA 1971, Sched 11, para 2(2), amended by the Criminal Justice Act 1982 and the Criminal Penalties (Increase) Order 1984). The submission of an incorrect certificate will only rarely invalidate any consent eventually granted (*Main* v *Swansea CC* (1985) 49 P & CR 26).

The authority must not determine the application until twenty-one days have elapsed since the last of the owners was informed of the application or since it was advertised in the press (whichever was the later). When it does determine the application, it must also take into account any representations made by any owners of the building (as defined above) made within the twenty-one-day period, and notify them of the outcome.

8.4 Procedure following the submission of an application

Before even starting to consider whether to grant or refuse listed building consent, the local planning authority must give wide publicity to the application. This should enable comments to be made both by those immediately affected (in particular those living and working in nearby properties) and by local and national bodies with access to specialist knowledge and wider experience. The various statutory requirements are summarised in Figure 8.3.

Figure 8.3 Listed building consent applications: publicity and consultation

A England (outside Greater London)
Grade I or II* building

Demolition	A B C D E F
Alteration or extension	A B E F

Grade II building

Total demolition	A B C D E
Partial demolition:	
most cases (see 8.4(*e*))	A B C D E
other cases	A B C D
Alteration or extension affecting exterior of building:	
where grant has been offered or is being considered	A B E
other cases	A B
Internal alterations:	
where grant has been offered or is being considered	E
other cases	(none)

B Greater London (except the Docklands UDC area)
Grade I or II* building

Demolition	A B C D F G
Alteration or extension	A B F G

Grade II building

Total demolition:	A B C D F G
Partial demolition:	
most cases (see 8.4(*f*), (*e*))	A B C D F G
other cases	A B C D F
Alteration or extension affecting exterior of building	A B F
Internal alteration	F

C Wales
Grade I or II* building

Demolition	A B C D H
Alteration or extension	A B H

Grade II building

Total or partial demolition	A B C D H
Alteration or extension affecting exterior of building	A B H
Internal alterations:	
where grant has been offered or is being considered	H
other cases	(none)

Key
A Local planning authority (LPA) to place notice on site (see 8.4(*b*))
B LPA to place advertisement in local newspaper (see 8.4(*b*))
C LPA to notify national amenity societies (see 8.4(*c*))
D LPA to notify Royal Commission on Historical Monuments (see 8.4(*d*))
E LPA to notify Secretary of State (DOE Regional Office), unless it intends to refuse application (see 8.4(*e*), (*h*))
F LPA to notify Historic Buildings and Monuments Commission (HBMC) (see 8.4(*e*), (*f*))
G HBMC to notify Secretary of State (see 8.4(*f*)), unle⁻ it intends to direct LPA to refuse application
H LPA to notify Secretary of State (Cadw-Welsh Historic Monuments), unless it intends to refuse application (see 8.4(*b*))

For applications in the London Docklands area, see 8.4(*g*). References to grants refer only to grants under the HBAMA 1953 (see 6.2(*a*)).

(a) Acknowledgment of application

The authority is to acknowledge receipt of the application immediately (TCP (LBCA) Regs 1987, reg 3(2) and Sched 1, Part I).

It must then check that the application is valid—that is, that it contains the required forms, and sufficient supporting material (drawings, photographs and other details as appropriate, see 8.3(*c*)). It may then ask the applicant for any further details it requires (TCPA 1971, Sched 11, para 1(1); TCP (LBCA) Regs 1987, reg 3(3)).

(b) Publicity by planning authority

The authority must publicise any application for listed building consent affecting a building of Grade I or II*, and any application which affects the exterior of a Grade II building, by inserting a notice in the local press and one on or near the building (TCP (LBCA) Regs 1987, reg 5(1), (3)). Each notice must state where the application (including any plans and photographs submitted) can be inspected. In the case of a listed building in large grounds, it would obviously be prudent for the authority to erect a notice at the boundary of a site as well as on the building itself.

The authority must not determine the application until at least twenty-one days have elapsed since the second of the two notices was published or erected. When it does determine it, it must take into account any representations made as a result of the notices within the twenty-one-day period.

(c) Notification to national amenity societies

The planning authority must notify the major national amenity societies of any application to demolish all or part of a listed building (of whatever grade), as soon as it is received (TCPA 1971, Sched 11, para 7(2), (3); direction in Circ 8/87, para 81). The societies which must be consulted in this way are the following:

The Ancient Monuments Society (St Andrew-by-the-Wardrobe, Queen Victoria Street, London EC4V 5DE; tel 01–236 3934);

The Council for British Archaeology (112 Kennington Road, London SE11 6RE; tel 01-582 0494);

The Georgian Group (37 Spital Square, London E1 6DY; tel 01-377 1722);

The Society for the Protection of Ancient Buildings (37 Spital Square, London E1 6DY; tel 01-377 1644); and

The Victorian Society (1 Priory Gardens, Bedford Park, London W4 1TT; tel 01-994 1019).

It might also be helpful for authorities to notify the Thirties Society (3 Park Square West, London NW1 4LJ; tel 01-381 9797) in appropriate cases, even though they are not on the official list.

Note that these addresses apply to applications in Wales as well as to those in England. The corresponding direction applying there is to be found in WO Circ 61/81, para 52.

The notification should include a copy of the relevant entry in the statutory list describing the building concerned, and should include appropriate supporting information. Clearly, where the application is, for example, for consent to demolish a Georgian building, it would be appropriate to send full details to the Georgian Society, but only a brief note to the Victorian Society. This can in some cases be a valuable means of bringing informed and articulate professional opinion and comment to bear on a particular proposal. The societies must also be informed of the outcome of all such applications.

As to the distinction between 'demolition' and 'alteration or extension', see 8.1(*d*); and note that the case of *R* v *North Hertfordshire DC* [1981] JPL 752, mentioned there, arose because of the contention of a neighbour that the planning authority should have notified the national amenity societies of an application for the 'extension' of a listed building. It was held in the High Court that in the circumstances of that case, the extension did involve sufficient demolition of the existing structure to amount to demolition of part of it, and that the societies should therefore have been notified.

(d) Notification to the Royal Commission on Historical Monuments

Planning authorities in England have also been directed to give notice of any application for listed building consent for total or partial demolition to the Royal Commission on Historical Monuments of England (Fortress House, 23 Savile Row, London W1X 1AB; tel 01-734 6010) (Circ 8/87, para 81). The purpose here is that the Commission should be alerted to the possible need to record the building for posterity should consent be given for its demolition (see 8.1(*b*)). It is not necessary for authorities to send to the Commission extracts from the statutory list, but it must in due course be notified of the outcome of the application (Circ 8/87, para 81).

In addition to needing listed building consent, works for the demolition of a listed building are not fully authorised until they have been notified to the Royal Commission (TCPA 1971, s 55(2)(*b*)). If consent is given to demolish (in whole or part), reasonable access must be given to the Commission's officers for a period of at least a month so that they can record the building, unless they state in writing that they do not wish to or have already done so (s 55(2)(*b*)).

Note that the Royal Commission on Historical Monuments of England, which was set up in 1908 with the aim of recording historic buildings in England, should not be confused with the Historic Buildings and Monuments Commission for England (also known as 'English Heritage'), set up in 1983. It is the latter which is referred to in this book as 'the Commission'.

In Wales, the corresponding body who must be notified is the Royal Commission on Ancient and Historical Monuments (Wales and Monmouthshire) (Edleston House, Queen's Road, Aberystwyth, Dyfed SY23 2HP; tel Aberystwyth (0970) 4381). The relevant direction in this case is in para 52 of WO Circ 61/81.

(e) Notification of applications to the Secretary of State and the Historic Buildings and Monuments Commission: outside London

The Secretary of State may in theory call in any application for his own decision (TCPA 1971, Sched 11, para 4(1)–(3)). But his ability to do so in practice is substantially limited by the extent to which he is aware of potentially controversial proposals. The application procedures are therefore designed to ensure that he is made aware of the more important cases. To avoid a flood of trivial applications being referred, however, he may direct which categories of application are *not* to be notified to him (Sched 11, para 7(1), (1A), (3), amended by LGA 1985 and HPA 1986).

As a result of the direction currently in force in England (in Circ 8/87, para 86.I), a planning authority outside Greater London must notify the Secretary of State of every application for listed building consent, unless it is going to refuse it, if it falls in any of the following categories:

(1) all applications affecting a building of Grade I or II*;
(2) all applications affecting a building (of any grade) for which a grant by the Commission has been given or is being considered (see 6.2(*a*); and

(3) most applications for the total or partial demolition of a
building of Grade II;

   (a) the total demolition of a 'principal building' (that is, a
   building included in the statutory list in its own right,
   including any object or structure fixed to it, but not a
   building or structure in its curtilage);

   (b) the total demolition of a 'curtilage building' (that is, a
   building or structure which has been in the curtilage of
   a principal building since 1948; see 2.5(*d*), (*e*)) if it is
   recorded in the statutory list;

   (c) the demolition of any part of a principal building where
   the volume of that part (together with the volume of
   any other part of the building that has been demolished
   since it was listed) is more than 10 per cent of the
   volume of the whole building, other than:
   —post-1914 parts of basically pre-1914 buildings, and
   —post-1948 parts of basically 1914–1939 buildings;

   (d) the demolition of any of the elevations of a principal
   building;

   (e) the demolition of substantially all of the interior of a
   principal building;

   (f) the demolition (in whole or in part) of any object or
   structure fixed to a principal or curtilage building, where
   it is recorded in the description of the building in the
   statutory list;

   (g) the demolition (in whole or in part) of any principal or
   curtilage building if an earlier application for the total
   or partial demolition of that building has within the
   previous five years been decided by the Secretary of
   State, either on appeal or because he called it in.

This direction is aimed to reflect the criteria for listing. It is
however somewhat tortuous, and problems could arise particularly
with regard to the '10 per cent demolition' category. As a result,
where a proposal is for partial demolition, a planning authority
must calculate the volume of the part proposed to be demolished,
the volume of any other parts already demolished since listing,
and the volume of the building at the date when it was first listed
(if known). It will also have to estimate the date of the building
and the date of the part to be demolished. It is not surprising that
the Secretary of State has suggested that 'authorities should not
spend too much time [on this]. If there is any doubt, the application should be referred' (Circ 8/87, para 85). In view of the

pressures on local authority time and staff resources, it is probable that the courts would interpret this direction as 'directory' rather than 'mandatory', so that only a blatant failure to comply with it would be sufficient to lead to a subsequent decision being invalidated (see *Howard* v *Bodington* (1877) 2 PD 203 per Lord Penzance at 211).

Notifications should be sent to the appropriate regional office of the Department of the Environment. The authority should send a copy of the application itself, together with recent photographs of the building where available, and copies of any representations received (particularly if any of the national amenity societies have responded; see 8.4(*c*)). If the Secretary of State wishes to call-in an application for his decision, he must do so within twenty-eight days after being notified of it, unless during that period he asks for more time (Sched 11, para 5, amended by LGA 1985 and HPA 1986).

The aim of the 1987 revisions to the notification procedures was to enable more applications to be decided as a matter of course by planning authorities, and thus to lessen delay. Local and national amenity groups will no doubt be keeping an eagle eye on them to see how they make use of their new powers. In addition, the Secretary of State is able to require a planning authority to refer to him any application, or any class of applications, for listed building consent, even if it falls within a category of applications which he would not normally see (Sched 11, para 7(1B), amended by HPA 1986). Thus an amenity group, for example, could ask him to call-in for his decision a particularly contentious application for the extension of a Grade II building.

Planning authorities outside London must also notify the Historic Buildings and Monuments Commission (at Fortress House, 23 Savile Row, London W1X 2HE; tel 01-734 6010) of all applications for listed building consent affecting buildings of Grade I or II* (including those applications which they may intend to refuse) as soon as they are received (para 7(2), (3), amended by HPA 1986; Circ 8/87, para 82(*a*)). The aim of this notification is to enable the Commission to become involved at the earliest possible stage, and to offer helpful comments before an authority has made up its mind, if it feels that a particular proposal is of sufficient importance. In extreme cases it can request the Secretary of State to call-in the application for his own decision (although in many cases he will have already had a chance to do so under the above arrangements for notifying him directly). However it has no power in cases outside London to give a binding direction to an authority as to how an application is to be determined.

(f) Notification to the Commission and the Secretary of State: Greater London except the Docklands

In Greater London, the London Division of the Commission performs the same role as the former Historic Buildings Division of the Greater London Council. In recognition of the high level of specialist experience and skill within the Division, it has been empowered to handle most applications without the involvement of the Secretary of State.

Accordingly, a London borough council does not have to notify the Secretary of State directly of any applications for listed building consent. Instead, it must notify the Commission of every application for consent, whether for the demolition, alteration or extension of all or any part of any listed building, of any grade, and regardless of whether it intends to grant or refuse it (TCPA 1971, Sched 11, para 7(2), (3), amended by HPA 1986; Circ 8/ 87, para 82(*b*)).

A borough council may refuse listed building consent regardless of any comments by the Commission (Sched 11, para 6(1), amended by LGA 1985). But it may not grant consent until the Commission has either:

(1) authorised it to determine the application as it sees fit; or
(2) directed it as to how the application is to be determined (para 6(2), amended by LGA 1985).

However, before allowing or directing the council to grant the application, the Commission must in turn notify the Secretary of State in the following cases:

(1) all applications for the total or partial demolition of buildings of Grade I or II* (but not merely for their alteration or extension; see 8.1(*d*)); and
(2) most applications for the total or partial demolition of a building of Grade II (exactly as for the corresponding provision outside Greater London, although note that the direction is numbered differently).

If the Secretary of State wishes to call-in such an application for his decision, he must do so within twenty-eight days after being notified of it, unless during that period he asks for more time (para 6(3), amended by LGA 1985, and para 7(1), (1A), (3), amended by LGA 1985 and HPA 1986; Circ 8/87, para 86.II).

If a borough council is directed by the Commission to refuse

an application, and it is unwilling to accept the direction, it has
the option of referring the whole matter to the Secretary of State
within twenty-eight days of receiving the direction (para 6(5), (6),
amended by HPA 1986). If the authority does not hear from
the Secretary of State within twenty-eight days of referring the
application to him (or such longer period as he requires), it must
comply with the original direction. Alternatively, he may call-in
the application for his decision.

*(g) Notification to the Commission and the Secretary of State:
London Docklands*

Applications for listed building consent within the area of the
London Docklands Development Corporation are made to and
determined by the Corporation (see 1.3(*a*), 8.3(*b*)).

Before determining applications, the Corporation must notify
the Secretary of State of them in the same cases as it would do if
it were a planning authority outside London (Circ 8/87, para
86.I; see 8.4(*e*)). In addition, the Corporation must notify the
Commission of any application for listed building consent, and
must take into account any representations made by it within
twenty-one (note, not twenty-eight) days of being notified, and
must also notify it of the decision eventually reached (LGPLA
1980, s 138; Circ 8/87, para 82(1)).

Urban development corporations other than those for the
London Docklands and Cardiff Bay areas are, incidentally,
subject to the same procedural rules as other non-London authorities (see 1.3(*a*)).

(h) Notification of applications to the Secretary of State for Wales

In Wales, a planning authority must notify the Secretary of
State of every application for listed building consent other than
one which it is proposing to refuse, unless it refers only to works
to the interior of a Grade II building. Even this must be referred
to him if it refers to a building in respect of which a Cadw (Welsh
Office) grant has been given or is currently being contemplated.
The current direction to this effect is in WO Circ 61/81, para 53.

8.5 Determination of applications

(a) Timetable

It may be helpful to summarise the various time limits contained
in the above discussion of procedures (see also Figure 8.4).

First, the planning authority must not determine an application for listed building consent until at least twenty-one days after the latest of the following:

(1) the notification by the applicant of other owners of the building (if any) (see 8.3(*d*));

(2) the publication of a notice in the local paper by the applicant, where he does not know of some or any of the other owners of the building (8.3(*d*));

(3) the placing of a notice by the authority on or near the building (8.4(*b*)); and

(4) the publication of a notice in the local paper by the local authority (8.4(*b*))

(TCP (LBCA) Regs 1987, regs 5(2), 6(3)).

Secondly, where the authority has notified the application to the Secretary of State (outside London or in the Docklands; see 8.4(*e*), (*g*), (*h*)), it must not determine it until either:

(1) at least twenty-eight days have elapsed since the notification, and nothing has been heard from him; or

(2) he has notified the authority that he does not wish to call-in the application (TCPA, Sched 11, para 5(1); see 8.5(*b*)).

If the Secretary of State realises that it will take him longer than twenty-eight days to decide whether or not to call-in the application, he may give notice to the planning authority that he requires more time. The authority is then only free to determine the application once it has heard again from him, however long it takes him to reach a decision (para 5(2), amended by HPA 1986).

Where an authority (outside London) has notified an application to the Historic Buildings and Monuments Commission for comment, it can be assumed that there is no comment if no response is received within twenty-eight days (Circ 8/87, para 82).

In Greater London, a borough council may not determine an application until either directed or authorised to do so by the Commission (see 8.4(*f*)). In cases where the Commission in turn has to notify the application to the Secretary of State, he must respond within twenty-eight days unless he asks for more time. There is no statutory time limit within which the Commission must respond to the initial notification by the authority; the reference in Circ 8/87 (para 82) to a response within twenty-eight days appears on the face of it to apply to Greater London as well as elsewhere, but clearly more time will be needed if the Commission has to wait to hear from the Secretary of State.

Figure 8.4 (Greater London) Listed building consent application: summary of procedure

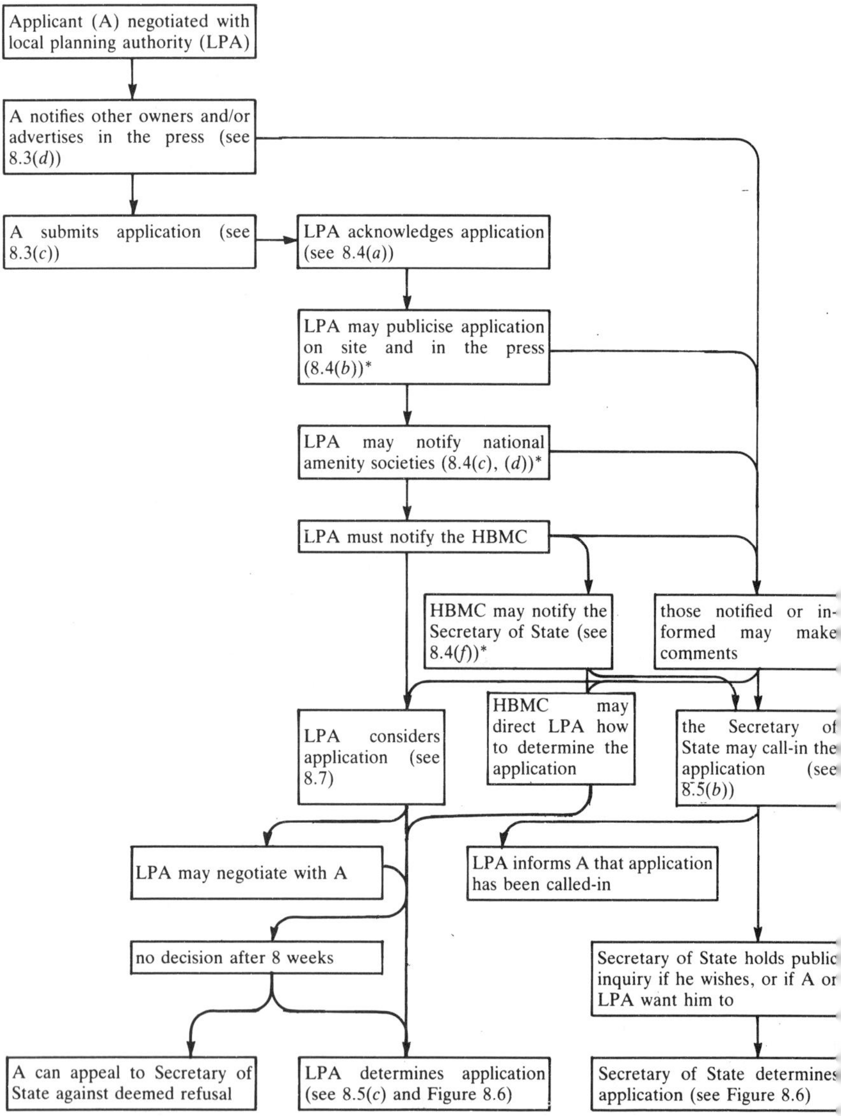
Applicant (A) negotiated with local planning authority (LPA)
A notifies other owners and/or advertises in the press (see 8.3(d))
A submits application (see 8.3(c))
LPA acknowledges application (see 8.4(a))
LPA may publicise application on site and in the press (8.4(b))*
LPA may notify national amenity societies (8.4(c), (d))*
LPA must notify the HBMC
HBMC may notify the Secretary of State (see 8.4(f))*
those notified or informed may make comments
LPA considers application (see 8.7)
HBMC may direct LPA how to determine the application
the Secretary of State may call-in the application (see 8.5(b))
LPA may negotiate with A
LPA informs A that application has been called-in
no decision after 8 weeks
Secretary of State holds public inquiry if he wishes, or if A or LPA want him to
A can appeal to Secretary of State against deemed refusal
LPA determines application (see 8.5(c) and Figure 8.6)
Secretary of State determines application (see Figure 8.6)

Notes:
1 This figure applies in Greater London other than the London Docklands area.
2 The stages indicated with an asterisk only occur in certain cases; see Part B of Figure 8.3.

Figure 8.4 (Outside London) Listed building consent application: summary of procedure

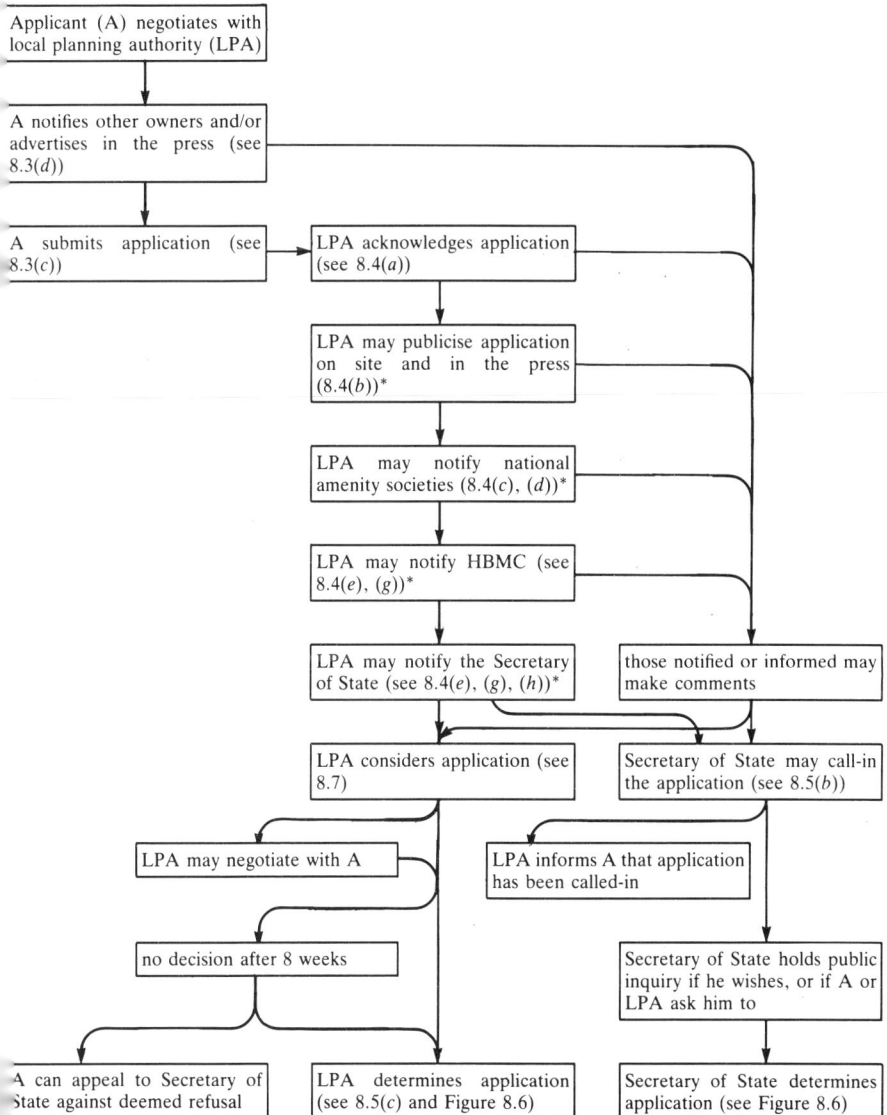

This figure applies in England outside Greater London, in Wales, and in the London Docklands area.
The stages indicated with an asterisk only occur in certain cases; see Parts A and C of Figure 8.3.

Finally, unless the Secretary of State calls-in the application for his own decision, the authority is under a duty to determine it within eight weeks. The eight-week period starts on the date on which the application was first received, or the date on which it was first agreed to be valid, if that was later (where, for example, the initial submission was accompanied by the wrong ownership certificate, or inadequate drawings) (TCP (LBCA) Regs 1987, reg 3(4)). This period may be extended by written agreement between the applicant and the authority.

Authorities have been urged to give decisions on listed building consent applications as quickly as possible after the various statutory periods for representations have expired, and to keep applicants informed about the progress of applications. 'Any potential difficulties about their proposals should be discussed with them [applicants] to try to resolve the problems in a mutually satisfactory way' (Circ 8/87, para 110). In practice, many applications take longer than eight weeks to determine; and authorities do not always notify applicants of likely delay, particularly if it will not be substantial.

Where the application is called-in by the Secretary of State (see below), the authority must inform the applicant of this within the eight-week period (or, again, a longer period if agreed).

If an applicant has not received by the end of the eight-week period (or whatever extended period he has agreed to) either a decision on his application or a notice that it has been called-in, he or she is entitled to appeal to the Secretary of State. Such an appeal is on the basis that the application is deemed to have been refused (Sched 11, para 9(1); and see 8.8(a)). Since many decisions take longer than eight weeks to be reached, it is only worth an applicant appealing under this provision where:

(1) it appears certain that the application is going to be refused, and he or she merely wishes to get the appeal started as soon as possible; or
(2) the consultation process has got out of hand, and the application is clearly going to take much longer than eight weeks to be dealt with by the planning authority; or
(3) it appears that the authority is unwilling to reach any decision at all (for example, because of fears of a compensation claim being made following a refusal).

It is in any event always worthwhile for the applicant and the relevant officer of the planning authority to keep in touch while the application is being processed. By doing this, it should be possible to minimise, and hopefully to avoid altogether, any disagreements and misunderstandings that might otherwise arise. If, however, it appears that an application is likely (or certain) to be refused, it may be prudent for the applicant to put in writing a summary of his or her case, to be considered by the relevant local authority committee before reaching a decision (see Figure 8.5 for an example).

(b) Call-in by the Secretary of State

As a result of an application being notified to him under the statutory procedures outlined above, or because of pressure from the Commission, national or local amenity societies, or even interested individuals, the Secretary of State may wish to decide it himself (TCPA 1971, Sched 11, para 4(1), (2)). If this happens, he will ask the planning authority to refer it to him, together with all supporting drawings, photographs and other details, and any representations that have been made by owners, amenity societies, neighbours, and others (para 4(3)). The authority may also wish to send him a statement of its own views on the application.

The authority must notify the applicant in writing that the Secretary of State has called-in the application.

Where an application is called-in, the Secretary of State treats it as if it were the subject of an appeal (see 8.8). That is, he first offers the applicant and the planning authority a chance to be heard at a public local inquiry if either wishes (Sched 11, para 4(4)). It is also likely that the Commission will become involved in such a case (NHA 1983, s 33). It may happen that one or other local authority is perfectly satisfied with the proposed works, and is therefore on the same 'side' as the applicant—with the other authority, the Commission, local or national groups, or individuals, or some combination of them, in opposition.

There is obviously no right of appeal against a called-in decision (para 4(5)), other than to the courts on a point of law (see 8.9). For an example of a called-in case, involving the partial demolition of a Grade I house near Harrogate, see [1985] JPL 332.

(c) Decision by planning authority

A planning authority (or, come to that, the Secretary of State) may either refuse an application for listed building consent, or grant it subject to conditions (even if only as to the duration of the consent; see 8.6(*b*)). Either way, the decision must be notified to the applicant in writing. It must include reasons for a refusal

Figure 8.5 Listed building consent application: supporting letter to local planning authority

Cllr Barker,
Chair, Planning and Development Committee,
Oxbridge City Council,
Civic Centre,
Oxbridge OB1 4EA   7 September 1988

Dear Cllr Barker,

142 London Road, Oxbridge: Applications nos TP/88/724,725/EL

I understand that your Committee are to consider the above applications (for planning permission and listed building consent) at their meeting on 16 September. They concern a proposal to refurbish and upgrade the interior of a fine Grade II listed building, and to replace a later extension to the rear with a more suitable modern one. The purpose of this work is to create a regional office for Universal Computer Products PLC, who are a successful and expanding company providing a number of jobs in your area.

You will be aware that the villas along the north side of this part of London Road were built in around 1853, in a somewhat florid Italianate style, to house the newly wealthy merchants of that period. Number 142, in common with most of the others, was converted into flats after the war. More recently (in about 1964) it was subdivided further into small bedsitters—largely used by student nurses from the nearby Hospital. These became increasingly seedy, and the house has been partly vacant since 1984. By the time our clients purchased a 99 year lease in 1987, the property was in a poor state of repair.

One or two of the villas in this group were demolished in the 1950s, but an application (by the former owner) to demolish No 142 was refused in 1984. Our clients are now very keen to save the building and restore it to its former glory.

The proposed works to the interior of the building are necessary partly by way of repair, in view of its current dilapidated state, and partly in order to bring it up to the standards of modern office accommodation elsewhere. We have however tried to retain all the principal internal features of any merit.

The existing rear extension is of no particular value, in that it appears to have been tacked on in the 1930s, to provide extra space for kitchens etc. Our proposal is to replace this with a slightly larger but more sensitively designed extension. This will also provide additional floorspace that will in turn reduce the need to alter the main building.

As to the change from residential to office use, a financial appraisal was submitted with the application, showing that the only viable alternative was to demolish the whole building. To refurbish it for residential use would not yield a high enough residual value to do more than cover the cost of the works.

In the light of the above, I trust that you will agree that this proposal should be welcomed as a way of bringing this important building back into productive use—and thus also of enhancing the character and appearance of the surrounding conservation area.

If you have any queries, please do not hesitate to get in touch.

Yours sincerely,

A. Harcourt

Oxbridge Design Group

or for any conditions imposed on a grant; and it must also include a statement of the applicant's rights to appeal against the refusal or any of the conditions (TCP (LBCA) Regs 1987, reg 3(5) and Sched 1, Part II).

Where consent is granted for the total or partial demolition of a building, the authority should remind the applicant of his obligation to allow access to officers of the Royal Commission on Historical Monuments to record the building (Circ 8/87, para 117; and see 8.4(*d*)). It should also send the applicant a copy of the form RCHM(E) (available from the Commission), on which he can give notice of his intention to demolish. A copy of the decision should be sent to the Royal Commission, as an advance warning. In addition, the national amenity societies who were initially notified of the application should also be informed of any decision on it (Circ 8/87, para 81; WO Circ 61/81, para 52).

Any consent that is granted generally lasts for the lifetime of the building (TCPA 1971, Sched 11, para 1(2)). There are however some exceptions to this:

(1) where the consent itself specifically states otherwise; or
(2) where works are not started within five years of the consent, or any other period specified (see below); or
(3) where the consent is revoked or modified, when compensation may be payable (see 8.11).

The first of these, which refers to what is in effect a temporary grant of consent, will not often be suitable. Where it is granted, it should normally be subject to conditions:

(1) that the works are carried out in such a way that they can be removed at the end of the temporary period without any adverse effect on the listed building; and
(2) that they are thus removed at the end of the period.

If the works remain, the owner would have committed a criminal offence, and could therefore be prosecuted and (presumably) made to remove them (TCPA 1971, s 55(4)).

A grant of listed building consent can be acted on by anyone interested in the building for the time being—again, unless it states otherwise (TCPA 1971, Sched 11, para 1(2)). A 'personal' grant of consent would not often be suitable, since the considerations to be taken into account by an authority determining an application for listed building consent (as opposed to one for planning permission) primarily concern the building, not its owners or occupiers (TCPA 1971, s 56(3)).

8.6 Conditions

(a) Generally

As with a decision on whether or not to grant planning permission, the ability to impose conditions often plays a most important part in a decision. Frequently, listed building consent would not be given at all unless conditions were imposed safeguarding the treatment of the building or requiring works to be carried out in a certain way.

Planning authorities, and the Secretary of State, have a general power to impose any conditions on a grant of listed building consent (TCPA 1971, s 56(4), substituted by LGPLA 1980). Some types of conditions are specifically provided for by statute; but that is specifically stated to be without prejudice to the general power to impose conditions. That general power cannot however be exercised without any limits. Thus 'The planning authority are not at liberty to use their powers for an ulterior object, however desirable that object may seem to them to be in the public interest' (per Lord Denning in *Pyx Granite Co Ltd* v *Minister of Housing and Local Government* [1958] 1 QB 554 at 572). Rather, the power to impose conditions must be exercised in pursuance of the aims of listed building control generally, that is, '[to preserve] the building or its setting or any features of special architectural or historic interest which it possesses' (s 56(3), amended by LGPLA 1980).

The courts will only intervene to overturn a condition if they consider that it is one which 'no reasonable authority, acting within the four corners of their jurisdiction, could have decided to impose'. To prove this 'would require something overwhelming' (*Associated Provincial Picture Houses* v *Wednesbury Corpn* [1948] 1 KB 223, per Lord Greene MR at 233 and 230; cited with approval in the House of Lords in *Fawcett Properties Ltd* v *Buckinghamshire CC* [1961] AC 636 at 661–2, 678–9 and 685).

As to the policy considerations dictating the choice of conditions, there is no general ministerial guidance equivalent to Circ 1/85 on conditions attached to grants of planning permission. However, some of the considerations in that Circular, suitably adapted, are relevant to conditions on listed building consent. Conditions should thus only be imposed where they are:

(1) necessary;
(2) relevant to [listed building control];
(3) relevant to the [works] to be permitted;

(4) enforceable;

(5) precise; and

(6) reasonable in all respects

(cf Circ 1/85, para 11). That Circular should be consulted for further comments on the practical application of those tests.

More specific, if limited, guidance is given in para 111 of and App VII to Circ 8/87. This generally concerns conditions following more or less those prescribed in the Act (see 8.6(b)–(d)). It does however provide suggested wording for other conditions, such as those with regard to:

(1) the precise techniques to be used in carrying out the permitted works (App VII, paras 3, 5);

(2) the recording of the building by a suitable institution (para 4) (this is as well as the requirement to give access to the Royal Commission in demolition cases; see 8.5(c)); and

(3) the detailed design of new fittings (windows, doors etc), to ensure that they harmonise with those in the existing building (paras 11, 12).

Further conditions may relate to temporary or personal consents (see 8.5(c)).

A breach of any condition attached to a grant of listed building consent (except, possibly, one with regard to the time limit within which works must be started; see below) is an offence liable to attract the same maximum penalties as carrying out work without consent at all (TCPA 1971, s 55(4), amended by HPA 1986; and see Chapter 9).

(b) Duration of consent

Every listed building consent granted since 1980 has been subject to an implied condition that the works permitted by it must be begun within five years of the date of the grant, unless there is an explicit condition stating a different time limit, which could be either longer or shorter (TCPA 1971, s 56A(1), (2), inserted by LGPLA 1980).

There is no provision setting out precisely what constitutes 'beginning' work in the context of listed building consent. Yet by analogy with the provisions applying to planning permissions subject to similar conditions (TCPA 1971, s 43), it would seem that, for works to be 'begun', it will be sufficient for an owner to have carried out almost any part of them.

If works are begun after the expiry of the time limit, this will amount to a breach of a condition (implied or explicit) on the listed building consent, imposed under s 56A. That is an offence under s 55(4) of the Act, but not under s 55(2), since the latter refers only to work being carried out in contravention of conditions imposed under s 56. It is thus not clear whether a successful prosecution could be mounted to stop work being carried out which had once been the subject of a now time-expired consent.

Once the works have been begun, their completion can be delayed indefinitely (*Spackman* v *Wiltshire CC* (1976) 33 P & CR 430). A planning authority cannot force an unwilling owner to complete works for which listed building consent has been granted by serving on him or her a completion notice (again, unlike the position with regard to planning permissions). Thus if, for example, listed building consent is granted for removing the existing windows from a building and replacing them with suitable alternatives, and the owner merely removes the existing ones without replacement, the only remedy open to the authority to achieve the completion of the works would be to prosecute him or her for not carrying them out in accordance with the consent (s 55(2); see Chapter 9).

(c) Subsequent approval of details

It has been possible since 1987 for a local planning authority to grant listed building consent subject to a condition reserving particular details for later approval (TCPA 1971, s 56(4B), inserted by HPA 1986). This gives statutory recognition to a type of condition which has probably been imposed in the past anyway.

This is not intended to be 'outline listed building consent' under another name, as is emphasised by the placing within the Act itself of the requirement that *every* application for consent must be accompanied by sufficient details to describe the works fully (TCPA 1971, Sched 11, para 1(1)(*b*), substituted by HPA 1986, replacing TCP (LBCA) Regs 1977, reg 3(1)). Thus, even if an applicant desires to obtain consent subject to such a condition, and the authority is willing to grant it, the initial application must still be accompanied by full details. However it does mean that, where enough information has been supplied for the general effect of the proposed works to be assessed, consent can now be granted even though more negotiation might be needed as to the details of a particular element of the proposal.

Such a condition should state whether the subsequent approval

is to be by the planning authority or by the Secretary of State
(s 56(4B)).

Where subsequent approval of details by the planning authority
is required, an application should be made as if for straightforward
listed building consent. If approval is not forthcoming, there is a
right of appeal against refusal or non-determination, as for a
straightforward application (Sched 11, para 8(1)(*b*), inserted by
HPA 1986). The only difference is that it is not possible for an
authority to seek the agreement of the applicant to take more
than eight weeks to determine the application; he or she is able
to appeal against non-determination after eight weeks as of right
(Sched 11, para 9(2), inserted by HPA 1986).

(d) Other statutory conditions

There are several other conditions which are specifically stated
in the Act to be capable of being attached to a grant of listed
building consent. These are:
   (1) that particular features of the building are to be preserved,
       either as part of it or after severance from it (TCPA 1971,
       s 56(4A)(*a*), as amended by LGPLA 1980);
   (2) that any damage caused by the works permitted is made
       good after they are complete (s 56(4A)(*b*));
   (3) that the building, or a specified part of it, is reconstructed
       following the execution of the works, with:
       —the use of original materials so far as practicable; and
       —such alterations of the interior of the building as may be
         specified (s 56(4A)(*c*)); and
   (4) that the building shall not be demolished until:
       —a contract for the carrying out of works of redevelopment
         of the site has been made; and
       —planning permission has been granted for that redevelop-
         ment (s 56(5), substituted by LGPLA 1980).
These are reasonably straightforward. The simple examples given
in App VII to Circ 8/87 of conditions which are acceptable in
appropriate circumstances are in most cases based on these statutory conditions. They include in particular sensible conditions
designed to ensure that the most important features of a building
are retained for re-use, either in the building as altered or rebuilt,
or in the building which replaces it on the same site, or elsewhere.
Nevertheless, the precise wording of conditions to be used in a
particular case will obviously need to be considered very carefully,
since many historic buildings are unique; and it will in many cases

be best if the conditions are drafted, or at least finalised, in conjunction with the person who will actually carry out the works, to avoid the possibility of any misunderstanding or dispute later on. For examples of appeal decisions where listed building consent was granted subject to such conditions, see [1987] JPL 299 (balusters to be retained after the demolition of a house), and [1985] (a Union Set—a double row of barrels—to be retained after the demolition of a brewery).

The last of the above statutory conditions, which was only introduced in 1980, is designed to ensure that premature demolition does not take place and leave an empty gap long before planning permission is sought and rebuilding starts. The Secretary of State has urged authorities to impose it in all cases where it is appropriate (see Circ 8/87, para 111). For an example, see the appeal decision at [1987] JPL 299. The use of such a condition will also be appropriate in cases where only the main facade of a building is to be retained in front of a completely rebuilt interior. Here it should be linked to a series of other conditions to ensure that the retention is in fact possible; see Circ 8/87, App VII, para 9 for a simple example.

(e) Applications to modify conditions

It has already been noted that conditions attached to a listed building consent are often very important. Nevertheless it may sometimes be desirable to seek to have a condition altered or removed.

From the point of view of the applicant, he may seek to have conditions varied or discharged where they have become too onerous—either because his circumstances have changed; or because the current owner is not the original applicant; or because the works already carried out have revealed that the remaining approved works are now likely to be unexpectedly expensive to complete. Examples of this might be where dry rot is more extensive than thought; or where other genuine structural problems arise (see Circ 8/87, para 114).

From the point of view of the planning authority, on the other hand, there may be occasions where the approved scheme was less than ideal, and where revised conditions may be appropriate once better solutions for the treatment of the building have been devised. It may also be sensible to reconsider conditions attached to the original consent if older and more interesting features are revealed once works have begun. An authority in such a case can only invite the applicant to submit an application to modify the relevant conditions. If the applicant is unwilling, the authority would have to modify the consent, which is possible, but which carries with it a possible liability to pay compensation (see 8.11).

Many authorities in the past were willing in such circumstances to entertain non-statutory applications to have conditions on listed building consent varied or removed, as with conditions attached to planning permissions. This received statutory recognition in a new section inserted into the 1971 Act (TCPA 1971, s 56B, inserted by HPA 1986). The advantage of this change, from the point of view of the applicant, is that it is now possible to apply for a condition to be modified without the risk of the consent itself being revoked. Where consent would not have been granted without a particular condition, an application to have that condition discharged would no doubt be refused.

The wording of the new provision allows for the planning authority to 'vary or discharge the conditions attached to the consent, and [to] add new conditions consequential upon the variation or discharge' (s 56B(3)). It is somewhat more restrictively worded than the corresponding new provision for applications to vary or discharge conditions attached to planning permissions, which allows the imposition of 'conditions differing from those subject to which the previous permission was granted' (TCPA 1971, s 31A(3)(a), inserted by HPA 1986). Only time will tell how the courts will interpret the phrase 'variation of condition', but it would clearly include the alteration of minor details (such as materials) specified in approved drawings.

Such an application may be made by anyone 'interested in' a listed building (TCPA 1971, s 56B(1), inserted by HPA 1986). That is, presumably, the applicant need not 'have an interest in' it; so a prospective purchaser, or even conceivably an amenity group, could apply. This can be contrasted with, for example, the enforcement provisions (TCPA 1971, ss 96(3)(b) and 97(1), substituted by LGPAA 1981) which use the latter phrase, which clearly has a more precise legal meaning. The more general phrase used in this new provision may lead to disputes as to locus standi. Thus in *Bearmans Ltd* v *Metropolitan Police District Receiver* [1961] 1 WLR 634 at 655 Devlin LJ said: 'The word "interested" is not a word which has any well defined meaning . . . it is essential . . . to look at the scope and purpose of the Act'. In a planning case concerning compensation payable under s 164 to any person 'interested' in land (*Pennine Raceway Ltd* v *Kirklees MC* [1982]

3 All ER 628), Eveleigh and Kerr LJJ held that someone with a mere contractual right to occupy land, probably not substantial enough to amount to a licence, was 'interested' in it; Stephenson LJ on the other hand preferred limiting the word to meaning 'holding a proprietary interest in' (that is, either a legal or an equitable interest, including possibly an interest arising as a result of estoppel). That narrower view was also supported in the earlier case of *Jones* v *Secretary of State for Wales* (1974) 28 P & CR 280.

The intention behind the new provision in s 56B is clear, however: 'it has been decided to restrict the making of the application to a person interested in the building to avoid applications by third parties who may try to have the consent altered without having the responsibility for carrying out the work' (Circ 8/87, para 78).

An application for the variation or discharge of a condition is (obviously) to specify the condition at issue; otherwise the procedural provisions follow almost exactly those applying to an ordinary application for consent (s 56B(2), inserted by HPA 1986; TCP (LBCA) Regs 1987, reg 4; Circ 8/87, para 78).

8.7 Matters to be taken into account in determining applications

(a) General considerations

A planning authority, or the Secretary of State, when determining an application for listed building consent, is under a duty to take into account any representations made:

(1) by owners of the building (see 8.3(*d*)) who were notified by the applicant or were alerted by the advertisement placed in the press (TCP (LBCA) Regs 1987, reg 6(4)(*a*)); or

(2) as a result of the notices placed on site and in the press by the authority (reg 2; see 8.4(*b*)).

The authority is only obliged to take into account such representations if they are made within the relevant twenty-one-day period (after the notification or advertisement). In practice it would be unwise to ignore any comments received, whether as a result of the publicity or otherwise, before the actual date of the decision.

As well as (and, in most cases, of much more significance than) these specific requirements, the local planning authority is under a general duty, in considering whether to grant listed building consent for any works, to

have special regard to the desirability of preserving
   the building, or
   its setting, or
   any features of special architectural or historic interest which it
   possesses. (TCPA 1971, s 56(3), amended by LGPLA 1980).

Note that there is no presumption that it *is* desirable to preserve
these things—it is merely incumbent on the authority to consider
the possibility of doing so. On the other hand, the Secretary of
State has made it clear that as a matter of policy, rather than law,
he considers that there is a presumption in favour of preservation—which will operate as a presumption against granting
listed building consent, at least for demolition or major alterations
(see Circ 8/87, para 91, quoted in full below). This is in contrast
to the presumption in favour of granting planning permission (in
Circ 22/80, para 2, and Circ 14/85, para 3).

(b) Advice by the Secretary of State

This book is primarily concerned with law and procedures,
rather than policy, but it would be incomplete without at least
some reference to the declared policy of the Secretary of State.
This will clearly be relevant where an application is refused, and
the applicant appeals against the refusal, or where it is called-in,
since it will then be the Secretary of State who will determine it—
and he is in general obliged to take into account his own declared
policy, or else to state explicitly why he chooses not to do so
on any particular occasion (*Sears Blok* v *Secretary of State and
Southwark LBC* [1982] JPL 248 and *JA Pye (Oxford) Estates Ltd*
v *West Oxfordshire DC and Secretary of State* [1982] JPL 577).
For an example of a decision where he explicitly declined to follow
his normal policy, see 8.7(*e*).

But the considerations which will influence him in such cases
are equally relevant to decisions by planning authorities, since—
although planning authorities may determine applications for
listed building consent as they see fit (subject to any directions by
the Historic Buildings and Monuments Commission)—they will
not wish to make decisions that are likely to be overturned on
appeal.

It has already been noted that one of the most important factors
determining whether or not an historic building can be preserved
or restored is whether a use can be found for it that is both
suitable for the building and financially viable (see 7.6(*b*)). The

Secretary of State's policy on this, in the context of applications to demolish listed buildings, is very clear:

[He] will not be prepared to grant listed building consent for the total or substantial demolition of a listed building unless he is satisfied that every possible effort has been made to continue the present use or to find a suitable alternative use for the building. He would normally expect to see evidence that the freehold of the building had been offered for sale on the open market. There would need to be exceptional reasons to justify the offer of a lease or the imposition of restrictive covenants which would unreasonably limit the chances of finding a new use for the building. He also expects local authorities to be guided by these considerations (Circ 8/87, para 89).

He has also provided guidance (in Circ 8/87, paras 90, 91) on the criteria to be taken into account by a local authority when considering an application, and by him and his inspectors when deciding appeals:

(a) the importance of the building, both intrinsically and relatively bearing in mind the number of other buildings of special architectural or historic interest in the neighbourhood. In some cases a building may be important because there are only a few of its type in the neighbourhood or because it has a fine interior, while in other cases its importance may be enhanced because it forms part of a group or series. Attention should also be paid to the contribution to the local scene made by a building, particularly if it is in a conservation area; but the absence of such a contribution is not a reason for demolition or alteration;

(b) in assessing the importance of the building, attention should be paid both to its architectural merit and to its historical interest. This includes not only historical associations but also the way the design, plan, materials or location of the building illustrates the character of a past age; or the development of a particular skill, style or technology;

(c) the condition of the building, the cost of repairing and maintaining it in relation to its importance, and whether it has already received or been promised grants from public funds. In estimating cost, however, due regard should be paid to the economic value of the building when repaired and to any saving through not having to provide alternative accommodation in a new building. Old buildings generally suffer from some defects but the effects of these can easily be exaggerated;

(d) the importance of any alternative use for the site and, in particular whether the use of the site for some public purpose would make it possible to enhance the environment and especially other listed buildings in the area; or whether, in a rundown area, a limited redevelopment might bring new life and make the other listed buildings more economically viable.

Generally, it should be remembered that the number of buildings of special architectural and historic interest is limited. Accordingly, the

Secretary of State is of the view that the presumption should be in favour of preservation except where a strong case can be made out for granting consent after application of the criteria mentioned.

This repeats word for word the guidance given ten years earlier (in Circ 23/77, paras 63, 64), which emphasises its significance.

(c) Proposals for demolition

Where consent has been sought for the demolition of a listed building, the first consideration will be the quality of the building to be demolished, both in its own right and in relation to its setting. See, for example, the appeals noted at [1986] JPL 141 (an important early cinema in the centre of Swansea, an area almost devoid of listed buildings and other buildings of distinction: to be retained), and [1987] JPL 297 (a redundant public house in Hampshire of no apparent interest or beauty: consent granted to demolish).

Where, as will often be the case, it is proposed to redevelop the site with another building, it appears (from *Kent Messenger Ltd* v *Secretary of State* [1976] JPL 372) that the following considerations are relevant:

(1) the cost of putting the listed building into good repair;
(2) the value of the building for any purpose if put into good repair;
(3) accordingly, the extent to which such restoration is an economic proposition;
(4) whether any, and if so what, replacement building is feasible; and
(5) the cost and value of any such replacement.

A similar approach was adopted in *Thanet DC* v *Secretary of State* [1978] JPL 251, where it was considered that the likely cost of restoration was such as to render the whole proposal impracticable.

Several recent appeals regarding redundant buildings also illustrate this principle. In 1985, listed building consent was granted for the demolition of the Bass No 2 Brewery at Burton-on-Trent, since no scheme that was financially viable could be found for its re-use ([1985] JPL 652). The following year, consent was refused for the demolition of the Maltings at Sleaford, to allow more time to seek alternative uses for the buildings, and for investigating the best form of redevelopment ([1986] JPL 55). By contrast, where listed building consent was sought for the demolition of a redundant brick-kiln in Reading, it was granted on the grounds that no

H

other use could be found for the building other than to restore it as a 'controlled' ruin having only local, and extremely limited, interest, and that this could not justify the high cost of both the restoration works themselves and the subsequent maintenance that would be required ([1984] JPL 121).

However, even where rehabilitation of a listed building is not economically viable for its owner, consent may still be refused where there is a strong possibility of it being purchased and restored by a new owner, such as an amenity group or a building preservation trust (see, for example, the appeal at [1984] JPL 679). Where a listed building forms only part of a site, it has recently been held that it is legitimate to consider the economic viability of redeveloping not just the building itself, but also the whole site (*Godden v Secretary of State* [1988] JPL 99).

In the light of this, it may well be sensible for an applicant to include with his application a financial appraisal, highlighting the matters listed above. A report by a building surveyor may also be useful to support any estimates of the cost of restoration or re-development. For examples of such analysis in the case of a substantial commercial development, see *Lichfield and Lintott on Period Buildings: Evaluation of Development-Conservation Options— A Manual for Practice (Henry Stewart Publications, May 1986)*.

As to the quality (as opposed to the financial viability) of any proposed redevelopment, the Secretary of State in *Kent Messenger* had taken the view that it was not a material consideration, but the High Court specifically left the question open. In *Godden*, Stuart Smith J considered that 'Where an area . . . was an obvious candidate for redevelopment in a potentially attractive area, then such potential development was a material consideration but it was probably not one to which great weight would be attached unless the nature of the development was reasonably well known. . . . But weight was a matter for the Inspector and the Secretary of State' ([1988] JPL 99 at 100–1).

(d) Proposals for alterations and extensions

Planning authorities are likely to scrutinise very carefully all applications for alterations and extensions to listed buildings. It has already been noted that planning authorities have been advised that they may intervene on design matters when determining planning applications more freely in conservation areas than elsewhere (see 7.4(*c*)). This applies even more to applications for listed building consent. 'The alteration of listed buildings requires the greatest skill and care in order to avoid damage to historic structures, to ensure that any additions are in keeping with other parts of the building and to see that any new external or internal features harmonise with their surroundings' (Circ 8/ 87, para 92).

A helpful digest of technical advice approved by the Historic Buildings and Monuments Commission is included as App IV to Circ 8/87. It covers a wide range of topics: external elevations, extensions, windows and their details, doors, roofs, shop fronts, interiors, outbuildings, garden ornaments, industrial buildings, ecclesiastical and other public buildings, bridges, theatres and cinemas, public houses and billiard halls, public parks, seaside piers, esplanades and promenades, and churchyards and cemeteries.

Amongst appeals which have been reported have been the following (listed building consent was refused in every case):

new replacement windows ([1987] JPL 806 and [1988] JPL 194);
plastic blinds on a Victorian shop front ([1986] JPL 928);
a PVC canopy outside a night club in a conservation area ([1985] JPL 669); and
a glazed door to enclose a brick storm porch ([1985] JPL 416).

Also of interest is the decision of the Secretary of State on a called-in listed building consent application and several associated appeals regarding a number of alterations to Sutton Place in Surrey (listed Grade I) ([1984] JPL 899). Amongst the issues considered relevant were the following:

(1) the contribution made by the building to the appearance and character of the general locality (in this case, limited);
(2) the purpose of the proposed works (some of the proposed alterations, for example, were to provide fire exits);
(3) the fact that some of the alterations had the effect of restoring the appearance of the building at an earlier date (see 9.4(c));
(4) the condition, age and quality of features to be removed or obscured by the alterations (here, wood panelling of various dates, to be covered with paint);
(5) the historical importance of the features (in this case, stained glass illustrating an aspect of the history of the ownership of the house); and
(6) the possibility of retaining some of the features in alternative locations.

Finally, where a proposal is for a package of alterations, it is possible for consent to be granted for some and refused for others. This can only happen where each group is clearly defined and could have formed the basis of a separate freestanding application of itself. In an appeal regarding a house in Kingsdown Parade in Bristol, for example, consent was granted for the construction of a mansard roof (to replace the existing decayed one), but refused for unsympathetic alterations to windows on the front facade ([1984] JPL 525).

(e) Special circumstances

It will be recalled that an authority, in determining an application for listed building consent, must have 'special regard' to the desirability of preserving the building, its setting and its features (TCPA 1971, s 56(3), amended by LGPLA 1980). However, the use of the phrase 'special regard' would seem to indicate that while the principal concern of the authority is to consider the desirability of preservation, that is not the only issue that it can take into account. This opens the way for it to bear in mind any other 'material considerations'—a phrase that is only used explicitly in connection with planning applications (s 29(1)), but which has been considered at length in the courts, most recently in *R v Westminster CC, ex parte Monahan* [1988] JPL 557 (see 7.6(*d*)).

In particular, as with planning applications, the personal circumstances of the owners or occupiers of a building may be relevant:

It would be inhuman pedantry to exclude from the control of our development the human factor. The human factor is always present, of course . . . It could, however, and sometimes should, be given direct effect as an exceptional or special circumstance. . . . If a planning authority was to give effect to them, a specific case had to be made and the planning authority had to give reasons for accepting it (*Great Portland Estates PLC v Westminster CC*, Lord Scarman, as reported in [1985] JPL 108 at 111).

Thus consent may occasionally have to be granted for the demolition of a building not with a view to the redevelopment of its site, but simply because its owner (even with the benefit of any grants available) cannot afford to keep it in a safe condition, let alone in good repair, and where as a result there is no alternative to demolition. The Secretary of State thus ended his decision letter, granting consent for the demolition of a Victorian Methodist church in Barnsley, with this slightly pathetic plea:

In all the circumstances of this unfortunate case [he] has concluded with regret that he would not be justified in adhering to his normal policy of withholding consent for demolition where it is not clear that all avenues for further use have been explored. He points out that a listed building consent is permissive and not mandatory, and trusts that in the event that, even at this late stage, some aid is offered which would enable the Church Council at least to retain the temporary scaffolding support, they would not exercise the consent ([1984] JPL 363 at 366).

8.8 Appeal to the Secretary of State

(a) Preliminaries

Figure 8.6 illustrates the various possible courses of action open to an applicant for listed building consent who receives an adverse decision—either a refusal, or a grant subject to onerous conditions—or no decision at all. Of these options, the first to be considered is almost always an appeal to the Secretary of State.

An applicant who is refused listed building consent by a local planning authority, or who considers that a condition attached to a grant of consent is unreasonable or onerous, may appeal to the Secretary of State within six months of the authority's decision (TCPA 1971, Sched 11, para 8(1)(a), amended by HPA 1986; TCP (LBCA) Regs 1987, reg 8(1)(a)).

It is also possible to appeal against the refusal of a local planning authority to approve details submitted as a result of a condition on a previous grant of listed building consent, or its refusal to vary or remove onerous conditions on such a consent; the same time limit applies (Sched 11, para 8(1)(b), substituted by HPA 1986; s 56B(2), inserted by HPA 1986).

There is, finally, a right of appeal against a deemed refusal if the authority fails to make any decision within eight weeks of receiving the application (or such longer period as has been agreed); again, the applicant must lodge the appeal within six months of the expiry of the relevant period (Sched 11, para 9(1), amended by HPA 1986; TCP (LBCA) Regs 1987, reg 8(1)(b); see 8.5(a)).

An extension of these six-month periods is possible, but only with the consent of the Secretary of State, which is unlikely to be forthcoming except in very abnormal circumstances.

As with refusals of planning permission, it is always sensible for an applicant to consider entering into (or continuing) negotiations with the planning authority, either as well as or instead of immediately submitting an appeal. If there are relatively few disputed

Figure 8.6 Listed building consent: possible responses to an adverse decision

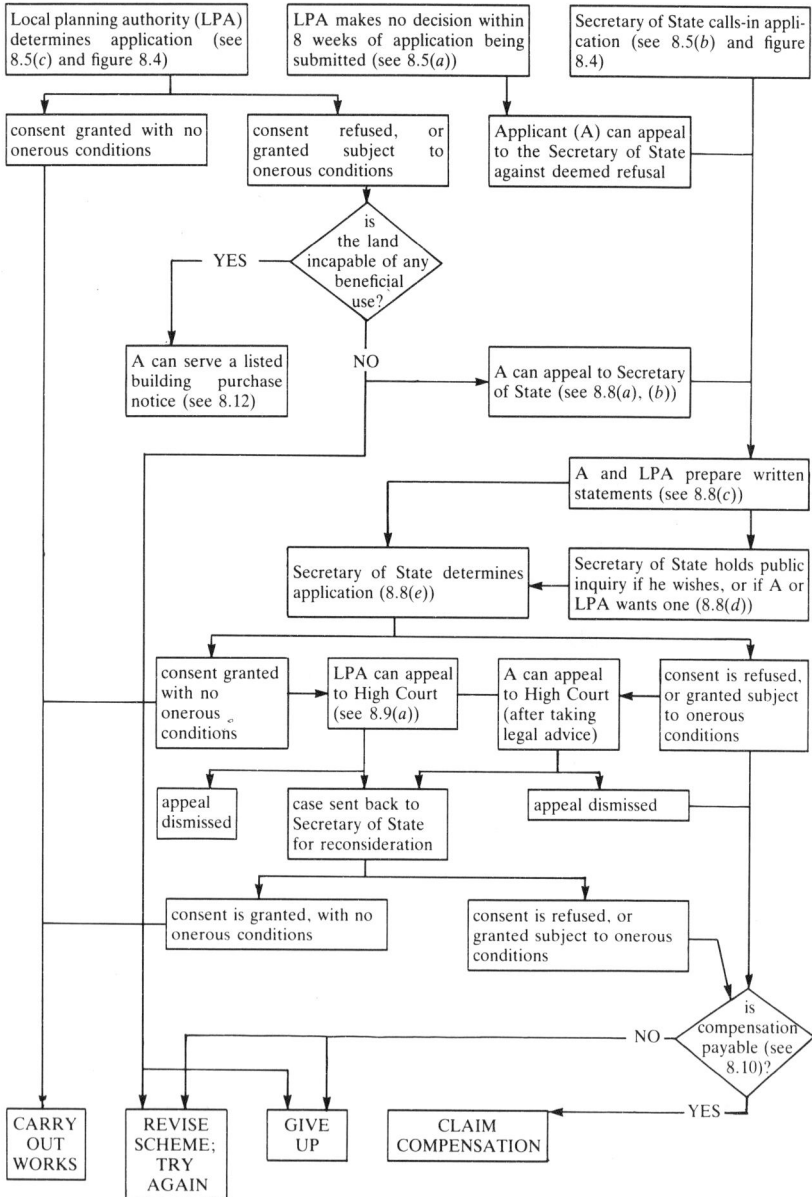

matters, even a successful appeal may not be worth the delay and expense that can be involved. Alternatively, since no fee is payable for listed building consent applications, it may be worth submitting a compromise application at the same time as submitting an appeal on the refused proposal. If the former is granted consent, it may obviate the need for proceeding further with the latter.

It is obviously not possible to appeal to the Secretary of State against a decision he himself has made on a called-in application.

(b) Procedure

Once an appeal has been decided on, the procedure is broadly as for an appeal against the refusal of planning permission. All the standard planning law texts cover this in some detail; therefore the procedure will only be described in outline here, with emphasis on those features peculiar to listed building consent appeals.

The broad statutory framework for listed building consent appeals decided by the Secretary of State is provided by para 8 of Sched 11 to the 1971 Act. Schedule 9 to the Act, covering those decided by inspectors, is applied to listed building consent appeals as to planning appeals (TCPA 1971, Sched 11, para (8(6))). The new inquiries procedure rules (which came into force on 7 July 1988)—both those applying to decisions by the Secretary of State and those covering decisions by inspectors—apply to listed building consent appeals (see below). But the new regulations as to procedure for appeals (decided on the basis of written representation) and the time limits set out in them, do not (TCP (Appeals) (Written Representations Procedure) Regulations 1987, reg 3(1)). The procedure for appeals not decided by inquiry therefore remains non-statutory.

It should be remembered that in many cases two appeals will be required, one against refusal of planning permission, and one against refusal of listed building consent. The six-month time limit will apply to both, and the two appeals will generally be dealt with, and decided, together. This applies, for example, where applications have been refused both for consent for the demolition of a listed building and for permission for the subsequent redevelopment of its site—in this case, both appeals will probably be decided by the Secretary of State following an inquiry. It also applies where both types of consent are required for the alteration or extension of a listed building, although here the decision may be by an inspector after an exchange of written representations.

The Department of the Environment and the Welsh Office (together referred to here as 'the Department') have issued a helpful publication entitled *Planning Appeals: A Guide*, which describes the procedure from the point of view of the appellant. It was designed primarily to cover appeals against refusal of planning permission, but it does apply broadly to listed building consent appeals as well. It was most recently updated following the procedural changes in 1988, and a copy of it is sent with every appeal form issued by the Department.

(c) Submission of appeal

The appellant must submit an appeal, on the form supplied by the Department (see Figure 8.7), to the Planning Inspectorate at Bristol or Cardiff as appropriate. He should also submit, with the form, a copy of:
(1) the application, and all relevant supporting material (including the ownership certificate) (see 8.3(*d*));
(2) any revised drawings or other material;
(3) the planning authority's decision (if any); and
(4) all relevant correspondence with the planning authority (both before and after the submission of the application)
(TCP (LBCA) Regs 1987, reg 8(2)). The appeal should also be accompanied by a further ownership certificate. This will probably contain the same information as was submitted with the original application, but it may not, since it refers to the position as it is twenty days before the date of the appeal, which may be many months after the date of the application. The appellant will also have to notify the owners once again and insert further press notices as appropriate.

The Department ask the appellant to send to the planning authority a further copy of the appeal form and of any other material submitted with it which the authority does not already possess. There is in fact no statutory authority for this since there is no provision in the TCP (LBCA) Regs 1987 corresponding to art 20(3) of the GDO (as substituted in 1987). But it is a sensible procedure, and saves time, and thus should normally be followed.

The appellant may use any ground of appeal that seems appropriate. Needless to say, the considerations influencing decisions by local planning authorities on applications for listed building consent (see 8.7) will be equally relevant to decisions on appeals.

Figure 8.7 Appeal against refusal of listed building consent

Department of the Environment

Town and Country Planning Act 1971
Town and Country Planning (Listed Buildings and Buildings In Conservation Areas) Regulations 1987
Appeal to the Secretary of State

FOR DOE USE ONLY
Date received
Date acknowledged

- Read the booklet 'Planning Appeals — A Guide' carefully, Appendix III in particular, before you start to complete this form.
- Please complete this form clearly and send one copy to the Department and one copy to the LPA.

A. Information about the appellant(s)

1. Full Name(s) ___ Universal Computer Products PLC

2. Address ___ UCP House, The Broadway,
LONDON   Postcode W15 7EX
Daytime Telephone Number 01-334 5778   Reference 1268/AG

3. Agent's name (if any) ___ Oxbridge Design Group
Agent's address ___ Abbey Chambers,
High Street,
OXBRIDGE   Postcode OB1 3QZ
Daytime Telephone Number Oxbridge 242167   Reference LR/AH

B. Details of the appeal

4. Name of local planning authority (LPA)

   Oxbridge City Council

5. Description of the works

   Internal alterations and refurbishment of main building; demolition of 1930s extension; construction of new extension at rear

6. (a) Address of the building ___

   142 London Road, Oxbridge

6 (b) National Grid Reference (see key on Ordnance Survey Map for instructions).
Grid letters: Grid Numbers e.g. TQ
TQ:17247938

7. Date and reference no. of application against which you are appealing.
6th June 1988   TP 8837253EL

8. Date of decision (if any).
16th September 1988

9. If the building is listed, state the grade of the building: I/II* or II (delete inappropriate).

10. Has a grant been made under sections 3A or 4 of the Historic Buildings and Ancient Monuments Act 1953?   YES / NO

11. Does the appeal relate to an application for conservation area consent?   YES / NO

1   TCP 201/LB (REV APRIL 88)

12. Are there any other applications relating to the same site either currently being considered by or about to be put before the LPA?   ~~YES~~ / NO

If YES, please describe briefly.

(Planning permission for the works that are the subject of this appeal was applied for and refused at the same time as listed building consent; an appeal against that refusal accompanies this one)

C. Procedure

(tick appropriate box)

13. Do you agree to the written procedure? (i.e. an exchange of written statements with the LPA plus a visit to the site by a Planning Inspector.)   YES [ ]   NO [✓]

If YES could the Inspector see the whole site clearly enough from the road or other public land?   YES [ ]   NO [ ]

D. Supporting Documents

- You must enclose a copy of each of the following with the appeal form sent to the Department. Otherwise your appeal may be seriously delayed.

[✓] • the application made to the local planning authority for listed building consent or conservation area consent in respect of the works;

[✓] • any Regulation 6 certificate submitted to the LPA, in accordance with Regulation 6 of the 1987 Regulations;

[ ] • the appropriate Regulation 6 certificate for this appeal (look at the Notes then tick a box to show which certificate you have enclosed);

    A [✓]   B [ ]   C [ ]   D [ ]   Notice 1 [ ]   Notice 2 [ ]

[✓] • each of the plans, drawings or documents sent to the LPA as part of the application they considered;

[✓] • the LPA's decision (if any);

[✓] • all other relevant correspondence with the LPA;

[✓] • a plan showing the site, marked in red, in relation to two named roads (preferably on an extract from the relevant 1:10,000 OS Map).

- You should also enclose copies of the following, if appropriate:

[✓] • any other plans, drawings and documents sent to the LPA, but which did not form part of the application (e.g. drawings for illustrative purposes);

[✓] • any additional plans or drawings relating to the application but not previously seen by the LPA. Number them clearly and note the numbers here: LR 16 - 18

- You must also complete and return to the Department the attached acknowledgement cards.

E. The Appeal

Please set out on Page 3 the full grounds of your appeal and sign the declaration below:

* I/We Appeal Against

A. i.   the decision of the local planning authority refusing ~~/granting subject to conditions,~~ listed building consent ~~or conservation area consent~~ for the works described above.

ii.   the decision of the local planning authority refusing to vary or discharge the conditions attached to a listed building consent or a conservation area consent, or in respect of the addition of new conditions consequential upon any such variation or discharge.

2

By the failure of the local planning authority to give notice of their decision within the appropriate period on an application for listed building consent or conservation area consent for the works described above.

* I/We confirm that I/we have enclosed a copy of each of the supporting documents indicated above and that I/we have clearly marked the relevant plans. I/We also certify that I/we have sent a copy of this appeal form and any supporting documents which were not seen as part of the application, to the LPA.

Signed _____ *A. Harcourt* _____ (on behalf of) _____ Oxbridge Design Group

Name (in block letters) _____ Albert Harcourt _____ Date 18th November 1988

* Strike out the items that do not apply in your case.

Grounds of appeal | This must be a clear and concise statement of your full case.

1. The local authority state that "the proposed works will lead to the loss of the fine interior of this Grade II building." In fact our proposals will notonly retain the main staircase and the principal rooms at the front, but will also remove some of the later unsympathetic alterations made to them as a result of the poor residential conversions. The other rooms, which will be substantially altered, are of no particular merit. See Appendix 2 to the attached Statement, which is an assessment of the quality of the building, by Dr Jacobs of the History of Art Department at Oxbridge Polytechnic.

2. It is also stated that "the existing rear extension must be retained as it is an unusual example of the Arts and Crafts style in this area" (reason for refusal 2). This is disputed - para 2.3 of the attached statement lists a number of buildings of similar style in the area. It is anyway a very debased example of the "Arts and Crafts style" - being in reality more "1930s speculative builder, vaguely after the manner of the Arts and Crafts style." This extension has been substantially altered since it was first built.

3. The third reason for refusal is that "the proposed new extension is un sympathetic to the listed building and its setting." This is a matter of opinion, but the extension has in fact been carefully designed to respect the main villa. Its style does not slavishly copy that of the main building, but rather echoes its rhythm of solids and voids, and its overall geometry, in a more modern idiom. It is also, in its use of glass, timber and brick-work, similar in feel to the orangery traditionally found alongside country houses. As to the setting of the building, the scheme involves a careful landscape treatment of the whole site (including the new parking area required by the local authority's standards for office developments) - which is considerably better than the unkempt jungle that exists at present.

4. The fourth reason for refusal, that "the proposal is contrary to the Council's office location policy", logically relates less to the refusal of listed building consent than to the refusal of planning permission (which is the subject of a separate appeal being submitted together with this one). It is however clear from the survey of the building and the detailed finan-cial appraisal submitted with this appeal (see Appendices 3 and 4 of the Statement) that, due to its condition, the only viable alternative to comm-ercial use is its demolition. The Council's local plan also envisages office use in otherwise unacceptable locations where this would enable a listed building to be restored (para 6.2.7).

These grounds of appeal are set out in full, together with further supporting material, in the attached Statement and Appendices.

continue overleaf, if necessary

3

The appellant's grounds of appeal, and supporting argument, and the planning authority's response, should be drafted accordingly. In particular, an appellant will need to be able to show—especially in the case of an application for consent for the total demolition of a listed building—that every avenue which could lead to its retention has been explored.

It is also possible—and sometimes (although not often) appropriate—for an appellant to claim that the building in question is not of special architectural or historic interest, and should not therefore be listed as such (Sched 11, para 8(2)). This ground is likely to become used more often as the number of listed buildings increases. It is also particularly relevant where the building is not listed but is subject to a building preservation notice (see Chapter 3).

(d) Inquiries

The Secretary of State is obliged to hold a public local inquiry if either the appellant or the local planning authority wishes it (TCPA 1971, Sched 11, para 8(4)). The procedure at such an inquiry is as for an inquiry into an appeal against the refusal of planning permission (TCP (Inquiries Procedure) Rules 1988, rule 3(1)(c); TCP Appeals (Determination by Inspectors) (Inquiries Procedure) Rules 1988, r 3(1)(b)). As noted above, one inquiry will often be held to deal with both types of appeal at the same time.

Where the Historic Buildings and Monuments Commission has given a direction to a London borough council as to how an application for listed building consent should be determined (see 8.4(f)), and this results in an appeal, the council may require the Commission to provide a statement setting out its reasons for the direction (Inquiries Rules 1988, rr 4(2)(b), (3)). Whether or not a formal direction was given, the Commission has a right to be heard at any inquiry referring to a listed building consent appeal in Greater London (other than one in the Docklands area) (r 11(1)(g)).

Conservation officers from the county council, where available, may be particularly useful at inquiries, both because of their specialist technical knowledge and as a result of their wider experience. Relevant consultants—building surveyors, archaeologists, millwrights, glass experts and many others—will also be useful, both to the planning authority and to the building owner.

(e) The decision

In line with the gradual delegation to inspectors of the power to make decisions on appeals against the refusal of planning permission, they have been able since 1986 to decide appeals against the refusal or conditional grant of listed building consent for the alteration or extension (but not the demolition) of a Grade II listed building in England (TCP (Determination of Appeals by Appointed Persons) (Prescribed Classes) Regulations 1981, reg 3(*d*), inserted by TCP (Determination [etc]) Regulations 1986).

The Secretary of State however, will still decide any appeal referring to a building (of any grade) if it has been the subject of a repairs grant from himself or from the Commission (Prescribed Classes), Regulations 1981–1986, reg 4(*e*)), although such grants are in practice only given to buildings of Grade II* or Grade I anyway. The Secretary of State for Wales still decides all listed building consent appeals in Wales (reg 4(*f*)).

The inspector, where he or she is not making the decision, will submit a report analysing the facts of the case to the Secretary of State. In *Godden* v *Secretary of State* [1988] JPL 99 (a case regarding the demolition of a listed building of considerable historic interest in Folkestone), Stuart Smith J is reported to have said that:

He felt that he should not approach consideration of the Inspector's report and reasons as if it were a statute or contract where each word or phrase may have to be carefully weighed, but liberally and according to its intent and purpose. Moreover, it was addressed to informed readers, those who had knowledge of the issues and the evidence given at the inquiry. It was also the decision of a technically qualified Inspector who had inspected the building and the site, and who not only might but was expected to use his own knowledge and expertise in reaching a decision where that knowledge and expertise was relevant (p 102).

The inspector and the Secretary of State will decide the appeal from first principles; they are not there merely to see whether the decision of the planning authority was justified on the basis of its stated reasons. The decision must be accompanied by proper and adequate reasons for it, which must be 'clear and intelligible and deal with the substantial points which had been raised' (*Godden* at p 102).

The inspector or the Secretary of State may vary the authority's decision in whole or in part, even if the part varied was not subject to appeal (Sched 11, para 8(3)). This can be important where an appeal is against conditions attached to listed building consent—

there is always a danger that the appeal might result in consent being refused altogether. The standard practice however is that appellants are informed if a refusal of consent is being notified in such circumstances (see *Planning Appeals: A Guide*, p 9).

As well as allowing or dismissing the appeal, either the Secretary of State or an inspector may vary the list by removing from it the building involved (Sched 11, para 8(3)(*b*); Sched 9, para 2(1)(*f*)). If, however, the building is not listed but is merely subject to a building preservation notice (see Chapter 3), the Secretary of State (but not an inspector) may direct that it is not to be included in the list, and notify the planning authority accordingly (s 58(5)).

8.9 Appeal to the courts

(a) Statutory right of appeal

The decision of the Secretary of State or his inspector on an appeal or on a called-in application is final with regard to issues of fact and policy (TCPA 1971, Sched 11, para 8(5)). But it is possible for anyone aggrieved by such a decision to appeal against it to the High Court, on the following grounds:

(1) that the decision was not within his powers under the Act; or

(2) that any of the relevant requirements have not been complied with in relation to it (TCPA 1971, ss 245(1), (3), 242(3)(*k*)).

The phrase 'a person aggrieved' has been considered at length in the courts. It undoubtedly includes the applicant/appellant; it almost certainly includes the Commission in listed building cases; and it probably includes anyone who made representations in writing or at the inquiry, such as a local amenity society (*Turner* v *Secretary of State* (1973) 28 P & CR 123). It is also likely to include a neighbour (*R* v *North Hertfordshire DC, ex parte Sullivan* [1981] JPL 752), though that case actually concerned an application for judicial review (see below), or a person living nearby (*Bernard Hollis* v *Secretary of State* [1983] JPL 164). The local planning authority directly concerned has a separate but similar right to appeal under s 245(2).

A local planning authority has also been able since 1987 to appeal under s 245 to the High Court against a decision taken by the Secretary of State on an application it has itself made for listed building consent to carry out works to its own buildings (TCPA 1971, Sched 21, amended by HPA 1986).

The grounds for such an appeal include almost any failure of the Secretary of State to comply either with specific procedural requirements or with any of the general principles of administrative law. This can include amongst other matters a failure to take into account representations from interested parties (especially those with a statutory right to be consulted), a failure to consider material facts, or a failure to give a clear and reasoned decision (*Godden* v *Secretary of State* [1988] JPL 99; see 8.8(*e*)). The classic formulation was given by Lord Denning MR in *Ashbridge Investments Ltd* v *Minister of Housing and Local Government* [1965] 1 WLR 1320 at 1326. But it does not include a disagreement with the substance of the decision, or the policy underlying it, however strongly or sincerely felt.

An appeal under these statutory provisions must be made within six weeks from the date on which the decision letter appealed against is put in the post (*Griffiths* v *Secretary of State* [1983] 2 AC 51). It is made by way of originating motion, notice of which must be served on the Secretary of State and on the authority, or, if the appeal is by the authority, on any party or parties who would be entitled to apply in their own right (RSC Ord 94, r 1(*d*)).

The outcome of such an appeal is that the matter is remitted to the Secretary of State for reconsideration. So, although countless applications and appeals are no doubt procedurally imperfect at some point (the complexity of the rules makes this almost inevitable), it is only worth considering an appeal to the courts if it is possible that the alleged error contributed substantially to the wrong decision being made.

(b) Application for judicial review

There is a further right to apply for judicial review of any decision by a planning authority, the Secretary of State or an inspector (RSC Ord 53). This is only available however in cases not covered by the statutory right of appeal (see above) (TCPA 1971, s 242(1)). It does not therefore cover decisions on appeals; but it would be available to challenge decisions by local planning authorities. Thus the application in *R* v *North Hertfordshire DC, ex parte Sullivan* concerned the propriety of a planning authority's decision to grant listed building consent for what was alleged to be demolition without first consulting the national amenity societies (see 8.4(*c*)).

It is necessary to seek leave to begin an application for judicial review. If leave is granted, application must be made by orig-inating motion 'promptly, and in any event within three months from the date when the grounds for the application first arose' (RSC Ord 53, r 4). To be successful, it will be necessary to show that the particular act or decision complained of was illegal, unreasonable, or procedurally improper (*Council of Civil Service Unions* v *Minister for the Civil Service* [1984] 3 All ER 935).

8.10 Compensation for refusal of listed building consent

There is in certain limited circumstances a right to claim compensation where listed building consent is refused or granted subject to adverse conditions. For this to apply, the works for which consent was refused must fulfil two criteria:

(1) they must constitute 'alteration or extension' of a listed building, not 'demolition' (see 8.1(*d*)); and

(2) either they are not 'development' at all (see 7.2(*a*)) or else they are automatically permitted by the GDO (see 7.3) (s 171(1)(*a*)).

In other words, they must be in the category of works for which listed building consent is required, but planning permission is not.

It has been noted (at 7.3(*b*)) that, because of changes intro-duced in the GDO 1988, the permitted development rights applying in the case of listed buildings are very restricted. As a result, there are now very few categories of works that are permitted development and also require listed building consent. The compensation provisions noted here are thus effectively limited principally to works which are not development at all, such as alterations to the interior of a listed building.

Secondly, compensation is only payable where listed building consent was refused, or granted subject to adverse conditions, by the Secretary of State—either on appeal, or because he decided the application in the first instance after calling it in (TCPA 1971, s 171(1)(*b*)). A mere refusal by the local planning authority is not enough.

The amount of the compensation payable is equal to the differ-ence between the value that the land would have had if listed building consent had been granted without any onerous conditions, and the value that it in fact has as a result of the decision giving rise to the claim (s 171(2)). In assessing the latter (existing) value, it is to be assumed:

(1) that any subsequent applications for listed building consent would be determined in the same way; and

(2) if the Secretary of State indicated in his decision that he would be willing to grant consent for some other works, that consent for those works was granted (s 171(3)).

It should be noted that it is the diminution in the value of the 'land' that is to be valued, not merely that in the value of the building.

A claim for compensation is to be made within six months of the Secretary of State's decision. It is to be submitted in writing, and delivered by hand or sent by post to the 'clerk' of the local planning authority which first determined the application (or which would have determined it if it had not been called-in by the Secretary of State) (TCP (LBCA) Regs 1987, reg 9).

The Government has stated its intention to abolish s 171 as part of its general review of the compensation provisions in the 1971 Act (*DOE Consultation Paper 1986*). It remains to be seen whether, and if so when, and in what form, this proposal will see the light of day.

8.11 Revocation or modification of listed building consent

(a) Procedure

It may occasionally happen that a local planning authority, 'having regard to the development plan and to any other material considerations', wishes to revoke or modify a listed building consent that has been granted, either by itself or by the Secretary of State. The procedure to be followed in such cases is set out in Part II of Sched 11 to the 1971 Act. Examples of occasions where modification of conditions might be desirable were noted at 8.6(*e*).

The authority should first make a revocation (or modification) order. It must then notify the owners and any occupiers of the building, and anyone else likely to be involved, such as architects, surveyors, builders, and (sometimes the most important!) demolition contractors. It should then normally submit the order to the Secretary of State for his confirmation, unless all those notified have stated in writing that they have no objection to it, in which case the expedited procedure can be used (see 8.11(*b*)) (TCPA 1971, Sched 11, para 10(2), (3)). There is then a period of (at least) twenty-eight days during which any of those notified can insist that he holds a public inquiry before he confirms the order. At such an inquiry, only the person requiring it to be held and the local authority have a right to appear, but presumably other interested parties would in practice be heard (para 10(3)). Whether or not there is an inquiry, the order only takes effect once the Secretary of State has confirmed it (with or without alterations).

The effect of an order is to revoke or modify consent for any works other than those already carried out (para 10(2), (4)). This means that the revocation procedure is scarcely if ever likely to be effective as an emergency measure to stop a building being demolished in reliance upon a listed building consent which the authority now regrets having given.

Where the Secretary of State wishes himself to revoke or modify a grant of listed building consent, after consultation with the planning authority, he is to make the draft order, and serve copies as above. If required to do so, he is to hold an inquiry before actually finalising the order (Sched 11, para 11, amended by LGPLA 1980).

Compensation is payable (under TCPA 1971, s 172) where listed building consent is revoked or modified, to anyone who can show that he has suffered loss or damage as a result. The measure of the compensation payable will be:

(1) the cost of works carried out subsequent to the grant of listed building consent and before the confirmation of the order, insofar as they are rendered abortive by the revocation or modification (s 172(1)(a); plus

(2) the cost of the preparation of drawings etc necessary to carry out the work, whether incurred before or after the grant of consent (s 172(2)); plus

(3) any other loss or damage directly attributable (such as any loss in the value of the land) (s 172(1)(b)).

A claim for compensation must be submitted to the appropriate local authority within six months of the revocation or modification taking effect (TCP (LBCA) Regs 1987, reg 9).

(b) Expedited procedure where no objections are made

Where all of those notified of the draft order revoking or modifying listed building consent have stated in writing that they do not object to it, the planning authority must advertise that fact in a local newspaper (Sched 11, para 12(1), amended by LGPLA

1980; TCP (LBCA) Regs 1987, reg 10). The advertisement must also specify:

(1) a period (of at least twenty-eight days) within which anyone else can object to the draft order and require the Secretary of State to hold an inquiry; and

(2) a further period (of at least fourteen days after the expiration of the twenty-eight-day period) at the end of which the order will take effect automatically if no such objections have been made (Sched 11, para 12(2)).

A copy of the advertisement must be sent to the Secretary of State within three days of its publication. Copies must also be sent to all those originally notified, presumably to give them a second chance to object (para 12(3), (4)). If no objections are made as a result of the advertisement and the notifications, and the Secretary of State does not request the authority to send the order to him for his confirmation, it takes effect automatically at the end of the fourteen-day period (para 12(5)).

This expedited procedure is not available to revoke or modify listed building consents granted originally by the Secretary of State (para 12(6)), and compensation is not payable (TCPA 1971, s 172(1)).

8.12 Listed building purchase notices

(a) Service of a notice

The listed building control procedure inevitably involves restricting to some degree the freedom of owners of listed buildings to do what they like with them. In most cases, however, it is still possible to use, or to sell, the building, and the associated land, albeit perhaps not in the way the owner might have liked, or with the same financial reward. In some cases it is possible to claim compensation (see 8.10). In a very few instances, an owner may be unable to use the building for anything, and thus be left with a valueless asset. In this case, he or she can seek to force the local authority to purchase the land, by serving on it a *listed building purchase notice*.

This is possible where an application for listed building consent is refused, or is granted but subject to onerous conditions, or is granted and then subsequently revoked or modified (see 8.11). However, the owner must be able to show that the land is 'incapable of beneficial use' as a result of the refusal, revocation or conditions (TCPA 1971, s 190(1), (2)). That is, it must be demonstrated:

(1) that the land is useless in its existing state; and
(2) where consent was granted subject to conditions or modified by the imposition of conditions, that it cannot be rendered capable of being used by the carrying out of the works for which the consent was granted, because of those conditions; and
(3) that there is no other purpose which would render it capable of being used beneficially for which planning permission and listed building consent has been or can be obtained.

It may sometimes happen that an old listed building has been allowed to decay, deliberately or otherwise, so that the only way in which its site can be used beneficially is by the building first being demolished. In such a case, if the planning authority refuses listed building consent, the site will be useless. Arguably, it is the decay, which is the owner's responsibility—or at any rate not the authority's—which has caused the impasse, not the refusal of consent. However, a listed building purchase notice which was served in just those circumstances was upheld in *Leominster BC v Minister of Housing and Local Government* (1971) 218 EG 1419; the local authority's argument that the Minister should have considered the history of the building's gradual decay was rejected.

As to the meaning of 'beneficial use' in general, the standard planning law texts should be consulted. See Circ 13/83 with regard to this and on purchase notices generally.

The 'land' to be considered in this case is the listed building itself, together with any adjacent land in the same ownership whose use is claimed by its owner to be inseparable from that of the building (s 190(3)).

Where the above conditions are satisfied, the owner must serve on the relevant authority a listed building purchase notice within twelve months of the decision, or later if the period is extended by the Secretary of State (TCP (LBCA) Regs 1987, reg 9). The relevant authority for this purpose is the district or London borough council (TCPA 1971, s 190(1)). For a model form of purchase notice, see App 1 to Circ 13/83.

(b) Procedure after service of notice

The procedure following the service of a listed building purchase notice is the same as that following the service of a purchase notice under s 180.

On receipt of the notice, the council may agree to purchase the land, or it may pass on the notice to another authority or statutory undertaker who is willing to purchase it (TCPA 1971, Sched 19, para 1(1)(*a*), (*b*)). If no authority can be found to purchase the land willingly, then the council on which the notice was first served must send it on to the Secretary of State (para 1(1)(*c*), amended by HPA 1986). He can confirm it, thus forcing the council to acquire the land, and if he has taken no action within nine months he is deemed to confirm it anyway. Alternatively he can confirm the notice in respect of part only of the land; or he can confirm it wholly or partially but substituting another public authority for the council on whom it was originally served (Sched 9, para 2(1), (2), (7)).

In any of these eventualities, the authority purchasing the land is deemed to be authorised to acquire it compulsorily under s 114, and to have served a notice to treat on the owner. The acquisition procedure thereafter follows the normal pattern of compulsory purchase. The valuation assumptions as to the compensation payable are complex; specialist advice should be obtained. In particular, if a listed building purchase notice is served as a result of listed building consent being revoked or modified, and the planning authority is therefore forced to pay compensation under s 172 (see above) as well as to purchase the land under s 190, then the price payable for the land is to be reduced by the amount of that compensation, to avoid double counting (Sched 19, para 4). The general assumptions applying wherever a listed building is compulsorily purchased apply here too (TCPA 1971, s 116; see 5.5(*f*)).

As an alternative to confirming the purchase notice, the Secretary of State can do one of the following:

(1) where the purchase notice was served as a result of listed building consent being refused, he can grant consent (and planning permission as well where appropriate) (Sched 19, para 2(3));

(2) where it was served as a result of consent being granted subject to onerous conditions, he can remove them (para 2(3));

(3) where it was served as a result of consent being revoked or modified, he can cancel or vary the revocation or modification order (para 2(4));

(4) where he considers that the site could be beneficially used for some other purpose, he can direct that any necessary listed building consent or planning permission should be granted if an application were to be made (para 2(5), (6)).

Chapter 9

Unauthorised Works to a Listed Building

9.1 Preliminary considerations

(a) Introduction

The previous two chapters have outlined in some detail the occasions on which consent is required for works to listed buildings. What happens however if such works take place without listed building consent, or in breach of conditions attached to it? The former would include major works (such as the total demolition of an important listed building), but also alterations that may be minor but which are still significant (such as changing the pattern of glazing bars on a house in a uniform terrace). Or consent might be granted for the demolition of part of an unsafe building but only subject to a condition that it must be reconstructed in the original materials—what if no further works take place after demolition? In the face of such problems, listed building control would be very weak if there were no effective means of enforcing control.

The first point to be made is that the carrying out of works to a listed building for which listed building consent ought to have been, but was not obtained, is a criminal offence. This is in contrast to the position regarding development for which specific planning permission is required but has not been obtained, which is only a breach of planning control. In the latter case, a criminal offence occurs only if an enforcement notice is issued and not complied with. It is therefore possible for a local authority (or an amenity group or, come to that, anyone interested) to mount a criminal prosecution (see 9.2 below).

The fact that Parliament has made a breach of the listed buildings code a criminal offence may reflect its view of the importance of our heritage, and the seriousness of unauthorised acts resulting

215

in the loss of any of it. More pragmatically, however, it also arises from the nature of such an offence. To erect a building without planning permission is no doubt an evil, but it is one which can readily be cured, by the simple expedient of an enforcement notice being served requiring the unauthorised building to be demolished. To knock down a fine old building, on the other hand, whether or not it is a great evil, is not an act which can easily be reversed; it is in many cases simply not possible to resurrect old buildings (even a reconstruction in facsimile is still lacking the 'age' which is often such a feature of a historic building). It is essential, therefore, if the law is to have any force at all, for it to be backed up by the availability of criminal sanctions.

The discussion in this chapter concentrates on criminal matters, as these are not covered elsewhere; but it should not be assumed from this that criminal procedure will be appropriate in every case, or even often, particularly in view of the large amount of time that is involved, and the relatively low penalties that are likely to be obtained.

Alternatively, where it is realistic to do so, the local planning authority could serve a listed building enforcement notice (see 9.4), although, as with the service of an 'ordinary' enforcement notice, this is entirely at its discretion. This has the advantage of enabling the authority to force the owner of the building to take practical steps to alleviate the effect of his or her misdeeds. There is no reason why an authority should not both mount a criminal prosecution and take enforcement action, thus securing at least the possibility of both punishment and restitution.

Finally, it is possible for a local authority to seek an injunction to halt unauthorised works in cases of urgency (see 9.5).

(b) Consent to retain works already carried out

First, however, there will always be some cases that are unsuitable either for prosecution or for enforcement action.

There will, for example, be cases where the works complained of are such that they did indeed technically require listed building consent, but where they were in fact very minor and quite unexceptionable. In such instances, it would probably be prudent for all concerned to take no further action at all.

In other cases, it may emerge that works have been carried out which were sufficiently major that they undoubtedly required consent, and for which consent would readily have been granted had it been sought. In this type of situation, it would be unreasonable for an authority to take punitive or enforcement action; but equally it would be imprudent for the owner to take no action at all—not least because problems may arise when the property subsequently changes hands. Here the right course of action is for the authority to invite the owner to submit an application to retain the works carried out, or for the owner to submit one voluntarily. Such an application, which has only been possible since 1980, is submitted and processed just like any other (TCPA 1971, s 55(2A), inserted by LGPLA 1980), although the fact that the works have already been carried out means that their effect on the building should be easier to ascertain, and that fewer details may therefore need to be submitted.

Finally under this heading, works may have been carried out to a listed building, without consent, which are not altogether satisfactory and which would therefore have been opposed had consent been sought. In some such cases, it may be right for the authority to take a firm line, and institute criminal or enforcement proceedings. It may not be appropriate, however, either because it is now unrealistic in all the circumstances to expect the building to be restored to its former state; or because to do so would be undesirable (where, for example, its former state was even worse than its present one); or because of personal or other special reasons (see 8.7(c)).

Here too the least undesirable course may be for an application to be submitted for listed building consent to retain the unauthorised works. In such a situation, it is then open to the authority, or the Secretary of State if the application is called-in, to grant consent subject to whatever conditions seem suitable to ensure that the effect of the works is minimised, and that any consequential damage is made good (see 8.6(d)). If the owner resents any of the conditions imposed, it is possible either to apply to the planning authority to have them varied (see 8.6(e)) or to appeal against them to the Secretary of State (see 8.8(a)).

Note that if listed building consent is granted to retain works which have already been carried out, it is not 'retrospective', that is, it does not absolve the owner from liability to criminal prosecution for the fact that consent was not obtained in the first place (see 9.2(a)). It does however halt any enforcement proceedings that may be under way (TCPA 1971, s 99A, inserted by LGPLA 1980; and see 9.4(d)).

9.2 Criminal prosecution: unauthorised works to a listed building

(a) Elements of the offence

There are two offences created by s 55 of the TCPA 1971. The first is contained in s 55(1):

> if a person executes or causes to be executed any works for the demolition of a listed building or for its alteration or extension in any manner which would affect its character as a building of special architectural or historic interest, and the works are not authorised under subsection (2) of this section, he shall be guilty of an offence.

In order for a prosecution for a criminal offence to be successful, it is necessary to prove each of its constituent elements. Conversely, if a defence against such a charge is to succeed, it is necessary either to show that at least one of those elements cannot be proved, or to rely on a specific defence provided for in statute. The burden and standard of proof required are considered further below (see 9.2(d)).

The elements of the offence created by s 55(1) are as follows:

(1) a person executes any works to a building, *or*
   a person causes to be executed any works to a building;
(2) the building is listed;
(3) the works are for the demolition of the building; *or*
   the works are for the alteration or extension of the building in a manner which would affect its character as a building of special architectural interest; and
(4) the works are not authorised under s 55(2).

The first and second elements are straightforward, and are merely matters of fact.

The third element is more awkward. The correct interpretation of the Act is in any event not entirely certain—is any unauthorised demolition an offence, or only such demolition as affects the special character of the building (see 8.1(b))? If (as is implied by the analysis there and above) the first of these views is right, what is the difference between 'demolition' and 'alteration' (see 8.1(d))? In any event, the Act introduces an element of subjective judgment here—what works 'affect the character' of a building? This is probably inevitable, but it must lead to problems of proof in borderline cases (see 8.1(c)).

As to the fourth element, works are authorised under s 55(2) if:

(1) the local planning authority or the Secretary of State has

granted listed building consent in writing for the execution of the works (s 55(1)(*a*), (3A), amended by LGPLA 1980); and

(2) the works are executed in accordance with the terms of:
—the consent, and
—any conditions attached to it under s 56 of the Act [that is, any condition other than one as to the duration of the consent] (see 8.6)
(s 55(1)(*a*)).

In addition, works involving total or partial demolition are not authorised unless notice of the proposal has been given to the Royal Commission on Historical Monuments and thereafter either:

(1) for at least one month following the grant of consent, and before the start of the works, reasonable access to the building has been made available to the Commission for the purpose of recording it; or

(2) the Commission has stated:
—that it has completed its recording of the building, or
—that it does not wish to record it

(s 55(2)(*b*), (3); and see 8.4(*d*), 8.5(*c*)).

This is reasonably straightforward; see the relevant sections of Chapter 8 for further details.

It has already been noted that listed building consent under s 55(2A) for the retention of works already carried out (see 9.1(*b*)) is not sufficient to avoid prosecution for an offence under s 55(1). But it must be open to doubt whether the courts would consider very seriously such a prosecution were it to be mounted after consent had thus been granted.

(b) Liability

The law has recently been usefully clarified with regard to the recurrent problem of unauthorised works being carried out to a listed building by someone who claimed that he or she did not know that it was listed. In *R v Wells Street Metropolitan Stipendiary Magistrate, ex parte Westminster CC* [1986] 1 WLR 1046, the City Council were concerned to bring about the prosecution of people caught in the act of removing valuable architectural features from a listed building in Wimpole Street. The stipendiary magistrate decided that committal proceedings could not be continued since there was no evidence that the accused knew that the building was listed. He accordingly refused to commit them for trial by jury. On the matter being referred to the High Court, however, Watkins LJ held that the carrying out of works to a listed building was an offence of 'strict liability', that is, that awareness of the listed status of the building was irrelevant. It was enough to prove that the act had been carried out. The case was accordingly remitted back to the magistrate to continue the hearing.

Strict liability normally applies to more minor offences, usually those punishable only by fine. In the case of listed buildings offences, it is theoretically possible to be imprisoned on conviction, but that would be at the discretion of the court, and is not of itself sufficient to require that proof of knowledge would always be needed to secure a conviction. In the course of his judgment, Watkins LJ relied on the decision of the Privy Council in *Gammon (Hong Kong) Ltd* v *A–G of Hong Kong* [1984] 2 All ER 503), which, significantly, concerned breaches of the Building Regulations (albeit in Hong Kong). Lord Scarman, in what is now the classic statement of the law on offences of strict liability, held (at p 507) that there is a presumption in law that mens rea (intent) is required before a person can be held guilty of any criminal offence, including a statutory offence. This presumption can be displaced only if this is clearly or by necessary implication the effect of the statute, and in addition only if it can be shown that the creation of strict liability will be effective to promote the objects of the statute by encouraging greater vigilance to prevent the commission of the prohibited act.

The *Westminster* decision is in line with an earlier judgment (also by Watkins LJ) that the carrying out of unauthorised works to a tree that is protected by a tree preservation order is an offence of strict liability (TCPA 1971, s 102, substituted by TCAA 1974; *Maidstone BC* v *Mortimer* [1981] JPL 112). The combined effect of these decisions is to indicate that a whole group of offences under the Planning Acts are offences of strict liability, including in particular damage to a listed building (under s 57(1); see 9.3), unauthorised demolition of a building in a conservation area (under s 55(5), applied by s 277A(8); see 10.6), and the carrying out of works to a tree in a conservation area without giving notice to the planning authority (under s 61A(1), inserted by TCAA 1974; see 11.1).

Where, as will usually be the case, the unauthorised works are carried out by a builder or demolition company, rather than by the owner in person, liability only attaches to the owner if he or she was vicariously liable for the acts of the contractor at the time the works were carried out. Thus where a protected tree was uprooted by an independent tree contractor, contrary to the express instructions of the owner, the owner was held not liable (*Groveside Homes* v *Elmbridge BC* (1987) 284 EG 940).

(c) Urgency of works as defence to prosecution

In appropriate cases, it has always been open to the owner of a listed building to demolish it on the grounds that 'the works were urgently necessary in the interests of safety or health, or for the preservation of the building' (TCPA 1971, s 55(6)). The owner must still inform the local authority 'as soon as reasonably practicable'. Since the authority has the power to grant listed building consent for the works already carried out (s 55(2A), inserted by LGPLA 1980; see 9.1(*b*)), such consent could then be subject to suitable conditions, and thus, in theory, the authority could require restoration of the building, or the making good of any damage.

In practice, of course, this has always been an obvious loophole since once a building has been totally demolished, it is easy for an owner to claim that its removal was 'necessary', but difficult for an authority—and sometimes even more difficult for a vigilant amenity group—to prove otherwise. It was therefore suggested in the Commons debate on the Housing and Planning Bill that the relevant subsection of the 1971 Act should be repealed. The view put forward for the Government in the Lords, however, was that 'we consider it is wrong to remove completely the defence offered by section 55(6) if demolition is involved; though we accept that in its present form it can be abused'. Accordingly a revised subsection was introduced, which imposes a much tougher duty on any building owner in this position.

For a defence under s 55(6) to be successful, it will now be necessary to prove all of the following:

(*a*) that works to the building were urgently necessary in the interests of safety or health or for the preservation of the building,

(*b*) that it was not practicable to secure safety or health or, as the case may be, the preservation of the building by works of repair or works for affording temporary support or shelter,

(*c*) that the works carried out were limited to the minimum measures immediately necessary, and

(*d*) that notice in writing justifying in detail the carrying out of the works was given to the local planning authority as soon as reasonably practicable

(s 55(6), substituted by HPA 1986).

This is reasonably self-explanatory. It leaves untouched the problem of an unscrupulous property owner who demolishes all or part of a listed building, thus removing the evidence. But it is probably as far as the law can go; and it is difficult to see how that particular problem could ever be entirely satisfactorily solved. The tightening-up of the law should certainly have a deterrent effect on the willingness of demolition companies to deal with 'unsafe' listed buildings on Friday nights. Since unauthorised demolition of a listed building, whether or not it is alleged to be unsafe, is a criminal offence, such companies would anyway be liable to prosecution under the Accessories and Abettors Act 1861 (s 8).

(d) Evidence

It is essential for anyone mounting a prosecution under the listed buildings provisions to ensure that the required evidence is available. Conversely, anyone wishing to avoid a conviction must know what case the prosecution has to establish, if he or she is to be able successfully to discredit it.

First, it will have to be proved that the works complained of were actually carried out. This should be relatively straightforward, although if the building has only recently been listed, it will be necessary to produce evidence of the date when the works were started. It must also be shown that the defendant carried them out, or alternatively that he caused them to be carried out. Thus it would be possible to prosecute the builder or demolition contractor under the first heading, and the owner of the building under the second. See 9.2(*b*) on liability generally.

Secondly, it will be necessary to prove that the building was actually listed. To this end, all the relevant paperwork will be needed; and it must be completely in order. In particular, it must be shown that the owner of the building was notified in writing when it was first listed, and that a copy of the list has been kept available for public inspection by the authority and by the Secretary of State at all times subsequently (as required by TCPA 1971, s 56(7), (8), amended by LGA 1972 and 1985). Thus it was held that liability under the tree preservation order legislation did not apply where a defendant was ignorant of the order because the local planning authority had failed to make it available for public inspection (*Vale of Glamorgan BC* v *Palmer* [1984] JPL 334). The requirement to place on deposit a certified copy of the order and the accompanying map (currently under TCP (Tree

Preservation Order) Regulations 1969, reg 5(1)) was held to be mandatory, and not merely directory, and the absence of the order and the map were fatal to the chances of a successful prosecution (see 11.2(*c*)).

Thirdly, it will be necessary to show that the works were either demolition or that they affected the character of the building as one of special interest, in order to prove that the Act has been contravened (TCPA 1971, (s 55(1)). The first will be a matter of fact, and easy to prove. The second will require expert evidence from an appropriately qualified witness (preferably one with specialist knowledge of the type of building in question, rather than merely any architect or surveyor).

Finally, it must be shown that the works were not authorised, as to which, see 9.2(*a*) and Chapter 8.

The burden of proof in a criminal trial lies in general on the prosecution, which must prove all the elements of the offence charged, to the normal criminal standard (sufficient for a jury to be 'satisfied beyond reasonable doubt so that they feel sure': *Ferguson* v *R* [1979] 1 WLR 94, PC). It is therefore up to the prosecution to prove that the works were carried out, that the defendant was responsible, and that the building was listed. It is also for the prosecution to prove (in appropriate cases) that the works affected the character of the building (*Gatland* v *Commissioner of Police of the Metropolis* [1968] 2 QB 279), that is, the defendant does not have to prove that the works did *not* affect its character.

But where a statute creates an exception or a defence, it is for the defendant to show that it applies in the particular case (Magistrates' Courts Act 1980, s 101; *R* v *Edwards* [1975] QB 27, CA). It is thus up to him or her to prove that the works were properly authorised, that is, that listed building consent had been granted and (in cases involving demolition) that the Royal Commission had been notified. It is not necessary (and, indeed, arguably it would not be logically possible) for the authority to prove that the works were not authorised. If the defence is based on the claim that the works were urgently necessary for safety or health (see 9.2(*c*) above), it is for the defendant to prove all the elements of that defence. In either case, where the burden of proof rests on the defendant rather than on the prosecution, the standard of proof required is merely the balance of probabilities (*R* v *Carr-Briant* [1943] KB 607, CCA).

(e) Procedure and penalties

Anyone is entitled to bring a prosecution in respect of unauthorised works to a listed building. In practice, of the few prosecutions that have been brought, most were by local authorities. But some of the most effective have been by amenity groups such as the Society for the Protection of Ancient Buildings. The cooperation of the local authorities (of both tiers), and possibly of the Historic Buildings and Monuments Commission, would in any event be invaluable to any other body (or individual) contemplating a prosecution.

An offence under s 55(1) is triable either way (TCPA 1971, s 55(5)). This means that the accused is first brought before the local magistrates, who must initially decide whether they consider that the case is suitable for summary trial (that is, trial before them rather than before a jury). Both the prosecution and the defence are asked if they have any views. If the magistrates consider that summary trial is preferable, they will offer the accused the option. If he or she also wants a summary trial, the magistrates will then proceed to hear the case. If the accused is found guilty (or pleads guilty), the maximum penalty is a prison sentence of up to three months, or a fine of up to 'the prescribed sum', or both (s 55(5)(*a*), amended by Magistrates' Courts Act 1980; Criminal Justice Act 1982; Criminal Penalties (Increase) Order 1984).

If on the other hand the magistrates consider that the case is not suitable for summary trial—possibly because of the limits on their powers of sentencing—or if the accused elects to be tried by a jury, the case will be committed to the Crown Court. If the accused is found guilty there, the maximum penalty is a prison sentence of up to twelve months, or an unlimited fine, or both (s 55(5)(*b*)).

The Act specifically provides that, in passing sentence, the Crown Court must in particular 'have regard to any financial benefit which has accrued or appears likely to accrue to [a person convicted] in consequence of the offence' (s 55). Thus if, in the circumstances of the *John Walker* case (see 2.2(*a*)), the building had been illegally demolished, the benefit accruing would have been £1.5 million—at 1973 prices. A fine of a few thousand pounds would thus not have been a great deterrent. In practice, however, fines imposed in the past have in most cases been derisory, although this seems to be gradually changing.

As an example of how this works, in 1985 a listed house in Royston was demolished during the night (according to the owners, to protect trespassing children from being injured as a result of its unsafe condition). A 'retrospective' application for listed building consent was submitted, and refused. The local authority considered that the magistrates' court would not impose high enough fines. It had in other cases only been able to secure fines of £100. It therefore opted for trial on indictment, and waited for a year in the queue to be heard in the Crown Court. In the end, the prosecution resulted in the conviction of both the owners of the building and the contractors who carried out the demolition. They were fined respectively £5,000 and £1,000, and ordered to pay the authority's legal costs (estimated at £14,000) as well as their own (£15,000)—a total bill of £35,000.

Sometimes, too, penalties can be imposed in other ways. Thus, when Monkspath Hall, Solihull (eighteenth century, listed Grade II) was demolished, allegedly by mistake, the bulldozer driver was fined £1,500, and the demolition company (of which he was a director) £2,000. The local council, which had employed them to demolish (unlisted) farm buildings across the road, then sued them under their contract, as a result of which the company had to pay for the cost of rebuilding and preserving the remaining parts of the Hall, estimated in 1985 at £200,000 (*Solihull BC* v *D Doyle Contractors (Birmingham) Ltd and Keenan*, reported as a news item in *The Times*, 7 November 1985).

(f) Non-compliance with conditions attached to consent

The second offence created by s 55 of TCPA 1971 is contained in s 55(4):

Without prejudice to subsection (1) of this section, if a person executing or causing to be executed any works in relation to a listed building under a listed building consent fails to comply with any condition attached to the consent, he shall be guilty of an offence.

The elements of this offence are as follows:
  (1) a person executes any works to a building, *or* a person causes to be executed any works to a building;
  (2) the building is listed;
  (3) the works are authorised under a grant of listed building consent; and
  (4) they have been carried out in breach of a condition attached to that consent.

Here, all the elements of the offence are relatively straightforward. There is only likely to be any dispute if the wording of the relevant condition is obscure. Hence it should be easier to achieve a conviction under this provision. See 8.6 on conditions generally.

Examples of situations in which a charge under s 55(4) rather than s 55(1) might be appropriate would include cases where demolition was not followed by reconstruction as required by a condition, or where items from the building were not retained after the completion of the works. In the case of alterations, s 55(4) might be invoked where works have been carried out using the wrong materials or to the wrong design.

The offence created by s 55(4) is triable either way, and carries the same penalties on conviction as an offence under s 55(1) (see 9.2(*e*)). It is also a defence to a charge under s 55(4) that the works carried out in breach of a condition were necessary for health and safety (s 55(6), substituted by HPA 1986); but the same requirements concerning proof apply as when this defence is used in response to a charge under s 55(1) (see 9.2(*c*), (*d*)).

(g) Unauthorised works to a building subject to a building preservation notice

Section 55 applies to a building in respect of which a building preservation notice has been served (see Chapter 3) as it does to a listed building (TCPA 1971, s 58(4)). It is therefore an offence either:

(1) to carry out works for the demolition of such a building, or for its alteration or extension in any way which affects its character as a building of special interest, without listed building consent having been granted (s 55(1), applied by s 58(4)), or

(2) where consent has been granted for such works, to carry them out in breach of any condition attached to it (s 55(4), applied by s 58(4)).

The elements of the offences under these provisions, and the statutory defence available in respect of a charge (under s 55(6); see 9.2(*c*)), are exactly the same as for the corresponding offence in connection with works to a building that is actually listed. The comments above therefore apply here too, except (obviously) that it will be necessary to prove that a building preservation notice has been properly served in respect of the building, rather than that it has been listed. In particular, the date on which the notice was actually served will need to be proved where it is critical (where, for example, the unauthorised works started at around the same time). Service through the post cannot be presumed (*Maltglade* v *St Albans RDC* [1972] 3 All ER 129).

(h) Alternative charges

Finally, it is worth considering what alternatives are available to charges under s 55(1) (unauthorised works to a listed building) or under s 55(4) (works carried out in breach of a condition). Note that these two may occasionally be alternatives to each other.

First, it may be difficult to prove that the works were either sufficiently substantial to amount to demolition or, if they were for the alteration of the building, that they affected its character. It may however be possible to prove that carrying out the works damaged the building, and was therefore an offence under s 57(1) (see 9.3). However, it should be borne in mind that the required mens rea is different—there must be an intention to cause damage for a successful prosecution under s 57. The maximum penalty is currently only £400. Nevertheless if it is felt to be appropriate to consider a charge under s 57 as an alternative to one under s 55(1), the indictment should be framed to contain both counts; the magistrates or (on indictment) the jury would then be able to convict on whichever count proves to be justified by the evidence. The procedure to be followed in such a case is now laid down in the Criminal Justice Act 1988 (s 41).

However, discretion is needed. If, for example, the impecunious owner of a listed building replaces the natural slates on the roof with asbestos slates, it may be impossible to secure a conviction either under s 55(1) (because the court does not consider that the works harmed the character of the building) or under s 57 (because there is no evidence that the owner intended to cause damage—quite the reverse: he wanted to reroof the building to prevent damage, but could not afford the correct slates). In such a case, it might be more appropriate for the authority to take enforcement action. It may be easier to convince an inspector at the appeal against the enforcement notice that the works affected the character of the building, and at least it might then be possible to get the slates restored, perhaps with a grant.

Note that, if the building is not listed but is subject to a building preservation notice, a charge under s 57 is not possible as an alternative to one under s 58 (s 58(4); see 9.2(*g*)).

Secondly, if it transpires that a building is not after all listed, or that a building preservation notice has not been properly served, it would be possible if the building is in a conservation area for the prosecution to seek to amend the indictment so as to allege that the offence is now under s 55 as applied by s 277A (as to which, see 10.6) rather than under s 55 simpliciter. Again, this would not be possible if the original charge was under s 57 rather than s 55, since the former is not applied to unlisted buildings in conservation areas (s 277A(8), substituted by HPA 1986).

9.3 Criminal prosecution: damage to a listed building

(a) Elements of the offence

Damage to a listed building is a criminal offence under TCPA 1971, s 57(1). The elements of the offence are as follows:
  (1) a person does or permits the doing of any act which causes or is likely to result in damage to a building, other than an act for the execution of 'excepted works';
  (2) he or she would be entitled to do or permit the doing of the act but for this section;
  (3) the building is a listed building other than:
      —an ecclesiastical building in ecclesiastical use, or
      —a scheduled monument; and
  (4) he or she has the intention of causing damage to the building.

The first of these is straightforward where the act complained of actually does cause damage to the building. A charge under this section might also be appropriate where works have been carried out to a listed building, causing damage, for which listed building consent was probably required but was not sought. It has the advantage that it is not necessary to prove that the works 'affected the character of the building' (see 9.2(d)).

'Excepted works' are defined to mean works for which specific planning permission or listed building consent has been granted (note—not merely works for which permission or consent has been sought (TCPA 1971, s 57(2)). To qualify under the first of these headings, the permission must have been granted in response to either a planning application or an appeal against an enforcement notice (see TCPA 1971, s 88B(3), inserted by LGPAA 1981), that is, it is not enough if the works are permitted development (see 7.3).

As to works 'likely to result in damage to' a listed building, one type of damage that could be envisaged here is work that is sufficiently substantial to harm the building (and possibly to lead to its decay and eventual demolition)—and therefore undesirable—but not substantial enough either to 'cause' damage, or to require listed building consent (see 8.1). Thus it could be difficult to show that the removal of a few slates from the roof of a redundant listed building, so as to let in the rain and eventually cause major structural problems, in itself actually 'caused' any damage. This could scarcely be said to affect the special character of the building, and thus require consent. But it might be possible to show 'beyond reasonable doubt' that it would be likely to result in damage.

To commit an offence under s 57, it is necessary to do a prohibited act, or to permit another to do so. It is not enough to unwittingly cause another to do it; knowledge or recklessness would be required (see *Sweet* v *Parsley* [1970] AC 132 at 162 per Lord Diplock). Further, the offence can only be committed by 'any person who, but for this section, would be entitled to do the act. That is, in general, it can only be committed by the owner or occupier of the land. Thus, in the case of a building occupied under a lease or licence, the terms of the occupancy agreement would need to be checked to see who would be entitled to do works to the building. If works causing damage are carried out by anyone not entitled to do them at all, the correct course would be to charge under s 1(1) of the Criminal Damage Act 1971, rather than under TCPA 1971, s 57.

The building damaged must be listed. As to the need to prove this, see 9.2(*d*). It is not enough that it is subject to a building preservation notice, or that it is in a conservation area. Nor will the section apply if it is an 'ecclesiastical building in ecclesiastical use' or a scheduled monument (as to which, see Chapters 13 and 14 respectively). If it is a scheduled monument, it would be possible in certain cases to bring a charge under the AMAAA 1979 (s 28; see 14.5(*c*)).

The final element to be proved if a prosecution is to be successful is that the person doing the prohibited act actually intended to cause the damage. It will not be enough merely to prove that he or she was reckless as to whether damage would be caused (contrast the wording of, for example, s 1 of the Criminal Damage Act 1971). As to the meaning of 'intend', see the Criminal Justice Act 1967, s 8, and standard texts on criminal law. On the other hand, knowledge that the building was listed would probably not need to be proved, following *R* v *Wells Street Metro-*

politan Stipendiary Magistrate [1986] 1 WLR 1046, although no case under s 57 has yet been reported.

(b) Procedure and penalties

The offence under s 57 can only be tried summarily (that is, before a magistrate; see 9.2(*e*)) (TCPA 1971, s 57(1)).

The maximum penalty on conviction is a fine of level 3 on the standard scale (s 57(1), amended by Criminal Justice Act 1982; Criminal Penalties (Increase) Order 1984).

If a person after being convicted of an offence under s 57(1) fails to take such reasonable steps as may be to prevent any damage or further damage resulting from the act which led to the conviction, he or she is guilty of a further offence under s 57(3). This is also only triable summarily and, if found guilty, the offender is liable to a fine of up to £40 for each day that the failure continues (TCPA 1971, s 57(3), amended by HPA 1986).

9.4 Listed building enforcement notices

(a) Enforcement generally

The general structure of the enforcement provisions in the 1971 Act is that the carrying out of development without planning permission is not a criminal offence, but merely a breach of planning control. If such a breach should come to the attention of the local planning authority, it has complete discretion as to whether or not to issue an enforcement notice (referred to in this Chapter as an 'ordinary' enforcement notice). If the authority does issue a notice, anyone served with a copy is entitled to appeal against it to the Secretary of State. However, unless such an appeal is allowed, it is then a criminal offence not to comply with the notice.

These same principles apply to works to a listed building carried out without listed building consent. The authority has complete discretion whether to issue a *listed building enforcement notice*. Again, subject to a right of appeal, non-compliance with the notice is then an offence.

The detailed provisions regarding the two types of enforcement notice are broadly similar. Since ordinary enforcement procedures have been dealt with extensively both in general books on planning law and in specialist texts such as CM Brand's *Enforcement of Planning Control* (Longman, 1988), the discussion in this chapter is only in outline, and concentrates particularly on those features which are peculiar to listed buildings.

There are in particular three aspects of the listed building enforcement notice procedures which should be borne in mind at the outset:

(1) the issue of a listed building enforcement notice is an alternative (or may be in addition) to the criminal prosecution of those responsible for allegedly unauthorised works (see 9.1(*a*));

(2) there is no time limit equivalent to the 'four-year rule' applying in some ordinary enforcement procedures—in this respect a listed building enforcement notice resembles an ordinary enforcement notice concerning an unauthorised change of use; and

(3) there is no 'stop notice' procedure—instead, an injunction must be served in cases of urgency (see 9.5(*a*)).

The provisions concerning the enforcement of both planning control and listed building control are to be found in Part V of the 1971 Act. This was almost entirely remodelled by the LGPAA 1981; all references in this chapter to ss 87 to 99A of the TCPA 1971 therefore refer to them as substituted or amended by the 1981 Act.

(b) Initial procedure

The planning authority may issue a listed building enforcement notice if:

(1) it appears that works have been carried out to a listed building without listed building consent or in breach of a condition attached to a grant of consent; and

(2) the authority considers it 'expedient' to do so having regard to the effect of the works on the special character of the building (TCPA 1971, s 96(1), (2)).

The most usual reason for enforcement action being taken is that complaints are made to the authority by amenity groups and members of the public. However, the authority cannot be forced to take action of any kind if it chooses not to do so, unless it can be shown that its refusal is unreasonable or arbitrary (*Perry* v *Stanborough (Developments) Ltd* (1977) 244 EG 551). If that does not seem to be the case, the only remedies available to a dissatisfied complainant would be a private prosecution of the person carrying out the works (which will not often be a realistic option) or a complaint to the ombudsman (which is not likely to achieve a great deal either).

Note that the authority is not required to consider merely

whether the effect of the works carried out on the character of the building is such that they required consent, but whether their effect was sufficient to justify enforcement action. Thus listed building consent should be sought for works which significantly improve the appearance of a building just as much as for those which detract from it; but if, in the former case, consent had not been sought before works were carried out, it would quite possibly not be 'expedient' for the authority to take enforcement action. It would of course be imprudent for an owner in such a situation to rely on an authority taking no action; and an application to retain the works should therefore be submitted (see 9.1(*b*)).

(c) Contents of notice

A listed building enforcement notice is to specify clearly:
(1) the alleged contravention (TCPA 1971, s 96(1)(*a*));
(2) what the authority wishes to see done about it (s 96(1)(*b*));
(3) the time in which that must be done (s 96(1)(*b*)); and
(4) the date on which the notice is to come into effect (s 96(4); and see 9.4(*d*)).

The general test which must be satisfied by any enforcement notice is 'does it tell [the recipient] fairly what he has done wrong and what he must do to remedy it?' (*Miller-Mead* v *Minister of Housing and Local Government* [1963] 2 QB 196 at 232 per Upjohn LJ).

As for the works which the authority wishes to be carried out to remedy the contravention, these can be of one or more of three kinds, specified in s 96(1)(*b*) as follows:

(i) for restoring the building to its former state; or
(ii) where the authority consider[s] that such restoration would not be reasonably practicable, or would be undesirable, for executing such further works specified in the notice as [it considers] necessary to alleviate the effect of the works which were carried out without listed building consent; or
(iii) for bringing the building to the state in which it would have been if the terms and conditions of any listed building consent which has been granted for the works had been complied with.

As to the first of these, the 'former state' refers to the state of the building immediately before the allegedly unauthorised works were carried out. Thus in his report on the appeal against listed building enforcement notices served in respect of Sutton Place, Surrey, the inspector noted drily that 'it seems to me that the "former state" of the building referred to in the notice means its state immediately prior to the removal of the stained glass and not, as suggested in the grounds of appeal, its state in the 16th century' ([1984] JPL 899; and see 8.7(*d*)).

It will often happen that the restoration of the building will either be impracticable, because of the irreversible nature of the works carried out, or undesirable, because the former state was even worse than it is now. The second category of remedial works was therefore added by the LGPAA 1981 to enable a planning authority to require the owner to carry out whatever further works might be desirable in all the circumstances. Where a notice specifies works in this category, they are deemed to be granted listed building consent if they are carried out in accordance with that specification (s 96(7)).

The drafting of any enforcement notice needs care, if it is not to be open to a successful appeal. This is particularly so with regard to the specification of the remedial works required by the authority (see 9.4(*g*)).

There is, curiously, no requirement that a listed building enforcement notice should either specify the reasons why it was issued or inform those who receive copies of their right to appeal against it, since there is no equivalent of s 87(12) applying to listed buildings, and Part II of the TCP (Enforcement Notices and Appeals) Regulations 1981 (SI No 1742) applies only to ordinary enforcement notices. It would however be good practice for an authority to include with every copy of a notice a copy of the booklet *Enforcement Notice Appeals—A Guide to Procedure*, together with the official appeal form (see 9.4(*e*)), as is normally done with ordinary enforcement notices.

(d) Issue and coming into effect of the notice

A listed building enforcement notice may be issued by the following authorities:

(1) *in urban development areas except Cardiff Bay*: the urban development corporation (see 1.3(*a*));

(2) *elsewhere in metropolitan counties*: the district or borough council (TCPA 1971, s 1(1)(*b*), substituted by LGA 1985);

(3) *elsewhere in Greater London*: either the borough council or the Historic Buildings and Monuments Commission (TCPA 1971, s 99B, substituted by LGPAA 1981);

(4) *elsewhere in national parks*: the county council or the joint planning board (LGA 1972, s 182(4));

(5) *the Broads*: the Broads Authority (TCPA 1971, s 273A, inserted by NSBA 1988); and

(6) *elsewhere*: the district or borough council (LGA 1972, Sched 16, para 25(1)).

In addition, the Secretary of State, after consultation with the local planning authority, as defined above, may issue a notice in respect of any listed building. If the building is in England he must also first consult the Commission. Where he does issue a notice, it has the same effect as one issued by a local authority (TCPA 1971, s 100, amended by NHA 1983 and LGA 1985). The use of this power is rare; but it could be appropriate where it is a local authority itself that has carried out the unauthorised works, or where the owner of the listed building in question was a foreign government (many of the embassies in London, for example, are listed).

Once the notice has been 'issued' by the local authority (that is, a resolution to that effect has been passed by the appropriate committee, sub-committee or officer acting under delegated powers) or by the Secretary of State, copies of it must be served within twenty-eight days on the owners and occupiers of the building and on anyone else who 'has an interest in it' (TCPA 1971, s 96(3)). As to the meaning of the latter phrase, see 8.6(*e*). In the unusual case of a building having been dismantled partially or wholly, a copy of the notice should also be served on whoever now owns most of the pieces (*R* v *Leominster DC, ex parte Antique Country Buildings Ltd* [1988] JPL 554). If works are actually in progress, it would also be prudent for the authority to serve copies on any builders, demolition contractors, architects, surveyors and others involved, and possibly to fix a copy to the building itself.

The notice comes into effect on a date stated in it, which must be at least twenty-eight days after copies of it were issued to those who had to receive them (s 96(3), (4)). At any time before that date, the local authority may withdraw it (although it can always issue another) or the owner may appeal against it to the Secretary of State (ss 96(5), (6), 97(1)). If an appeal is made, the notice then only comes into effect once the appeal has been withdrawn or 'finally determined' (s 97(9)). The effect of these provisions is that the notice comes into effect:

(1) on the date stated in it, or
(2) if there is an appeal against the notice, which is subsequently withdrawn, on the date of the withdrawal, or
(3) if the appeal is not withdrawn, when the Secretary of State makes his decision on it, or

(4) if a further appeal to the High Court is made against his decision, when that appeal is withdrawn or decided, or
(5) if the High Court refers the case back to the Secretary of State, when he makes any second decision

(*Dover DC* v *McKeen* [1985] JPL 627; *R* v *Kuxhaus* [1988] JPL 545).

If listed building consent is subsequently granted under s 55(2A) to retain all or some of the works which are the subject of the enforcement notice, the notice will then cease to have effect as far as it relates to those works (s 99A, inserted by LGPLA 1980).

(e) Appeal against listed building enforcement notice

An appeal may be made either by anyone having an interest in the building, or by anyone occupying it by virtue of a licence (TCPA 1971, s 97(1); TCPA 1984, s 4(2)). It may be made on the appropriate form issued by the Department of the Environment (similar to the one used for appealing against the refusal of consent; see Figure 8.7), although the use of this is not mandatory. It must be sent so as to reach the Secretary of State by the date on which the notice would otherwise be due to come into effect, and no extensions of that time limit are allowed in any circumstances (*Howard* v *Secretary of State for the Environment* [1975] QB 235; *Lenlyn Ltd* v *Secretary of State* [1985] JPL 482; *R* v *Secretary of State, ex parte Jackson* [1987] JPL 790). It should accordingly be sent by first-class post and recorded delivery to the Planning Inspectorate at Bristol or Cardiff as appropriate. The envelope should be clearly marked 'Enforcement Notice Appeal', to ensure that there is no delay.

Whether or not the official form is used, the appeal must be in writing. The appellant need not specify the grounds which are being relied on (see 9.2(*f*), (*g*) and Figure 9.1) when the appeal is first made; it is in theory adequate to state no more than the address of the building and the name of the local authority involved. But it is helpful to all parties if at least some statement accompanies the appeal. One must in any event be provided within twenty-eight days of it being requested by the Secretary of State, specifying the grounds relied on and stating briefly the facts on which it is proposed to rely in support of each of those grounds (s 97(2)–(4); TCP (Enforcement Notices and Appeals) Regulations 1984, reg 5). In a case to be decided after a public inquiry, the planning authority must then submit a statement of its case at least twenty-eight days before the date appointed. In other cases,

Figure 9.1 Grounds of appeal against a listed building enforcement notice

(*a*) That the building is not of special architectural or historic interest.

(*b*) That the matters alleged to constitute a contravention of s 55 of this Act [which specifies the need for works to be authorised: see 8.1(*a*)] do not involve such a contravention.

(*c*) That the contravention of that section alleged in the notice has not taken place.

(*d*) That works to the building were urgently necessary in the interests of safety and health or for the preservation of the building,
that it was not practicable to secure safety or health or, as the case may be, the preservation of the building by works of repair or works for affording temporary support or shelter, and
that the works carried out were limited to the minimum measures immediately necessary.

(*e*) That listed building consent ought to be granted for the works, or that any relevant condition of such consent which has been granted ought to be discharged, or different conditions substituted.

(*f*) That copies of the notice were not served as required by s 96(3) of this Act [see 9.4(*d*)].

(*g*) Except in relation to such a requirement as is mentioned in s 96(1)(*b*)(ii) or (iii) of this Act [see 9.4(*c*)], the requirements of the notice exceed what is necessary for restoring the building to its condition before the works were carried out.

(*h*) That the period specified in the notice as the period within which any step required thereby is to be taken falls short of what should reasonably be allowed.

(*i*) That the steps required by the notice for the purpose of restoring the character of the building to its former state would not serve that purpose.

(*j*) That steps required to be taken by virtue of s 96(1)(*b*)(ii) of this Act [see 9.4(*c*)] exceed what is necessary to alleviate the effect of the works executed to the building.

(*k*) That steps required to be taken by virtue of s 96(1)(*b*)(iii) of this Act [see 9.4(*c*)] exceed what is necessary to bring the building to the state in which it would have been if the terms and conditions of the listed building consent had been applied with.

Source: TCPA 1971, s 97(1), as substituted by LGPAA 1981 and amended by HPA 1986

the authority must produce a statement within twenty-eight days of being asked to do so by the Secretary of State (1984 Regulations, reg 6).

The Secretary of State has power to dismiss an appeal or quash an enforcement notice (without any inquiry) where one side or the other fails to produce a statement when asked to do so (s 97(5), (7)). In any other case, a public local inquiry must be held if either the appellant or the local authority wants one. The procedure at such an inquiry will be broadly as for one into a normal appeal (s 97(6); TCP (Enforcement) (Inquiries Procedure) Rules 1981). If an appellant relies on more than one ground of appeal, but only provides supporting information in respect of some of them, the appeal may be decided without any consideration being given to the other grounds (s 97(8)).

The power to decide listed building enforcement notice appeals has been delegated to inspectors in almost all cases referring to works for the alteration or extension of Grade II buildings in England (TCPA 1971, s 97(10), Sched 9; TCP (Determination of Appeals by Appointed Persons) (Prescribed Classes) Regulations 1981, regs 3(c), 4(c)–(f), inserted by TCP (Determination [etc]) Regulations 1986).

(f) Grounds of appeal (a) to (f)

The only grounds that can be used in an appeal against a listed building enforcement notice are set out in the Act (TCPA 1971, s 97(1); see Figure 9.1).

Ground (a) is a straightforward matter of fact and opinion, as to which professional witnesses should be called. If the Secretary of State agrees, he will be able to remove the building from the list, so that listed building consent is no longer required for the works (s 97A(4)(c)). Ground (b) on the other hand is largely a matter of law and depends largely on the matters set out earlier in this book. Again, professional advice will be needed if this ground is relied on. If either of these or ground (c) (as to which no comment is needed) is successfully relied on, the only option open to the Secretary of State would be to allow the appeal and quash the notice (s 97A(1)).

Ground (d) has been redrafted in line with the redrafting of s 55(6) of the Act; as to that, see 9.2(c). It will now be much more difficult to rely successfully on this ground alone. Factual evidence will be needed as to the condition of the building prior to the works, and professional evidence (from, say, a building surveyor or structural engineer) as to the cost and feasibility of both the works that were carried out and any alternatives that may be suggested.

As to ground (*e*), the issues at stake will be those that are relevant to an ordinary application for listed building consent (see 8.7) or at an appeal against the imposition of conditions (see 8.6).

Ground (*f*) refers to the mechanics of service of the notice (as to which, see 9.4(*d*)). However, even if it can be proved that a copy of the notice was not served on a person who should have had one, the Secretary of State may disregard that if he considers that neither that person nor the appellant was substantially prejudiced by the error (s 97A(3)). So, for example, it may not be enough to show that a mortgagee was not served with a copy of the notice, as was the case with the enforcement notice in the Stagbatch case ([1987] JPL 798; see 9.4(*g*) and 9.5(*b*)). Anyone who appeals to the Secretary of State against a notice cannot then appeal to the courts on the grounds that it was not properly served on him or her (TCPA 1971, s 110(2)).

(g) Grounds of appeal (g) to (k)

Grounds (*g*) to (*k*) concern the details of the steps specified in the notice as required for alleviating the effect of the unauthorised works. Reliance on one or more of these is much more likely to lead to a successful appeal. But note that ground (*h*) (insufficient time) should never be used on its own except as a last resort, for, although it is frequently accepted by the Secretary of State, it almost invariably leads to the notice being varied so as to allow for a longer period in which to carry out the specified works. It thus merely postpones the inevitable.

Grounds (*g*) and (*i*) are only applicable in respect of works specified under s 96(1)(*b*)(i); that is, where the authority has required that the building should be restored to the state in which it was immediately prior to the unauthorised works being carried out (see 9.4(*c*)). The first, (*g*), is a claim that what is required is excessive. The second, (*i*), is a claim that it would not even achieve the stated purpose anyway; but reliance on that ground, even if successful, is likely to lead to the notice being varied rather than quashed.

A notorious example of the successful use of ground (*g*) in practice was the case of the Grosvenor Hotel in Bath. The building, which was listed Grade I, had originally been roofed with stone tiles. At some later date, these had been replaced with natural Welsh slates. These in turn had gradually deteriorated, and the owners had therefore patched up its roof over the years in a piecemeal fashion so that approximately two thirds of it was now covered in Welsh slates, and one third in asbestos slates, but some parts in various other materials including corrugated sheeting. They then decided to completely reroof the building, using asbestos slates. The builders were starting to do this when the local authority issued a listed building enforcement notice, requiring them to stop work, and reroof the whole building in natural slates.

The owners appealed to the Secretary of State against the notice on a number of grounds including (g). He allowed the appeal on that ground, but only because he felt:

(1) that the steps specified in the notice were more than was required to restore the building 'to its former state', which was by implication neither with its original roof of stone tiles, nor with its later roof entirely of Welsh slates, but with its patchwork roof as it had been prior to the recent reroofing; and

(2) that it would not be possible for the notice to be amended so as to require the roof to be reinstated to that previous patchwork condition.

The City Council then appealed to the High Court (*Bath CC v Secretary of State for the Environment and Grosvenor Hotel* [1983] JPL 737). On the first point, Woolf J, as he then was, agreed with the Secretary of State:

. . . the power which was given could not be properly used to achieve what the planning authority, for the best of reasons, would like to achieve here, namely a result which would be an improvement so far as this roof was concerned from a situation which existed prior to the unauthorised works being carried out. At that time there were asbestos slates and although the company, no doubt, were very wrong in carrying out the work which they did without consent, the object of the new provision was not to provide a punishment for them in the form of a requirement to carry out work which was over and above the work which was required to remedy the works which were done without consent (pp 740–1).

On the second point, however, he disagreed with the Secretary of State, since he felt that the notice could be amended, but whether that would be desirable in this case would be a matter for him (the Secretary of State) and the City Council. The notice was accordingly remitted to him for further consideration, and he decided that ground (*g*) succeeded, and that the notice should therefore be quashed (see [1984] JPL 285).

On the other hand, in the appeal against the listed building enforcement notice served by Leominster District Council requiring the reconstruction of Stagbatch Barn ([1987] JPL 798; for the facts, see 9.5(*b*)), the Secretary of State noted that Woolf J had said in the *Bath* case (at p 741):

> If works were carried out without the necessary building consent then it may be that an indirect consequence was that the person carrying out those works which were necessary to comply with a proper enforcement notice will have to carry out more work than was strictly required by the . . . notice. That would not be a ground for challenging [its] validity because the person carrying out the works should be in the best position to know what steps were needed to rectify the breach of the listed building provisions which he had committed . . .

He therefore considered that in this case it was not unduly onerous to require the owners to rebuild the barn, particularly since it had been carefully packed and stored ready for re-erection elsewhere.

Grounds (*j*) and (*k*) raise similar considerations to ground (*g*), in relation to works required under s 96(*b*)(ii) and (iii).

(h) Outcome of the appeal

In determining an appeal, the Secretary of State or the inspector may do one or more of the following:

(1) quash the enforcement notice (s 97A(1));

(2) correct any minor defect in the drafting of the notice, or vary its terms (s 97A(2));

(3) grant listed building consent for all or part of the works carried out (s 97A(4)(*a*));

(4) discharge any condition attached to a listed building consent, and substitute another (s 97A(4)(*b*)); or

remove the building from the statutory list (s 97A(4)(*c*)).

As to correcting or varying the notice, this can only be done if to do so would not cause injustice. Thus, for example, in a decision letter by the Secretary of State regarding the unauthorised installation of replacement windows, window frames and doors, he stated:

> [he] has regard to the term 'sliding casement' in the schedule to the enforcement notice, which it is agreed could be misunderstood. The Council would appear to be seeking replacement of the 3 UPVC windows with traditional timber windows of the horizontal sliding sash type. The Secretary of State is thus of the view that the enforcement notice as

served by the Council is imprecise, but that it can be varied. Accordingly the appeal against the listed building enforcement notice has been considered on that basis ([1987] JPL 804).

It is then possible for either the local authority or anyone served with a copy of the notice to appeal against the decision of the Secretary of State to the High Court on a point of law. This may be by way of either a statutory appeal (under TCPA 1971, s 246(1)(*b*), amended by LGPAA 1981) or an application for judicial review (see 8.9). However, the appeal may not be on any of the grounds on which an appeal to the Secretary of State could have been based (see 9.4(*f*), (*g*)) (s 243(1)(*b*)).

(i) Subsequent procedure

Once the notice has finally come into force, and all possibility of appeal has been exhausted, the remedial works specified in it must be carried out within the stated time limit, subject to any extension that may have been won on appeal, or that may have been allowed by the planning authority (s 98(5)). This is the responsibility of the person who was the owner of the building at the time when copies of the notice were served. If the works are not carried out, he or she is liable to be prosecuted for non-compliance. This is an offence triable either way (as to which, see 9.2(*e*)). The maximum penalty is a fine of up to 'the prescribed sum' on summary conviction, or an unlimited fine on indictment (TCPA 1971, s 98(1), amended by Magistrates' Courts Act 1980; Criminal Penalties etc (Increase) Order 1984).

Where the person being prosecuted no longer owns the building, but took all reasonable steps to secure compliance with the notice while he was still the owner, he or she can take steps to have the successor in title prosecuted instead (s 98(2), (3)).

Following a conviction for non-compliance, if the required works are still not carried out, the person convicted may be prosecuted again. This further offence is also triable either way, and the maximum penalty on summary conviction is a fine of up to £200 for each day following the first conviction that the works remain to be completed or on indictment an unlimited fine (s 98(4), amended by HPA 1986).

Finally, if all else fails, the planning authority may enter the land, carry out the required works itself, and reclaim the cost of doing so from whoever is currently the owner of the land, together with a reasonable sum in respect of its establishment charges (s 99(1); LGA 1974, s 36). This is recoverable as a simple contract debt (TCPA 1971, s 111). The current owner may in turn recover it from whoever was responsible for the unauthorised works in the first place (s 99(2)).

9.5 Injunctions

(a) General principles

There will inevitably be a few cases where urgent action is required to stop a listed building being demolished or substantially altered in the very near future—possibly in the next twenty-four hours; or to halt unauthorised works which are actually in progress.

In such situations, it will be of limited use to institute criminal proceedings: even if the offenders are successfully prosecuted, it will usually be much too late to stop the works being completed. It will also be useless to issue a listed building enforcement notice on its own. If the works have not started, there has been no breach to be enforced; and if they are under way, it may not be possible to resurrect the building. In the latter case, however, if there is any possibility of the effect of the works being remedied, a notice should still be issued, even if it eventually proves ineffective.

Where an ordinary enforcement notice is issued to stop undesirable development being carried out without planning permission, it is possible to issue a 'stop notice' (under TCPA 1971, s 90) which has the effect of bringing the enforcement notice into effect within three days. There is no equivalent procedure with listed building enforcement notices—possibly reflecting the fact that it is possible to do a lot of demolition even in only three days! Instead, it is possible for a local authority to seek an injunction restraining the owner of the building (or anyone else who may be thought suitable) from carrying out, or continuing, any unauthorised works to it. If such an injunction (known as quia timet) is granted, and its terms are then flouted, a further action can be brought for contempt of court. The courts consider actions for contempt very seriously, and it is thus likely that any penalties imposed at that stage would be severe, including, in appropriate cases, imprisonment (as in *Maidstone BC* v *Batchelor* (1983) (unreported): contempt of court for flouting an injunction issued to uphold a tree preservation order).

The power of a local authority to seek an injunction to enforce planning law (under LGA 1972, s 222) has been used increasingly frequently in recent years. 'The terms of section 222 are sufficiently explicit to enable a local authority to bring proceedings in [its] own name and to contradict the view that [its] powers . . . are limited to requesting the Attorney-General to allow proceedings to be instituted in his name at the relation of the local authority' (*Stoke-on-Trent CC* v *B & Q (Retail) Ltd* [1984] AC 754 per Lord Templeman at 773).

Note that an injunction under these powers can only be sought by a local authority as such, and not by an amenity group, or the Historic Buildings and Monuments Commission, or even an urban development corporation. The inability of the latter emerged when the London Docklands Development Corporation attempted, unsuccessfully, to seek an injunction to stop Rank Hovis demolishing some redundant silos by the Thames which were subject to a building preservation notice (*London Docklands Development Corpn* v *Rank Hovis McDougall Ltd* [1986] JPL 826).

An injunction will, understandably, only be granted where it is really necessary. The correct approach has been expressed by the Court of Appeal (in *Runnymede BC* v *Ball and others* [1986] JPL 288, as summarised by Millett J in *Runnymede BC* v *Smith and others* [1986] JPL 592 at 597):

the court should bear in mind that the duty of a local planning authority under the planning legislation was not merely to enforce penalties for past offences but was also to do all within [its] power to ensure, through properly observed planning control, the natural amenities of [its] area; and that the local planning authority could take the view, in an appropriate case, that it was necessary to resort to relief at civil law in order to prevent irreparable damage, which might well not be prevented by the process of a magistrates' court.

This overrides the test (previously much quoted, after its first appearance in *Stafford BC* v *Elkenford Ltd* (1976) 121 SJ 34) of whether the act complained of is a 'deliberate and flagrant breach of the criminal law'. More recently, it has been held that an injunction should be granted only if it appeared that the unlawful operations would continue unless and until effectively restrained by the law, and that nothing short of an injunction would be effective (*Wychavon DC* v *Midland Events (Special Events) Ltd* (1987) 86 LGR 83 at 89, cited with approval in *City of London Corpn* v *Bovis Construction Ltd* (1988) *The Times*, 21 April).

In any event, a quia timet injunction would in principle be an appropriate remedy where a listed building is about to be or is being demolished, since the damage will usually be both irreparable and unable to be prevented in any other way.

(b) Procedure

An application for an injunction in these circumstances is best brought in the Chancery Division of the High Court. The first step, if time permits, is for the authority to issue a notice of motion informing the defendants (the owners of the building and all others concerned) that the court will be moved by counsel for an interlocutory injunction in the terms specified in the notice. This notice must be served at least two days before the motion is heard. The motion will then be heard in open court, and the injunction will, if granted, take effect immediately.

Where greater speed is required, the authority should apply at once to the court on an ex parte basis (that is, without the defendants being present). In extreme cases, where the court is not sitting, application may be made at any time to a judge at his or her home; the authority's solicitors should telephone the Royal Courts of Justice who will be able to put them in touch with a judge available for the hearing of urgent applications. The authority will have to produce an affidavit as to the merits of its case, and an undertaking both to serve the notice of motion on the defendants as soon as possible (that is, in the following twenty-four hours) and to compensate them if it transpires that it was not entitled to the relief sought. If it is successful, the court will issue an interim injunction which will be effective only for a short period (usually five days or a week), until an inter partes application can be heard, so that the defendants can state their case.

Although an injunction is in principle an appropriate remedy to be used in a listed buildings case, it is an entirely discretionary one. Whether it will in fact be granted in any particular instance will be determined at the inter partes hearing according to the principles set out in *American Cyanamid Co* v *Ethicon Ltd* [1975] AC 396. Thus the party seeking the injunction (in this case, the authority) must show:

(1) that there is a serious question to be tried: this should not be too difficult if the works are about to start or are under way, although there will need to be proof; and where the works are already well advanced (particularly in the case of

demolition), it must be shown that it will be possible for their effect to be reversed;

(2) that an award of damages will not compensate the authority for the loss of or damage to the building (which will plainly be the case, since it is seeking the injunction on behalf of the public, not in its own right); and

(3) that damages would compensate the defendants if it subsequently transpired that its case was defective (if, for example, it turned out that the building was not in fact listed, or that a building preservation notice had not been properly served).

If an award of damages will adequately compensate the defendants in the event of the authority eventually losing, the court should then grant the injunction. If, on the other hand, an award of damages will not compensate the defendants, the court must decide where the public interest lies; and usually it will favour the maintenance of the status quo, which in a listed building case will also result in it granting the injunction.

The operation of these principles is illustrated by the case of Stagbatch Barn in Herefordshire. It came to the attention of the local authority on 5 August 1986 that a listed medieval cruck barn had been dismantled, and that its timbers were about to be exported to the USA. An injunction was granted ex parte that same day; and the local authority issued a listed building enforcement notice on 8 August requiring its re-erection (as to which, see 9.4(g)). The injunction was renewed on 11 August after an inter partes hearing by Hoffman J (reported as *Leominster DC* v *British Historic Buildings and SPS Shipping* [1987] JPL 350). He considered the application of the *Cyanamid* guidelines, and decided that the balance of convenience plainly favoured the retention of the timbers within the country until the matter could be resolved.

Although the Stagbatch case is not directly to point, because it concerns the export of a building which had already been demolished (which will not often occur), it is submitted that the same principles would surely apply where demolition or other unauthorised works are about to happen or are currently taking place.

Chapter 10

Demolition of Unlisted Buildings in Conservation Areas

10.1 Conservation area consent

(a) Background

When conservation areas were first introduced (see Chapter 4), there was no control over the demolition of buildings within them, except, obviously, those that were listed. This was altered by the TCP (Amendment) Act 1972, which provided that a local authority could control the demolition of a particular unlisted building in a conservation area, by making with respect to it a direction under s 8 of that Act. The effect of such a direction was similar to that of a building preservation notice (see Chapter 3), in that it applied to the building most of the provisions of the listed buildings code (as amended by Sched 2 to the 1972 Act).

However, the control mechanism under the 1972 Act proved in practice to be very cumbersome, and was little used. Two years later it was therefore replaced by the present system, introduced in the TCAA 1974. This in turn was slightly modified by the HPA 1986 and the TCP (Listed Buildings and Buildings in Conservation Areas) Regulations 1987. As a result, consent is now needed for the demolition of almost any building within a conservation area.

Until 1987 there had been some uncertainty about the name of this consent. It was variously referred to as 'listed building consent' (which was confusing, since the buildings involved were by definition not listed), 'consent under s 277A of the 1971 Act' or, more recently, 'conservation area consent' (introduced for the first time, apparently unintentionally, in the TCPA 1984). The 1987 Regulations, sensibly, have now come down firmly in favour of the third of these terms (TCPA 1971, s 55(3A), as substituted by TCP (LBCA) Regs 1987, reg 12 and Sched 3).

The scheme of the legislation is to apply almost all the

provisions of the 1971 Act regarding 'listed building consent' to 'conservation area consent', subject to any variation that may be prescribed in regulations. The sections of the Act which are thus applied to unlisted buildings in conservation areas are listed in TCPA 1971, s 277A (as amended by HPA 1986), which is reproduced as Part A of the Appendix to this book. Those sections have in some cases been modified in their application to unlisted buildings; and the modifications have been set out as Sched 3 to the TCP (LBCA) Regs 1987. As a result of those, the only really significant difference between listed building consent and conservation area consent is that conservation area consent is not required for the alteration or extension of an unlisted building, but only for its demolition.

Sections 55 and 56 of the Act, which are the most important provisions regarding listed building control, are set out (as modified by the Regulations to apply to conservation areas) as Part C of the Appendix.

(b) The need for conservation area consent

Conservation area consent is thus needed from the local planning authority for almost any works for the demolition of all or part of any unlisted building within a conservation area (TCPA 1971, s 277A(2), inserted by TCAA 1974).

It is not however needed for the following.

(1) the demolition of a listed building (for which listed building consent is needed instead; see 8.1(*b*)) (s 277A(1)(*a*));

(2) the demolition of an ecclesiastical building in ecclesiastical use (see 13.2(*a*)) (ss 277A(1)(*b*), 58(2)(*a*));

(3) the demolition of a scheduled monument (for which scheduled monument consent is needed instead; see 14.3) (ss 277A(1)(*b*), 58(2)(*b*), substituted by AMAAA 1979); or

(4) the demolition of a building in any of the exempted categories set out in a direction by the Secretary of State (see 10.2(*a*)).

Consent is in general needed for works for the demolition of part of a building (TCPA 1971, s 290). But where the part to be 'demolished' is very insignificant, the works may amount to 'alteration' rather than 'demolition'; they may then require planning permission (see 7.2), but they will not require conservation area consent. The distinction between these two terms has already been considered (see 8.1(*d*)), together with the unhelpful dictum of Comyn J in *R* v *North Hertfordshire DC, ex parte Sullivan* [1981]

JPL 752 at 754: 'not every piece of work by way of alteration or extension necessarily amounts to demolition'. In this context it may be that a useful test is to consider the effect of the proposed works on the character and appearance of the area, rather than just on that of the building itself.

In one appeal case at Brighton, for example, the removal of almost two metres of stucco cornice from an unlisted building in a conservation area was held by the Secretary of State ('as a matter of fact and degree') to be 'work on too small a scale to be regarded as demolition within the meaning of the Act' (DOE Ref APP/5202/F/77/22). But this opinion appears to have been considerably influenced by the location, where the absence of the cornice 'would not be particularly noticeable given the diverse frontage details of the other properties in this street'. A similar alteration, but in a uniform terrace, might well have produced a different result.

It would seem too that in practice the demolition of any part of the interior of an unlisted building is regarded as 'alteration', so that it does not need conservation area consent. This may be intellectually indefensible in some cases, but makes sense in terms of the objective of the Act, which is to protect the character and appearance of areas, not that of buildings.

The need for conservation area consent and planning permission is summarised in Figure 10.1.

10.2 Exceptions to the need for conservation area consent

(a) Directions by the Secretary of State

The Secretary of State has power to make directions exempting certain categories of demolition from the need for conservation area consent to be obtained (s 277A(4)–(6), inserted by TCAA 1974).

The direction now applying to England (in para 97 of DOE Circ 8/87) is reproduced as Part B of the Appendix to this book. It is in a number of respects significantly different from (and simpler than) its predecessor (in para 71 of Circ 23/77).

The direction applying to Wales, on the other hand, (in para 70 of WO Circ 61/81) is identical to the old English direction. It is likely that it will be revised in due course, and it may well be that any new direction will be more or less identical to the current English one, not least to avoid the references to the GDO 1977

Figure 10.1 Works to an unlisted building in a conservation area: consents needed

Type of works	Conservation area consent	Planning permission
1 Demolition of: building whose total vol is less than 115 cu m; wall etc less than 1m high on highway, or 2m elsewhere	Not needed	Never needed in practice (see 7.2(*d*))
2 Total or partial demolition of agricultural building	England: not needed for post-1914 building Wales: never needed	Never needed in practice (see 7.2(*d*))
3 Total or partial demolition of industrial building	Needed except where building (or part) to be demolished is small (see 10.2(*b*))	Rarely needed in practice (see 7.2(*d*))
4 Demolition works required by certain other legislation (see 10.2(*c*))	Not needed	Never needed in practice (see 7.2(*d*))
5 Total demolition of any other building	Always needed	Never needed in practice (see 7.2(*d*))
6 Partial demolition of any other building	England: always needed Wales: almost always needed (see 10.2(*b*) for exceptions)	Only needed if associated with other development
7 External alteration or extension of building (not 'permitted development'; see 7.3)	Only needed where the works involve partial demolition (see 10.1(*b*))	Always needed
8 External alteration or extension of building (permitted development)	Only needed where the works involve partial demolition (see 10.1(*b*))	Needed only where required by an Article 4 direction (see 7.4) or by a condition on a previous permission
9 Minor external alteration to building (not 'development'; see 7.2(*a*))	Not needed	Never needed
10 Alteration to interior of building	Never needed in practice (see 10.1(*b*))	Never needed
11 Erection of new building	Never needed	Almost always needed
12 Works to religious building	Not often needed (see 13.2)	As for 5 to 11 above
13 Works to scheduled monument in conservation area	Never needed; but scheduled monument consent is usually needed (see 14.3)	As for 5 to 11 above

which has now been replaced. By way of comparison, the equivalent direction applying in Scotland (in Annex IV of SDD Circ 17/1987) is generally similar to the new English direction.

(b) Minor demolition works

The first group of categories of demolition works which are exempted from the need for conservation area consent comprises various minor works which are presumably reckoned to be generally harmless (DOE Circ 8/87, para 97(a)–(d); WO Circ 61/81, para 70(a), (b)). This represents a mechanism similar to 'permitted development', whereby planning permission is granted automatically for certain types of generally harmless development (see 7.3). But note that there is no equivalent of the 'Article 4 direction' procedure (see 7.4), so it is not possible for a local authority to bring within control any demolition in the exempted categories, except by seeking to have the building concerned listed or serving on it a building preservation notice (see Chapter 3).

Conservation area consent is thus not needed in England for the demolition of the following categories of unlisted building:
  (a) any building whose *total* volume is less than 115 cu m, or any part of such a building;
  (b) any gate, wall, fence or railing less than 1 m high fronting a highway or open space or 2 m high elsewhere;
  (c) any agricultural building erected after 1914;
  (d) up to 10 per cent (or 500 sq m if greater) of any industrial building.

This usefully avoids the tortuous provision in the old direction linking demolition rights with permitted development rights under the GDO, which used to cause a number of problems in practice (and which still applies in Wales; see below). It means that, for example, features such as cornices or gables cannot now be demolished without consent, except where they are so insignificant that their removal amounts to 'alteration' (see 10.1(b)).

Category (a) allows the demolition without specific consent of small structures (such as garden sheds). Note that this is almost the only instance where the meaning of 'building' does not include 'part of a building', so that the removal of part of a larger building (even though the part to be removed may be under 115 cu m in volume) still requires consent, unless it is excepted under any of the other headings.

Category (d) is slightly unclear. It refers to the demolition of:

any part of [an industrial building], provided that such part (taken with any other part which may have been demolished) does not exceed ten per cent of the cubic content of the original building . . . or 500 square metres of floor space, whichever is the greater.

Does the phrase 'original building' refer to the building as it was first built, or to it as it was at 1 July 1948 (the meaning in the GDO)? As for 'any other part which may have been demolished'—demolished since when? Since the building was built, or since 1948, or since it was first included in a conservation area, or since the direction was made (April 1987)? The most probable answer to the first question would seem to be 1948, since that would tie in with a number of provisions elsewhere in planning legislation (for example, TCPA 1971, ss 23(2)–(4) and Sched 8, as well as GDO 1988, art 2). As to the second question the most satisfactory answer would be either 1948 or when the building was included in the area.

The above notes (and the text of Part B of the Appendix) represent the position taking account of an amendment to the direction within Circular 8/87 as originally published, which was issued shortly after the Circular itself to correct some minor drafting errors.

In Wales, category (*a*) applies as in England. But categories (*b*) to (*d*) do not. Instead, conservation area consent is not needed in Wales for the demolition of:

any [unlisted] building if development consisting of the erection of that building:
> would be development permitted by classes I, II, IV, VI or VIII of Schedule 1 to the General Development Order and article 3 of that Order [development within the curtilage of a dwellinghouse, sundry minor operations (including the construction of gates and walls), temporary buildings, agricultural development and minor industrial development]; or
> would be so permitted but for [an Article 4 direction]
(WO Circ 61/81, para 70(*b*)).

As to the classes of permitted development referred to here, they refer to the (now superseded) GDO 1977. They are roughly—but not exactly—equivalent to Parts 1, 2, 4, 6, and 8 of Sched 2 to the GDO 1988 (see Figure 7.1). One example of demolition exempt from the need for conservation area consent under this heading would be the removal of a garden shed, or of a front garden wall less than a metre high, since the erection of either of these would be permitted development under Class I.3 or II.1

respectively. The position is less clear, however, with regard to partial demolition of larger buildings. It would seem that the alteration or extension of a dwellinghouse or an industrial building, although (in certain circumstances) permitted development under Class I.1 or VIII, might not constitute the 'erection' of a building (*Whyte* v *Bruce* (1900) 37 SLT 614). The undoing of such an alteration, and possibly the removal of such an extension, might therefore not be exempt from the need for consent. But this is far from clear; see correspondence in the JPL at [1982] 667, [1984] 327 and [1987] 308.

(c) Demolition authorised under other procedures

The second group of exceptions refers to various circumstances where demolition can be authorised under other procedures.

Conservation area consent is thus not needed in England (by virtue of DOE Circ 8/87, para 97(*e*)–(*k*)) for demolition works required by any of the following:

(*e*) a discontinuance order;

(*f*) a s 52 agreement;

(*g*) an enforcement notice or a listed building enforcement notice;

(*h*) a condition attached to a planning permission (but not, since 1987, where the permission was in effect granted to a planning authority by itself for its own works; see 7.5(*e*));

(*i*) a demolition order under the Housing Act 1985 (see 5.9(*b*));

(*j*) a compulsory purchase order under the 1985 Act (but, since 1987, only where the order has been approved by the Secretary of State) (see 5.9(*b*)); and

(*k*) a pastoral scheme or a redundancy scheme under the Pastoral Measure 1983 (providing for the demolition of a redundant Church of England church; see 13.5).

The presumption here is that further consent is unnecessary, since in most of these cases the demolition works will have already been either authorised or indeed required by the local authority, which will have presumably taken into account their effect on the appearance of the conservation area (as required by TCPA 1971, s 277(8)).

Category (*f*) is unfortunately drafted, in that it refers only to an agreement under TCPA 1971, s 52, whereas agreements having a similar effect are in fact often made under other legislation, such as s 33 of the Local Government (Miscellaneous Provisions) Act 1982. In any event, for this exemption to operate, the agreement must actually 'require' the demolition of the building, rather than merely facilitate the development of its site (*Windsor and Maidenhead RBC* v *Brandrose Investments Ltd* [1983] JPL 374 at 375).

The effect of the recent change to category (*h*) is that a local planning authority can no longer give itself planning permission for a new building in a conservation area, and incorporate as a condition a requirement that the existing building on the site should be demolished. In such a case, conservation area consent must now be obtained from the Secretary of State (TCPA 1971, s 277A(7)(*a*), inserted by TCAA 1974). The change to category (*j*) ensures that a local authority cannot demolish a house in a conservation area that has been acquired by agreement under Housing Act powers. Again, it must first obtain the approval of the Secretary of State.

All these categories apply to Wales (although lettered (*c*) to (*i*), rather than (*e*) to (*k*)), except that the changes made in 1987 and noted in the previous paragraph do not apply (WO Circ 61/81, para 70(*c*)–(*i*)).

10.3 Applications for conservation area consent

(a) Submission of application

The sources of the procedural rules regarding conservation area consent are as for listed building consent (see 8.3(*a*)), although the 1971 Act is slightly modified in its application to conservation areas by Sched 3 to the TCP (LBCA) Regs 1987. Accordingly, the details in Chapter 8 regarding the submission and processing of applications for listed building consent apply also to those for conservation area consent, subject to modifications noted here; that chapter should be consulted for details of the relevant statutory and other authorities. The comments in Circ 8/87 regarding listed building consent applications are specifically extended to apply to conservation area consent except where otherwise stated (para 94).

An application for conservation area consent should be made to the appropriate local planning authority (see 8.3(*b*)). It should be on the form supplied by the authority—there is no standard one; and it is likely that, until the new terminology of 'conservation area consent' is universally accepted (see 10.1(*a*)), some authorities will continue to issue listed building consent forms for use with conservation area applications. The supporting details required will be as for an application for listed building consent to demolish a listed building (8.3(c)). Ownership certificates, and associated notification and advertisement, will be required as for listed building and planning applications. The authority must take into account any representations made by any owners thus notified (TCP (LBCA) Regs 1987, reg 6; see 8.3(d)).

(b) Procedure following submission of application

On receipt of an application for conservation area consent, the planning authority must acknowledge it, and check that it is in order (see 8.4(a)). It must also publicise the application by placing a notice on site and in the local press, and take into account any representations made as a result (TCP (LBCA) Regs 1987, reg 5(1), (2); and see 8.4(b)).

Authorities are not required to notify the Royal Commission on Historical Monuments of conservation area applications, nor any of the national amenity societies; the direction in para 81 of DOE Circ 8/87 (para 52 of WO Circ 61/81) does not apply to unlisted buildings. But there is no reason why it should not notify one or more of them of any particular application if it wishes—for example, where proposed demolition in a conservation area affects the setting of a listed building of a particular period. And there is no requirement for the Secretary of State to be notified either.

Similarly, an authority outside London is not required to send any application for conservation area consent to the Historic Buildings and Monuments Commission, although of course it may if it wishes. Within Greater London, however, the London Division of the Commission must be notified of every application for conservation area consent, whether it is made to a borough council or to the London Docklands Development Corporation. Further, the local planning authority must not determine the application until twenty-eight days have elapsed after the Commission was notified, and must take into account any representations made by it (TCPA 1971, Sched 11, para 6, as substituted in respect of unlisted buildings in conservation areas by TCP (LBCA) Regs 1987, Sched 3). Note that the Commission is not empowered to direct the authority how to determine the application; it may merely comment. Moreover, it is not required to consult the Secretary of State before making any such comment.

(c) The decision

The timetable for determining applications for conservation area consent is as for listed buildings (see 8.5(*a*)). There is the same right of appeal against the failure of an authority to determine an application within eight weeks of it being submitted. The Secretary of State also has power to call-in any conservation area application for his own decision if he wishes (see 8.5(*b*)).

There is no need for either the authority or the applicant to notify the Royal Commission of any decision to grant consent for demolition; TCPA 1971, s 55(2)(*b*) does not apply to unlisted buildings (TCP (LBCA) Regs 1987, Sched 3). But the Historic Buildings and Monuments Commission must be notified of the outcome of every conservation area application in London (TPCA 1971, Sched 11, para 6, applied by 1987 Regs, Sched 3).

Conservation area consent can either be refused or granted subject to conditions.

As to conditions generally, see 8.6; most of those suitable for consent for the demolition of a listed building will be suitable for use in conservation areas. In particular, all conservation area consents last for five years unless stated otherwise (s 56A, inserted by LGPLA 1980 and applied by s 277(8); see 8.6(*b*)). It is possible for a planning authority to impose a condition requiring specified works to be approved later, and for an applicant to apply later to have any condition modified or varied (ss 56(4B), 56B, inserted by HPA 1986 and applied by s 277(8); see 8.6(*c*), (*e*)), although neither power is likely to be used particularly often in the context of conservation area consent.

It may be appropriate in cases of demolition followed by redevelopment to accompany any consent that may be granted with an agreement enforceable under s 33 of the Local Government (Miscellaneous Provisions) Act 1982. 'In the past, unsightly gaps have appeared in conservation areas as a result of premature demolition, and unsatisfactory redevelopment has been allowed, primarily in order to fill such gaps' (Circ 8/87, para 95). In such cases, it may also be suitable to impose a condition that the building is not to be demolished before a contract has been made and planning permission has been granted for the construction of its replacement (under TCPA 1971, s 56(5), inserted by LGPLA 1980 and applied by s 277(8); and see 8.6(*d*)).

(d) Matters to be taken into account in determining applications

In assessing whether or not consent should be granted, authorities have been advised by the Secretary of State (in Circ 8/87, para 94) that they should have regard to the desirability of preserving or enhancing the character or appearance of the conservation area in which the building is situated. This follows the wording of subs (8) of s 277 of the 1971 Act (as substituted by TCAA 1974). This, however, conflicts with subs (1) of the same section, which states that by definition a conservation area is an area the character or appearance of which it *is* desirable to preserve or enhance. Thus the authority may consider the desirability of preserving and enhancing an area if it wishes (and as it is indeed required to do by subs (8)), but the outcome of such consideration is a foregone conclusion.

It would seem therefore that the duty of the planning authority is rather to consider whether the proposed works actually *contribute towards* the preservation or enhancement of the area's character, since that is, by definition, a desirable aim (see also *Steinberg* v *Secretary of State*, (1988) *The Independent*, 2 December). In other words, if a proposal is to demolish an eyesore which at present spoils the area, consent should be granted; if on the other hand it is to demolish a building that is in itself unremarkable but that fits in perfectly as part of a pleasant, homogeneous area, it should be refused. The key factor to be considered is thus undoubtedly the appearance and character of the area, not that of the building itself.

Where (as is often the case) the demolition of a building is to be followed by the redevelopment of the site, the Secretary of State has stated (in Circ 8/87, para 95) that '[he] considers that consent to demolish should normally be given only where there are acceptable and detailed plans for that redevelopment'. He also drew attention to *Richmond-upon-Thames LBC* v *Secretary of State* (1978) 37 P & CR 151, in which Sir Douglas Frank, sitting as deputy judge of the High Court, held that the function of giving consent to demolish an unlisted building in a conservation area could not be performed without seeing what was to be substituted and how it would fit into the area. Arguably, however, if the demolition of an existing building in a conservation area contributes nothing to the preservation or enhancement of the character of the area, consent should be refused; and the consideration of any replacement building then becomes irrelevant.

Also relevant here will be the considerations raised in *Kent Messenger Ltd* v *Secretary of State* [1976] JPL 372 and *Thanet DC* v *Secretary of State* [1978] JPL 251 on the economics of the replacement building—the first of these was considered by the judge in the *Richmond* case (above)—and *Godden* v *Secretary of State* [1988] JPL 99 on the redevelopment of larger areas. See also 8.7(*c*).

(e) Special cases

Applications by local authorities themselves to demolish their own unlisted buildings in conservation areas must be made to the Secretary of State (TCPA 1971, s 277A(7), inserted by TCAA 1974); as with listed buildings, they cannot grant themselves deemed consent (see 8.2(*e*) for further details).

Thus, for example, the Greater London Council was able in 1982 to prevent (at least for a while) the demolition of Kensington Town Hall by the local council by including it within a conservation area. At the time the designation order came into effect, half of the building had been perfectly lawfully demolished. As a result of the designation, before the demolition works could be completed, the Borough Council then had to seek consent from the Secretary of State, which in the event he readily gave. (He had also declined to list the building a few years earlier.)

Proposals by Government departments to demolish their unlisted buildings in conservation areas, on the other hand, do not require consent as such. Instead, as with works that would otherwise require planning permission or listed building consent, developing departments notify the local planning authority of their proposals under the procedure set out in Circ 18/84 (see 8.2(*c*)).

10.4 Remedies following the refusal of conservation area consent

(a) Appeals

The statutory provisions (described in 8.8) regarding appeals against the refusal of listed building consent apply virtually without alteration to appeals against the refusal of conservation area consent (or the grant of consent but subject to onerous conditions or the failure of the authority to make any decision within eight weeks).

There is a specific ground of appeal against the refusal of listed building consent that 'the building is not of special . . . interest,

K

and should be removed from the list' (TCPA 1971, Sched 11, para 8(2)); but there is no corresponding provision applying to conservation area appeals. Indeed, no specific grounds of appeal are mentioned. But there is no reason why, for example, an appellant should not include as a specific ground of appeal the following:

(1) 'that the area in which the building lies is not an area of special architectural or historic interest, and ought not to be designated as a conservation area'; or

(2) 'that the character and appearance of the area in which the building lies are not desirable to preserve and enhance, and that it ought not to be designated as a conservation area'.

Either or both of these might in some cases be a perfectly proper line of argument.

The decisions on all appeals against the refusal of conservation area consent in England may now be taken by inspectors (TCP (Determination of Appeals by Appointed Persons) (Prescribed Classes) Regulations 1981, reg 3(*d*), inserted by TCP (Determination [etc]) Regulations 1986). In Wales, all decisions must still be taken by the Secretary of State (regs 3(*d*), 4(*f*)).

The rights of appeal to the courts against decisions of local authorities, the Secretary of State or his inspectors are the same in connection with conservation area consent as they are in connection with listed buildings (see 8.9).

(b) Compensation

There is no right of compensation for the refusal of conservation area consent, or its grant subject to onerous conditions. Section 171 does not apply to unlisted buildings.

(c) Conservation area purchase notices

If conservation area consent is refused, granted subject to onerous conditions, revoked or modified, and land is thereby rendered 'incapable of beneficial use', the owner may serve on the local authority a *conservation area purchase notice*. The entitlement to serve such a notice and the procedure after one has been served correspond exactly to those applying where a listed building purchase notice is served (TCPA 1971, s 190, applied by TCP (LBCA) Regs 1987, reg 12(*a*) and Sched 3; and see 8.12).

10.5 Revocation or modification of conservation area consent

Either a planning authority or (since 1987) the Secretary of State may revoke or modify a conservation area consent once it has been granted. Again, the procedure and entitlement to compensation are as for the revocation or modification of listed building consent (TCPA 1971, Sched 11, Part II, and s 172, applied by TCP (LBCA) Regs 1987, Sched 3; and see 8.11).

10.6 Unauthorised demolition

(a) Application for consent for demolition already carried out

It is possible to submit an application for conservation area consent to authorise demolition works already carried out (TCPA 1971, s 55(2A), inserted by LGPLA 1980 and applied by TCPA 1971, s 277A(8)). Such consent, if granted, does not render immunity from criminal prosecution, but it would be sufficient to halt any enforcement action that might be under way (s 99A, inserted by LGPLA 1980).

(b) Criminal prosecution

The demolition of an unlisted building in a conservation area, except in the circumstances mentioned in 10.1(*b*), is a criminal offence (under s 55(1) as applied by s 277A(8)). The same considerations would generally apply as to proceedings under s 55(1) in connection with listed buildings (see 9.2).

The onus would thus be on the authority (or whoever mounted the prosecution) to prove that the demolition had taken place, and that the building was in a conservation area. In proving the latter, particular care would be needed to ensure that the relevant paperwork (including copies of the advertisement in the local newspaper and the *London Gazette*, as required by s 277(6)) was in order; the procedures followed by some authorities in designating conservation areas might not stand up very well in the light of cross-examination (see *Vale of Glamorgan BC* v *Palmer* [1984] JPL 334).

It would also seem in the light of the decision of the House of Lords in *R* v *Hunt* [1987] 1 All ER 1 (overturning the decision of the Court of Appeal at [1986] 2 WLR 225) that the onus was on the prosecution to prove in appropriate cases that the demolition was not in one of the excepted categories in s 277A(1) (see 10.1(*b*)). This could be particularly relevant where the demolition was claimed to be within one of the categories in the Secretary of State's directions (see 10.2).

It would be up to the accused, on the other hand, to prove either:

(1) that he or she had obtained conservation area consent; or
(2) that the works were urgently necessary [etc] (and all the other items required by s 55(6); see 9.2(*c*)).

It is also an offence to carry out demolition works for which conservation area consent has been given without complying with a condition attached to the consent (s 55(4), applied by s 277A(8); and see 9.2(*f*)).

Both of the offences under s 55 are triable either way, and carry the same maximum penalties as the corresponding listed building offences (s 55(5), applied by s 277A(8); see 9.2(*e*)). It would seem that both of them are strict liability, that is, it would not be necessary for the prosecution to prove that the accused knew that the building was in a conservation area (*R* v *Wells Street Metropolitan Stipendiary Magistrate, ex parte Westminster CC* [1986] 1 WLR 1046).

It is not an offence to 'damage' an unlisted building in a conservation area, unless that damage amounts to demolition of part of the building. Section 57 applies to listed buildings only.

(c) Conservation area enforcement notices

As an alternative to prosecuting those responsible for the unauthorised demolition of an unlisted building in a conservation area, it is possible for a planning authority to issue a *conservation area enforcement notice*, if it considers it expedient to do so in the light of the effect of the allegedly unauthorised works on the character and appearance of the area (s 96(1), applied by s 277A(8) and modified by TCP (LBCA) Regs 1987, reg 12 and Sched 3). See 9.4(*a*), (*b*) on enforcement generally.

The provisions as to the contents of a conservation area enforcement notice, its issue and its coming into effect follow precisely those applying to a listed building notice (see 9.4(*c*), (*d*)).

The procedure as to appeals and their aftermath is also the same for conservation areas as for listed buildings (see 9.4(*e*), (*h*), (*i*)). The grounds of appeal (see Figure 9.1) are the same, with two exceptions (s 97(1), applied by s 277A(8) and modified by TCP (LBCA) Regs 1987, Sched 3):

(1) Ground (*a*) becomes: 'That retention of the building is not necessary in the interests of preserving or enhancing the

character of the conservation area in which it is situated';
and

(2) Ground (*i*) ('That the steps required by the notice for the
purpose of restoring the character of the building to its
former state would not serve that purpose') does not apply.

The grounds of appeal suggested in connection with appeals
against refusal of consent (see 10.4(*a*)) could not be used here,
since the list of grounds in s 97 is exhaustive. Anyone contemplating carrying out demolition works and justifying them on those
grounds should therefore apply for consent and appeal against
any refusal, rather than carry on regardless and appeal against
any subsequent enforcement notice.

The decisions on all appeals against conservation area enforcement notices in England may now be taken by inspectors (TCP
(Determination of Appeals by Appointed Persons) (Prescribed
Classes) Regulations 1981, reg 3(*c*), inserted by TCP (Determination [etc]) Regulations 1986). In Wales, all decisions are still
taken by the Secretary of State (regs 3(*c*), 4(*f*)).

(d) Injunctions

It would be possible to use injunctions to halt the unauthorised
demolition of unlisted buildings in conservation areas in the same
circumstances as apply in the case of works to listed buildings (see
9.5). It could be more difficult to persuade a court to issue an
injunction in connection with an unlisted building; but it might be
possible, particularly in the case of a persistent offender.

Chapter 11

Trees and Gardens

11.1 Trees in conservation areas

(a) Notice to be given to the local authority before carrying out works

It is the character and appearance of conservation areas as a whole that local authorities are required to preserve and enhance, not just that of the buildings within them. A major element in the character and appearance of many areas is the trees and gardens within them. The latter, inevitably and rightly, are not suitable for any but very limited 'control', although the best gardens in England are now at least recorded (see 11.4). However, ill-considered works to trees may not only lead to the loss of the trees themselves, but also ruin the appearance of the area surrounding them and spoil the setting of any buildings nearby. Since this is particularly unfortunate in conservation areas, whose appearance is (by definition) both special and worth preserving, local authorities have been given at least some powers to control works to trees there.

Accordingly, anyone proposing to carry out any works to a tree that is in a conservation area must almost always give written notice of at least six weeks to the local planning authority (TCPA 1971, s 61A(1)–(3), inserted by TCAA 1974). This requirement, which seems to be relatively unknown by owners of property in conservation areas (or at any rate is not widely observed), was introduced by the TCAA 1974, the same Act that provided for effective control over demolition in conservation areas (see 10.1(*a*)).

The works to be notified under this provision are the 'cutting down, topping, lopping, uprooting, wilful damage, or wilful destruction' of any tree (ss 61A(1), 60(1)(*a*), inserted by TCAA

1974). As to the meaning of 'destruction', see 11.1(*d*); and regarding the vexed question of what is a 'tree', see 11.2(*a*).

(b) Exceptions to the need to notify the local authority

There are, inevitably, a number of exceptions to this general requirement, set out in regulations made under s 61A(4)–(5). It is thus currently not necessary to notify the authority in any of the following circumstances (TCP (Tree Preservation Order) (Amendment) and (Trees in Conservation Areas) (Exempted Cases) Regulations 1975, reg 3):

  (i) the cutting down, uprooting, topping or lopping of a tree
    —because it is dying, dead, or dangerous; or
    —in order to comply with an Act of Parliament; or
    —so far as may be necessary to prevent or abate a nuisance (TCPA 1971, s 60(6));

  (ii) the cutting down of a tree in accordance with a plan of operations approved by the Forestry Commission (TCP (Tree Preservation Order) Regulations 1969, model order, Sched 2, paras (1), (2)); or
    the cutting down, uprooting, topping or lopping of a tree:
    —where carried out or required by any one of a variety of statutory undertakers, river authorities, airport authorities etc;
    —in order to carry out development for which planning permission has been granted (but not merely in order to carry out permitted development; see 7.3); or
    —which is a fruit tree in an orchard or garden cultivated for fruit production
    (model order, Sched 2, para (3));

  (iii) the cutting down of a tree in accordance with a felling licence under the Forestry Act 1967;

  (iv) the cutting down, uprooting, topping or lopping of a tree on land owned by a local authority with its consent;

  (v) the cutting down, uprooting, topping or lopping of:
    —a tree with a diameter of not more than 75 mm at 1.5 m above ground level; or
    —a tree with a diameter of not more than 100 mm at that height where the act is to improve the growth of other trees.

Most of these categories are straightforward. They mean, in particular, that it is not necessary to notify the local authority of proposed works to a fruit tree, or to a small tree (as defined above) (reg 3(ii), (v)).

Nor is notification needed where a tree is to be removed because it is dead or dangerous (reg 3(*i*)). However, where works are carried out in any of the circumstances in category (i), although it is not necessary to notify the authority, another tree must normally be planted (see 11.3) (s 61A(8)).

Problems may arise with works which are claimed to be necessary 'to prevent or abate a nuisance'. A tree will often be a 'nuisance' in the every day sense of the word; but what is envisaged here is a 'nuisance' at law. Thus damage, amounting to a nuisance, may be caused by either the penetration of roots from one property to another (as in *Davey* v *Harrow Corpn* [1958] 1 QB 60 and *Bunclark* v *Hertfordshire CC* (1977) 243 EG 455) or the overhanging of branches (as in *Lemmon* v *Webb* [1895] AC 1 and *Smith* v *Giddy* [1904] 2 KB 448). But whilst at common law the property owner suffering the nuisance is entitled to the self-help remedy of abatement, no action would lie unless damage results; and it would seem that the exemption from control under the TCPA 1971 would similarly apply only where there is actual damage, rather than merely an encroachment over a neighbour's air space (*Sun Timber Company* v *Leeds CC* (1980) Leeds Crown Court (unreported)).

(c) Procedure

Notice must be given to the local district or borough council in writing, specifying the trees concerned and the works proposed (TCPA 1971, s 61A(3)(*a*)). It is also advisable to state the reasons for the works, and whether any replanting is proposed. Some authorities issue a standard form for this purpose; others are content for notice to be given by letter. Once notice has been given, the works must not be carried out until either the appropriate authority has granted consent or no response has been received after six weeks have elapsed (s 61A(3)(*b*)).

The appropriate authority for the purpose of granting consent under s 61A(3)(*b*) is as follows:

(1) *in urban development areas other than Cardiff Bay*: the urban development corporation (see 1.3(*a*));
(2) *in national parks*: the county council or the special planning board (LGA 1972, s 182(4), Sched 17);
(3) *elsewhere in Greater London and the metropolitan areas*: the

district or borough council (TCPA 1971, s 1(1)(*b*), (*c*), substituted by LGA 1985);

(4) *the Broads*: the Broads Authority or the county council (TCPA 1971, ss 1(1)(*a*) [substituted by LGA 1985] and 273A [inserted by NSBA 1988]);

(5) *elsewhere*: the district, borough or county council (s 1(1)(*a*), substituted by LGA 1985).

Where consent is granted, there is no provision for any conditions to be attached. Where on the other hand an authority wishes to refuse consent for the works, or wishes to impose any conditions on a grant of consent, the only way in which this can be done is for it first to make a tree preservation order (see 11.2(*a*)), and then refuse consent under that order. There is then a right of appeal against such refusal (11.2(*e*)).

Where no response is received, a further notification will be required if the works are to be carried out more than two years after the original notice (s 61A(3)(*b*)).

Finally, where a tree in a conservation area is subject to a tree preservation order, it is necessary to obtain consent under the order for any works proposed, rather than to give notice under s 61A (s 61A(2)) (see 11.2(*d*)).

(d) Unauthorised works

It is an offence under s 61A(1):

(1) to carry out any works to a tree in a conservation area without giving notice to the authority, unless the works are in one of the exempted categories listed in 11.1(*b*); or

(2) to carry out any such works where consent has been refused.

Note that none of the exempted categories includes the wilful damage or destruction of any tree. This therefore remains an offence. The 'destruction' of a tree has been held to include the carrying out of any act, such as severing its root system, as a result of which it ceases to have any further use as an amenity, that is, it is no longer worth preserving (*Barnet LBC* v *Eastern Electricity Board* [1973] 1 WLR 430).

This offence is probably one of strict liability, that is, it would not be a necessary ingredient that the accused was aware that the tree was within a conservation area (see 9.2(*b*)). The required mens rea for a conviction for wilful damage or destruction would seem to be 'wilfulness' as to the damage, rather than knowledge as to the existence of the conservation area designation.

If the unauthorised works consist of:

(1) the cutting down, uprooting or wilful destruction of a tree; or

(2) the wilful damage, lopping or topping of a tree in such a manner as is likely to destroy it,

the offence is triable either way, and is subject to a fine of up to 'the prescribed sum' on summary conviction, or an unlimited fine on indictment (see also 9.2(*e*)) (TCPA 1971, s 102(1), (4), substituted by TCAA 1974 and amended by Magistrates' Courts Act 1980; Criminal Penalties etc (Increase) Order 1984). Where an offender is convicted in the Crown Court, the court must bear in mind in determining the appropriate fine any financial benefit that has accrued or is likely to accrue as a result of the offence (as with unauthorised works to listed buildings) (s 102(1)(*b*)). Thus if the removal of a tree unlocks a development site, the fine should in theory be substantial. In practice, however, possibly even more than with other offences described in this book, any fines imposed are likely to be very small, especially in the magistrates' courts.

If the unauthorised works consist of any other topping or lopping of a tree, the offence is triable only summarily, and the maximum penalty on conviction is a fine of up to level 4 on the standard scale (s 102(2), (4), amended by Criminal Justice Act 1982; Criminal Penalties etc (Increase) Order 1984).

Finally, where unauthorised works are carried out leading to the loss of a tree, a replacement must be planted (see 11.3) (s 61A(8)).

11.2 Tree preservation orders

(a) Preliminaries

As well as the limited general protection given to trees under s 61A, and occasionally as a result of it (see 11.1(*c*)), it will sometimes be appropriate for individual trees or groups of trees to be specially protected. This is in part achieved through local authorities being given powers to make *tree preservation orders*. These are inaptly named, for no amount of legislation can 'preserve' a tree beyond its natural lifespan. However they at least provide some control over unsuitable works being carried out which would damage or destroy the health or appearance of selected trees.

A local authority may make tree preservation orders where it appears to be expedient to do so in the interests of 'amenity' (as to which, see 5.7(*e*)) (TCPA 1971, s 60(1), amended by TCAA 1974). A detailed discussion of the circumstances where the making of an order would be appropriate is beyond the scope of this book; but some relevant advice is given in the Memorandum to Circ 36/78 (which is very informative on trees and forestry generally); see paras 41–3.

The general duty of planning authorities to preserve and enhance the appearance of conservation areas (s 277(8), substituted by TCAA 1974) will mean that they should consider making orders covering the trees in them. Suitable occasions for this will be when notice is given to them of proposed works to trees, under the s 61A procedure (see 11.1(*c*)) and, more positively, when they are surveying their areas in connection with preparing local plans and enhancement proposals under s 277B (see 4.4).

Authorities are also under a special duty to consider the desirability of making orders when granting planning permission for development on sites containing existing trees (s 59). This would apply particularly where an authority is considering an application for planning permission or listed building consent for works to a listed building, since it is then under a duty to consider the desirability of preserving the setting of the building, which may well include trees (s 56(3)). Finally, it may be appropriate to make orders to protect new trees to be planted in connection with development (often as a result of a condition attached to the planning permission) (s 59). Where orders are made in any of these circumstances to protect trees from damage or loss as a result of impending building works, they will almost always need to be made under the s 61 procedure (see 11.2(*c*)).

It has recently been held in the High Court that, in the light of the amended legislation whereby there is no right of appeal to the Secretary of State against the making of an order (see 11.2(*c*)), it is particularly important for a local authority to give proper consideration to the making of the order in the first place, and not to take into account any immaterial considerations (*Bellcross Co Ltd* v *Mid Bedfordshire DC* [1988] 15 EG 106). Since the only material consideration is 'amenity', it would be improper to take into account, for example, the desire to impede an unpopular development taking place on a site currently occupied by trees of no particular amenity value.

The definition of what is a 'tree' has proved notoriously difficult. In one old case, it was stated that reference to trees generally means 'wood applicable to buildings and does not include orchard trees' (*Bullen* v *Denning* (1826) 5 B & C 842 at 851). It is doubtful whether this would apply in the present circumstances, as an orchard tree could almost certainly be subject to a tree preservation order; but the definition does have something to commend it, as works to orchard trees are exempt both from the need for notice to be given to the local authority under s 61A (see 11.1(*b*)) and from the need for consent under any order (see 11.2(*d*)). More recently, Lord Denning has suggested that a distinction might be drawn between mature trees and saplings, with only trees having a diameter greater than seven inches or eight inches being protected by a woodland tree preservation order (see 11.2(*b*)) (*Kent CC* v *Batchelor* (1976) 33 P & CR 185 at 189).

But a contrary view was expressed by Phillips J in *Bullock* v *Secretary of State for the Environment* (1980) 40 P & CR 246, when he upheld an order in respect of a coppice; he preferred to let the word bear its normal meaning—whatever that is! Trees with a diameter not exceeding 75 mm at a height of 1.5 m above the ground are specifically excluded from the operation of s 61A (see 11.1(*b*)), so by implication plants of lesser dimensions can still sometimes be 'trees'. It is possible in certain circumstances for tree preservation orders to be placed on trees from the moment of their planting (see, for example, ss 60(3), 62(2)); it is difficult to conceive of a definition that would include such saplings but exclude a number of other plants that are clearly not trees. The Secretary of State has merely said that he considers it to exclude shrubs and hedges (although not hedgerow trees) (Memorandum to Circ 36/78, para 44).

(b) Form of a tree preservation order

The form of a tree preservation order is provided for in regulations (s 60(5)). The regulations currently in force are the TCP (Tree Preservation Order) Regulations 1969, which were amended by the TCP (Tree Preservation Order) (Amendment) [etc] Regulations 1975 and 1988. An order is thus to be in the form, or 'substantially' in the form, of the model order set out as the Schedule to these (reg 4).

The body of the order, together with the second and third schedules to it, is to set out the requirement for consent to be obtained, the procedure for obtaining it and various consequential provisions as to replacement planting, compensation and so forth (see 11.2(*d*), (*e*), (*f*)). This will in practice follow the text of the model order, except that the model order, since it dates from 1969, is drafted with reference to the TCPA 1962, the Civic Amenities Act 1967 and the TCPA 1968, and should be updated to include the corresponding provisions of the TCPA 1971.

The first schedule to the order is to specify the trees to be protected by the order (which area is also to be shown on a map). They are to be categorised into trees specified individually, trees specified by reference to an area, groups of trees, and woodlands. These classifications can be significant when it comes to the requirement to plant replacement trees (ss 62, 103, amended by TCP (Amendment) Act 1985; *Bush* v *Secretary of State for the Environment* [1988] JPL 108; see 11.3).

(c) Procedure for making a tree preservation order

A tree preservation order can be made by the following local authorities:

(1) *urban development areas other than Cardiff Bay*: the urban development corporation (see 1.3(*a*));
(2) *national parks*: the county council (or special planning board) or the district council (TCPA 1971, s 60(1), (1A)(*d*), LGA 1972, s 182(5));
(3) *elsewhere in Greater London and the metropolitan areas*: the district or borough council;
(4) *elsewhere*: either:
 — the county council, where it is determining a planning application, or in respect of land in two districts, or on its land (ss 60(1), 1(1)(*a*), 60(1A)(*a*)–(*c*)), or
 — the district council (ss 60(1), 1(1)(*a*)).

The procedure for making an order is set out in the 1969 Regulations. The authority must, after making the draft order, have it available for public inspection, and send copies to the district valuer and the Conservator of Forests. More importantly it must send copies to the owners and occupiers concerned and anyone else entitled to fell any of the trees affected by the order (such as tree surgeons, builders and surveyors) together with a notice stating the reasons for the making of the order, and explaining their right to object to the authority (reg 5). It has been suggested, sensibly, that where an order might affect the interests of neighbouring owners or where there is likely to be public interest, consideration should be given to the display of a site notice or other suitable publicity (Memorandum to Circ 36/78, para 51).

Objections can then be made to the authority, which can if it wishes hold an inquiry to consider them. It may then confirm the order with or without modifications, but if any modifications have been made, those who were initially notified must be told (regs 7–9). This is a slightly bizarre procedure, since the only right of objection to an order is to the authority that made it, which is only likely to result in the order being modified if it contains a factual error (such as the species of a tree being incorrectly specified). Presumably it will be possible to overturn an order if it can be shown that an authority had resolved to turn a deaf ear to all objections; it has a duty 'to listen to any objector who shows that he may have something new to say' (*R* v *Secretary of State for the Environment, ex parte Brent LBC* [1982] QB 593).

The order in theory takes effect only once it has been confirmed (s 60(4), substituted by LGPLA 1980). However, where it appears to the authority that the order should take effect at once, it can insert in the order a direction (under s 61) to achieve this. It must then also explain to the owners and occupiers concerned that this means that the order comes into effect immediately, so that consent is needed for any works to the trees involved from the date of the order (reg 5(*c*)(*v*)). Since orders will often be made in circumstances where their purpose will be frustrated if they do not come into effect immediately, it is difficult to see any particular merit in the s 60(4) procedure. Where the s 61 procedure is used, the order must however be confirmed within six months, or else it lapses.

Once an order has been confirmed, its validity cannot be challenged except by application to the High Court (TCPA 1971, ss 242(1)(*d*), (2)(*c*), 245(3)). Such an application must be made within six weeks of the date of the confirmation of the order (s 245(2); *R* v *Secretary of State for the Environment, ex parte Ostler* [1977] QB 122); although Professor Wade comments that it is not apparent why a tree preservation order should not be challengeable after six weeks (*Administrative Law*, 5th ed, Oxford, 1982, p 615). In any event, the order continues in force until the end of any legal proceedings (s 245(4)).

Even when the order is in force, a copy of it must still be retained for public inspection by the local authority that made it (model order, art 5(*a*)). If it is not, any subsequent prosecution for a breach of the order may fail (*Vale of Glamorgan BC* v *Palmer* [1984] JPL 334).

(d) Need for consent under the order

Where works are to be carried out for the cutting down, topping, lopping, uprooting, wilful damage, or wilful destruction of a tree that is protected by a preservation order, consent must normally be obtained from the local authority (s 60(1)(*a*), amended by TCAA 1974). Consent may also be required by an order to cause or permit a tree to be cut down (*R v Bournemouth JJ, ex parte Bournemouth Corpn* (1970) 21 P & CR 163).

Consent will not however be required in any of the following cases:

(1) the cutting down, uprooting, topping or lopping of a tree:
—because it is dying, dead or dangerous, or
—in order to comply with an Act of Parliament, or
—to prevent or abate a nuisance
(TCPA 1971, s 60(6), amended by TCAA 1974);

(2) the cutting down of a tree in accordance with a plan of operations approved by the Forestry Commission (s 60(8); model order, Sched 2, paras (1), (2)); or

(3) the cutting down, uprooting, topping or lopping of a tree:
—where carried out or required by any one of a variety of statutory undertakers, river authorities, airport authorities etc;
—in order to carry out development for which planning permission has been granted (but not merely in order to carry out permitted development; see 7.3); or
—which is a fruit tree in an orchard or garden cultivated for fruit production
(model order, Sched 2, para (3)).

These are identical to the first two categories listed in 11.1(*b*); see the comments on them there.

Where works are carried out in the first category (because the trees are dying, dead or dangerous, or in order to comply with an Act of Parliament, or to prevent or abate a nuisance), consent is not required, but a replacement tree must be planted (see 11.3) (s 62(1)).

Finally, where the volume of timber to be felled is such that a felling licence is required (under Forestry Act 1967, s 9), an application should be made not to the local authority but only to the Forestry Commission (s 10).

(e) Procedure for applying for consent

An application for consent to carry out works to a tree protected by a tree preservation order is to be made to the same authority that made the order. Usually the authority will have a standard form, but sometimes a letter will suffice. Either way, the application should contain the following details:

(1) the location, size and species of the trees concerned;
(2) the works to be carried out;
(3) the reason for the works; and
(4) any replanting proposed (model order, art 3).

There is no fee payable.

Consent can be refused or granted subject to conditions; and conditions may in particular be imposed requiring one or more trees to be planted to replace the one that is to be removed (see 11.3) (art 4). There is then a right of appeal against the planning authority's decision to the Secretary of State, who will (if required to do so by either party) hold an inquiry (art 8 and Third Sched).

If the decision to refuse consent or to grant it subject to onerous conditions leads to a loss in the value of the land, this is generally recoverable from the planning authority by way of compensation under art 9 of the model order (TCPA 1971, s 174). The quantum of such compensation is not limited to the commercial value of the timber which cannot now be realised (*Bell* v *Canterbury CC* [1986] JPL 844). No compensation is however payable if a certificate is issued by the authority (as it frequently will be), under art 5 of the order, to the effect that:

(1) the decision was in the interests of good forestry; or
(2) the trees concerned are of outstanding or special amenity value.

As a result of widespread concern following the decision of the Court of Appeal in the *Canterbury* case, such a certificate may now be issued in connection with woodlands as well as in other situations (art 5, as amended by TCP (Tree Preservation Order) (Amendment) Regulations 1988).

(f) Unauthorised works

It is an offence under TCPA 1971, s 102:

(1) to carry out works to a tree that is subject to a tree preservation order without obtaining consent from the local authority, unless the works are in one of the exempted categories listed in 11.2(*d*); or

(2) to carry out any such works where consent has been refused. The considerations which apply here are identical to those applying to offences under s 61A; see 11.1(*d*) for further comment. In particular, the penalties are identical (s 102(1), (2)); and an offender must plant trees to replace any that have been lost (see 11.3) (s 62(1)).

The offence is one of strict liability, that is, ignorance of the order is no defence (see 9.2(*b*)) (*Maidstone BC* v *Mortimer* [1981] JPL 112). The only exception to this is where the planning authority had failed to keep a copy of it available for inspection (*Vale of Glamorgan BC* v *Palmer* [1984] JPL 334). And an owner is not liable for unauthorised works carried out to trees on his or her land by independent contractors acting against express instructions (*Groveside Homes* v *Elmbridge BC* (1987) 284 EG 940).

A threatened breach of a tree preservation order can be restrained by the use of an injunction, even where no prosecution for breach of the order has been instituted (see 9.5) (LGA 1972, s 222; *Kent CC* v *Batchelor* (1976) 33 P & CR 1985; *Kent CC* v *Batchelor (No 2)* [1979] 1 WLR 213; *A–G* v *Melville Construction Co Ltd* (1968) 20 P & CR 131).

11.3 Replacement trees

(a) The requirement to plant a replacement

It has been noted that a replacement tree must be planted in any of the following circumstances:
(1) where a tree that is either in a conservation area or subject to a tree preservation order is removed in any of the circumstances in the first category in the lists in 11.1(*b*) and 11.2(*d*) (principally, where the tree is dead or dangerous, or where the works are necessary to prevent or abate a nuisance);
(2) where a tree in a conservation area is removed without notice being given to the local authority (see 11.1(*d*)); or
(3) where a tree that is subject to a preservation order is removed without the consent of the authority (see 11.2(*f*)).
Where this requirement applies, a tree 'of an appropriate size and species' must normally be planted 'at the same place' as the tree that has been removed as soon as is reasonable (TCPA 1971, ss 61A(8), 62(1)). However, this requirement can be dispensed

with or varied if the authority is notified and states in writing that it is agreeable.

The appropriateness of the size and species would presumably be determined in the light of all the circumstances after the removal of the previous tree: where, for example, an old oak tree was removed from a small, recently created suburban garden, its replacement should obviously not be another large oak. Similarly, the replacement would in many cases have to be 'near' the same place as the old tree, since its remaining roots will often render planting 'at' exactly the same place either impossible (without enormous expense) or undesirable, and it would be absurd for the authority to be notified in every such case. Where the tree that was removed was included in a tree preservation order, the 'place' means the area specified on the plan attached to the order; in the case of an 'area' order, this will give scope for some latitude in the location of the replacement (see comment on *Bush* v *Secretary of State and Redditch BC* [1988] JPL 108 at 111).

Furthermore, if trees have been removed that were subject to a tree preservation order as part of a woodland, they must be replaced with the same number of trees 'on or near the land on which the trees removed, uprooted or destroyed stood' or on such other land as may be agreed between the local planning authority and the owner of the land, and (in either case) in such places as may be designated by the local planning authority' (s 62(1A), inserted by TCP (Amendment) Act 1985).

(b) Enforcement of the requirement

If a new tree is not planted when it is required, the planning authority may serve on the owner of the land concerned at any time within the following four years a notice under s 103, requiring the planting of a tree or trees of a size and species to be specified (TCPA 1971, s 103(1)). Note that the duty to plant passes with the ownership of the land, and can be enforced by the authority accordingly (ss 61A(9), 62(3)).

A notice under s 103 can also be used to enforce any condition on a consent granted under a tree preservation order, whereby a replacement must be planted (s 103(1)).

The notice will take effect on a date specified in it, which must be at least twenty-eight days after it is served on the owner of the land concerned (s 103(2)). At any time before it comes into effect, the owner may appeal to the Secretary of State against the notice, on the following grounds (s 103(3)):

(*a*) that the requirement to replant does not apply;

(*b*) that the size or species specified, or the time within which the planting is to be carried out, is unreasonable;

(*c*) that the planting is not required in the interests of amenity, or would be contrary to good forestry practice; or

(*d*) that the location for the planting is unsuitable.

The appeal is to be in writing, including the grounds on which it is based; and either the owner or the planning authority can insist on an inquiry. The notice is of no effect until the appeal is finally determined (as to which, see 9.4(*d*)). The Secretary of State or the inspector can uphold or quash the notice, or can vary it if that can be done without causing injustice to either party (s 103(3A)–(4), inserted by LGPAA 1981).

If the notice is upheld, with or without variations, and the trees are still not planted, the authority can enter the land, do the work itself, and reclaim the cost from the current owner of the land, together with a reasonable sum in respect of its establishment charges (ss 103(5), 91(1), LGA 1974, s 36). This is recoverable as a simple contract debt (TCPA 1971, s 111). The current owner may in turn recover it from whoever was responsible for the replanting requirement arising in the first place (ss 103(5), 91(2)). It seems that it would be possible for the authority to plant only some of the required trees under this provision (*Arcam Demolition and Construction Co Ltd* v *Worcestershire CC* [1964] 1 WLR 661).

Where the tree that was removed was subject to a tree preservation order, the one that replaces it will be subject to the same order from the moment it is planted (s 62(3)).

(c) Replanting of woodlands

Where consent is given under a tree preservation order for the felling of woodlands, the authority must normally require the land to be replanted (model order, art 6). Where this is to be done in a manner which may be conducive to amenity, but is not in accordance with good forestry practice, the Forestry Commission may not give the financial assistance that would otherwise be available under s 4 of the Forestry Act 1967. In such a case, the owner may claim compensation from the planning authority, equal to the amount by which he or she is as a result out of pocket (TCPA 1971, s 175). Note, however, that s 4 was repealed by the Forestry Act 1979, s 3(2) and Sched 2. See now s 1 of the 1979 Act.

11.4 Gardens

Gardens are a major feature of both conservation areas and the setting of many listed buildings. They clearly cannot be 'preserved', although they will often contain individual trees suitable for tree preservation orders, and the need for consent to be obtained to fell those trees will give at least some protection to the gardens as a whole. Similarly, many important gardens contain objects that will be listed by virtue of being within the curtilage of a listed building (see 2.5(*d*)). The ground itself will not be listed (*Cotswold DC* v *Secretary of State and Pearson* [1985] JPL 407, but any 'structures' such as walls, statues, staircases, gazebos, temples, hahas and (probably) terraces. The need for listed building consent to alter or remove these features will also help to protect the garden itself.

In addition, however, given the limited degree of protection it would be a pity if there was not at least some record of the best gardens.

Accordingly, when the Historic Buildings and Monuments Commission was set up in 1983, it was given a new power, to compile a register of gardens of special historic interest in England (HBAMA 1953, s 8C, inserted by NHA 1983). A copy of each entry in the register is to be sent to the owner and occupier of the garden concerned, the district and county planning authority for the area, and the Secretary of State.

By March 1988, the Commission had published all forty-four county volumes of a Register of Historic Parks and Gardens. These volumes list over 1,200 parks and gardens which range from major man-made landscapes like Blenheim to quite small gardens such as the one hectare garden at Marsh Court in Hampshire. The register has no statutory force, but its purpose is to record and grade gardens which still retain their historic interest, 'so that highway and planning authorities, and developers, know that they should try to safeguard them when planning new road schemes and new development generally' (Circ 8/87, para 15).

All enquiries about the register should be made to the Commission.

Chapter 12

Advertisements

12.1 The need for control

One feature of the urban scene which causes particular concern in some conservation areas is inappropriate advertising. This may be in the form of traditional advertisement hoardings, or may be on shop fascias, canopies, placards, displays at petrol stations, estate agents' boards, flags or even balloons. Flyposting, too, can be a problem in some urban areas.

The display of insensitively designed or sited advertisements can also spoil the appearance of a listed building, or detract from its setting. The erection of an advertisement of any size on or attached to a listed building would of course require listed building consent, as it would almost undoubtedly be an alteration which affected the special character of the building, and would therefore be subject to detailed control. However if the advertisement is not actually attached to the building, it would not require listed building consent (*Cotswold DC v Secretary of State and Pearson* [1985] JPL 407), even though it might ruin its setting.

The display of outdoor advertisements has always been exempt from normal planning control (see currently TCPA 1971, ss 22(4), 64). It is instead controlled under special regulations made under powers in the Planning Acts (s 63, amended by HPA 1986). The regulations currently in force are the TCP (Control of Advertisements) Regulations 1984; references in this chapter are to these. They have been amended several times since they were first made, and it is expected that new, consolidating regulations incorporating these and other amendments will be laid before Parliament early in 1989.

12.2 The mechanics of control

(a) The need for consent

Lack of space precludes a detailed examination of the precise mechanics of the control. Briefly, however, 'express consent' is required from the local authority for the display of any advertisement unless either:

(1) it falls outside the scope of the Regulations altogether; or
(2) it is granted 'deemed consent' by the Regulations.

Even if it is within one of these classes, it may of course require listed building consent if it is attached to a listed building (see 12.1).

An advertisement will be excluded from control altogether if it is within one of the following categories (reg 3):

(1) advertisements on enclosed land (such as a station forecourt or a football stadium);
(2) unilluminated advertisements inside a building (such as a shop);
(3) advertisements that form part of the fabric of a building (such as the name of a shop in ornamental tiles);
(4) advertisements on vehicles (such as buses);
(5) unilluminated advertisements on goods to be sold and on vending machines; and
(6) some balloon advertisements.

Deemed consent is granted automatically by the Regulations for the following:

(1) various official signs and advertisements (regs 9, 10);
(2) advertisements displayed on a site used for advertising on 1 April 1974 (reg 11, substituted by Amendment No 2 Regulations 1987; and see *Arthur Maiden Ltd* v *Lanark CC (No 2)* [1958] JPL 422; *Mills and Allen Ltd* v *City of Glasgow DC* [1980] JPL 409);
(3) other advertisements inside a building (reg 12);
(4) advertisements for which express consent had been granted, after that consent has expired (reg 13); and
(5) unilluminated advertisements in certain specified classes (reg 14, as amended by Amendment Regulations 1987 and Amendment (No 2) Regulations 1987), as follows:
  I   functional advertisements by public bodies;
  II   miscellaneous small signs; small notices advertising trades and professions (such as doctors' brass plates); signs relating to churches, hotels and so on;

III   estate agents' boards; site boards at building sites; advertisements for fetes, sales, and other temporary events;

IV   signs on business premises, advertising the business itself or the goods or services available there (see *Arthur Maiden Ltd* v *Lanark CC* (No 1) [1958] JPL 417;

V   ground-level signs on forecourts of business premises (see *Heron Service Stations* v *Coupe* [1973] 1 WLR 502, HL);

VI   advertisements on flags;

VII   posters on hoardings surrounding building sites;

VIII directional signs in certain experimental areas;

IX   four-sheet poster panels displayed on purpose-designed highway structures;

X   Neighbourhood Watch signs; and

XI   temporary signs to housebuilders' sites.

All the classes in reg 14 are subject to various limitations as to size and location. Advertisements in Class VII (only) are also granted deemed consent if they are illuminated. Further classes are to be introduced, including certain illuminated advertisements on business premises and in retail parks.

One category of advertisement with deemed consent that has caused particular problems is estate agents' boards. However, as a result of changes made in 1987 (which took effect on 28 October 1988), the maximum size of estate agents' boards that may be displayed on residential property without express consent has now been drastically reduced to one board of 0.5 sq m in area, or two joined boards together of 0.6 sq m, for each sale (reg 14(1), Class III(*a*), substituted by Amendment No 2 Regulations 1987). It has been held by the House of Lords that this deemed consent is limited to one board (or one pair of joined boards) in total per sale or letting, regardless of how many agents are instructed. However, if a subsequent board is erected only the subsequent agent is liable to prosecution (*Porter* v *Honey* [1988] 1 WLR 1420, overturning [1988] JPL 632).

An authority may prevent the display of a particular class of advertisements which could otherwise be displayed with deemed consent, by requesting the Secretary of State to make a direction (under reg 15) requiring that express consent be obtained. The use of this power may be appropriate in a conservation area. Some authorities in London, for example, managed to control the proliferation of estate agents' boards using reg 15 directions. But the Secretary of State apparently refused to make a similar direction in respect of boards in the centre of Bath, arguably a more deserving case. The need to seek special control over that particular category of advertisement may now not recur, however, since the changes to the rules noted above.

It seems that it is not possible for an authority to attach a condition to a grant of planning permission requiring express consent to be obtained for advertisements which could otherwise be displayed with deemed consent ([1988] JPL 204).

(b) Applications for consent

In cases where express consent is required, an application must be made to the local planning authority, on a form supplied by it and accompanied by the appropriate fee. It is then processed in much the same way as an application for planning permission or listed building consent, and consent is either granted subject to conditions or refused (regs 5–7, 17–21).

When considering whether or not to grant consent for the display of advertisements, a planning authority may only take into account two considerations—'amenity' and public safety (reg 5). Matters such as the commercial need for a particular advertisement are therefore totally irrelevant. The need to consider amenity means that the authority is required to consider the effect of a proposed advertisement 'in the light of the general characteristics of the locality, including the presence therein of any feature of historic, architectural, cultural or similar interest' (reg 5(2)(a)). One such feature would be any listed building that was affected by a proposed advertisement. The authority is required to have special regard to the desirability of preserving the character and appearance of conservation areas when exercising any of its powers under the 1971 Act, of which the control of advertisements is one (TCPA 1971, s 277(8), substituted by TCAA 1974; and see 12.3(a)). As to the meaning of the word 'amenity' generally, see also 5.7(e).

If consent is refused by the local authority, it is possible to appeal to the Secretary of State (reg 22). In determining any appeal, he will be guided by the same considerations. Consent was, for example, granted on appeal for an illuminated projecting sign outside a listed building in a conservation area in Liverpool: it was considered that, because of its size, its traditional design and its subdued colouring, it would not appear out of character with the building in particular or the area generally ([1983] JPL 269). Where a listed house in the Forest of Dean had been converted for use as an office, consent was granted on appeal for the display of individually applied lettering and for a small brass plaque, but refused for a solid fascia sign ([1988] JPL 204; and see also [1988] JPL 323). On the Secretary of State's policy generally, see Circ 11/84.

More recently, however, a decision by the Secretary of State to grant consent for a carefully designed non-illuminated advance warning sign was overturned by the courts because, although he had considered the effect of the proposed sign on the setting of a nearby listed building, he had not considered its effect on the conservation area. In particular, he had ignored the comment of his Inspector that 'too great a multiplicity of individual signs is likely to prove both unsatisfactory and detrimental to the exceptionally attractive landscapes of the South Hams' (*South Hams DC* v *Secretary of State* [1988] 3 PLR 57).

(c) Unauthorised display of advertisements

A person displaying an advertisement in contravention of the Regulations is liable on summary conviction to a fine of up to level 3 on the standard scale (currently £400) (TCPA 1971, s 109(2), amended by Criminal Justice Act 1982; Criminal Penalties etc (Increase) Order 1984 reg 8, amended by Amendment Regulations 1987).

The liability for the offence obviously attaches to the person actually responsible for the advertisement. The owner and occupier of the land on which it is displayed and the owners of the business or product being advertised can also be prosecuted unless they can show that they did not know of the existence of the advertisement (s 109(3); *Preston* v *British Union for the Abolition of Vivisection* (1985) *The Times*, 24 July).

If after being convicted a person does not remove the offending display, he or she is liable to a further fine on conviction of £20 per day (TCPA 1971, s 109(2), amended by HPA 1986; reg 8). But this does not apply where, following an initial conviction, the unauthorised advertisement appears again after a reasonable break (*Kensington and Chelsea RBC* v *Elmton Ltd* (1978) 246 EG 1011).

In addition, a local authority (district or borough council) may remove or obliterate any placard or poster displayed in contravention of the Regulations. Where it does not identify who is responsible, this can be done at once; where it does, that person only has to be given two days' notice (s 109A, inserted by Local Government (Miscellaneous Provisions) Act 1982). This procedure, which enables an authority to control flyposting, has been little used. It appears to be very straightforward, and would be appropriate where unauthorised posters are disfiguring a listed building, or spoiling the setting of one or the appearance of a conservation area.

12.3 Special control in sensitive areas

(a) Conservation areas

The 1971 Act itself specifically states that regulations may make special provision with respect to the control of advertisements in conservation areas (TCPA 1971, s 63(3)(a), substituted by HPA 1986). In fact, however, the 1984 Regulations apply to land in conservation areas almost exactly as elsewhere, with only three minor exceptions:

(1) express consent is required for the display of an advertisement on a tethered balloon for any length of time (which elsewhere requires consent only if the display is for more than ten days in any year) (reg 3(3));

(2) express consent is required for the display of advertisements on hoardings surrounding building sites (which elsewhere has deemed consent) (reg 14, Class VII, and reg 27(5)); and

(3) express consent will be required for the new classes of deemed consent to be introduced for business premises and retail parks (see 12.2(a)).

These exceptions also apply to land in national parks, areas of outstanding natural beauty and areas of special control of advertisements (see 12.3(b)).

In general, local planning authorities have been advised to 'use their powers under the Control of Advertisements Regulations flexibly, taking account of the fact that many conservation areas include thriving commercial centres, whilst ensuring that advertising displays do not detract from the appearance of areas of architectural and historic interest' (Circ 8/87, para 67). Specific advice has been given on the display of poster advertising in conservation areas. This is reckoned to be generally appropriate only in the predominantly shopping and business parts of such areas; care needs to be taken in the choice of panel sizes, and the detailed location of panels, to avoid disfiguring the area (Circ 11/ 84, Annex, App C, para 14).

On the other hand, it has been explicitly recognised in the courts that the control of advertisments is one of the functions of a planning authority which must be carried out with special attention being given to the desirability of preserving or enhancing the character or appearance of any conservation area involved (*South Hams DC* v *Secretary of State* [1988] 3 PLR 57 at 59; *Westminster CC* v *Secretary of State* [1988] 3 PLR 104 at 105; and see 4.3(*b*)). In addition, in the first of those cases, Mr David Widdicombe QC (sitting as a deputy High Court judge) commented (at 60): '[it was] said that the conservation area was covered by the reference . . . to the area of special control of advertisements, but this cannot be correct. An area of special control may well . . . cover many areas which are not designated as conservation areas. Conservation is a separate and additional control, as is recognised by s 277(8) of the Act.'

(b) Areas of special control of advertisements

The definition by a local authority of an *area of special control* of advertisements may also be appropriate within all or part of a conservation area. This is an area within which the control of advertisements is much stricter than elsewhere (reg 27).

Except in rural areas, however, the approval of the Secretary of State is needed before an area of special control can be defined. He has advised authorities that, in seeking that approval, the mere fact of conservation are a designation will by itself not be enough. The tighter control must be justified by reference to the special characteristics of the area which make it desirable—for example, a small enclave, within an otherwise commercial town-centre, which has important architectural, archaeological, historical or visual characteristics, such as the precincts of a cathedral or other significant church, or a group of listed buildings, or an important market square. Also see the comments above on the *South Hams* case.

On areas of special control generally, see Circular 11/84 (Annex, paras 34–8).

(c) Discontinuance notices

Where an advertisement is being displayed with the benefit of 'deemed consent' (see 12.2(*a*)), an authority may serve a discontinuance notice on the owner and occupier of the land and on the advertiser, requiring the advertisement to be removed.

This power is to be used by the authority if it considers it to be expedient 'in the interests of amenity or public safety' (reg 16(1)). In particular, it may serve a notice to halt the display of an advertisement in one of the classes in reg 14 only if it considers that it 'is required to remedy a substantial injury to the amenity of the locality or a danger to members of the public'. It might well be expedient for an authority to use this procedure where a particular advertisement is disfiguring a conservation area or the setting of a listed building.

It is however possible for an advertiser to appeal to the Secretary of State against a discontinuance notice (reg 22(5)). If the advertisement to be discontinued was being displayed on 1 August 1948, any expenses incurred in complying with the notice can be recovered from the planning authority by way of compensation under TCPA 1971, s 176. However this right does not extend to reclaiming the present value of any future loss of income.

As an example of the use of this procedure, in the *Westminster* case (above) the Council were trying to bring about the improvement of the appearance of the Pimlico Conservation Area through the removal of illuminated box signs on hotels, and their replacement with more suitable signs. This was considered to be a perfectly reasonable aim; and it was noted that reg 5(2)(*a*) provided that, in exercising its powers under the Regulations in the interests of amenity, an authority was entitled to assess the general characteristics of an area disregarding any advertisements already being displayed there. The Secretary of State, in dealing with any appeal against a discontinuance notice in such a case, therefore, should not just consider the merits or otherwise of the particular advertisement concerned, but should also bear in mind the prospective removal of others in the area.

Chapter 13

Religious Buildings

13.1 Background

Among the most notable of all Britain's historic buildings must be its churches and cathedrals. Over half (approximately 8,500) of the buildings of the Church of England date from before the Reformation; almost all of these are listed, and many more are in conservation areas. A further 3,700 post-Reformation buildings are listed, including the Wren churches, and many fine examples of Victorian architecture. There are also around 1,200 listed non-conformist churches and chapels in England alone. The Methodists have an estimated 500 listed chapels (including a dozen of Grade I or II*), and a further 900 in conservation areas, largely from the Victorian period. The Quakers and the Unitarians have higher proportions of churches of architectural interest, particularly of the eighteenth century. The Roman Catholics, too, have many listed buildings, particularly in the larger cities.

The categories of churches which are considered by the Department of the Environment to be eligible for listing are as follows:

   (i) churches of recognisably pre-Reformation date;

   (ii) most churches built between the Reformation and 1818;

   (iii) churches built between 1818 and 1914 that are of definite quality and character;

   (iv) a selection of churches built between 1914 and 1939;

   (v) important examples of regional church types;

   (vi) churches containing major paintings, glass, sculpture, monuments or fittings;

   (vii) churches materially associated with historic events or people of national importance; and

   (viii) churches having group value, especially as an integral part of a planned scheme

(*Guidance notes to those concerned with survey for listing*, 1985).

Buildings falling within categories (v) to (vii) will usually be listed anyway by virtue of also falling within one of the earlier categories. In addition it may be noted that, as part of the move to list post-war buildings, a handful of post-1939 churches are now being listed. Coventry Cathedral, for example, was listed Grade I in March 1988.

Listed Church of England churches used to be graded A, B and C, rather than I, II* and II; but in lists issued since August 1977 the 'secular' grading system (see 2.1(*c*)) has sensibly been used for religious buildings of all faiths and all denominations, whether in use or redundant. There are inevitably a very much higher proportion of listed churches classified as Grade I or II* than is the case with listed buildings generally: out of the 13,500 churches which had been listed by the end of 1987, some 2,650 are Grade I (43 per cent of all Grade I buildings).

Religious buildings of non-Christian faiths are selected for listing on the same basis as any other buildings (see 2.1(*b*)). Not many have yet been listed, although, for example, there is a grade II* listed mosque in Fournier Street, Spitalfields (in East London) which was originally a Huguenot chapel, and was then used successively as a Methodist chapel and a synagogue, reflecting the changing ethnic make-up of the local area. And since there are now some 315 synagogues, 300 mosques, and 260 Hindu or Sikh temples registered in England and Wales, it is inevitable that some must be in conservation areas.

13.2 Works to churches in use: 'secular' control

(a) Listed building consent and conservation area consent

In spite of their architectural and historic importance, religious buildings that are in use are largely outside the scope of normal listed building and conservation area control. The basic rule is thus that listed building consent is not required for the alteration, extension or demolition of a listed building if it is 'an ecclesiastical building which is for the time being used for ecclesiastical purposes or would be but for the works' (TCPA 1971, s 56(1)(*a*)).

The term 'ecclesiastical building' is not defined, other than by noting that it does not include 'a building used or available for use by a minister of religion wholly or mainly as a residence from which to perform the duties of his office' (s 56(1)). This exception is to reverse the ruling in *Phillips* v *Minister of Housing and Local Government* [1965] 1 QB 156. More generally, the phrase has been considered in the leading case on this subject (*A–G, ex rel Bedfordshire CC* v *Howard United Reformed Church Trustees, Bedford* [1976] AC 363). Lord Cross in that case at p 376 first stated clearly that 'ecclesiastical' does not mean 'Anglican', that is, it certainly includes the free churches and the Roman Catholic Church. He further agreed at pp 377–8 with the Court of Appeal that a building that is now vacant but which was used as a church and has never been used for any other purpose is still an 'ecclesiastical building'. Unfortunately he declined to consider questions such as whether the expression extended to synagogues and mosques, or whether the ownership of the building was relevant, or whether it makes a difference if the building had not originally been built as a church. As to the first of these, see 13.7.

Similarly, the term 'ecclesiastical purposes' is not defined. The Court of Appeal in *Howard* considered that the term meant 'church purposes as distinct from social purposes', and thought that the use of the building for church meetings, elders' meetings, and a carol service, but for no other worship, was sufficient to constitute 'use for ecclesiastical purposes' ([1974] 3 All ER 273 at 277). Lord Cross considered that it was 'a vague phrase which might mean only purposes connected with the use of the building for corporate worship or might extend to any purposes which the church authorities might think likely to foster Christian fellowship among the members of the congregation' ([1976] AC 363 at 377).

The practical effect of this is that listed building consent is not required for the alteration or extension of a listed ecclesiastical building of any denomination provided that it is used for ecclesiastical purposes (however defined) both before and after the works. Further, it would seem that consent is not required where an ecclesiastical building is to be partly demolished, provided that ecclesiastical use is to continue in the part of the building that remains. This would have allowed the Catholic Archdiocese of Liverpool to demolish St Francis Xavier's Church, even though it was listed, because one small chapel was to be retained for worship. This did not in fact take place, owing to vociferous public protest. But those who tried to save the Jesmond Methodist Church in Newcastle were not so fortunate: it was demolished, without listed building consent, two years after it was listed, because the attached Sunday School building was retained.

Similarly, conservation area consent is not needed for the demo-

lition of an unlisted ecclesiastical building in a conservation area
if it is in ecclesiastical use (TCPA 1971, s 277A(1)(*b*), inserted by
TCAA 1974). Thus to demolish only part of a church, of any
denomination, that is in a conservation area does not currently
require conservation area consent, provided that 'ecclesiastical
use' (see above) continues in what remains of the building after
the works are complete (ss 277A(1)(*b*), 58(2)).

(b) Changes in the law

The exemption from listed building control of works to churches
in use, sometimes referred to as the 'ecclesiastical exemption', is
not surprisingly resented by many in the conservation lobby, and
defended vigorously by the churches.

The main justifications for the exemption are:

(1) the imposition of secular control would be a threat to
religious freedom; and

(2) the various religious authorities operate schemes to control
works to their own buildings, which are claimed to be
adequate substitutes.

As to the first of these, the churches would argue that religious
freedom has been hard-won in this country, and therefore
deserves special consideration. To have secular control over the
interior design of a sanctuary, for example, implies secular control
over the pattern of worship within it; and this would be unacceptable to many, particularly those of the non-conformist and Catholic traditions, who were subject to considerable social, legal and
political disabilities until comparatively recently.

As against which, it could equally be argued that control over
works to *any* historic building is an interference with the freedom
of its owner, and that the churches should be subject to the same
control as others.

As to the second argument, the Church of England's faculty
system (see 13.3) has been modified over the years, becoming
gradually more responsive to public opinion both within and
outside the Church. But it is still in the eyes of many an inadequate
substitute for listed building control. The control mechanisms
operated by the other Christian denominations, although no doubt
operated in good faith, are logically of no more consequence than
the internal controls of any other owner of a number of listed
buildings, such as British Rail or the major banks, and are no
guarantee that works will be suitable. The relevant internal rules
and procedures of the four main Christian denominations other

than the Church of England, who between them have almost as many buildings as are owned by the Anglican churches, are described in 13.4.

In the light of such criticism, a new section was inserted into the 1971 Act (as s 58AA) by the HPA 1986, enabling the Secretary of State to provide by order that the exemption would no longer apply to certain categories of works to listed churches. At the time of writing, consultations are still taking place between the Government and the Churches, and it seems probable that no order will be made until 1989 at the earliest. However, the broad intention of the Government, as outlined by its spokesman in the Lords debate on the 1986 Bill and restated in Circ 8/87 (para 103(i)), is that:

proposals that would materially affect the architectural or historic interest of a church *not* belonging to the Church of England such as a spire, tower or cupola should require listed building consent but that the exemption should continue to apply to proposals which would have a lesser effect.

In other words, listed building consent will be needed for the demolition of all *or a significant part of* a listed non-Anglican ecclesiastical building. The precise wording of the order will need to be studied carefully to see just how far this will extend.

It will be noted that the owner of the largest number of listed ecclesiastical buildings, the Church of England, is likely to remain outside the secular system of control; although the new enabling power in s 58AA does not specifically mention it, and a future Secretary of State could (at least in theory) bring Anglican buildings, provided that they remain in ecclesiastical use, into line with those of other denominations, without requiring new primary legislation.

Additionally, it is envisaged that works to buildings and structures (church halls, major monuments, etc) within the curtilage of listed churches and which are thereby deemed to be listed may well be brought within the scope of listed building control (s 58AA(2)(c); Circ 8/87, para 103(iv)).

The Secretary of State's powers under s 58AA are also applied (by s 277A(8)) so as to enable him to make an order providing that conservation area consent will in certain circumstances be needed for the partial demolition of a church remaining in use. As with consent for works to listed churches, the wording of any order to be made is still uncertain at the time of writing. Nor has there been any explicit indication as to the possible scope of any

L

order, either in Ministerial statements to Parliament or in advice by the Department of the Environment. In view of the statements made on listed building consent, however, it is probable that conservation area consent will be required for the partial demolition of a religious building not belonging to the Church of England in the same circumstances as listed building consent would be required, that is, where the works would involve the loss of a significant feature of the building (see above). It would seem to be very unlikely that conservation area consent will be required for any demolition (total or partial) of Church of England buildings.

Finally, the Church of England and the Churches Main Committee (which represents all the main denominations) have given an undertaking that all churches will consult the local planning authority before carrying out any significant external works which remain exempt from listed building control. In addition, they will, in England, also consult the Historic Buildings and Monuments Commission (Circ 8/87, para 103 (iv)). How this will operate in practice remains to be seen.

(c) Planning permission

Local planning authorities do already have considerable scope for considering the desirability of at least some works to churches, since they require planning permission as much as works affecting any other building type. This is regardless of the religion or denomination of the building, and regardless of whether it is listed, scheduled, or in a conservation area. Permission is thus needed for almost any external alterations to a church; it is only internal works that are entirely outside the secular jurisdiction (see 7.2(b)). In determining any planning application for works affecting a listed church or its setting, an authority must have special regard to the desirability of preserving it, or any features of special interest that it possesses (TCPA 1971, s 56(3), amended by LGPLA 1980). In determining an application for works in a conservation area, it must consider the desirability of preserving the character and appearance of that area (s 277(8), substituted by TCAA 1974).

13.3 Works to churches in use: procedures of the Church of England

(a) Faculties

The ecclesiastical exemption originated in 1913 in response to assurances given by the then Archbishop of Canterbury as to the Church's future good conduct. Parliament at that time accepted that secular control was not necessary in view of the Church of England's own faculty system of control over works to its buildings.

The principles of the system are set out in the Faculty Jurisdiction Measure 1964 (the 1964 Measure). The detailed procedures are in the Faculty Jurisdiction Rules 1967, which were recently amended by the Faculty Jurisdiction (Amendment) Rules 1987. Measures and Rules are passed by the Church of England's General Synod, but have the force of Acts of Parliament and statutory instruments. Those concerning faculties are set out in full as appendices to *Faculty Jurisdiction of the Church of England* (Sweet & Maxwell, 1988) by GH Newsom, himself a chancellor of three dioceses. That book should be consulted for full details. Note that a new Care of Churches Measure is likely to be considered by the Synod in 1989 or 1990, to replace the 1964 Measure.

In outline, a faculty is required for almost all works of any consequence to consecrated buildings of the Church of England or to unconsecrated buildings for the time being used for worship, and for alterations to the contents of such buildings. A faculty is also required for any works on land (consecrated or otherwise) within the curtilage of a Church of England church (1964 Measure, s 7). As to the definition of 'curtilage', see 2.5(*e*); some of the cases cited there in fact arose in connection with the faculty jurisdiction.

A faculty is not however required in the following instances:

(1) for works to a cathedral, or to an 'ecclesiastical peculiar' (that is, a Church of England church that is neither a cathedral nor a parish church) (see 13.3(*f*));

(2) where contents are moved from one church to another as a result of a sharing agreement under the Sharing of Church Buildings Act 1969 or a pastoral scheme under the Pastoral Measure 1983 (see 13.5(*a*)); or

(3) for the felling of timber in a churchyard, (although consent will of course be required from the local authority if the

trees are within a conservation area or are subject to a tree preservation order) (see 11.1 and 11.2).

(b) Faculties for demolition works

The demolition of a Church of England church may normally be authorised only by means of a pastoral or redundancy scheme (see 13.5). But it may be authorised by a faculty in the following cases:

(1) the total demolition of a church if another church is to be erected on the site;

(2) partial demolition of a church if the part remaining is to be used for worship;

(3) works necessary for the repair, alteration or reconstruction of the church or any part of it; or

(4) works necessary under a dangerous structures order (1964 Measure s 2(4), amended by Building Act 1984; see 5.8(*a*)).

In either of the first two cases the proposal must be advertised, the case must be heard in public, and the advice of both the diocesan advisory committee and the Council for the Care of Churches must be obtained (see 13.3(*c*)), (s 2(1), (2), (3)(i)). In the third case, the Council must be informed, and the chancellor must consider any advice it gives (s 2(3)(ii)).

In the first case, or in the fourth case if the building is to be totally demolished, listed building consent must be obtained if the church is listed; the exemption from the need for such consent applies only where the demolition is carried out as part of a pastoral or redundancy scheme (see 13.5) (Redundant Churches and Other Religious Buildings Act 1969). Similarly, if the church is not listed but is in a conservation area, conservation area consent must be obtained. In any other case, where the building will be only partially demolished, 'secular' consent is not required, since the building will still be in use after the completion of the works. This applies even where all that is left is, for example, an underground crypt (*Re St Luke's, Cheetham* [1977] 3 WLR 969).

(c) Faculties: procedure

An application for a faculty is made to the chancellor of the appropriate diocese (area), who will be advised by the relevant archdeacon, and by the diocesan advisory committee (the DAC).

In the great majority of cases, however, the applicants, normally the incumbent (rector or vicar) and churchwardens, and their professional advisers will have discussed the proposal thoroughly with the archdeacon and with the committee long before it reaches the chancellor. The committee (which must be appointed for every diocese: 1964 Measure, s 13) is available to give advice to any interested parties on matters concerning church buildings. It consists of the archdeacons within the diocese and others with a special knowledge of art, architecture and related matters. It was agreed by the Church in 1986 that the Historic Buildings and Monuments Commission, local planning authorities and the national amenity societies will in future be represented in the membership of diocesan advisory committees (Circ 8/87, para 103(iii)). The Council for the Care of Churches in London is also available to advise in important or difficult cases, or on request.

Where a proposal has been the subject of proper professional and other advice, and (in appropriate cases) consultation with all interested parties, the actual grant of a faculty is a mere formality. But where proposals are contested (which only occurs infrequently) or are otherwise of major consequence, all interested parties may state their case before the chancellor at a hearing of the diocesan consistory court. Chancellors, incidentally, are lawyers, usually judges or senior barristers, experienced in these matters.

Faculties can be applied for by the incumbent, the churchwardens, the parochial church council, by anyone else resident in the parish or on the church electoral roll, or the archdeacon (1964 Measure, s 9; Parochial Church Council (Powers) Measure 1956, s 4). Applications must be widely publicised (1967 Rules, r 5, substituted by 1987 Rules). They can then be opposed by any 'interested person'. This category was widened considerably by the 1987 Rules, so that it now includes, as well as those already mentioned, the local planning authority, the national amenity societies, and any other person or body appearing to have a lawful interest in the proceedings (r 5A). The 'local planning authority' is not defined, but would probably mean at least the district or borough council, and probably also the county council or planning board in a national park, as well as any urban development corporation (see 1.3(*a*)). The statutory amenity societies are those who must be consulted on listed building consent applications (excluding the Royal Commission on Historical Monuments; see 8.4(*c*)) (r 2(1)). The last category would presumably include the Historic Buildings and Monuments Commission, and any local amenity society; but only at the discretion of the diocesan registrar. Note that this means that such bodies and societies no longer have to act through the good offices of a sympathetic parishioner.

The chancellor is not bound to take advice of the diocesan advisory committee, or of any of the other bodies or individuals mentioned above. However there is a right of appeal against his or her decision—in cases involving doctrine or ceremonial to the Court of Ecclesiastical Causes Reserved, and in other cases to the Court of Arches or the Chancery Court of York as appropriate.

Where work is carried out without a faculty, or contrary to the terms of one, a confirmatory faculty may be applied for, usually by the incumbent and the parish council, to regularise the position. Alternatively, however, if unauthorised works are carried out to which someone (for example, a parishioner) objects, a faculty may be sought by the objector to restore the church to its former state.

Fees may be charged for applications (according to orders made under the Ecclesiastical Fees Measure 1986). In routine cases, however, these are often either waived or paid by the diocesan board of finance. The chancellor may also make awards of costs in appropriate cases (Ecclesiastical Jurisdiction Measure 1963, s 60).

(d) Faculties affecting listed buildings

It has already been noted that many Church of England buildings are listed (see 13.1). Where alterations are proposed to one of these, the fact of the listing may well be relevant in determining whether the chancellor will be willing to grant a faculty. It will therefore also be relevant in considering the manner in which such proposals are designed and presented.

Thus in *Re St Mary's, Banbury* [1985] 2 All ER 611, Boydell Ch decided against allowing a major change in a listed church:

On balance, the petitioners have satisfied me, in principle, that they should be permitted to construct lavatories in the porches; but I am not prepared to grant the faculty on the basis of the plans and other material adduced at the hearing. This is a Grade A [now Grade I] listed building; and any proposal to alter the structure of such a building must be approached with the same care and be subject to the same detailed consideration as would be necessary if the churches were to lose their ecclesiastical immunity and if, therefore, this were an application for listed building consent under the Town and Country Planning Act 1971 (at p 618).

He accordingly directed a further and more detailed petition on the subject. This point was then developed by the Dean of the Arches when the case went before him on appeal:

When a church is listed as a building of special architectural or historic interest, a faculty which would affect its character as such should only be granted in wholly exceptional circumstances, these circumstances clearly showing a necessity for such a change ([1987] Fam 136).

This reference to 'proved necessity' was criticised by the Court of Ecclesiastical Causes Reserved in *Re St Stephen's, Walbrook* [1987] 3 WLR 726, since no such concept appeared in TCPA 1971, s 56(3), which directed secular authorities on the considerations to be borne in mind in granting listed building consent. Sir Anthony Lloyd noted that 'the fact that an ecclesiastical building is listed is a relevant consideration in deciding whether or not to grant a faculty', and Sir Ralph Gibson said:

The right approach, in my view, is to exercise the discretion as I think Parliament intended that it should be exercised, namely in accordance with established principles; and that includes, of course, having full regard to all the circumstances including the interest of the community as a whole in the special architectural or historic attributes of the building and the desirability of preserving the building and any features of special architectural or historic interest that it possesses. The discretion, however, is to be exercised in the context that the building is used for the purposes of the Church, that is to say in the service of God as the Church, doing its best, perceives how that service is to be rendered.

(e) Minor works

No special consent is needed for trivial alterations to Church of England churches, such as the introduction of new books (although that is not always regarded as 'trivial'), routine maintenance, or burials in the churchyard (although a faculty is required for the erection of a monument).

Slightly more significant works can be carried out with an *archdeacon's certificate*, rather than a faculty as such (Faculty Jurisdiction Measure 1964, s 12). Examples of works that could be approved in this way include minor repairs to the building or its contents (including redecoration and alterations to any existing heating system), if they do not involve either substantial change to its structure or alterations to its external or internal appearance. If any objections are lodged, a faculty must be applied for such works as for any others. The archdeacon's certificate procedure used to be simpler and cheaper than an application for a faculty, but it is now in some dioceses falling into disuse in favour of the archdeacon approving works under powers delegated to him by the chancellor.

(f) Quinquennial surveys

The synod of each diocese is required (by the Inspection of Churches Measure 1955) to establish a scheme to ensure that an inspection of the fabric of every parish church is carried out, at least (in theory) once every five years, by an architect appointed in accordance with the scheme and approved by the diocesan advisory committee (see above). The architect is to make a report and send copies both to the archdeacon and to the parochial church council of the church concerned. The cost of the inspection is usually, but not always, paid from a special fund set up under the scheme. If a church council does not itself arrange for an inspection to be carried out, the archdeacon can require it to do so, and, if necessary, he can arrange it himself (1955 Measure, s 2).

This is a valuable arrangement, since it alerts the vicar and church council to impending problems, and enables them, finances permitting, to arrange for appropriate maintenance or repairs to be carried out, obviating the need for more expensive works later on.

(g) Cathedrals and other non-parochial churches

As already noted, cathedrals (including parish church cathedrals, such as Sheffield) are outside the scope of the faculty procedure. They are instead governed by their own statutes, made under the provisions of the Cathedrals Measures 1963 and 1976. Cathedral chapters normally consult the Cathedrals Advisory Commission (set up under the terms of the 1963 Measure, and reconstructed in 1981) on works of any substance; and the Commission may offer comments as it sees fit. But it has no binding authority, and chapters may in practice do as they wish. The General Synod has however approved the Care of Cathedrals Measure, which is likely to obtain royal assent in 1989 or 1990; this is expectecd to provide for the setting up of a Cathedrals Fabric Commission to replace the present, non-statutory Commission, as well as tightening up procedures generally. In the meanwhile cathedrals are virtually autonomous, being outside both the faculty system, with its elaborate consultation procedures, and the secular system. This is perhaps particularly unfortunate as they are amongst the finest historic buildings in

Europe, and any ill-considered alterations could be extremely unfortunate. On the other hand, they receive no financial assistance from central Government (either directly or via the Historic Buildings and Monuments Commission).

Less clear, and less satisfactory, is the status of the 'peculiars'. These are Church of England buildings which are neither parish churches (and thus under the faculty jurisdiction) nor cathedrals. They include numerous chapels at schools, colleges, cemeteries, prisons and similar establishments, some of which (such as some of the Oxford and Cambridge college chapels) are of considerable architectural interest. They also include the royal chapels (such as St George's Chapel in Windsor and Westminster Abbey) and the Temple Church, which are of great importance. These appear to be subject neither to any clearly defined ecclesiastical system of control, nor to the 'secular' system, although in practice a number of the peculiars operate as if they were subject to the latter, and thus apply for listed building or conservation area consent as appropriate.

13.4 Works to churches in use: procedures of other Christian denominations

(a) The Methodist Church

The basic administrative unit of Methodism is the circuit. This consists of a group of local churches, and a team of ministers under the direction of a superintendent. These are in turn organised in districts, of which there are twenty-nine in England and Wales, broadly equivalent to Anglican dioceses. The life of the Church is closely regulated through the annual Conference, which passes 'standing orders' which become mandatory for each of the 7,500 local churches.

The Methodist Church Act 1976 provides that the Trustees for Methodist Church Purposes are the custodian trustees for virtually all Methodist property: chapels, halls, manses (ministers' houses) and investments. But the Act also provides that the managing trusteeship is in the hands of the local church councils in the case of chapels and their associated buildings (Sunday schools and so on), and of the circuit meeting in the case of manses.

Before any works can be carried out to a building, other than of a purely decorative or maintenance character, permission must be sought through a hierarchical system of the circuit, the District Synod, and finally the Methodist Church Property Division.

The Property Division acts under its own Board, appointed by the Conference, and has full administrative responsibility for all property affairs throughout the churches. All property schemes are carefully scrutinised, and those involving listed buildings receive special care. The Division is however always having to balance demands for conservation against the need to refurbish buildings as it sees best for the present and future mission of the Church.

In particular, the Division has since the late sixties kept careful records of those chapels which are listed and it has a special 'Listed Buildings Fund' to provide financial assistance for them. It also published in 1974 a guidance booklet on the care of listed chapels, and in 1988 it established a working party to prepare and issue further advice on the problems and opportunities associated with them.

A Standing Order was issued in 1965 requiring that quinquennial inspections be carried out of all Methodist church properties (not just chapels). Managing trustees are required to ensure that any inspection under the Standing Order is carried out by an architect, building surveyor or other appropriately qualified person, who is adequately covered by professional indemnity insurance against any liability arising from the inspection.

For further details, contact the Methodist Church Property Division (Central Buildings, Oldham Street, Manchester M1 1JQ; tel 061-236 5194).

(b) The Baptist Union

Baptist churches are each entirely independent and self-governing, to a greater extent than Methodist churches. As with them, however, all church property is held in trust, by the local church as managing trustee. In most cases, the Baptist Union Corporation Ltd (set up under the terms of the Baptist Trust Act 1951) is the custodian trustee but some of the area associations (roughly equivalent to Anglican dioceses and Methodist districts) have their own trust corporation.

Any proposal for building works to a Baptist church should therefore be approved both by the local church and by the custodian trustee. The latter will however mainly be concerned to examine it from the point of view of safety and structural soundness, and to ensure that the local church is obtaining proper professional advice. In practice, the local church can go its own way more or less as it wishes. If the proposal does not require planning permission (as would be the case with any purely internal works), the custodian trustee does not even need to be consulted.

For further details, consult the Baptist Union of Great Britain and Northern Ireland (4 Southampton Row, London WC1B 4AB; tel 01–405 9803).

(c) The United Reformed Church

The United Reformed Church was formed in 1972 as a result of the unification of the Presbyterian and Congregational Churches (under the terms of the United Reformed Church Act 1972).

The procedure whereby works to buildings of the United Reformed Church are approved involves a hierarchical structure similar to those in the Methodist and Baptist Churches. Once a proposal has been approved by the local church, it must then be agreed by the District Council (not the local authority). In most provinces, it must then be approved by the Provincial Grants and Loans Committee, which in turn passes it on to the appropriate trustees, which may be either the central board of trustees, or one for the province (which it will be depends on the constitution of the church concerned). The procedure does however slightly vary as between provinces.

It may be recalled that the *Howard* case (see 13.2(*a*)), the leading case in this area of law, concerned the demolition of a Congregational church. (It happened at about the time the United Reformed Church was set up.) The climate of opinion has since changed somewhat, however, and most provincial authorities are now aware of the conservation issues, and attempt to bear them in mind when considering proposals for works to alter or demolish churches.

(d) The Roman Catholic Church

Slightly surprisingly, perhaps, the Roman Catholic Church, which has the appearance to outsiders of being the most authoritarian of the denominations discussed here, in fact has the least control over what happens to its buildings.

The Catholic Church in England and Wales is organised into twenty-one dioceses. Each diocese is almost entirely autonomous and its bishop has authority to make whatever arrangements he thinks fit for such matters as the approval of works to churches. General resolutions are from time to time passed by the Bishops'

Conference, which meets twice a year, and which has specialist departments and committees dealing with particular topics; the laity (and indeed the clergy other than the bishops) are only represented on the committees, not on the Conference itself. However resolutions passed by the Conference are not always translated into action quite as smoothly as might be desirable. In particular, in response to criticism from organisations such as the Victorian Society, much thought is being given to the whole issue of works to historic churches; at present, for example, there is no estimate of how many Catholic churches are listed or in conservation areas; but this is being attended to.

The procedure in most dioceses at present, then, is that a priest wishing to carry out any works to a church should obtain the approval of the Diocesan Liturgy Commission. This body will normally consider the suitability of the works from the point of view of aesthetics and history as well as in the light of other criteria. If the proposed works are likely to be expensive (the precise limit varies between dioceses), they must also be approved by the Diocesan Finance Officer, even if the cost is to be met from local sources.

This consultation process is however not laid down in formal rules (as with the Church of England) or by standing orders (as with the Methodists). It is primarily enforced through the sanction of the bishop's disapproval in the event of works being carried out without consultation with the diocesan bodies, and through the necessity for the Finance Officer to approve any works before he will authorise the spending of any money. The procedure in certain dioceses varies somewhat from that described here. For further details, the relevant diocesan authorities should be consulted, or the Liturgy Office in London (39 Eccleston Square, SW1V 1PL; tel 01-821 0553).

13.5 Redundant Church of England buildings

(a) Pastoral schemes

As well as the routine procedures for ensuring that Church of England buildings are regularly surveyed, and that any alterations that may be proposed in the course of their regular use are approved (see 13.3), there is provision for the continuous review of the arrangements for pastoral care within each diocese as a whole and in each parish, and for the making of any proposals for changes that may be considered appropriate as a result of such a review. The significance of this in the present context is that such changes may (and often do) involve alterations to parish churches, changes in their use, construction of new ones or demolition of existing ones. However since these will often concern not just the church communities involved but also the wider community (including, amongst others, local authorities and amenity societies), there are elaborate arrangements to ensure that at each stage all such views are heard (even if they are not always listened to).

The relevant procedure is set out in the Pastoral Measure 1983 (the 1983 Measure), which consolidated with minor amendments and replaced the Pastoral Measure 1968 and the Pastoral (Amendment) Measure 1982. The latter had considerably strengthened the provisions of the 1968 Measure in that, among other things, much more specific duties were laid down as to the need to consider the architectural, historic and aesthetic importance of the buildings involved. In addition, greater flexibility in decision making was allowed to the relevant authorities, although not without any loss of the rights of parishioners and others to express their views.

A pastoral committee is to be set up for each diocese, and it is to prepare as necessary *pastoral schemes* for the rearrangement of parishes, clergy, churches and vicarages, and for other related matters. The committee is to send such schemes in draft to the bishop, after consulting all 'interested parties' (1983 Measure, s 3). These are principally the vicars, patrons and church councils of the parishes involved, the archdeacons and, usually, the local planning authority (in this context, the district or borough council: s 87). In any case where a proposal, if implemented, would result in a church being declared redundant, the committee is required (by s 3(7)) not merely to consult the local planning authority, but actually to ascertain its views. In such a case, the committee must also consult the Council for the Care of Churches, which must then prepare a report on:
  (1) the historic interest and architectural quality of the churches involved and of others in the area;
  (2) the historic interest and aesthetic quality of their contents; and
  (3) the special features of any churchyards involved (s 3(8)).
The bishop may amend the proposed scheme, with the agreement of the pastoral committee, and will then send it on to the Church

Commissioners (s 4). Where a proposal provides for a redundancy, the Commissioners must consult with the Advisory Board for Redundant Churches if it involves alterations to or the demolition of any church, or its transfer to the Redundant Churches Fund (s 5(2)). The Commissioners will then prepare a draft scheme and send copies to all interested parties. They will consider any comments made, finalise the scheme, and send it for formal approval by Her Majesty in Council (ss 6–10).

Where a church is to become redundant as a result of a pastoral scheme, the scheme itself will not normally provide for its future use or for its demolition (s 28). However a pastoral scheme may make such provision where the redundant church is to be replaced by a new place of worship (which will not necessarily, or often, be a new building) and where one of the following conditions are satisfied (s 46):

(1) the Advisory Board states that the church is of no merit; or

(2) it is satisfied with a proposal to move its principal features to another church; or

(3) the Commissioners are satisfied (in spite of any advice to the contrary given by the Advisory Board) 'for reasons regarded by them as sufficient' that the church should be demolished; or

(4) they are satisfied as to the future use proposed for the church.

In addition (even where a replacement church is not, yet, available), a pastoral scheme may provide for an alternative use if there is one already known which is acceptable to the Commissioners. Finally, a scheme may provide for a church to be transferred to the Redundant Churches Fund where no alternative use is likely to be found, and where the building is 'of such historic and archaeological interest or architectural quality that it ought to be preserved in the interests of the nation and the Church of England' (s 47). The fund, financial jointly by the Church Commissioners and the Historic Buildings and Monuments Commission, now looks after 240 former parish churches.

Except in the specific cases mentioned above, a pastoral scheme will only provide that a church is to become redundant. The ultimate fate of the building in most cases has to be the subject of a *redundancy scheme* (s 48).

(b) Redundancy schemes

A redundancy scheme will provide for the future of a building that has been declared to be redundant in a pastoral scheme, in one of the following ways (1983 Measure, s 51):

(1) an alternative use for the building;
(2) the transfer of the building, if it is of great interest (see above), to the Redundant Churches Fund;
(3) the diocesan board of finance to retain control of it; or
(4) the demolition of the building.

The scheme will also, in practice, make other related provisions as to the future of any land attached, and the disposal of the proceeds of any sale.

A scheme must not normally be made for at least six months after the formal declaration of redundancy (that is, the approval of the pastoral scheme), but it must be made within three years from then, unless that would be impracticable (s 50(1)). During the waiting period, the church council has no further responsibility for the redundant building, except to assist the diocesan board of finance (which takes full charge of it) with its preservation. The quinquennial inspection (see 13.3(*f*)) is no longer required. The Church Commissioners may however, before the six month period is up, prepare a draft redundancy scheme providing for either:

(1) the demolition of the building (if the Advisory Board for Redundant Churches is satisfied that it is of no interest at all); or
(2) an approved alternative use (s 49).

The Commissioners, before preparing a draft redundancy scheme that involves any demolition of the building (in whole or in part) or any architectural or structural changes to it, must consult the Advisory Board. They must, in any event, consult the bishop, and serve a copy of the draft scheme on the following (among others):

(1) the diocesan board of finance;
(2) the Advisory Board;
(3) the Redundant Churches Fund (if it is proposed to transfer the building to the Fund); and
(4) the local planning authority (see 13.5(*a*)).

They must also advertise the draft scheme in a local paper, stating where it can be inspected in detail (s 50). They must bear in mind all the comments made, and they may then decide to proceed with the scheme or to amend it—in the latter case, they must then start the whole process all over again.

304 LISTED BUILDINGS AND CONSERVATION AREAS

Once a redundancy scheme is confirmed by Her Majesty in Council, the faculty procedure (see 13.3(*a*)) will no longer apply and, except in the case of buildings transferred to the Redundant Churches Fund, the legal effects of consecration will cease (1983 Measure, s 61).

At any stage of the process, the board of finance or the Redundant Churches Fund may transfer a redundant building to the Secretary of State or, with his agreement, to the Historic Buildings and Monuments Commission (1983 Measure, s 66, amended by NHA 1983).

(c) Exemption from 'secular' control

The total or partial demolition of a redundant Church of England building within the terms of a pastoral or redundancy scheme is exempt from listed building control. This is not because of the 1971 Act, but by virtue of the Redundant Churches and Other Religious Buildings Act 1969 (s 2, amended by TCPA 1971). That Act is entirely outside the scope of the new provisions in TCPA 1971, s 58AA (see 13.2(*b*)), and remains in force. Similarly, the demolition of a Church of England church in a conservation area under the terms of a redundancy or pastoral scheme does not require conservation area consent, by virtue of the Secretary of State's Direction in para 97, (*k*) of Circ 8/87 (see 10.2(*c*)).

However, as a result of concern over the possibility that this could be thought to lead to abuse, the Government has agreed with the Church of England as follows (see Circ 8/87, para 103(ii)):

. . . the Church Commissioners have agreed *always* to ask the Secretary of State for the Environment whether he wishes to hold a non-statutory local public inquiry into any proposal to demolish, wholly or partially, a listed church (or a non-listed church in a conservation area) in circumstances where the Historic Buildings and Monuments Commission, the Advisory Board for Redundant Churches, the local planning authority *or* a national amenity society give reasoned objections to that proposal. What is more, the Church Commissioners have undertaken to accept a recommendation from the Secretary of State following such an inquiry that the church is of sufficient importance to be vested in the Redundant Churches Fund or, in cases where the recommendation was not that the building should go to the Fund, to make further efforts to find an alternative use and to engage in further consultation with the Secretary of State before using the Pastoral Measure powers to demolish. In considering the recommendation which he will make, following a non-statutory

inquiry, the Secretary of State will take into account the financial implications of retaining a church building as well as the architectural and
historic interest of the church and other planning and social factors.

Finally, it may be noted that planning permission is of course
needed for a change of use of a church, or a major part of one.
This may be significant where an architecturally important church
is made redundant:

Redundant churches pose a sensitive problem as there are many people
who sincerely believe that a once-consecrated building should not be used
for purposes which they regard as incompatible with years of worship.
Nevertheless, unless funds are available to retain a redundant church in
good repair, the acceptance of a suitable alternative use may be the only
means to preserve both the building itself and its contribution to the
character and appearance of the area, and a reminder of its earlier
purpose (Circ 8/87, para 21).

13.6 Redundant churches of denominations other than the Church of England

Works for the demolition, alteration or extension of listed
ecclesiastical buildings of denominations other than the Church
of England that are no longer in use are in general subject to the
normal requirement for listed building consent to be obtained. In
particular, the total demolition of a redundant church that is listed
requires listed building consent, since clearly 'ecclesiastical use',
however defined, cannot continue in it once the works are
complete. Indeed the *Howard* case itself (see 13.2(*a*)) concerned
just such a situation—the trustees of a Congregational church
in Bedford wished to demolish the Howard Church, since its
congregation had been united with that of a neighbouring church.
It was held that, in such a case, listed building consent was
certainly required.

Similarly, conservation area consent will be required for the
total demolition of an unlisted church in a conservation area if it
belongs to a denomination other than the Church of England.

A preservation trust, sponsored by the Historic Buildings and
Monuments Commission, is currently being set up to take over
the finest Non Conformist and Roman Catholic churches which
are no longer required for worship. This will form a badly needed
counterpart to the Church of England's Redundant Churches
Fund (see 13.5(*a*)).

13.7 Religious buildings of other faiths

The exemption from listed building control described above applies to 'ecclesiastical buildings' (TCPA 1971, s 56(1)(*a*)). It has already been noted that this term has not been defined; and in particular that the House of Lords (in the *Howard* case [1976] AC 363; see 13.2(*a*)) specifically refused to say whether the ecclesiastical exemption extends to synagogues or mosques. The new provision introduced by the HPA 1986 makes it clear for the first time (at least implicitly) that it does encompass 'buildings of different [that is, presumably, including non-Christian] religious faiths' (TCPA 1971, s 58AA(2)(*b*), inserted by HPA 1986).

It remains to be seen how non-Christian buildings will be treated in any order made by the Secretary of State under the powers given to him in s 58AA. It is however, difficult to see buildings of at least the main faiths being treated any less favourably than those of non-Anglican Christian denominations.

More problematic will be buildings owned by fringe religions and cults. Decisions relating to the status of such organisations for purposes of charity law have tended to take a broadminded approach. See, for example, *Thornton* v *Howe* (1862) 31 Beav 14 at 19–20 per Sir John Romilly MR: 'the Court of Chancery makes no distinction between one sort of religion and another. . . . although this Court might consider the opinions sought to be propagated foolish or even devoid of foundation, it would not, on that account, declare it void . . .' That case concerned the followers of Joanna Southcote, who claimed that she was with child by the Holy Ghost, and would give birth to a second Messiah; and it may well be that the decision was influenced by the law as it then was (and in particular the Statute of Mortmain), as a result of which, because the sect was held to be a religion, and therefore charitable, a gift to it failed. But the judgment remains. On the other hand, the objects of the Church of Scientology have been held not to be for the advancement of religion (*R* v *Registrar General, ex parte Segerdal* [1970] 2 QB 697); nor are those of a masonic lodge (*Re Porter* [1925] Ch 746).

Chapter 14

Ancient Monuments

14.1 Introduction

(a) Background

The principle of scheduling 'ancient monuments' is much older than that of listing buildings or designating conservation areas. The first Ancient Monuments Protection Act, with a Schedule identifying just 68 sites throughout Britain, was passed in 1882, before many of the buildings that are now listed had even been built. By March 1988 there were estimated to be 12,674 scheduled monuments in England. These were in the past selected on a slightly ad hoc basis, and the current county lists are as a result somewhat unbalanced in the range and quality of monuments recorded. Their geographical distribution is also very uneven, even in rural areas, with over 1,302 in Cornwall alone and a mere 86 in Bedfordshire. There were a further 2,539 scheduled monuments in Wales (a very much higher proportion of the number in England than is the case with listed buildings).

Since 1984, the task of scheduling monuments in England and controlling works to them has in practice fallen largely to the Ancient Monuments Division of the Historic Buildings and Monuments Commission—in this chapter referred to as 'the Commission'—subject to overall direction by the Secretary of State. In February 1986, as the resurvey of buildings for listing was drawing to a close, the Commission announced the setting up of the Monuments Protection Programme, aimed at scheduling a further 45,000 sites in the next five to ten years. This would bring the total number of scheduled monuments in England to nearly 60,000, compared to an estimated 635,000 sites reckoned to be of archaeological interest. A resurvey in Wales is likely to happen in due course, but not in the immediate future.

307

The great majority of scheduled ancient monuments are archaeological sites or monuments whose importance resides in their buried archaeological deposits as well as any standing remains. They are located frequently in agricultural land in the countryside. Others are ruins or buildings for which there is often no present-day economic use readily apparent. A survey carried out by the English Tourist Board in December 1985 revealed that, out of 12,763 ancient monuments in England (of which the vast majority were scheduled), roughly 90 per cent were within one of the following ten categories (listed in order of frequency):

burial mounds and megalithic monuments

camps and settlements

castles and fortifications

deserted villages and moated sites

Roman ruins

[disused] ecclesiastical buildings

crosses and inscribed stones

bridges

linear earthworks

industrial monuments

The legislation regarding ancient monuments was consolidated and amended by the AMAAA 1979, which came into force (as far as ancient monuments were concerned) in October 1981. It replaced the Ancient Monuments Consolidation and Amendment Act 1913, the Ancient Monuments Act 1931, most of the Historic Buildings and Ancient Monuments Act 1953, and the Field Monuments Act 1972, and the Schedule to the 1882 Act. It has itself been significantly amended by the NHA 1983, so as to take into account the creation of the Commission, and references in this chapter to the AMAAA 1979 are thus to that Act as amended by the NHA 1983.

The related topic of archaeological areas (which are the subject of Part II of the 1979 Act) is covered in the following chapter (see 15.3).

(b) Classification of monuments

There are several different categories of monuments referred to in the 1979 Act, as follows:

scheduled monuments

monuments that are included in the Schedule prepared by the Secretary of State (see 14.2(*a*))

ancient monuments

scheduled monuments; and

any other monuments that are of sufficient public interest (see 14.4(*a*))

protected   scheduled monuments; and
monuments   any other ancient monuments that are in public
                ownership or guardianship (see 14.5(*c*)).

14.2 Scheduled monuments

(*a*) *Eligibility for scheduling*

A scheduled monument is defined as being any 'monument' (see below) that is included in a schedule of monuments compiled by the Secretary of State (AMAAA 1979, s 1(10)).

A monument is eligible for inclusion in the Schedule if:
(1) it was included, or proposed for inclusion, in a list of monuments under the provisions of the 1913 and 1931 Acts (see 14.1(a)) (s 1(2)); or
(2) it appears to the Secretary of State (after consultation with the Commission in the case of a monument in England) to be 'of national importance' (s 1(3)).

The first category is now of historical interest only, as the new county lists (see 14.2(*d*)) include all monuments scheduled up to the end of 1987 under either previous or current legislation. As to the second, this is a less precise criterion for inclusion than applies to the selection of listed buildings (which must be 'of special architectural or historic interest': TCPA 1971, s 54(1)), but it does indicate that a monument that is of only minor or local interest should not be scheduled. This is reflected in the fact that applications for scheduled monument consent are always dealt with by the Secretary of State, whereas most applications for listed building consent are determined by local authorities.

The Secretary of State's own view appears to be that the Schedule is to consist of 'ancient monuments of national importance by virtue of their historic, architectural, traditional, or archaeological interest' (Circ 8/87, para 49). This is not stated in the 1979 Act as such, although it does echo the phrase used in a slightly different context in s 61(12)(*b*) (which adds 'artistic' interest; see 14.4(*a*)); but that is referring to monuments suitable for financial assistance or public control.

The term 'monument' is also defined, as follows:
(1) any building, structure or work, whether above or below the surface of the land, other than an ecclesiastical building for the time being used for ecclesiastical purposes (see 13.2(*a*)) (s 61(7)(*a*), (8));

(2) any site comprising the remains of any such building, structure or work (s 61(7)(*b*));

(3) any cave or excavation (s 61(7)(*a*));

(4) any site comprising the remains of any cave or excavation (s 61(7)(*b*)); and

(5) any site comprising, or comprising the remains of, all or part of any vehicle, vessel, aircraft or other movable structure, where its situation in that particular site is a matter of public interest (s 61(7)(*c*), (8)(*a*)), other than a site protected under the Protection of Wrecks Act 1973 (s 61(8)(*b*)).

'Remains' in this context includes 'any trace or sign of the previous existence of the thing in question' (s 61(13)).

The Act also provides that a 'monument' (and presumably also, therefore, a scheduled monument) includes:

(1) any machinery attached it, if it could not be detached without being dismantled (s 61(7));

(2) its site (s 61(10)(*a*)); and

(3) any part of the monument as so defined (s 61(10)(*b*)).

A monument that is occupied as a dwelling (other than by a caretaker and his or her family) is not to be included in the Schedule (s 1(3)), although a number have been. Nor is an ecclesiastical building in use to be scheduled, since it is excluded from the definition of a monument (see above). It was after all in connection with the ancient monuments legislation that the ecclesiastical exemption first arose (see 13.3(*a*)). As to what kinds of monuments have in fact been scheduled, see 14.1.

(b) Production of schedule

The Secretary of State is empowered to include any monument in the Schedule if it seems to him to be of national importance, subject to the exclusions already noted (see 14.2(*a*)) (AMAAA 1979, s 1(3)). He may also amend or delete any entry in the Schedule (s 1(5)). In either case, he must consult the Commission before taking any action with respect to a monument in England. He is also given specific powers to authorise anyone (including, obviously, his officers and those of the Commission) to enter any land on or under which he knows or has reason to believe that there is an ancient monument (s 26).

After including or excluding a monument, he must then notify its owner and, where different, its occupier. He must also inform the local authorities (county and district/borough councils) covering the area, and the Broads Authority in its area (s 52A inserted by NSBA 1988). It would also be prudent for any local planning authority (such as a national park planning board or urban development corporation) to be notified, even though this is not strictly required, since authorities other than district or borough councils are excluded from the definition of 'local authority' in s 61(1). In England, this notification is to be done by the Secretary of State informing the Commission, which in turn is to inform the owner, occupier and authorities (ss 1(6A), 1A(1)); in Wales he is to do it directly (s 1(6)). From time to time he is to notify the Commission of all the scheduled monuments in an area, and it is to publish a list of them (ss 1(7A), 1A(2)). In Wales, he is to publish such lists himself (s 1(7)). Any entry of a monument in the Schedule is to be a local land charge (s 1(9)).

In practice, as with the listing procedure (see 2.2), most of the work in the Monuments Protection Programme (see 14.1) will be done by the Commission's own inspectors, but some is expected to be delegated to specialists from elsewhere. No doubt, quite apart from the Programme, other monuments will be added to the Schedule from time to time as appropriate. Once a revision to the Schedule has been approved by the Commission, it is then passed on to the Department of the Environment, which in turn has to approve it with or without modifications. The Commission can then carry out the necessary notifications, as above.

In Wales, the procedure is more or less similar, except that the leading role there is taken by Cadw—Welsh Historic Monuments, which is constitutionally part of the Welsh Office and thus under the direct control of the Secretary of State. However, since the resurvey of buildings for listing is only in its early stages, it is likely that any resurvey of monuments in Wales will not be taking place for several years yet.

(c) Consequences of scheduling

The main consequences of a monument being scheduled are as follows:

(1) almost any works to it require scheduled monument consent (see 14.3);
(2) it may be the subject of acquisition or guardianship procedures (14.4); and
(3) it is a criminal offence to damage it or to use a metal detector on its site (14.5).

In addition, works to a scheduled monument will be zero-rated for value added tax provided that scheduled monument consent is needed and has been obtained (see 6.8(*a*)). General rates will usually not be payable in respect of a scheduled monument, since it will in most cases not be rateably occupied (see 6.8(*b*)).

(d) Where to find information

The Historic Buildings and Monuments Commission maintains accurate and up-to-date records of all scheduled monuments in England (as it is required to do by s 1A(2), (3)). It has recently reviewed these, and is expecting to have published by the end of 1988 lists for each county, including all monuments scheduled up to the end of 1987. These county lists are available (price £2.50 each, apparently regardless of the number of monuments recorded) from the Ancient Monuments Division of the Commission at Fortress House, 23 Savile Row, London W1X 2HE (tel 01–734 6010). The Commission should also be consulted to ascertain whether a particular monument has been scheduled since the publication of the relevant county list.

In Wales, similar information is available from Cadw—Welsh Historic Monuments, Brunel House, 2 Fitzalan Road, Cardiff CF2 1UY (tel 0222–465511).

14.3 Works to scheduled monuments

(a) Need for scheduled monument consent

Scheduled monument consent is required from the Secretary of State for the carrying out of almost any works to a scheduled monument (AMAAA 1979, s 2(1),(3)). In particular, it is required for the following (specified in s 2(2)):

(*a*) any works resulting in:
—the demolition or destruction of a scheduled monument, or
—any damage to it;
(*b*) any works for the purpose of:
—removing or repairing a scheduled monument or any part of it, or
—making any alterations or additions to it;
(*c*) any flooding or tipping operations on land in, on or under which there is a scheduled monument.

To carry out such works without consent, or in breach of the terms or conditions of any consent that has been obtained, is a criminal offence (s 2(1)). See 14.5(*a*) on unauthorised works generally.

It will be appreciated that this is a much broader category of operations than those for which planning permission or listed building consent is required. In particular, it includes 'making any alterations' to the monument, which must be read bearing in mind that 'a monument' is defined to include its site (s 61(10)(*a*)).

The Secretary of State (after consulting the Commission) may, however, grant consent by order for specific categories of works (s 3(1)). This is a mechanism similar to 'permitted development' whereby planning permission is granted automatically for certain classes of development (see 7.3). The order currently in force is the Ancient Monuments (Class Consents) Order 1981, which was marginally amended in 1984. Under this, scheduled monument consent is granted (and a specific application is therefore not necessary) for works in the following classes:

I   Agricultural, horticultural or forestry works, being works of the same kind as works previously executed in the same field or location during the period of five years immediately preceding the coming into operation of [the] order [9 October 1981]; but not including subsoiling, drainage works, the planting or uprooting of trees, hedges or shrubs, or any other works likely to disturb the soil below the maximum depth affected by normal ploughing.

II   Works executed more than ten metres below ground level by [British Coal or its licensees].

III [Certain essential works of repair or maintenance executed by the British Waterways Board].

IV   Works for the repair or maintenance of machinery, being works which do not involve a material alteration to a monument.

V   Works which are essential for the purposes of health or safety.

VI   Works executed by [the Commission].

Class VI is particularly significant when it is remembered that over 400 monuments—including many of the most important ones—are in the care of the Commission. Such works, where they are 'development', will also normally be permitted automatically by the GDO (GDO 1988, Sched 2, Part 26; see 7.3(*e*)).

The general consent granted by the Order may be revoked in any particular case by a direction made under s 3(3), similar in effect to an Article 4 direction (see 7.4). If such a direction is made, and consent is subsequently applied for and granted subject to onerous conditions or refused, compensation will be payable by the Commission (in England) or by the Secretary of State (in Wales) (s 9(1), (2)(*a*), (3)).

Works by Government departments affecting scheduled monuments in Crown ownership do not require scheduled monument consent (s 50). They should instead be notified to the Department of the Environment (Heritage Sponsorship Division) or Cadw—Welsh Historic Monuments (Circ 18/84, para 36). The procedure will be similar to that applying to works to listed buildings in Crown ownership (see 8.2(c)), except that it is the Secretary of State who is notified, rather than the local authority.

Works by local authorities require consent from the Secretary of State just as do those by anyone else.

(b) Submission of application

All applications for scheduled monument consent are to be made to the Secretary of State, not to the local planning authority. The procedure is set out in AMAAA 1979, Sched 1, Part I and in the Ancient Monuments (Applications for Scheduled Monument Consent) Regulations 1981.

An application is to be made on the form prescribed in Sched 1 to the Regulations, and must be accompanied by plans and drawings sufficient to identify the monument and describe the works proposed (reg 2(1), (2)). By the nature of ancient monuments, the works may need to be described in considerable detail to enable their effect on the monument to be adequately ascertained. The Secretary of State can always ask for further information if he wishes (reg 2(3)).

It should also be accompanied by a certificate as to the ownership of the monument, similar to that needed with an application for planning permission or listed building consent (see 8.3(d)) (AMAAA 1979, Sched 1, para 2(1); 1981 Regulations, reg 3, Sched 2). Here, unlike the position with regard to those applications, the Secretary of State does have jurisdiction to entertain an application for scheduled monument consent if it is not accompanied by a certificate (compare TCPA 1971, s 27(1) and TCP (LBCA) Regs 1987, reg 6(1)). There is no fee payable.

The application should be sent to:

Department of the Environment, HSD3, Room 242, Lambeth Bridge House, Albert Embankment, London SE1 7SB; or

Cadw—Welsh Historic Monuments, Brunel House, 2 Fitzalan Road, Cardiff CF2 1UY.

On receiving an application, the Secretary of State will (in England) immediately send a copy to the Commission (AMAAA 1979, Sched 1, para 2A).

(c) Determination of application

Before making a decision on any application for scheduled monument consent, the Secretary of State:

(1) must give an opportunity to be heard (at either a public local inquiry or some other hearing) to the applicant;

(2) may give such an opportunity to be heard to anyone else if it seems expedient to do so;

(3) must consider any report made by the person holding any such inquiry or hearing;

(4) must consider any representations made by owners or occupiers notified by the applicant (see above);

(5) may give publicity to the application, but must consider any representations arising if he does so;

(6) must consider any representations made by any other person for any other reason;

(7) must consult with the Commission in England

(AMAAA 1979, Sched 1, para 3(2), (3)).

However, there is no obligation on either the Secretary of State or the Commission to publicise the application at the site or in the local press or to notify anyone of it, even the local authority. This is a surprising lacuna, which Parliament would do well to rectify at some suitable opportunity.

Consent may be granted for all or some of the works proposed, and any decision must be notified to the applicant and to anyone who made representations (para 3(1),(4)). Consent may be subject to any conditions considered suitable (s 2(4)) and, in particular, conditions as to the manner in which or the persons by whom the works are to be carried out.

It may also be a condition of consent that access must be given (in England) to anyone authorised by the Commission or (in Wales) to the Secretary of State or anyone authorised by him, before the works are started, to examine the site and the monument itself and to carry out archaeological excavations as appropriate (s 2(5)). In addition, whether or not such a condition is imposed, anyone authorised by the Commission (in England) or by the Secretary of State (in England or Wales) may enter the land:

(1) to inspect the works in progress or the condition of the land and the monument once they have been completed (ss 6(2), 6A(2)); or

(2) to inspect the land (and any buildings or objects on it) to

observe and record any objects of archaeological or historic interest that may be found during the works (s 6(4)).

This applies where the works concerned are authorised either by a specific grant of scheduled monument consent under s 2(3) or by a general class consent under s 3(1) (see 14.3(*a*)) (ss 6(6), 6A(5)).

Any consent granted lapses automatically after five years (or any other period specifically stated), unless within that period the works authorised have been executed, or at least 'started' (as to which, see 8.6(*b*)) (s 4(1), (2)).

(d) Considerations taken into account in determining applications

It seems that the only two considerations taken into account by the Commission in advising the Secretary of State on whether or not to grant scheduled monument consent are:

(1) whether the proposed works will damage the monument; and

(2) whether they would constitute an inappropriate addition to the monument.

There were some 773 applications for scheduled monument consent in England during 1987, which represents around 6 per cent of the number of monuments. Of those, only 15 were refused; but many were the subject of detailed discussions between the applicant and the Commission.

Most proposals requiring consent are for works which might appear to be relatively minor, such as altering the pattern of ploughing, or erecting a small structure on the site of a monument. There is in practice, however, an overwhelming presumption in favour of the preservation of a scheduled monument, and any proposal is therefore looked at very critically.

(e) Revocation or modification of consent

The Secretary of State may, if he wishes, revoke or modify a grant of scheduled monument consent (AMAAA 1979, s 4(3)). He may, in particular, modify the period within which the works authorised by the consent must be started (s 4(4)). The procedure for revoking or modifying consent is set out in AMAAA 1979, Sched 1, Part II.

In England, after consulting with the Commission, the Secretary of State must serve on the owner and occupier of the monument a notice of his proposal, together with his reasons for doing so. Where the proposal is to revoke consent, or to modify its scope so as to exclude some works, the notice will have the effect of halting immediately those works which are now unauthorised (Sched 1, para 5). The owner and occupier then have twenty-eight days in which to object and, if they do, there must be an inquiry if they wish. The Secretary of State must then consider any objections made, and may then give the direction modifying or revoking the consent (para 6). Notice of the direction must be given to the owner and occupier (para 7).

Compensation can be claimed in such cases. The amount payable will be the value of any expenditure rendered abortive, together with any loss or damage arising from the revocation or modification of consent (s 9(1), (2)(b), (c)).

(f) The need for other types of consent

Planning permission is needed for development affecting ancient monuments as in any other case, and the effect of a proposal may of course be a perfectly valid reason for permission being refused. Thus, in *Hoveringham Gravels Ltd* v *Secretary of State* [1975] QB 754, Lord Denning MR said (at 763):

> But now I turn back to the extraction of sand and gravel for commercial purposes. . . . Even if there had been no preservation orders, they would never have got planning permission for that purpose. . . . They actually applied for planning permission—long before any preservation orders were made—and were refused. The cause of this refusal . . . lies in the very nature of Berry Mound Camp itself. It was known to the planning authorities to be an iron age fort of great archaeological interest, so much so that it was of national importance that it should be preserved and not destroyed. That was a perfectly legitimate reason for refusing planning permission. It was just as legitimate to refuse for archaeological reasons as for amenity reasons.

Note that this would apply whether or not the monument was actually 'scheduled'.

Since the coming into force of the new GDO (5 December 1988), planning authorities are now required to consult the Commission (or, in Wales, the Secretary of State) before granting planning permission in any case where proposed development is likely to affect the site of a scheduled ancient monument (GDO 1988, art 18 (1) (n); and see Circ 8/87, para 52).

The criteria for the selection of monuments are different from those for selecting buildings for listing, but inevitably there is some degree of overlap, and some structures are therefore both scheduled and listed. To avoid duplication of controls, however, which would result in unneccessary bureaucracy and delay, it is provided that listed building consent is not needed as well as scheduled monument consent for works to a listed building that is also a scheduled monument (TCPA 1971, s 56(1)(*b*), substituted by AMAAA 1979; and see 8.2(*b*)).

Similarly, conservation area consent is not needed as well as scheduled monument consent for the demolition of a scheduled monument that happens to be in a conservation area (TCPA 1971, s 277A(1)(*b*), inserted by TCAA 1974; s 58(2)(*b*), substituted by AMAAA 1979; and see 10.1(*b*)).

(g) Compensation for refusal of scheduled monument consent

Compensation is payable where scheduled monument consent is refused, but only in very limited circumstances.

The first is where scheduled monument consent is refused for the carrying out of works affecting a monument or its site for which planning permission has already been granted (AMAAA 1979, s 7(2)(*a*), (3)), but only where:

(1) the permission was granted before the monument was scheduled; and

(2) it was still valid at the date on which the consent was refused.

The second is where consent is refused for works which are not 'development' (see 7.2(*a*)), or which are 'permitted development' (7.3(*a*)) (AMAAA 1979, s 7(2)(*b*)). Compensation is not normally payable under this heading where the works for which consent is refused are such that they would result in the demolition or destruction of the monument. However it is payable if consent is refused for agricultural or forestry operations, even if they would lead to such a result (s 7(4)).

The third situation giving rise to a liability for compensation is where a monument is included in the Schedule and, as a result, consent is now required to continue the current use of its site (for example, for waste tipping or mineral extraction). Compensation is then payable if consent is refused, resulting in the continuation of that use being impossible (s 7(2)(*c*), (5)).

The net effect of these provisions is to preserve any value attaching to the land by virtue of either:

(1) an express planning permission granted before the monument is scheduled, or

(2) any right to carry out works that do not require planning permission.

Otherwise, compensation is limited to works necessary to continue the use of the site that was in existence at the date it was scheduled. Thus in the *Hoveringham Gravels* case (see above), consent was (in effect) refused both for gravel working and for agriculture, but compensation was only payable for the second refusal, since the agricultural works proposed would have been permitted development.

If consent is refused for any works, and compensation is as a result actually received, then it must be paid back if consent is subsequently granted for the same works (s 8)—which is not unreasonable.

14.4 Care and ownership of ancient monuments

(a) Introduction

Ancient monuments are mostly in private hands. Many, for example, are in or underneath fields that are part of working farms. Since it would be unreasonable for a private landowner to have to meet the full costs of maintaining, say, an iron-age hill fort or a medieval ruined chapel, it is more appropriate for the most significant monuments (such as Stonehenge, or the Welsh castles) to be in public ownership or care.

Accordingly, discretionary grants are available for the upkeep of ancient monuments. There are also special provisions whereby they can in appropriate cases be taken into public care—either by acquisition, or under a guardianship or other agreement.

Note that unless specifically stated otherwise, these provisions apply not just to 'scheduled monuments' (see 14.2(*a*)), but also to any *ancient monument*—which term includes 'any other monument which in the opinion of the Secretary of State is of public interest by reason of the historic, architectural, traditional, artistic or archaeological interest attaching to it' (AMAAA 1979, s 61(12)). Note too that, whereas monuments must be 'of national importance' to be eligible for scheduling (see 14.2(*a*)), they only have to be 'of public interest' to be categorised as 'ancient monuments' suitable for financial assistance or public control. The latter would seem to be a significantly lower standard.

(b) Grants for ancient monuments

The Commission has power (under AMAAA 1979, s 24(3A)) to defray or contribute towards the cost of any of the following, in connection with any ancient monument in England:

its acquisition by any person or body; or

its preservation, maintenance and management (including the removal elsewhere of all or part of it to ensure its preservation). 'Maintenance' in this context includes fencing, repairing, and covering in a monument, and doing anything else needed to repair it or to protect it from decay or injury (s 13(7)).

The Commission spent £1.4 million on such grants in 1986–87. It states that the criteria for assistance are as follows:

> Grants are given to owners of ancient monuments for major repairs or management works, but not for routine maintenance. The standard rate of grant is 40 per cent. . . . but may be higher where necessary. Eligible works can include restoration of earthworks after erosion, repointing, roof repairs and major consolidation and stabilisation schemes. (*Grants for Monuments, Historic Buildings and Conservation Areas*, HBMC leaflet, 1988.)

Since the date of that statement, the rate of grant to local authorities, which used to be 25 per cent, has risen to 40 per cent.

In addition, the Commission is empowered to give financial assistance towards the cost of any archaeological investigation work in England (s 45(1A)). Most of the £7.2 million spent under this heading in 1986–87 went on rescue archaeology (see Chapter 15), but some was spent on new excavations.

The Secretary of State for Wales has identical powers (ss 24(1), (2), 45(1)).

Application forms and further details are available from the Ancient Monuments Division of English Heritage and from Cadw—Welsh Historic Monuments (see 14.2(*d*)).

Any local authority (in England or Wales) may also give a grant to assist with the cost of the preservation, maintenance or management of any ancient monuments in its area (s 24(4)), or any archaeological investigation (s 45(2)).

(c) Works to preserve a scheduled monument

As well as or instead of giving grant aid to others to preserve, maintain or manage monuments, or to carry out any archaeological investigation work, the Commission (in England), the Secretary of State (in Wales) or any local authority may undertake or assist in any such activities on their own account (ss 24, 45).

Alternatively the Commission or the Secretary of State may in appropriate cases give advice on, or superintend, the carrying out of any works to an ancient monument—either free or for a charge, and either at the request of the owner or otherwise (s 25).

Further powers are available in connection with a monument that is actually scheduled. The Commission (in England) or the Secretary of State (in Wales) may enter any land with the consent of its owner and occupier, to put up notices or posts on or near a monument so as to preserve it from accidental or deliberate damage (ss 6(5), 6A(4)). In cases of urgency, either the Secretary of State (in England or Wales) or the Commission (in England, if authorised by the Secretary of State) may enter on any land to carry out any works to preserve a monument, after giving at least seven days' notice to the owner (s 5).

(d) Acquisition by the Secretary of State, the Commission or a local authority

Where private owners are unwilling or unable to cooperate in maintaining or preserving a monument, the only option may be to take it into public ownership. This may be suitable anyway for the most important monuments, as one means of ensuring that the public are able to gain access to them.

First, the Secretary of State (in England or Wales) may acquire any 'ancient monument' (see 14.4(a)) by compulsory purchase (s 10). He may acquire any land in the vicinity of the monument— or any easement, such as a right of way, over such land—needed for access to it or for the maintenance of its amenities (ss 15, 16). The procedure is as set out in the Acquisition of Land Act 1981. The Secretary of State has undertaken never to use this power except where it is the only way of preserving a monument.

Secondly, an ancient monument in England may be acquired by agreement or as a gift by the Secretary of State (after consulting with the Commission), the Commission, or a local authority (s 11(1)–(3A)). A Welsh monument may be acquired by the Secretary of State or a local authority (s 11(1), (2)). This provision also extends to the acquisition of any land associated with the monument or any easement over such land (ss 15, 16).

Once a monument is in the ownership of one of the above public bodies, it may then be passed to any of the others as appropriate (s 21).

The Commission (or, in Wales, the Secretary of State) may be willing to assist a local authority to purchase a monument when it is considered to be of exceptional interest and when preservation by other means is not possible.

It may also be noted in passing that a local authority is not able to acquire the site of an ancient monument or other object of

M

archaeological interest either in order to carry out repairs to a house unfit for human occupation (under HA 1985, s 192; see 5.9(*a*)) or for slum clearance. Nor may it acquire such a site for the provision of housing, except by compulsory purchase, which ensures that the Secretary of State has to give his approval (HA 1985, s 608).

(e) Guardianship and other agreements

As an alternative to outright acquisition of a monument, it is also possible for a private owner to enter voluntarily into an agreement with the Secretary of State, the Commission or a local authority whereby the public body is constituted by deed to be the guardian of the monument (AMAAA 1979, s 12(1)–(2)). The owner for this purpose is the owner of the freehold, or a leasehold with at least forty-five years unexpired, or a life interest in possession; and if such an owner is not also the occupier of the land containing the monument, the occupier must be party to the deed (s 12(3), (4)). This provision too extends to any land associated with the monument or any easement over such land (ss 15, 16).

In addition, either the Secretary of State (in England or Wales) or the Commission (in England) may purchase or accept as a gift any object associated with a monument in their guardianship (HBAMA 1953, s 5(2)(*b*), (3A)). They may also accept a capital endowment to provide income for the upkeep of such a monument (HBAMA 1953, ss 8(1)(*c*), 8A(1)(*c*); and see 5.6(*b*)).

A guardianship arrangement does not alter the ownership of the monument, but it does transfer from the owner to the guardian the (sometimes extremely onerous) responsibility for its upkeep and maintenance. To this end, the guardian is given full control and management of it, except as provided for in the guardianship deed (AMAAA 1979, s 13). Guardianship arrangements have been a feature of all ancient monuments legislation since 1913; but the compulsory guardianship arrangements of the past, which proved unsuccessful in practice, have been dropped in favour of the present voluntary scheme. They are in practice the way in which the Commission and Cadw have control over many of the monuments in their care.

The guardianship of a monument may be transferred between the Secretary of State, the Commission and a local authority as seems appropriate (s 21).

It is possible for any owner (as defined above) to terminate the guardianship, and theoretically possible for the guardian to do so if satisfied that the monument will be properly looked after in the future (s 14).

There is also a more limited power (in s 17) whereby the Secretary of State, the Commission or a local authority may enter into an agreement with the occupier of land including a monument, providing for:

(1) the maintenance and preservation of the monument, or the carrying out of specified works to it;
(2) the provision of public access to the monument;
(3) the restriction of the use of the land, or the prohibition of unsuitable activities on it; and
(4) the making of appropriate payments to the occupier.

The owner of the land (if not the same person as the occupier) may, but need not be, party to such an agreement.

(f) Public access to ancient monuments

The public must be allowed access to any monument in the ownership or guardianship of the Secretary of State, the Commission or a local authority—that being, after all, one of the main points of such public control (s 19).

The provision of such access may however be limited or excluded altogether for a time, by virtue of regulations made by the owner or guardian of the monument. Such regulations may also make appropriate provisions for the preservation of the monument, and for admission charges (s 19(2)–(5)). Such regulations may also be made with respect to any monument owned or controlled by the Secretary of State for any other reason.

The Secretary of State, the Commission or a local authority may provide facilities for the public in connection with any ancient monument in public control, and may make whatever charge seems appropriate (s 20). The provision of such facilities, if it amounts to development, will usually either require planning permission or need to be notified to the local planning authority (see 7.3(e)).

14.5 Offences involving ancient monuments

(a) Introduction

If unauthorised works are carried out to a scheduled monument, there is no provision in the 1979 Act for 'enforcement action' to

be taken, as there is with unauthorised development (see 9.4(*a*));
an ancient monument often cannot by its nature be 'restored'.
The only measure that could possibly be effective, either as a
punishment or as a deterrent, is therefore criminal prosecution.
Accordingly, the Act provides for several offences of carrying out
unauthorised works to a scheduled monument (see 14.5(*b*)), and
for further offences of damaging a protected monument (14.5(*c*))
and using a metal detector (14.5(*d*)). For each of these offences
there are specific defences available.

As to the effectiveness of these provisions, thirty-seven cases
of damage to scheduled ancient monuments were apparently
reported to English Heritage during 1986–87. They resulted from
unauthorised works or the unlicensed use of metal detectors.
Prosecutions were undertaken in nine cases. Five resulted in
convictions and fines, the most notable being the fine imposed on
the Marquess of Hertford following damage caused by ploughing
the site of Alcester Roman Town.

(b) Unauthorised works to a scheduled monument

The first offence is to carry out any unauthorised works resulting
in:
(1) the demolition or destruction of a scheduled monument, or
(2) any damage to it (AMAAA 1979, s 2(2)(*a*)).
It should be borne in mind when considering this that the definition of a 'monument' includes any part of it, and all or part of
its site (s 61(10)). It is a defence to a charge under this heading
to prove:
(1) that the accused 'took all reasonable precautions and exercised all due diligence to avoid or prevent damage to the
monument' (s 2(7)); or
(2) that he did not know that and had no reason to believe:
—that the monument was within the area affected by the
works, or
—that the monument was scheduled (s 2(8)).
The second of these defences means that it is only to a limited
extent an offence of strict liability. To avoid a conviction it is not
enough for an accused to show that he was unaware that the
monument was likely to be affected, or that it was scheduled; he
must also prove (on the balance of probability) that he had no
reason to believe that it was.

The second offence is to carry out any unauthorised works for
the purpose of:

(1) removing or repairing a scheduled monument or any part of it, or

(2) making any alterations or additions to it (s 2(2)(*b*)).

There is no need (as there is with the corresponding listed buildings offence) for the prosecution to prove that the alteration affected the special character of the monument as one of archaeological or historic interest. Since the 'monument' includes its site, the scope of 'alterations or additions' must be considerable, although some very minor works will of course be permitted by the general class consent under s 3 (see 14.3(*a*)).

The third offence is to carry out any unauthorised flooding or tipping operations on land in, on or under which there is a scheduled monument (s 2(2)(*c*)). Here too it is a defence to prove that the accused did not know and had no reason to believe that the monument was within the area affected by the works or that it was scheduled (s 2(8)).

It is of course a defence to any of these charges to prove that the works were authorised—that is, that they had received scheduled monument consent from the Secretary of State and that they had been carried out in accordance with the terms and conditions of such consent (s 2(3)). Where the works were given consent, but were carried out in breach of any condition attached to it, that is a further offence; but it is a defence to such a charge to prove that the accused took 'all reasonable precautions and exercised all due diligence to avoid contravening the condition' (s 2(6)).

Finally, it is a defence to a charge on any of the above offences to prove:

that the works were urgently necessary in the interests of safety or health and
that notice in writing of the need for the works was given to the Secretary of State as soon as reasonably practicable (s 2(9)).

This is easy to claim after the event, and difficult for the prosecution to disprove, and thus represents an unfortunate loophole which could be exploited by an unscrupulous owner of a monument. It is in fact drafted identically to the corresponding provision in the listed buildings code (TCPA 1971, s 55(6)), as it was before being tightened up by the HPA 1986 (see 9.2(*c*)).

All of the above offences are triable either way (see 9.2(*e*)) (s 2(10)). A person found guilty of any of them is liable:

(1) on summary conviction, to a fine of up to the 'statutory

maximum' (currently £2,000: s 61(1), amended by Magistrates' Courts Act 1980; Criminal Penalties etc (Increase) Order 1984); or

(2) on conviction on indictment, to an unlimited fine.

If the unauthorised works constitute serious 'damage' to a scheduled monument, it may be preferable to frame a charge under s 28 (see 14.5(c)), as this carries a higher maximum sentence. On the other hand, for a charge under s 28 to succeed, the required mens rea of intent or recklessness must be proved.

Finally, it must be remembered that the monument must actually be scheduled for a charge under s 2 to be possible. It is not enough to be an 'ancient monument' (see 14.4(a)) or a 'protected monument' (14.5(c)).

(c) Damage to a protected monument

Anyone who without lawful excuse destroys or damages a protected monument is guilty of an offence (under AMAAA 1979, s 28(1)) if he or she:

(1) knows that it is a protected monument; and
    either intends to destroy or damage the monument, or
(2) is reckless as to whether it would be destroyed or damaged.

This applies to acts done by anyone, including the owner, other than those for which scheduled monument consent has been obtained (s 28(2)). A *protected monument* is defined for this purpose as any monument which is either:

(1) a scheduled monument (see 14.2(a)) or
(2) under the ownership or guardianship of the Secretary of State, the Commission or a local authority (14.4(d), (e)).

Unlike the offence of damaging a listed building (see 9.3), this is not an offence of strict liability, in that it must be proved that the defendant knew the monument was protected. On the other hand, it will in many cases be difficult for an accused to prove the absence of such knowledge, where there are signs and other evidence. Equally, it is not necessary to prove 'intent'; mere recklessness is sufficient. The wording of the offence follows that used in s 1 of the Criminal Damage Act 1971, so that the necessary state of mind is as described by Lord Diplock in *R* v *Caldwell* [1982] AC 341 at 354.

The offence under s 28 is triable either way (s 28(4)). It attracts on summary conviction a fine of up to the 'statutory maximum' (see 14.5(b)), or a prison sentence of up to six months, or both. On conviction or indictment, the maximum penalty is an unlimited fine, or imprisonment for up to two years, or both. Where, as a result of such a conviction, a compensation order is made under s 35 of the Powers of Criminal Courts Act 1973, it may in appropriate cases be in favour of the guardian of the monument rather than the owner (s 29).

In some cases, it might also be appropriate to consider a charge of attempted damage (under Criminal Attempts Act 1981, s 1(1)). This would attract a fine of up to £2,000 or six months' imprisonment (1981 Act, s 4(1)(c)).

Any person authorised by the Secretary of State, the Commission or a local authority may refuse to admit to a monument under public control anyone who seems likely to damage the monument or upset the public visiting it (AMAAA 1979, s 19(6)). This enables the appropriate authorities to deal with either individual troublemakers or groups (such as the peace convoy at Stonehenge) which might be likely to cause problems.

More generally, any breach of regulations made to control access to public monuments (see 14.4(f)) is an offence, attracting a fine of up to level 3 (s 19(7), amended by Criminal Justice Act 1982; Criminal Penalties etc (Increase) Order 1984).

(d) Use of metal detectors at the site of a protected monument

It is an offence to use a metal detector at the site of any 'protected monument' (see 14.5(c)), without the written consent of the Commission (in England) or the Secretary of State (in Wales) (AMAAA 1979, s 42(1)). Anyone charged with this offence is liable on summary conviction to a fine of up to £200. The mere possession, as opposed to the use, of a metal detector at a protected site might be triable either as an offence of attempt (under Criminal Attempts Act 1981, s 1(1)) or as one of possessing an article for use to damage property (under Criminal Damage Act 1971, s 3(a)).

The real problem, however, is not the use of a metal detector but the subsequent removal of any objects discovered with it. Accordingly it is a more serious offence to remove from such a site, without written consent, any object of archaeological or historical interest (note: not 'special' interest) discovered with the use of a metal detector (s 42(3)). This is triable either way, and attracts on summary conviction a fine of up to the 'statutory maximum' (see 14.5(b)), or, on conviction on indictment, an unlimited fine.

Consent granted by the Commission or the Secretary of State—

in practice in the form of a 'licence'—can be either unconditional or subject to conditions; and a failure to comply with any conditions is an offence attracting the same penalties as failure to obtain consent at all (s 42(4), (5)).

It is a defence to proceedings under s 42 to prove:

(1) that the metal detector was being used for purposes other than to locate objects of archaeological or historical interest (s 42(6)); or

(2) that the accused had taken all reasonable steps to discover whether the site was a protected monument, and as a result did not believe that it was (s 42(7)).

Chapter 15

Rescue Archaeology

15.1 Background

The problems of development affecting the site of a known ancient monument have already been considered (see 14.3(*f*)). Rather different considerations arise however where redevelopment is proposed on a site which is already built on, but which is known or suspected to be of archaeological significance. Such a situation occurs often in connection with redevelopment in the centre of older cities (and not least in the City of London).

In such a case, it is of course possible for the local planning authority to refuse planning permission for the redevelopment solely or partly on archaeological grounds. The site can then be scheduled by the Secretary of State under the ancient monuments legislation (see 14.2), so that scheduled monument consent has to be obtained before the development can proceed. However, if consent is refused, compensation will have to be paid (under AMAAA 1979, s 7(2)(*c*); see 14.3(*g*)). This procedure will therefore only be appropriate where the site is known to be of outstanding archaeological value.

Rather than redevelopment being altogether blocked, it is more realistic in most cases for the start of building works to be delayed, so that archaeological excavations can be carried out before the site is once more covered up. In practice some developers may be willing to give such facilities, and an informal agreement will often be the best way to achieve a satisfactory arrangement, since the developer's cooperation is clearly vital. In a number of areas, such voluntary arrangements are already well established, and developers have agreed in some cases not only to provide access to sites but also to finance the excavation and the analysis, preservation and display of the finds. Very often neither central Government nor local authorities need to or should be involved other than on an advisory basis. Grants may well be available in appropriate cases from the Historic Buildings and Monuments Commission ('the Commission'), from Cadw—Welsh Historic Monuments, or from a local authority (see 14.4(*b*)) (AMAAA 1979, s 45).

15.2 Conditions on planning permissions

Where developers are unable or unwilling to enter into voluntary agreements to provide access to archaeologists, an alternative course of action is to grant planning permission for the redevelopment subject to suitable conditions.

This practice has been approved by the Secretary of State, and two examples of those considered acceptable are included in App A to the Annex to Circ 1/85.

No development shall take place until fencing has been erected, in a manner to be agreed with the local planning authority, about [*insert name of monument*]; and no works shall take place within the area inside that fencing without the consent of the local planning authority (model condition 37).

This type of condition would be appropriate where the redevelopment will not actually cover the part of the site to be fenced, so as to preserve the archaeological interest of the site as far as possible. It would also be suitable where that part of the site will be built on last (for example, as a car park), so as to give as much time as possible for any finds to be recorded.

The developer shall afford access at all reasonable times to any archaeologist nominated by the local planning authority, and shall allow him to observe the excavations and record items of interest and finds (model condition 38).

This could be used where the redevelopment, when completed, will completely obliterate the archaeological remains, so that there may be at least a brief last chance for them to be recorded.

The Secretary of State has however pointed out that conditions should not require work to be held up while archaeological investigation takes place (Circ 1/85). Such a requirement could not reasonably be the subject of a s 52 or similar agreement either (see Circ 22/83).

15.3 Areas of archaeological importance

(a) The designation of an area

Where an area is of great archaeological significance, and where as a result the need to facilitate investigation outweighs the problems of delaying development, it is possible for it to be formally designated as an *area of archaeological importance*, under Part II of the AMAAA 1979 (as amended by NHA 1983).

The power to designate an area of archaeological importance (under s 33) can be exercised by:

(1) *in Greater London*: the Secretary of State (after consultation with the Commission), a borough council (after notifying the Commission), and the Commission itself;

(2) *elsewhere in England*: the Secretary of State (after consultation with the Commission), or a county or district council or the Broads Authority (after notifying the Commission); and

(3) *in Wales*: the Secretary of State or a county or district council.

A proposal to designate an area should be advertised in the *London Gazette* and in a local newspaper. If it is the Secretary of State who is proposing to make a designation order, he should not do so before six weeks have elapsed since the publication of the advertisements, and should in any event first consult with the local authorities in the area and (in England) with the Commission (AMAAA 1979, Sched 2, paras 1–7). If it is a local authority or the Commission who wishes to designate an area, it must submit a draft designation order to the Secretary of State for his confirmation (again, after the expiry of the six-week period) (paras 8–15A). A designation order must be in the form of a map. Further press advertisements must be published when the order is made or confirmed, and it will then come into force after a further period of six months has elapsed (para 16). As with the designation of a conservation area, those living or working in an area of archaeological importance do not have to be informed, but the designation is a local land charge (s 33(5)).

The view of the Government when this procedure was first introduced (in April 1982) was that designation of areas should only be undertaken selectively, in areas of great archaeological importance where cooperation is poor or non-existent. Five areas have now been designated, comprising the historic centres of Canterbury, Chester, Exeter, Hereford and York.

For each archaeological area, the Secretary of State (after consulting with the Commission in England) is to appoint an 'investigating authority', on such terms as he thinks fit (s 34). If no appointment is made, or the office falls vacant, the functions of the investigating authority are exercisable by the Commission or Cadw—Welsh Historic Monuments (s 34(4)). The intention is that the investigating authority would normally be a body such as the archaeological unit of the local university, museum, or council.

(b) Development in an area of archaeological importance

Once an area of archaeological importance has been designated, any developer wishing to carry out on any site within it any operations which disturb the ground, or any flooding or tipping operations, must serve on the local borough or district council an *operations notice* (s 35(1)–(5)). If the operations involve the clearance of the site, the developer must serve a further notice on the investigating authority once the site is clear (s 35(7)).

The 'developer' for these purposes is anyone with a relevant interest in the site, or a statutory undertaker, or a body with powers to enter the land under compulsory purchase procedures (s 36). If the council itself is the developer, it must serve the relevant notices on the Secretary of State (s 35(5)(c)). The form of an operations notice, and indeed of all notices to be served under this procedure, is prescribed in the Areas of Archaeological Importance (Forms of Notice etc) Regulations 1984.

The requirement to notify the investigating authority does not however apply where the authority itself has already given its consent to the proposed works (s 37(1)). Nor does it apply where the works have been exempted by order of the Secretary of State (s 37(2)). The current order is the Areas of Archaeological Importance (Notification of Operations) (Exemption) Order 1984, which lists eleven categories of exempted operations, the most important being:

(1) landscaping and gardening up to a depth of 600 mm below ground level (class 2);

(2) tunnelling or other works at a depth of more than 10 m (class 3);

(3) certain routine operations carried out by various statutory undertakers and similar bodies (classes 5 to 9);

(4) operations on a site for which another operations notice has been served less than five years ago (class 10); and

(5) operations which have been granted scheduled monument consent (class 11).

It will be seen that this list still leaves most types of development needing to be notified; and in particular minor works such as small extensions to buildings, which might not even need planning permission, will need to be the subject of an operations notice.

After the operations notice has been served, the investigating authority can enter the site to determine whether archaeological excavation would be worthwhile, and generally to watch operations (s 38(1)). At any time within four weeks of the notice, it can in turn serve a notice on the developer, the local authority, the Secretary of State and (in England) the Commission, stating its intention to excavate (s 38(3)). It then has a right to investigate the site for a period of four months and two weeks, starting on either:

(1) a date six weeks after the service of the operations notice; or

(2) the date the site has been cleared, as notified under s 35(7) (see above); or

(3) any earlier date agreed between the developer and the investigating authority (s 38(4)).

If nothing has been heard from the investigating authority six weeks after the service of the operations notice, the developer may proceed with impunity. The investigating authority still has a right to excavate, but only in such a way as not to impede the development (s 38(5)).

The effect of this procedure is that a developer can be sure that, although there is a possibility that it will not be possible to touch the site for up to six months after serving an operations notice, the time allowed for excavations cannot be extended beyond that six-month period without his or her voluntary agreement.

(c) Offences involving areas of archaeological importance

It is an offence (under AMAAA 1979, s 35(1)) for a developer to carry out any operations in an area of archaeological importance, other than those exempted by order of the Secretary of State (see 15.3(*b*)), without having served an operations notice, or within six weeks of having served one. It is also an offence (under s 35(8)) to carry out operations after a site has been cleared without having notified the investigating authority of the clearance under s 35(7).

In proceedings for an offence under s 35, it is a defence for the accused to prove:

(1) that he or she took all reasonable precautions and exercised all due diligence to avoid or prevent disturbance of the ground (s 37(5)); or

(2) that he or she did not know and had no reason to believe that the site of the operations was within an area of archaeological importance (s 37(6)(a)); or

(3) that the operations were urgently necessary in the interests of safety or health, *and*

that notice in writing of the need for the operations was given to the Secretary of State as soon as reasonably practicable (s 37(6)(b)).

The offence is triable either way (see 9.2(e)) (s 35(9)). A person found guilty is liable:

(1) on summary conviction, to a fine of up to 'the statutory maximum' (see 14.5(b)); or

(2) on conviction on indictment, to an unlimited fine.

Finally, the various offences arising from the use of a metal detector apply to an area of archaeological importance exactly as they do to the site of a protected monument (see 14.5(d)) (s 42).

See 9.2 and 14.5 generally on criminal offences.

Appendix

Demolition in Conservation Areas

A   Town and Country Planning Act 1971, s 277A, as inserted in 1974 and amended in 1980, 1985 and 1986

Control of demolition in conservation areas

277A—(1) This section applies to all buildings in conservation areas other than—
  (*a*) listed buildings;
  (*b*) excepted buildings within the meaning of section 58(2) above; and
  (*c*) buildings in relation to which a direction under subsection (4) below is for the time being in force.

  (2) A building to which this section applies shall not be demolished without the consent of the appropriate authority.

  (3) [*Repealed*]

  (4) The Secretary of State may direct that this section shall not apply to a description of buildings specified in the direction. [*See B below*]

  (5) A direction under subsection (4) above relating to a description of buildings may be given either to an individual local planning authority or to local planning authorities generally.

  (6) The Secretary of State may vary or revoke a direction under subsection (4) above by a further direction under that subsection.

  (7) The appropriate authority for the purposes of this section is—
  (*a*) in relation to applications for consent made by local planning authorities, the Secretary of State; and
  (*b*) in relation to other applications for consent, the local planning authority or the Secretary of State.

  (8) The following provisions of this Act have effect in relation to buildings to which this section applies as they have effect in relation to listed buildings, subject to such exceptions and modifications as may be prescribed by regulations—
    sections 55 to 56C and 58AA and Parts I and II of Schedule 11 (requirement of consent to works; application for and revocation of consent), [*See C below*]
    sections 96 to 100 (enforcement),
    section 172 (compensation where consent revoked or modified),

335

section 190 and Schedule 19 (purchase notice on refusal of consent),
sections 242, 243, 245 and 246 (validity of orders, proceedings for
review and appeals),
section 255 (contributions by local authorities and statutory
undertakers),
section 266(1)(*b*), (4) and (5) (application to Crown land), and
section 271 and Part VI of Schedule 21 (application of provisions to
works by local planning authority).

(9) Any such regulations may make different provision—
(*a*) in relation to applications made by local planning authorities, and
(*b*) in relation to other applications.

(10) Any proceedings on or arising out of an application for [conservation area consent] made while this section applies to a building shall
lapse when it ceases to apply to it, and any [conservation area consent]
granted with respect to the building shall also lapse. However the fact
that this section has ceased to apply to a building shall not affect the
liability of any person to be prosecuted and punished for an offence
under section 55 or 98 of this Act committed by him with respect to the
building while this section applied to it.

(11) The functions of a local planning authority under this section shall
be exercisable—
(*a*) in Greater London or a metropolitan county, by the local planning
authority;
(*b*) in any part of a National Park outside a metropolitan county, by
the county planning authority; and
(*c*) elsewhere, by the district planning authority.

B   Direction by the Secretary of State in paragraph 97 of Department of the Environment Circular 8/87

In pursuance of his powers under section 277A(4) and (5) of the 1971
Act and of all other powers enabling him in that behalf, the Secretary
of State for the Environment as respects England, hereby directs as
follows:—

(1) Section 277A [*see A above*] shall not apply to the following descriptions of buildings:—
(*a*) any building with a *total* cubic content not exceeding 115 cubic
metres or any part of such a building, and in this sub-paragraph
'building' does not include part of a building;
(*b*) any gate, wall, fence or railing which is less than 1 metre high where
abutting on a highway (including a public footpath or bridleway) or
public open space, or 2 metres high in any other case;
(*c*) any building erected since 1 January 1914 and used, or last used,
for the purposes of agriculture or forestry;
(*d*) any part of a building used, or last used, for an industrial process,
provided that such part (taken with any other part which may have
been demolished) does not exceed ten per cent of the cubic content

of the original building (as ascertained by external measurement) or 500 square metres of floor space, whichever is the greater;

(*e*) any building required to be demolished by virtue of any provision of an agreement made under section 51 of the Act;

(*f*) any building required to be demolished by virtue of any provision of an agreement made under section 52 of the Act;

(*g*) any building in respect of which the provisions of an enforcement notice served under section 87, section 96 or section 100 of the Act require its demolition, in whole or part, however expressed;

(*h*) any building required to be demolished by virtue of a condition of a planning permission granted under section 29 of the Act, other than a permission deemed to be granted to a local planning authority by virtue of regulation 4(5) or regulation 5(4) of the Town and Country Planning General Regulations 1976 (SI 1976, No 1419);

(*i*) any building to which a demolition order made under Part IX of the Housing Act 1985 applies;

(*j*) any building included in a compulsory purchase order made under the provisions of Part IX of the Housing Act 1985 and confirmed by the Secretary of State;

(*k*) a redundant building (within the meaning of the Pastoral Measure 1983) or part of such a building where demolition is in pursuance of a pastoral or redundancy scheme (within the meaning of that Measure).

(2) In this direction:—

'the Act' means the Town and Country Planning Act 1971;

'forestry' means the growing of a utilisable crop of timber; and

'industrial process' means any process for or incidental to any of the following purposes, namely:—

(*a*) the making of any article or part of an article, or

(*b*) the altering, repairing, ornamenting, finishing, cleaning, washing, packing or canning, or adapting for sale, or breaking up, or demolition, of any article, or

(*c*) without prejudice to the foregoing paragraphs, the getting, dressing or treatment of minerals,

being a process carried out in the course of trade or business, and for the purposes of this definition the expression 'article' means an article of any description, including a ship or vessel.

C Town and Country Planning Act 1971, ss 55 and 56, as amended in 1979, 1980 and 1986

as applied to unlisted buildings in conservation areas by section 277A(8) of the Act and paragraph 13 of and Schedule 3 to the Town and Country Planning (Listed Buildings and Buildings in Conservation Areas) Regulations 1987

Control of works for demolition [of unlisted buildings in conservation areas]

55—(1) Subject to this Part of this Act, if a person executes or causes to be executed any works for the demolition of an unlisted building in a conservation area, and the works are not authorised under subsection (2) of this section, he shall be guilty of an offence.

(2) Works for the demolition of an unlisted building in a conservation area are authorised under this Part of this Act if—

(*a*) the local planning authority or the Secretary of State have granted written consent for the execution of the works and the works are executed in accordance with the terms of the consent and of any conditions attached to the consent under section 56 of this Act.

(*b*) [*Does not apply*]

(2A) If written consent is granted by the local planning authority or the Secretary of State for the retention of works for the demolition of an unlisted building in a conservation area, which have been executed without consent under subsection (2) of this section, the works are authorised under this Part of this Act from the grant of consent under this subsection.

(3) [*Does not apply*]

(3A) Consent under subsection (2) or (2A) of this section is referred to in this Part of this Act as 'conservation area consent'.

(4) Without prejudice to subsection (1) of this section, if a person executing or causing or causing to be executed any works in relation to an unlisted building in a conservation area under a conservation area consent fails to comply with any condition attached to the consent, he shall be guilty of an offence.

(5) A person guilty of an offence under this section shall be liable—

(*a*) on summary conviction to imprisonment for a term not exceeding three months or a fine not exceeding the prescribed sum or both; or

(*b*) on conviction on indictment to imprisonment for a term not exceeding twelve months or a fine, or both;

and, in determining the amount of any fine to be imposed on a person convicted on indictment, the court shall in particular have regard to any financial benefit which has accrued or appears likely to accrue to him in consequence of the offence.

(6) In proceedings for an offence under this section it shall be a defence to prove the following matters—

(*a*) that works to the building were urgently necessary in the interests of safety or health or for the preservation of the building,

(*b*) that it was not practicable to secure safety or health or, as the case may be, the preservation of the building by works of repair or works for affording temporary support or shelter,

(*c*) that the works carried out were limited to the minimum measures immediately necessary, and

(*d*) that notice in writing justifying in detail the carrying out of the works was given to the local planning authority as soon as reasonably practicable.

Provisions supplementary to s 55

56—(1) Section 55 of this Act shall not apply to works for the demolition, alteration or extension of—

(a) an ecclesiastical building which is for the time being used for ecclesiastical purposes or would be so used but for the works; or

(b) a building for the time being included in the schedule of monuments compiled and maintained under section 1 of the Ancient Monuments and Archaeological Areas Act 1979.

For the purposes of this subsection, a building used or available for use by a minister of religion wholly or mainly as a residence from which to perform the duties of his office shall be treated as not being an ecclesiastical building.

(2) [*Repealed*]

(3) [*Does not apply*]

(4) Conservation area consent may be granted subject to conditions.

(4A) Without prejudice to the generality of subsection (4) of this section, the conditions subject to which conservation area consent may be granted include conditions with respect to—

(a) the preservation of particular features of the building, either as part of it or after severance therefrom;

(b) the making good, after the works are completed, of any damage caused to the building by the works;

(c) the reconstruction of the building or any part of it following the execution of any works, with the use of original materials so far as practicable and with such alterations of the interior of the building as may be specified in the conditions.

(4B) Conservation area consent may be granted subject to a condition reserving specified details of the works (whether or not set out in the application) for subsequent approval by the local planning authority or, in the case of consent granted by the Secretary of State, specifying whether the reserved details are to be approved by the local planning authority or by him.

(5) Conservation area consent for the demolition of an unlisted building in a conservation area may be granted subject to a condition that the building shall not be demolished before a contract for the carrying out of works of redevelopment of the site has been made, and planning permission has been granted for the redevelopment for which the contract provides.

(6) Part I of Schedule 11 to this Act shall have effect with respect to applications to local planning authorities for conservation area consent, the reference of such applications to the Secretary of State and appeals against decisions on such applications; and Part II of that Schedule shall have effect with respect to the revocation of conservation area consent by a local planning authority or the Secretary of State.

Index